DUCATI

Gold Portfolio
1978-1982

D1573078

Compiled by
R.M.Clarke

ISBN 1 85520 3804

BROOKLANDS BOOKS LTD.
P.O. BOX 146, COBHAM,
SURREY, KT11 1LG. UK

A -D78BGP

Printed in Hong Kong

Brooklands Books

MOTORING

BROOKLANDS ROAD TEST SERIES

Abarth Gold Portfolio 1950-1971
AC Ace & Aceca 1953-1983
Alfa Romeo Giulietta Gold Portfolio 1954-1965
Alfa Romeo Giulia Berlinas 1962-1976
Alfa Romeo Giulia Coupés 1963-1976
Alfa Romeo Giulia Coupés Gold Port. 1963-1976
Alfa Romeo Spider 1966-1990
Alfa Romeo Spider Gold Portfolio 1966-1991
Alfa Romeo Alfasud 1972-1984
Alfa Romeo Alfetta Gold Portfolio 1972-1987
Alfa Romeo Alfetta GTV6 1980-1986
Allard Gold Portfolio 1937-1959
Alvis Gold Portfolio 1919-1967
AMX & Javelin Muscle Portfolio 1968-1974
Armstrong Siddeley Gold Portfolio 1945-1960
Aston Martin Gold Portfolio 1948-1971
Aston Martin Gold Portfolio 1972-1985
Aston Martin Gold Portfolio 1985-1995
Audi Quattro Gold Portfolio 1980-1991
Austin A30 & A35 1951-1962
Austin Healey 100 & 100/6 Gold Port. 1952-1959
Austin Healey 3000 Gold Portfolio 1959-1967
Austin Healey Sprite Gold Portfolio 1958-1971
Barracuda Muscle Portfolio 1964-1974
BMW 1600 Collection No.1 1966-1981
BMW 2002 Gold Portfolio 1968-1976
BMW 316, 318, 320 (4 cyl.) Gold Port. 1975-1990
BMW 320, 323, 325 (6 cyl.) Gold Port. 1977-1990
BMW M Series Performance Portfolio 1976-1993
BMW 5 Series Gold Portfolio 1981-1987
BMW 6 Series Gold Portfolio 1976-1989
Bricklin Gold Portfolio 1974-1975
Bristol Cars Gold Portfolio 1946-1992
Buick Automobiles 1947-1960
Buick Muscle Cars 1965-1970
Cadillac Allanté 1986-1993
Cadillac Automobiles 1949-1959
Cadillac Automobiles 1960-1969
Caprice 1965-1976 ☆ Limited Edition
Charger Muscle Portfolio 1966-1974
Checker ☆ Limited Edition
Chevrolet 1955-1957
Impala & SS Muscle Portfolio 1958-1972
Chevrolet Corvair 1959-1969
Chevy II & Nova SS Muscle Portfolio 1962-1974
Chevy El Camino & SS 1959-1987
Chevelle & SS Muscle Portfolio 1964-1972
Chevrolet Muscle Cars 1966-1971
Chevy Blazer 1969-1981
Chevrolet Corvette Gold Portfolio 1953-1962
Chevrolet Corvette Sting Ray Gold Port. 1963-1967
Chevrolet Corvette Gold Portfolio 1968-1977
High Performance Corvettes 1983-1989
Camaro Muscle Portfolio 1967-1973
Chevrolet Camaro & Z28 1973-1981
High Performance Camaros 1982-1988
Chrysler 300 Gold Portfolio 1955-1970
Chrysler Valiant 1960-1962
Citroen Traction Avant Gold Portfolio 1934-1957
Citroen 2CV Gold Portfolio 1948-1989
Citroen DS & ID 1955-1975
Citroen DS & ID Gold Portfolio 1955-1975
Citroen SM 1970-1975
Cobras & Replicas 1962-1983
Shelby Cobra Gold Portfolio 1962-1969
Cobras & Cobra Replicas Gold Portfolio 1962-1989
Cunningham Automobiles 1951-1955
Daimler SP250 Sports & V-8 250 Saloon Gold P. 1959-1969
Datsun Roadsters 1962-1971
Datsun 240Z 1970-1973
Datsun 280Z & ZX 1975-1983
DeLorean Gold Portfolio 1977-1995
Dodge Muscle Cars 1967-1970
Dodge Viper on the Road
Edsel 1957-1960 ☆ Limited Edition
ERA Gold Portfolio 1934-1994
Excalibur Collection No.1 1952-1981
Facel Vega 1954-1964
Ferrari Dino 1965-1974
Ferrari Dino 308 & Mondial Gold Portfolio1974-1985
Ferrari 328 • 348 • Mondial Gold Portfolio 1986-1994
Fiat 500 Gold Portfolio 1936-1972
Fiat 600 & 850 Gold Portfolio 1955-1972
Fiat Pininfarina 124 & 2000 Spider 1968-1985
Fiat X1/9 Gold Portfolio1973-1989
Fiat Abarth Performance Portfolio 1972-1987
Ford Consul, Zephyr, Zodiac Mk.I & II 1950-1962
Ford Zephyr, Zodiac, Executive, Mk.III & Mk.IV 1962-1971
Ford Cortina 1600E & GT 1967-1970
High Performance Capris Gold Portfolio 1969-1987
Capri Muscle Portfolio 1974-1987
High Performance Fiestas 1979-1991
High Performance Escorts Mk.I 1968-1974
High Performance Escorts Mk.II 1975-1980
High Performance Escorts 1980-1985
High Performance Escorts 1985-1990
High Performance Sierras & Merkurs
Gold Portfolio 1983-1990
Ford Automobiles 1949-1959
Ford Fairlane 1955-1970
Ford Ranchero 1957-1959
Ford Thunderbird 1955-1957
Ford Thunderbird 1958-1963
Ford GT40 Gold Portfolio 1964-1987
Ford Bronco 1966-1977
Ford Bronco 1978-1988
Goggomobil ☆ Limited Edition
Holden 1948-1962
Honda CRX 1983-1987
Imperial 1955-1970 ☆ Limited Edition
International Scout Gold Portfolio 1961-1980
Isetta 1953-1964
Iso & Bizzarrini Gold Portfolio 1962-1974
Kaiser • Frazer 1946-1955 ☆ Limited Edition
Jaguar and SS Gold Portfolio 1931-1951
Jaguar XK120, 140, 150 Gold Port. 1948-1960
Jaguar Mk.VII, VIII, IX, X, 420 Gold Port. 1950-1970
Jaguar Mk.1 & Mk.2 Gold Portfolio 1959-1969
Jaguar C-Type & D-Type ☆ Limited Edition
Jaguar E-Type Gold Portfolio 1961-1971
Jaguar E-Type V-12 1971-1975
Jaguar S-Type & 420 ☆ Limited Edition
Jaguar XJ12, XJ5.3, V12 Gold Portfolio 1972-1990
Jaguar XJ6 Series I & II Gold Portfolio 1968-1979
Jaguar XJ6 Series III Perf. Portfolio 1979-1986
Jaguar XJ6 Gold Portfolio 1986-1994
Jaguar XJS Gold Portfolio 1975-1988
Jaguar XJS Gold Portfolio 1988-1995
Jeep CJ5 & CJ6 1960-1976
Jeep CJ5 & CJ7 1976-1986
Jensen Cars 1946-1967
Jensen Cars 1967-1979
Jensen Interceptor Gold Portfolio 1966-1986
Jensen Healey 1972-1976
Lagonda Gold Portfolio 1919-1964
Lamborghini Countach & Urraco 1974-1980
Lamborghini Countach & Jalpa 1980-1985
Lancia Aurelia & Flaminia Gold Portfolio 1950-1970
Lancia Fulvia Gold Portfolio 1963-1976
Lancia Beta Gold Portfolio 1972-1984
Lancia Delta Gold Portfolio 1979-1994
Lancia Stratos 1972-1985
Land Rover Series I 1948-1958
Land Rover Series II & IIa 1958-1971
Land Rover Series III 1971-1985
Land Rover 90 110 Defender Gold Portfolio 1983-1994
Land Rover Discovery 1989-1994
Land Rover Story Part One 1948-1971
Lincoln Gold Portfolio 1949-1960
Lincoln Continental 1961-1969
Lincoln Continental 1969-1976
Lotus Sports Racers Gold Portfolio 1953-1965
Lotus Seven Gold Portfolio 1957-1974
Lotus Caterham Seven Gold Portfolio 1974-1995
Lotus Elan Gold Portfolio 1962-1974
Lotus Elan Collection No. 2 1963-1972
Lotus Elan & SE 1989-1992
Lotus Europa Gold Portfolio 1966-1975
Lotus Elite & Eclat 1974-1982
Lotus Turbo Esprit 1980-1986
Marcos Cars 1960-1988
Maserati 1965-1975
Matra 1965-1983 ☆ Limited Edition
Mazda Miata MX-5 Performance Portfolio 1989-1996
Mazda RX-7 Gold Portfolio 1978-1991
Mercedes 190 & 300 SL 1954-1963
Mercedes G Wagen 1981-1994
Mercedes S & 600 1965-1972
Mercedes S Class 1972-1979
Mercedes 230 • 250 • 280SL Gold Portfolio 1963-1971
Mercedes SLs & SLCs Gold Portfolio 1971-1989
Mercedes SLs Performance Portfolio 1989-1994
Mercury Muscle Cars 1966-1971
Messerschmitt Gold Portfolio 1954-1964
MG Gold Portfolio 1929-1939
MG TA & TC Gold Portfolio 1936-1949
MG TD & TF Gold Portfolio 1949-1955
MGA & Twin Cam Gold Portfolio 1955-1962
MG Midget Gold Portfolio 1961-1979
MGB Roadsters 1962-1980
MGB MGC & V8 Gold Portfolio 1962-1980
MGB GT 1965-1980
MGC & MGB GT V8 ☆ Limited Edition
MG Y-Type & Magnette ZA/ZB ☆ Limited Edition
Mini Gold Portfolio 1959-1969
Mini Gold Portfolio 1969-1980
High Performance Minis Gold Portfolio 1960-1973
Mini Cooper Gold Portfolio 1961-1971
Mini Moke Gold Portfolio 1964-1994
Mopar Muscle Cars 1964-1967
Morgan Three-Wheeler Gold Portfolio 1910-1952
Morgan Plus 4 & Four 4 Gold Portfolio. 1936-1967
Morgan Cars 1960-1970
Morgan Cars Gold Portfolio 1968-1989
Morris Minor Collection No. 1 1948-1980
Shelby Mustang Muscle Portfolio 1965-1970
High Performance Mustang IIs 1974-1978
High Performance Mustangs 1982-1988
Nash & Nash-Healey 1949-1957 ☆ Limited Edition
Nash-Austin Metropolitan Gold Portfolio 1954-1962
Oldsmobile Automobiles 1955-1963
Oldsmobile Muscle Cars 1964-1971
Oldsmobile Toronado 1966-1978
Opel GT Gold Portfolio 1968-1973
Opel Manta 1970-1975 ☆ Limited Edition
Packard Gold Portfolio 1946-1958
Pantera Gold Portfolio 1970-1989
Panther Gold Portfolio 1972-1990
Plymouth Muscle Cars 1966-1971
Pontiac Tempest & GTO 1961-1965
Pontiac Muscle Cars 1966-1972
Pontiac Firebird & Trans-Am 1973-1981
High Performance Firebirds 1982-1988
Pontiac Fiero 1984-1988
Porsche 356 Gold Portfolio 1953-1965
Porsche 911 1965-1969
Porsche 911 1970-1972
Porsche 911 1973-1977
Porsche 911 SC & Turbo Gold Portfolio 1978-1983
Porsche 911 Carrera & Turbo Gold Port. 1984-1989
Porsche 924 Gold Portfolio 1975-1988
Porsche 928 Performance Portfolio 1977-1994
Porsche 944 Gold Portfolio 1981-1991
Range Rover Gold Portfolio 1970-1985
Range Rover Gold Portfolio 1986-1995
Reliant Scimitar 1964-1986
Renault Alpine Gold Portfolio 1958-1994
Riley Gold Portfolio 1924-1939
Rolls Royce Silver Cloud & Bentley 'S' Series
Gold Portfolio 1955-1965
Rolls Royce Silver Shadow Gold Port. 1965-1980
Rolls Royce & Bentley Gold Port. 1980-1989
Rover P4 1949-1959
Rover P4 1955-1964
Rover 3 & 3.5 Litre Gold Portfolio 1958-1973
Rover 2000 & 2200 1963-1977
Rover 3500 1968-1977
Rover 3500 & Vitesse 1976-1986
Saab Sonett Collection No.1 1966-1974
Saab Turbo 1976-1983
Studebaker Gold Portfolio 1947-1966
Studebaker Hawks & Larks 1956-1963
Avanti 1962-1990
Sunbeam Tiger & Alpine Gold Portfolio. 1959-1967
Toyota Land Cruiser 1956-1984
Triumph Dolomite Sprint ☆ Limited Edition
Triumph TR2 & TR3 Gold Portfolio 1952-1961
Triumph TR4, TR5, TR250 1961-1968
Triumph TR6 Gold Portfolio 1969-1976
Triumph TR7 & TR8 Gold Portfolio 1975-1982
Triumph Herald 1959-1971
Triumph Vitesse 1962-1971
Triumph Spitfire Gold Portfolio 1962-1980
Triumph 2000, 2.5, 2500 1963-1977
Triumph GT6 Gold Portfolio 1966-1974
Triumph Stag Gold Portfolio 1970-1977
TVR Gold Portfolio 1959-1986
TVR Performance Portfolio 1986-1994
VW Beetle Gold Portfolio 1935-1967
VW Beetle Gold Portfolio 1968-1991
VW Beetle Collection No.1 1970-1982
VW Karmann Ghia 1955-1982
VW Bus, Camper, Van 1954-1967
VW Bus, Camper, Van 1968-1979
VW Bus, Camper, Van 1979-1989
VW Scirocco 1974-1981
VW Golf GTI 1976-1986
Volvo PV444 & PV544 1945-1965
Volvo Amazon-120 Gold Portfolio 1956-1970
Volvo 1800 Gold Portfolio 1960-1973
Volvo 140 & 160 Series Gold Portfolio 1966-1975
Westfield ☆ Limited Edition

Forty Years of Selling Volvo

BROOKLANDS ROAD & TRACK SERIES

Road & Track on Alfa Romeo 1964-1970
Road & Track on Alfa Romeo 1971-1976
Road & Track on Aston Martin 1962-1990
R & T on Auburn Cord and Duesenburg 1952-84
Road & Track on Audi & Auto Union 1952-1980
Road & Track on Audi & Auto Union 1980-1986
Road & Track on Austin Healey 1953-1970
Road & Track on BMW Cars 1966-1974
Road & Track on BMW Cars 1975-1978
Road & Track on BMW Cars 1979-1983
R & T on Cobra, Shelby & Ford GT40 1962-1992
Road & Track on Corvette 1953-1967
Road & Track on Corvette 1968-1982
Road & Track on Corvette 1982-1986
Road & Track on Corvette 1986-1990
Road & Track on Ferrari 1975-1981
Road & Track on Ferrari 1981-1984
Road & Track on Ferrari 1984-1988
Road & Track on Fiat Sports Cars 1968-1987
Road & Track on Jaguar 1950-1960
Road & Track on Jaguar 1961-1968
Road & Track on Jaguar 1968-1974
Road & Track on Jaguar 1974-1982
Road & Track on Jaguar 1983-1989
Road & Track on Lamborghini 1964-1985
Road & Track on Lotus 1972-1981
Road & Track on Maserati 1975-1983
R & T on Mazda RX-7 & MX-5 Miata 1986-1991
Road & Track on Mercedes 1952-1962
Road & Track on Mercedes 1963-1970
Road & Track on Mercedes 1971-1979
Road & Track on Mercedes 1980-1987
Road & Track on MG Sports Cars 1949-1961
Road & Track on MG Sports Cars 1962-1980
Road & Track on Mustang 1964-1977
R & T on Nissan 300-ZX & Turbo 1984-1989
Road & Track on Pontiac 1960-1983
Road & Track on Porsche 1951-1967
Road & Track on Porsche 1968-1971
Road & Track on Porsche 1972-1975
Road & Track on Porsche 1975-1978
Road & Track on Porsche 1985-1988
R & T on Rolls Royce & Bentley 1950-1965
R & T on Rolls Royce & Bentley 1966-1984
Road & Track on Saab 1972-1992
R & T on Toyota Sports & GT Cars 1966-1984
R & T on Triumph Sports Cars 1953-1967
R & T on Triumph Sports Cars 1967-1974
R & T on Triumph Sports Cars 1974-1982
Road & Track on Volkswagen 1951-1968
Road & Track on Volkswagen 1968-1978
Road & Track on Volkswagen 1978-1985
Road & Track on Volvo 1957-1974
Road & Track on Volvo 1977-1994
R & T - Henry Manney at Large & Abroad
R & T - Peter Egan's "Side Glances"
R & T - Peter Egan "At Large"

BROOKLANDS CAR AND DRIVER SERIES

Car and Driver on BMW 1955-1977
Car and Driver on BMW 1977-1985
C and D on Cobra, Shelby & Ford GT40 1963-84
Car and Driver on Corvette 1978-1982
Car and Driver on Corvette 1983-1988
C and D on Datsun Z 1600 & 2000 1966-1984
Car and Driver on Ferrari 1955-1962
Car and Driver on Ferrari 1963-1975
Car and Driver on Ferrari 1976-1983
Car and Driver on Mopar 1956-1967
Car and Driver on Mopar 1968-1975
Car and Driver on Mustang 1964-1972
Car and Driver on Pontiac 1961-1975
Car and Driver on Porsche 1955-1962
Car and Driver on Porsche 1963-1970
Car and Driver on Porsche 1970-1976
Car and Driver on Porsche 1977-1981
Car and Driver on Porsche 1982-1986
Car and Driver on Saab 1956-1985
Car and Driver on Volvo 1955-1986

BROOKLANDS PRACTICAL CLASSICS SERIES

PC on Austin A40 Restoration
PC on Land Rover Restoration
PC on Metalworking in Restoration
PC on Midget/Sprite Restoration
PC on MGB Restoration
PC on Sunbeam Rapier Restoration
PC on Triumph Herald/Vitesse
PC on Spitfire Restoration
PC on Beetle Restoration
PC on 1930s Car Restoration

BROOKLANDS HOT ROD 'MUSCLECAR & HI-PO ENGINES' SERIES

Chevy 265 & 283
Chevy 302 & 327
Chevy 348 & 409
Chevy 350 & 400
Chevy 396 & 427
Chevy 454 thru 512
Chrysler Hemi
Chrysler 273, 318, 340 & 360
Chrysler 361, 383, 400, 413, 426, 440
Ford 289, 302, Boss 302 & 351W
Ford 351C & Boss 351
Ford Big Block

BROOKLANDS RESTORATION SERIES

Auto Restoration Tips & Techniques
Basic Bodywork Tips & Techniques
Camaro Restoration Tips & Techniques
Chevrolet High Performance Tips & Techniques
Chevy Engine Swapping Tips & Techniques
Chevy-GMC Pickup Repair
Chrysler Engine Swapping Tips & Techniques
Engine Swapping Tips & Techniques
Ford Pickup Repair
How to Build a Street Rod
Land Rover Restoration Tips & Techniques
MG 'T' Series Restoration Guide
MGA Restoration Guide
Mustang Restoration Tips & Techniques
Performance Tuning - Chevrolets of the '60's
Performance Tuning - Pontiacs of the '60's

MOTORCYCLING

BROOKLANDS ROAD TEST SERIES

AJS & Matchless Gold Portfolio 1945-1966
BSA Twins A7 & A10 Gold Portfolio 1946-1962
BSA Twins A50 & A65 Gold Portfolio 1962-1973
BMW Motorcycles Gold Portfolio 1950-1971
BMW Motorcycles Gold Portfolio 1971-1976
Ducati Gold Portfolio 1960-1974
Ducati Gold Portfolio 1974-1978
Ducati Gold Portfolio 1978-1982
Laverda Gold Portfolio 1967-1977
Moto Guzzi Gold Portfolio 1949-1973
Norton Commando Gold Portfolio 1968-1977
Triumph Bonneville Gold Portfolio 1959-1983

BROOKLANDS CYCLE WORLD SERIES

Cycle World on BMW 1974-1980
Cycle World on BMW 1981-1986
Cycle World on Ducati 1982-1991
Cycle World on Harley-Davidson 1962-1968
Cycle World on Harley-Davidson 1978-1983
Cycle World on Harley-Davidson 1983-1987
Cycle World on Harley-Davidson 1987-1990
Cycle World on Harley-Davidson 1990-1992
Cycle World on Honda 1962-1967
Cycle World on Honda 1968-1971
Cycle World on Honda 1971-1974
Cycle World on Husqvarna 1966-1976
Cycle World on Husqvarna 1977-1984
Cycle World on Kawasaki 1966-1971
Cycle World on Kawasaki Off-Road Bikes 1972-1979
Cycle World on Kawasaki Street Bikes 1972-1976
Cycle World on Norton 1962-1971
Cycle World on Suzuki 1962-1970
Cycle World on Suzuki Off-Road Bikes 1971-1976
Cycle World on Suzuki Street Bikes 1971-1976
Cycle World on Triumph 1967-1972
Cycle World on Yamaha 1962-1969
Cycle World on Yamaha Off-Road Bikes 1970-1974
Cycle World on Yamaha Street Bikes 1970-1974

MILITARY

BROOKLANDS MILITARY VEHICLES SERIES

Allied Military Vehicles No.2 1941-1946
Complete WW2 Military Jeep Manual
Dodge Military Vehicles No.1 1940-1945
Hail To The Jeep
Military & Civilian Amphibians 1940-1990
Off Road Jeeps: Civ. & Mil. 1944-1971
US Military Vehicles 1941-1945
US Army Military Vehicles WW2-TM9-2800
VW Kubelwagen Military Portfolio 1940-1990
WW 2 Jeep Military Portfolio 1941-1945

RACING

Le Mans - The Jaguar Years - 1949-1957
Le Mans - The Ferrari Years - 1958-1965
Le Mans - The Ford & Matra Years - 1966-1974

CONTENTS

ACKNOWLEDGEMENTS

Brooklands Books' Gold Portfolio series are aimed at enthusiasts who enjoy reading historical magazine stories and road tests about a particular make or model of machine. Finding these older literary pieces, however, can be frustrating as well as time consuming, as readers will know. For forty years we at Brooklands have tried to fill this need by collating these hard-to-find articles, firstly for cars and more recently on motorcycles, and presenting them in this format for the dedicated collector.

This is the third title in the Ducati series, and relates solely to the vee twins. It covers the period when toothed belts and pulleys replaced the shafts and bevel gears used previously for the operation of the valve gear. It was also during this period that the company encountered serious financial problems, which led to their acquisition by Cagiva in 1985.

The assembly of all of the information contained within this volume would not have been possible without the generous assistance given by the world's leading motorcycle magazine publishers. Brooklands Books are therefore greatly indebted to all of the following, who so kindly gave their consent for the reproduction of their copyright material: *Bike, The Biker, Cycle, Cycle World, Motorcycle Mechanics, Motor Cycling, Motorcycling, Motorcycle Sport, Motorcyclist Illustrated, Superbike* and *Two Wheels*.

R.M. Clarke

The Darmah 900SD model, introduced in 1977, proved to be the mainstay of Ducati production for the next five years. It represented an attempt to provide a somewhat more civilised version of the earlier 864cc twins, having a 'softer' engine and using electrical equipment of improved quality and an electric starter. Now a large capacity Ducati vee twin could be purchased at a price comparable with that of Japanese motorcycles of similar size - and with the added advantage of desmodromic valve gear. Although the Darmah's performance lacked the edge of that of many of its predecessors, it nonetheless attracted many who desired a nicely styled sports touring bike with the charm that only a vee twin engine can provide.

One of Ducati's most outstanding achievements occurred during 1978, when Steve Wynne of Sports Motorcycles persuaded Mike Hailwood to return to the Isle of Man. The TT Formula One Championship had been created in 1976 and Ducati agreed to supply Wynne with a new F1 900NCR for Hailwood to ride. Despite not having ridden in the Island for 11 years, Hailwood won at an average speed of 108.51mph, breaking the lap record by 9mph! Ducati commemorated this success by manufacturing a Mike Hailwood Replica, which made its debut at the 1979 London Show. Though not a true replica in the generally accepted sense of the word, its distinctive red and green livery left no doubts about what had inspired it.

When Ducati reluctantly came to the conclusion that there was no money to be made from their vertical twins, they turned their attention towards a 500cc vee twin. To take advantage of modern technology and at the same time effect production economies, they abandoned the use of vertical shafts and bevel gear pinions to drive the overhead valve gear. Instead, they changed to toothed belts and pulleys, already being used successfully by the motor industry. Their first design embodying this change appeared in 1980, the 500cc Pantah 500SL, which had a 90 degree cylinder angle. Later came the 600SL, achieved by overboring the cylinders.

Jeff Clew

DUCATI 900SD DARMAH

CYCLE WORLD TEST

In a world of mass-produced, all-purpose missiles, it's heartening to see there's still room for something as specialized and soul-stirring as a Ducati.

Measured against the current crop of light-to-light pavement scorchers, these unique motorcycles may look to be a trifle short on oomph—but that's a conclusion one discards as soon as the pavement begins to develop kinks. This year's unprecedented batch of rockets—the Kawasaki Z1-R, Yamaha XS11, Suzuki GS1000 and almighty Honda CBX—tends to make us lose sight of all the qualities that make superbikes super. Go-power is part of it, of course. But so is the ability to get around fast turns without wrestling matches. And it's here that the Ducati

more than holds its ground, even against the sophisticated suspension componentry of something like the GS1000. Where the GS1000 inspires confidence in its rider, the Ducati inspires a sense of oneness. If the Suzuki's good manners make you feel like an instant expert, the Ducati makes you feel like a centaur.

Although the foregoing is particularly applicable to the almost-racer 900SS model, it's true of all Ducatis, including the 900 Sport Desmo Darmah tested here. "Darmah" means tiger, and even though this new addition to the Ducati street lineup is hauling around substantially more weight than the SS model, there's definitely a tiger lurking under that snazzy bright red clothing. You can feel its tautness, even on the freeway; like some superbly conditioned athlete, the bike conveys a sense of always being poised for action and always having some little extra held in reserve.

The Darmah is perhaps the most impressive update on the Ducati big bike street line since the first 750s were introduced six years ago. Intended as a somewhat streetified version of the SS, it includes all sorts of civilizing touches like all-new instrumentation, all-new electronic ignition, a new shifting mechanism for the 5-speed gearbox, a new electric starter, new horn, bigger battery, stronger alternator, double wall exhausts, Campagnolo cast alloy wheels and extra slick styling.

The price for all these amenities is about 60 lb. over the SS, a burden that takes a small bite out of performance, as you might expect. Nevertheless, the stock Darmah, as delivered, is a (barely) 12-sec. bike, which puts it close to some fast company. This performance can be improved considerably with substitute mufflers and bigger bore carbs, but the point is that out of the crate the Ducati will pull itself along quite respectably.

The Civilized Desmo Duck is Still Dynamite

Like some superbly conditioned athlete, the bik

The factor that makes the Darmah's performance noteworthy is its source, a 90-deg. ohc V-Twin, a powerplant that goes back to motorcycling's infancy yet manages to compete on reasonably equal footing with the high-rev Multis favored in most of today's hot street setups. As its full name implies, our Darmah's breathing is aided by desmodromic valve control, as adapted by Ducati's slightly legendary—and still active—Dr. Fabio Taglioni (see accompanying story).

There are students of motorcycle engine design who believe that bikes will ultimately return to V-Twins once the current Multi-Madness has run its course. The Darmah's powerplant makes an excellent case in favor of this theory. Although it lacks the wild rush that's characteristic of something like the new Honda Six, it is nevertheless strong enough to make this bike hard to catch when the going gets twisty. And unlike the Fours and Sixes, the Ducati's 863.9cc V-Twin (the 900 comes from an optimistic rounding off of the odd number) delivers power almost from idle. There's Harley-like torque lurking in those alloy barrels, but with virtually no trade-off in primary vibration. In fact, perhaps the most remarkable thing about this engine is how smooth it is. V-Twins, in theory, cancel out virtually all primary vibrations, but not all of them manage this in practice. With the exception of the Duck. At freeway cruising speeds—around 3500 to 4000 rpm—it's easy to tune the V-Twin out—if you want to. But chances are you won't want to. The engine has a lovely beat and a sound all its own. One of the irreverents around here said it behaved and sounded "like a Harley with overhead cams." Dr. T. isn't gonna like that.

Everyone agreed, though, that besides being a substantial performer the Ducati V-Twin *felt* like a motorcycle engine with-

onveys a sense of always being poised for action

out conveying any of the old-time discomforts associated with such items. It arrived from Jim Woods' Glendale shops in an excellent state of tune, desmo valve train shimmed and winkler-capped to perfect tolerances.

There followed an interval of torrential rain during which the Ducati was run for periods of about five minutes at intervals of about two hours: We didn't want to ride it in the rain, but we could at least *listen* to it every once in awhile. This ritual had its logical conclusion in a set of fouled plugs.

With fresh plugs installed, the Ducati started as willingly as anything in the house. It requires a short time at full choke (the control lever is handily located just below the speedo), a blip on the throttle, and then a short warm-up period (no choke) while it fusses and spits a bit. Too much throttle blipping will bring on flooding: both the 32mm Dellorto carbs are equipped with accelerator pumps. The drill is easy once you're accustomed to it.

Internal engine lubrication is accomplished by a gear-driven pump that draws oil from the bottom of the engine up through the heads and valve train. Return is accomplished by gravity. Besides a regular filter cartridge, the engine employs centrifugal filtration with various particles accumulating around an access plug below the crank. The V-Twin's oil capacity is 10 pints plus, which helps the engine run cool. This is particularly important for the rear (upright) cylinder, which is somewhat shielded from cooling air.

The weight of all that oil also aids in keeping the Duck's center of gravity close to the ground.

Helical-cut gears operate the Ducati's primary drive and the clutch is a wet, multi-plate setup that is a versatile and fussless ally. But the 5-speed gearbox (lubricated in common with the engine) is the biggest news item in the drivetrain. When the first 750cc Ducatis arrived, they came with European gear shifts on the right side of the bike. By the time the 860 Ducks hit these shores, in 1975, the shift was on the left side, but it was a cobbled up rig involving a crossover shaft. On the Darmah, the shift mechanism has been re-engineered with the lever shaft working directly into the transmission. The result is smooth, positive shifting up and down the range. Neutral is a bit tricky to locate at times, but this presents no real difficulties.

A #530 drive chain transfers power

Nippondenso instruments and switches adorn the Darmah. Ignition switch is between lower instrument lights, covered by small rubber boot.

from transmission to rear wheel, and this setup is peculiar to Ducati in that tension adjustment is made—awkwardly—at the swing arm pivot rather than at the rear hub. Properly adjusted, which was the way our test bike arrived, this chain drive is remarkably free of slop, which helps make the Ducati the responsive machine it is.

The Bosch electrical system is as up-to-date as tomorrow, entailing, among other things, four-stage automatic ignition advance. A tiny AC generator lurking under the left side cover accomplishes this, moving the advance from 6 deg. at idle (900

DESMODROMOLOGY

It sounds a bit like Jabberwocky, but desmodromic valve actuation is post-Lewis Carroll and a good deal less mysterious—once you understand it.

Desmodromy means positive valve control; one cam follower pushes the valve open, another one pulls it shut. Which means no valve springs. Which means no valve float, no broken valve springs and, theoretically, higher performance potential.

Although Ducati is the only firm to run desmodromic valve systems on production bikes, the concept antedates the advent of these machines by over 30 years. The first positive valve control system was patented by an Englishman, F. H. Arnott, in 1910 and was later adapted to the French Delage Grand Prix cars for the 1914 season.

Delage had only limited success with the system, as did several other auto firms experimenting with positive valve control during the Twenties and Thirties—Arnott, Peugeot, Brewster and Ballot notable among them. But in 1954, Mercedes installed desmodromic valve control on its W196 Grand Prix machines, and later its 300SLR sports/racers. This time the success was hardly limited. During the 1954 and '55 seasons the Mercedes cars were virtually unbeatable, totally dominating GP and endurance racing until the firm withdrew from competition following Pierre Levegh's tragic crash at LeMans in 1955.

The success of the Mercedes desmos hardly went unnoticed, of course, and one enthusiastic observer was Dr. Fabio Taglioni, who had joined Ducati Meccanica in 1954. The Bologna firm was just getting started in motorcycle production, but the combination of Mercedes successes and Dr. Taglioni's enthusiasm (he'd been sketching up desmo systems for motorcycle application since 1948) led Ducati to set its sights on Grand Prix racing. It looked like a good chance for a small company to attract attention to itself.

And so it proved to be. "Dr. T.", as he is known to Ducati faithful, had his first desmo engine, a 125cc Single, running in

1955 and the race bike was ready to go for the 1956 Swedish Grand Prix.

That race really put Ducati on the map, because with Degli Antoni up the newcomer won its first time out, beating the previously unbeatable MV Augusta team in the process.

Despite its encouraging start, and a class win in the Barcelona 24-Hour Grand Prix d'Endurance later the same year, Ducati wasn't prepared to mount an all-out Grand Prix effort until 1958. This wound up being something of a disappointment to Dr. T., inasmuch as the 125cc title went to MV Augusta and Carol Ubbiali once again, but it was the making of the Ducati legend. Ducatis won the Belgian, Swedish and Monza Grands Prix, taking the first five places at the latter.

The following season was the end of factory Grand Prix racing for Ducati, although some excellent one-off machines followed, such as the 250cc desmo Twin campaigned very successfully in Britain by Mike Hailwood that same year. Other companies looked at the possibility of adapting the desmo design to their own bikes—Norton's Bert Hopwood came up with an interesting desmo variation for the company's famous Manx Single—but none of them ever made a commitment to the system.

Ducati was even more alone when it introduced desmo versions of its street bikes in 1968. And so it remains today.

The Ducati system illustrated here differs from the one first installed by Dr. T. on the four-cam racing Singles. It entails over-and-under cam followers. The upper arm operates on the top of the valve stem to open it. The lower, equipped with a fork that brackets the stem, lifts up against a collar fitted on the stem. There are two sets of followers and hence four lobes on each cam, two for intake, two for exhaust.

Adjusting the desmo Duck introduces the newcomer to a marvelous world of shims and winkler caps. It is time-consuming—not only do you have to remove the heads to adjust the valve clearances, you might just find yourself honing shims on a

whetstone as they come only in increments of .008 in.—but for bikers with a love of engine innards this is probably a selling point.

Below the heads, current desmo and non-desmo Ducati engines are exactly alike. A driveshaft with beveled gears at either end transfers power from the bottom of the engine to the top. And even the heads appear very similar, since they're based on the same casting as the garden variety valve spring edition.

Desmodromic valves were dreamed up in the beginning because valve springs were totally unreliable at high rpm. But advances in metallurgy during the past decade or two have brought along valve springs that are good at extremely high revs—witness some of the production racers flying around out there right now.

Which brings us to the Big Question: Does this slightly exotic system of valve operation offer any advantages over more conventional systems?

The answer is yes. Valve spring salvation is no longer the big concern, but there are some other pluses. First, operating a heavy duty valve spring soaks up a certain amount of horsepower. The Kawasaki KZ1000, for example, employs valve springs with a seat pressure of 65 lb. and 100 lb. compressed. On Dr. T.'s 125cc road racers, the difference between desmo and valve spring engines was worth 3 hp (for a total of 19). On the fabled Mercedes racers it was worth about 30.

Next, are there drawbacks to offset the advantages? Again, yes. A desmo system is bound to be complicated and bulky and heavy. While there appear to be good reasons for going the desmo route, one must note that the Honda RCB, the Laverda V-6 and such take-no-prisoners car engines as the Ferrari flat 12 and the Cosworth V-8 all use valve springs. It's hard to fit a desmo design with rows of little cylinders. In the big leagues cylinders equal power, so the valve spring is still the leader.

Incidentally, you will notice clothespin-type springs in the illustrations accom-

rpm) to 16 deg. at 1800 rpm, 28 deg. at 2800 rpm and 32 deg. from 4000 rpm on up. A pair of coils fires the plugs, and the system worked smoothly throughout our test.

The electric starter has been beefed up, and is backed by a bigger 36 AH Yuasa battery which, in turn, is replenished by a 200 watt alternator. The kickstarter hasn't been removed from electric starting Ducatis yet—it pivots below and in front of the right side rider's footpeg—but this device is best left out of service; it can be the source of some nasty shin bites.

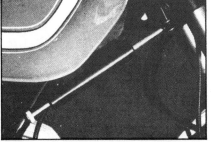

Steering damper is mounted on right side of bike. It's a necessary part of the Ducati's running gear.

Lights are first rate, particularly the Bosch H4 quartz-halogen headlamp that comes as standard equipment. We'd like to see this on all street bikes.

All the electronic gear, including fuses, stows neatly under the big, sculptured 4-gal. fuel tank.

The rock solid frame is unchanged from the first of the 860 models. It begins as a double cradle affair but stops short, with the two downtubes bolted to the engine block, which thus becomes a frame member as is current practice with the new Hondas. This arrangement seems to work

Valves Without Valve Springs—and it Works

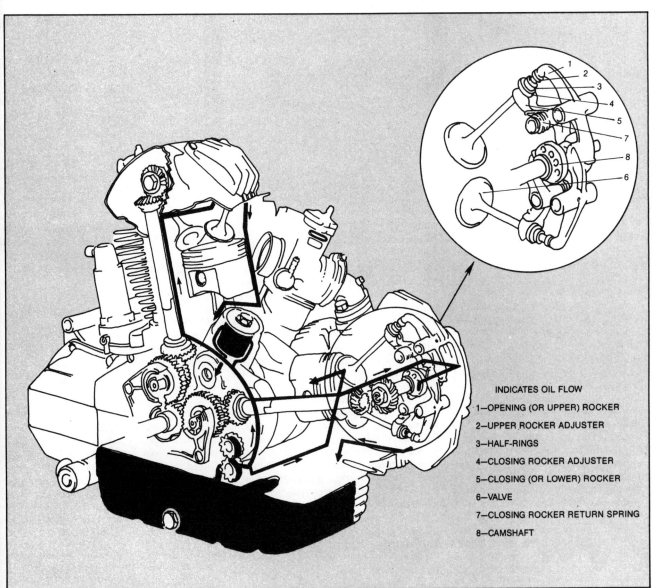

INDICATES OIL FLOW

1—OPENING (OR UPPER) ROCKER

2—UPPER ROCKER ADJUSTER

3—HALF-RINGS

4—CLOSING ROCKER ADJUSTER

5—CLOSING (OR LOWER) ROCKER

6—VALVE

7—CLOSING ROCKER RETURN SPRING

8—CAMSHAFT

panying this story. These are only for pushing the valve the last few thousandths onto its seat, a function otherwise accomplished by compression. If you're planning to race a Ducati, your first step is removal of these springs, which are prone to breakage.

Another important advantage of the desmo valve setup is that it permits the use of wilder cams. Since the followers are in continuous contact with the cams, much steeper ramps may be used on the lobes. Ducati's high lift Imola racing cams, for example, can't be used with the valve spring version of the engine.

There are demonstrable benefits, yes; but one of the big pluses of the desmo powerplant goes on inside the head of the rider. Just knowing you've got all that intriguing, intricate machinery whirring along together perfectly makes all the pains of its possession worthwhile.—*Tony Swan*

very well; we found no flex the first time around in 1975 and the arrangement seems flex-free on the Darmah. If there's any fault to find with the Darmah layout, it's that the combination of long wheelbase and 31-deg. rake make for unhandiness at low speeds in tight going: The bike wants to fall over. But this is a trade-off for the Duck's ability to eat up as many miles of fast, swoopy roadway as you care to feed it.

Suspension is Ceriani forks in front, Marzocchi shocks at the rear with five preload settings. These provide a ride and suspension response that rates as firm but well short of stiff and rarely what you'd call uncomfortable.

Although response was generally positive and free of any hint of wallowing or dive, we did encounter a certain amount of low frequency front-end oscillation, particularly in fast right-hand sweepers. The presence of a beefy steering damper made it plain that something like this might be coming, so it didn't exactly come as a surprise the first time it showed up, nor was it particularly alarming. The damper offers seven adjustments, and we'd dialed in four clicks before we got the bike to behave with complete steadiness at high speeds.

The source of this slow wobble is something of a mystery. It may come from altered geometry—the Darmah uses 12-in. rear shocks, an inch lower than those employed on the previous 860. We've also heard some negative speculation concerning the tires in regard to this problem, but the rubber doesn't really strike us as a source of trouble. The bike arrived with Michelin M45's at both ends, and these proved excellent in every way, hot or cold. Like the handsome Campagnolo cast wheels, these tires are an example of the excellent factory-installed equipment that makes this motorcycle such a desirable thing to possess.

The Brembo brakes are formidable. They are discs, of course, with cast iron rotors and double-piston calipers, two in front and one in the rear. Cast iron is good to see here, as the mass manufacturers have been using stainless steel rotors and have been having some problems finding a pad material which works against stainless in the rain. Iron doesn't have this drawback and the Darmah brakes worked beautifully, wet or dry. Leverage in front was that elusive balance between heavy and all-locked-up. The rear could use a bit less leverage, as one needs a few days' practice before a feather foot becomes a habit.

Atop the bike, there's more of the same. The traditional Smiths instruments have given way to Nippondenso gauges and switches, which is a big improvement. The various warning lights still show some hysterical tendencies—the neutral light on our bike was willing to click on in either first, neutral, or second, take your pick—but overall the Ducati's dashboard and switches have been brought forward a full decade.

Grips are firm rubber, very similar to those used by Yamaha, and are comfortable even for extended use in heavy going.

We wouldn't go so far as to call the saddle really comfortable, but it's certainly in step with the sporting nature of the beast. Lightly padded and backed by fiberglass, the whole thing lifts off for access to the little storage bin in the upswept tail section (wherein resides a rather ordinary collection of tools). Just sitting on that lean saddle gives one the feeling of counting down at Imola, a feeling reinforced by the rider's knees' indents at the rear of the tank. (It also gives the impression of sitting directly atop the Uncle Sam strap, which is an accurate impression. No

Rear shocks are Marzocchi with five preload adjustments. Mufflers shown here are standard. Conti racing mufflers, available through dealers, improve performance substantially.

DUCATI 900SD DARMAH

SPECIFICATIONS

List price ....$3500 approx.
Engine ....sohc desmodromic V-Twin
Bore x stroke ....86 x 74.4mm
Piston displacement 864cc
Compression ratio 9.3:1
Carburetion ....(2) 32mm Dellorto
Air filtration ....treated paper
Ignition ....Bosch CDI
Claimed power ....na
Claimed torque ....na
Lubrication system ....wet sump
Oil capacity..............................10.6 pt.
Fuel capacity ....4.0 gal.
Recommended fuel ....premium
Starting system ....electric, kick
Electrical system ..12v 200w alternator
Clutch ....wet, multi-disc
Primary drive ....helical gear
Final drive ....# 530 chain
Gear Ratios, overall:1
  5th...4.92
  4th...5.54
  3rd...6.67
  2nd...8.66
  1st...12.40
Suspension, front.........telescopic fork
Suspension, rear ....swing arm
Tire, front...........................350H-18
Tire, rear 4.25/85V-18
Brake, front..............dual 10.9-in. disc
Brake, rear ....10.8-in. disc
Total brake swept area ....265 sq. in.

Brake loading
  (160-lb. rider) ....2.5 lb./sq. in.
Wheelbase ....61.0 in.
Fork rake angle ....31.0 deg.
Trail ....na
Handlebar width ....27.9 in.
Seat height ....31.0 in.
Seat width ....7.0 in.
Footpeg height ....12.5 in.
Ground clearance.....................6.5 in.
Curb weight
  (w/half-tank fuel)..................500 lb.
Weight bias, front/rear,
  percent 46/54

PERFORMANCE

Engine speed @ 60 mph ......3877 rpm
Power/weight ratio,
  (160-lb. rider) ....na
Fuel consumption ....41.7 mpg
Speedometer error:
  30 mph indicated, actually 28.9
  40 mph indicated, actually 38.7
  50 mph indicated, actually 48.6
  60 mph indicated, actually 58.5
Braking distance
  from 30 mph..........................31.5 ft.
  from 60 mph........................134.0 ft.
Standing start
  ¼-mile ......12.98 sec. @ 101.23 mph
Speed after
  ½ mile ....111 mph

FRONT FORKS

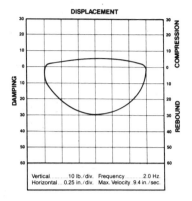

DISPLACEMENT

Vertical..........10 lb./div. Frequency.........2.0 Hz.
Horizontal...0.25 in./div. Max. Velocity 9.4 in./sec.

Ceriani straight-leg fork
Fork travel ....5.0 in.
Engagement ....6.4 in.
Spring rate ....30/55 lb./in.
Compression damping force..........5 lb.
Rebound damping force ....29 lb.
Static seal friction ....28 lb.

The combination of high seal friction
and low damping rates makes for a stiff
ride, but one which yields good control
and stability. An increase in compliance
and comfort, with no loss in control,
may be had by installing slicker seals
and using heavier-than-stock fork oil.

REAR SHOCKS

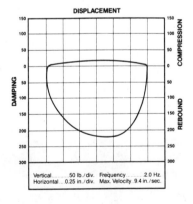

DISPLACEMENT

Vertical..........50 lb./div. Frequency.........2.0 Hz.
Horizontal...0.25 in./div. Max. Velocity 9.4 in./sec.

Marzocchi shock,rebuildable
Shock travel ....2.7 in.
Wheel travel ....3.6 in.
Spring rate..........................130 lb./in.
Compression damping force.......14 lb.
Rebound damping force ....220 lb.

Spring and damping rates are in keeping with the sporting nature of this bike.
While softer shocks and springs would
lessen the feedback through the Darmah's firm seat, the trade-off would not
be worthwhile in terms of control and
stability in the corners.

Tests performed at Number One Products

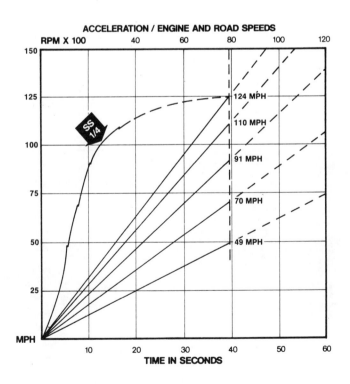

ACCELERATION / ENGINE AND ROAD SPEEDS

RPM X 100

SS 1/4

124 MPH
110 MPH
91 MPH
70 MPH
49 MPH

MPH

TIME IN SECONDS

The 900's piston is domed, with eyebrows for valve clearance. Compression ratio on the Darmah is 9.3:1, up from 9.0:1 on previous editions of the 860.

Ducati's overhead cams are driven by bevel gears. Power is transferred from crank to heads via gear-driven shafts. Tach drive shares cam drive on forward head.

reflection on Ducati and nothing a good sharp jackknife wouldn't cure.)

Although the combination of low seat height and high footpeg height (for max cornering clearance) make the riding position seem a trifle awkward for the first few minutes, this impression lasts only until you arrive at the first set of turns; from then on, the bike feels right.

The handlebars are something of a compromise, more of the civilizing that's part of the Darmah theme. These are quite similar to the ones used on the first 860, with just a little less rise. The relationship of rider to saddle, footpegs, foot controls and bars is a surprisingly comfortable semi-racing crouch, although for taller riders the position might be a bit on the fetal side.

But once the scenery accelerates, there isn't much time to think about the subtleties of your tuck; you'll be too involved with the heady sensations the Duck generates as you swoop from side to side or lay over for some mighty sweeper.

The Ducati will drag its centerstand quite easily, particularly on the left side of the bike, and the exhausts come next. But

by the time you begin grinding these items, you've already left a whole flock of Multis toiling along raggedly behind you.

Although some riders commented on the Darmah's extra weight as a noticeable drawback for back road barnstorming, it still behaves like a Ducati, requiring little in the way of rider acrobatics to get it around turns. You can still think it through the turns; it may be that you have to think *harder* than was the case with the SS, but high speed control is still effortless.

The Darmah is perhaps the most impressive update on the Ducati big bike line since the first 750s were introduced six years ago

There are flaws other than those already mentioned, of course. Little things, like a kickstand cunningly hidden under the gear shift, or those tiger decals that smell strongly of hasty afterthought. And good-sized drawbacks, such as the bike's true purpose. Civilized or not, this machine is designed for men who want to explore the outer limits of their ability to manage a

motorcycle at high speed, filling the slack periods between excursions by honing shims and ordering spare parts. Try selling *that* set of appeals to your girl friend or wife.

But we don't buy superbikes because they're practical or tame. We buy them because they're exciting, because they transport us to a realm that few of our fellow travelers ever visit.

Judged by this standard, it's hard to position the new Darmah far from the head of its illustrious class. Class. It's got plenty of that, along with enough flash to put some of the hairier machines on the trailer. The big load of improvements given to this new offering from Dr. T. and his pals in Bologna make it a contemporary bike in every sense, and Dr. T.'s special project—desmodromic valves—continue to set it apart from anything else on the market.

It's not for everyone. The price and the demands of maintenance help to isolate the Ducati in the marketplace.

But for the man who has a place in his collection for one of the ultimate personal sports bikes of the day, well, here it is. ◨

Duck's 200-watt alternator is chain driven off left side of engine. Excellent electrics are Bosch.

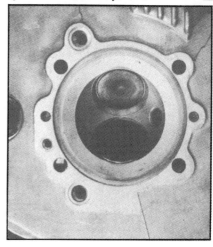

Desmo valve train differs from conventional in that valves are pulled shut as well as pushed open (note forked end of cam follower operating against valve stem collar). Clothespin-type spring snaps valve against seat; compression alone accomplishes this task on racing Ducks.

Valves are 40mm intake, 36mm exhaust.

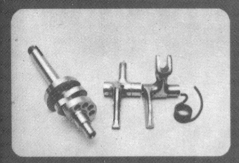

The full race camshaft operates via standard camshaft followers, they are more than strong enough.

Teflon coated 11:1 piston (right), standard (centre) and endurance 8:1 (left).

Due to the heavier crankpin and piston the crank has to be re-balanced.

Hailwood's T.T. Ducati
A works motor, plus Sports Motorcycles race-craft
by Dave Walker

The external flywheel is lightened and polished: the primary drive gears are special factory jobs.

A close ratio five speed gear cluster is fitted, many of the gears are drilled for lightness.

Running with a dry clutch means a special mag. alloy casting for the primary drive.

MIKE HAILWOOD could have had any machine he wanted for the Isle of Man Formula One race — he chose Ducati. To be more precise he chose Sports Motorcycles' Ducati and, as I found out when I visited them in Manchester, there is a big difference. I, like many others, was under the impression that the Hailwood "works" TT bike was to be supplied ready to go by the factory and Sports Motorcycles' job was simply to add the petrol. As I very quickly found out this is far from the truth for Steve Wynne has built the motor up from scratch, incorporating all his own hard earned modifications learned from racing Ducatis.

When the engine arrived from the factory it was fitted with race cams, gas flowed heads and a dry clutch set up. The bulk of the motor remained standard. Starting at the heart of the engine, the crankshaft,

Steve has found that the big-ends will fail when the engine is used hard. Finding the answer was expensive.

Since there is plenty of metal around the crankpin an oversize pin was made up and pressed into the standard flywheel. The standard rods are retained, but machined out to accept the new big end rollers. The finish on the rods is superb, like a mirror, but Steve wouldn't take credit for it: the rods are polished as standard.

With the new big end assembly fitted the engine will be a lot more reliable but Steve knows from his own experience that the next problem is to prevent the piston breaking up. The answer in this case is better pistons. Simple answers can also prove expensive because the new pistons had to be bought in from America. They are Teflon

1 A new crankpin is turned up and the standard rod bored out, to prevent big end failure.

2 This is what happens when you exceed 8,200 rpm with the standard piston; very expensive.

3 With the special clutch cover the oil filler is blanked off. The clutch is alloy on this machine.

4 A small error in each of these camshaft drive gears adds up to very inaccurate cam timing.

5 Extra keyways, cut offset in the bevel gears, means two more chances of spot on cam timing.

6 The hydraulic steering damper is located on alloy brackets, again to save weight.

Hailwood's T.T. Ducati

coated and a lot stronger than standard: with a raised crown on the top of the piston bringing compression ratio up to 11 to 1, they need to be.

Steve Wynne and the big Ducati which is now nearing completion for its historic appearance in the Island.

The barrels had to be bored to plus 40thou to accept the new pistons. This is not to increase the capacity, it's simply to fit the piston which does not come in a smaller size. The slight oversize also helps the compression ratio.

Naturally with the larger big end and heavier pistons the crankshaft had to be rebalanced. Rather than add weight to the crankweb, Steve removed it from the crankpin area of the flywheels. The flywheels were also polished around the crankpin. The small external wheel, just outboard of the primary drive gear, was lightened by reducing its width.

The cylinder heads were prepared at the works but started life as the standard Desmo unit. Both ports were opened out and gas flowed, but most of the attention was paid to the inlet which is opened out to within a hair's breadth of breaking through the cast-

ing. It feeds out into the cylinder around a 2mm oversize inlet valve. The combustion chamber was also polished but the shape remains standard. On the outlet side the exhaust valve is also 2mm oversize.

There is nothing very special about the camshaft which is the Imola, or full race cam. Timing is quoted by the factory as 65-95/95-55 degrees but Steve has found quite large discrepancies from one cam to another. To overcome this two extra keyways have been machined into the timing bevel gears, and this, combined with offset keys, allows the cams to be set up spot on.

When you consider that the factory quote their figures as + or − 5 degrees, you begin to understand what Steve is getting at. The main advantage of the desmodromic valve gear is the control it gives over valve acceleration. The valve can be fired off of its seat, straight to full lift without having to worry about valve float pulling the follower away from the cam face. Once fully open the valve can be left there until the last minute when it can be slammed almost shut, then gently lowered back onto its seat. The main advantage is, therefore, the amount of time the valve can spend at full lift for any given set of timing figures.

While it is true to say the desmodromic valve operation helps the free revving of the engine, it is not a licence to spin the motor at the speed of light. With its very long stroke, piston speed is the limiting factor for this big V-twin. Don't run away with the idea that the Ducati 860 is an old fashioned long stroke motor, at 86 x 74.4mm it IS oversquare. Having only two cylinders the stroke has to be longer than average to get the capacity, yet maintain a realistic bore to stroke ratio.

On the carburation side there are no fancy magnesium body instruments to be found. Breathing is through a pair of 40mm Dell'Orto carbs the same as can be found on any 900 SS production machine. Steve has found, through many hours of experimenting, that they perform best when the bellmouth length is reduced by half. This appears to give the best overall inlet tract length.

You can get a pretty fair idea of just how

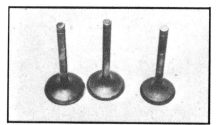

7 Two millimeter oversize valves are used on the inlet and exhaust. Standard valve in centre.

8 Since there are no valve springs this ramp on the camshaft closes the valve.

9 The clutch has sintered bronze plates and an alloy drum. These drilled units are from last year's bike.

13 The crankcase is drilled for this quick filler oil plug. The fairing obscures the original.

14 This crankcase web can be drilled with two half inch holes to help drainage from flywheel.

15 To get the best overall inlet tract length the standard bellmouths are cut in half.

19 Weight reduction can become an obsession, even the gearbox sprocket has been drilled!

20 The rear shock absorbers are Girling gas units, the latest road type with pre-load adjusters.

21 The clear section in the fuel tank allows the pit crew an instant check on petrol.

Hailwood's T.T. Ducati

efficient the engine is when you consider the fuel consumption which is an astonishing 40mpg at racing speeds! Helping here is a Lucas Rita ignition system. Steve found that when running with contact breakers the ignition could wander by as much as two degrees during a short race. The electronic set up doesn't vary at all and Lucas arranged for the "magic box" to be fitted with quick release jack plugs. If the ignition does give any trouble on the Island the whole set up can be replaced instantly.

Although the standard Ducati is now fitted with electronic ignition, much of it is located under the crankcase clutch cover — where it's difficult to get at in the event of trouble.

The primary gear, taking the power to the gearbox, is a special lightweight job from the factory. The driven gear is normally part of the clutch drum but on this motor it's separate, allowing the clutch drum to be fabricated from aluminium alloy. Before Steve got the alloy job from the factory he used the standard unit, but drilled it so full of holes it looked like a piece of Swiss cheese.

Like most racing machines the clutch runs dry, the friction plates being made from sintered bronze. When we road tested the Ducati Darmah we thought that the clutch might prove something of a weak spot if slipped excessively. This engine has the clutch springs from the Ducati 450 single

fitted, and Steve tells us this is also a good mod for the road bikes.

Since the clutch does run dry, a new casting was required on that side of the crankcase. The factory cast this from magnesium alloy along with the little cover which stops the rider's toes getting mangled in the works.

A close ratio gear cluster is fitted but Steve had to modify the fourth gear somewhat. He has found that when the motor is race tuned and the gearbox thrashed to within an inch of its life, fourth gear jumps out. This always seems to happen as the motor approaches maximum revs, which is a bit like sitting on a grenade.

To prevent this happening three of the selector dogs were machined away. This doesn't sound right; until you know how the standard gearbox works. In an attempt to reduce gearbox backlash three short dogs are fitted between the main ones. These don't help the initial engagement, they simply reduce the backlash on the over-run. These were ground away and the original main dogs cut a little deeper. This is strictly a racing mod; the box never gives any trouble on a tuned road machine.

The chassis is exactly the same as the one used last year. It is based on the 750 road bike design but has extra bracing struts around the steering head. Naturally, the tube is a special lightweight type.

The rear swinging arm is very interesting,

being a cross between the 750 and the 860 set ups. Like the standard road 750 the pivot at the chassis end is fixed. On the 860 it is mounted on eccentric adjusters. To tension the chain an eccentric spindle is fitted to the rear end of the fork, similar to the 860, but at the "wrong" end.

Ducati seemed to have been carried away with the idea of eccentric adjusters. The footrests are fitted with them, allowing the riding position to be tailored to the rider during actual track testing. The engine forms part of the frame structure and helps to keep the centre of gravity low down.

Although I obviously couldn't ride the bike, I was allowed to sit on it and play make-believe racers for a little while. It feels like a 250 — with an all up weight of around 370 lb, I should think it handles like one as well. The riding position fits like a glove, thanks to a very clever seat and tank design.

On the suspension side, Girling gas shocks are to be fitted to the rear, not the motocross type, but the new road shock absorber. The spring rates will depend on Mike Hailwood's test session. Up front, Marzocchi forks lead the way. The legs carry two Brembo calipers, and these clamp down onto standard diameter cast iron discs. In an effort to reduce the unsprung weight, and help heat dissipation, no less than 140 holes have been drilled, and countersunk, radially in each disc. A good mod for DIY types who are handy with a Black and Decker.

That was the state of the bike when I left Steve Wynne polishing the twin filler caps with his shirt sleeve, and quietly smiling to himself, as every proud father has a right to.

16

10 The standard gear on the left has three of its dogs machined away. The remaining ones are cut deeper.

11 The selector drum, for the close ratio five speed box, is peppered with holes to reduce weight.

12 Lucas Rita electronic ignition replaces the contact breaker set up on the 750 style crankcases.

16 The cast iron disc has 140 holes drilled in it. This reduces weight and helps cooling.

17 Short circuit scratchers don't need an oil cooler but in long races it's essential.

18 The rear set footrests are mounted on eccentric adjusters for instant adjustment.

22 For home tuning the inlet needs to be as big as possible. If you should break . . .

23 . . . through at the top of the port, it can be repaired with Araldite, like this.

24 When cleaning up the exhaust, avoid the bottom of the port, it's very thin just here.

ROAD MODS

With Mike Hailwood riding for them John Sear and Steve Wynne, the men behind Sports Motorcycles, could be forgiven for sticking their heads into the clouds, and having a little less time for the average mortal. If they were just businessmen instead of motorcyclists that might well have happened. While I was being shown around the bike the 'phone rang; a Ducati Darmah owner wanted some information on tuning his road bike. He wasn't a customer of Sports Motorcycles, but Steve still spent the best part of thirty minutes giving a fellow Ducati enthusiast a list of worthwhile mods.

Would they mind us passing on these hard earned tips to the general public, and their production racing competition? No, they wouldn't, the more quick Ducati twins around the better as far as they were concerned.

Starting at the engine, Steve says they would go plenty quick enough, if they were only set up as the designer originally intended. Camshaft timing is the main problem. If you invest in a degree disc and a dial gauge, you can find a fair bit more top speed by correcting the valve timing. This takes time and you will probably have to make up off-set keyways to put matters right.

The heads can be ported and polished by the average home tuner — but don't overdo it. The walls can get rather thin at the top of the inlet. If you should break through, you can effect a repair with Araldite. The idea is to get them: "as big, and as straight, as possible", and smooth out any obvious lumps and bumps. Polishing the port to a mirror finish is a harmless pastime, but don't expect any extra power — just plain smooth is good enough.

On the exhaust side the port can be cleaned up, but leave the bottom of the port alone. It is the pipe length that really helps the power. After making up countless systems, Steve found the best pipe length to be 24ins. These should feed into the standard silencer. With pipes this length you will have to make the one from the top cylinder a high level job.

The carbs from the 900 SS are the best units for maximum power but they are not a must. Whatever the size of your carbs will benefit from being shortened. Nothing as subtle as squashing them in a vice, you simply cut the bellmouth in half.

The engine will also run better at high rpm if the carbs are rubber mounted. There are no kits available, so car radiator hose and home made adaptors are the order of the day. It is easiest to fit the rubber between the manifold and the head, rather than the manifold and the carb. However you do it, keep the overall inlet tract length the same.

The heads are not fitted with gaskets but the seal can be guaranteed by lapping the head with fine grinding paste. Unless you have an old barrel that you can break the fins off you will have to get a suitable collar made up. Anything the same diameter as the barrel spigot can be used as long as its surface is flat.

Steve says you can get a useful gain in acceleration by reducing the width of the external flywheel by 50 per cent.

Although after these mods the motor should produce the sort of power the designer intended, it won't go any faster because the clutch is going to slip. Clutch springs from the 450 single are the answer.

As I said earlier, the latest 860 engine is fitted with its own electronic ignition. If you have a 750 with contact breakers and coils, the Lucas Rita set up is worth considering. Set the 750 timing to 10 degrees static.

If you just happen to be stripping your engine there is also a mod for the crankcases. Steve recommends drilling a couple of half inch holes in the bottom of the case baffle plate which improves drainage from the flywheel back into the sump.

The gearbox is quite up to hard road use without any mods. If you want to improve the change action a little you can gently radius the detent holes in the gear change plate.

On the chassis side there are one or two mods you can make to improve the already good road holding. An obvious mod is to swop the rear dampers. The standard set up on the Ducati twins is a little on the hard side for this country, and Steve recommends 13in Girling gas shocks with the 100lb rate springs.

At the front end the sting can be taken out of the Ceriani forks by removing the preload spacer from under the top nuts. These should be replaced with Triumph twin valve springs! They just happen to be the right diameter and give the front fork springs a little progressive action.

DUCATI 500

DUCATI 500

HOW TIME alters one's perspectives. Since the Laverda and Ducati 500s were introduced and reported on last August (See *Motorcyclist Illustrated* October 1977) Moto Guzzi have introduced a transverse V-twin, Moto Morini have produced a 500 on the lines of their famous '3½' range, and Ducati have a Taglioni designed longitudinal V-twin in their traditional style out of the Taglioni stable. But most of all, Honda have flung down their own gauntlet into the suddenly exploding new sales arena with a transverse V-twin of formidable worth.

When the pair in question were evaluated they were the only new 500s around in production, and they were filling a long standing gap left by the demise of the old Tiger 100. Admittedly the Japanese had come out with machines of their own, but they lacked that special, heady mix of lightweight handling with heavyweight power that only a 500 seems able to supply so satisfyingly. Since then, although the Honda CX500 has established itself, with good reason, as a remarkably fine motorcycle, it has not the Italian motorcycles' vivacity. Neither is the Honda a truly sporting machine inasmuch as it is equipped with no inbuilt incentive to persuade a rider to try, or to give him the itch to go racing properly.

Suddenly, we have a saturated market, to such an extent that the Guzzi/Ducati UK concessionaires have decided their new 500s to be commercially unviable, so are not importing them. Yet, apart from Honda's

For sheer looks, it would be hard to beat the Ducati in its bright red and white coachwork.

LAVERDA 500

DAVE MINTON

The Laverda is most un-Italian insofar as it has both an excellent finish and good electrics.

CX500, no 500s are selling as well as they really should in Britain. This is something I find hard to understand because, while so manageable in every sense of the word, they are precious little slower in practical terms than the litre-plus monsters around.

Saturated we might be in potential choice, but restricted in actual, for the above reason, presumably. Intruding into the subject, although in a very secondary manner, is the impression suggested by contact with the first machines ridden and reported on, in which a wobble marred the Laverda and vibration the Ducati. Since then, other models of the same type have been tried and found to be free of their forerunner's troubles. Should anyone dare to imagine the truth of this I suggest he tries one for himself to discover the truth.

Our Ducati 500 Sport came from Amington Motorcycles in Tamworth who, immediately the test machine was returned to them, stripped it for inspection preceeding racing assembly. During this time it was discovered that one piston had been fitted wrong way around and was not only spoiling combustion, but balance as well. An offer was made for a further test to be carried out, but by this time a visiting Italian, bristling with rage at the implications of my critisism, had offered his own model for evaluation. Half an hour was enough to invalidate much of what I had disliked about the vibratory attitude of the 500 Sport. While still not smooth, what vibration remained was by no means uncomfortable or destructive any longer. Unlike our pre-production test model, this Italian owned machine also provided its rider with the smoother advantages of a correctly balanced crankshaft.

Slater Bros., Laverda importers, had also discovered the reason for the stability imperfections of their Alpino, and make no mistake about it, imperfection it was, *not* weakness. The bike was designed for TT100s, but they were unavailable for production line machines, which left the factory with some very inferior alternative tyres instead. Further rides of Alpinos equipped with TT100 tyres have proved how incorrect was my first opinion when I began wondering about inadequate frame stiffness and the like. Finally, while still available to special order, the original Alpino (the name has been changed from Alpina as a concession to correct Italian) has been superceeded by the Alpino S, handsomely liveried in black with gold pin striped paintwork.

Inside the engine things have changed as well. Sporty they always were, but now they are positively racy, with compression up an atmosphere to 10:1, a sharper camshaft, and revised carburation to suit. Exactly what the power is Laverda prefer to keep to themselves but unofficial sources put it at around 48 bhp at 8500 rpm (crankshaft figures), where it once was 44 bhp. Ducati are equally coy about their baby, too, but once again, unofficial figures suggest something around 44 bhp at 8500 rpm.

Previously Laverda claimed the 500 would outperform their chunky old SF 750, something I responded to with considerable doubt, a good SF being an extraordinarily long legged beast overlooked by far too many as ''old fashioned''. Around the bends, by all means would an Alpino cut ahead, but now I am convinced that, even in a straight line the Alpino S would outpace an SF. Laverda claim a top speed of approximately 118 mph, and it would seem plausible. Unfortunately, the circumstances of the all-too short ride on the Alpino S disallowed such things as top speed checks, but 105 mph came up very fast indeed, with more coming along behind.

Despite being Italian in the very best sense of the word, the Alpino S displayed those niceties of Japanese motorcycling, too, in which the entire group of ancillary components, and the details and the paint and metal finishes, lose their individual identities as they contribute to such an harmonious whole. Whether you like Japanese machines or not they do offer the buying public absolute completeness. Unfortunately few others, save BMW and Laverda do. There

Laverda employ four valves per cylinder on the Alpino to aid efficient breathing. Motor's external appearance is still rather Japanese-like — but with an air of real quality. Power is now up to around 48bhp.

is always that air of careless slop that, while appealing to fly-spattered buffs, holds no water with the majority who patently prefer charm to guts.

In taking the bull by the horns and combining both philosophies Laverda have shown a fine example to their Latin counterparts, yet one that we British appear confused by, to the evident disadvantages of Laverda! It has all the appearance of a Japanese machine — meaning nicely trimmed — and is therefore judged as one, so it appears to be expensive. Madness, madness; where have our perspectives warped these days? The

bike reeks Latin splendour, and moves accordingly, with a pace and grace that would set the average Japanese so far behind its rider wouldn't know whether it was birthday or breakfast time.

Mind you, so would the Ducati 500, but it, sadly, conforms to the old traditions of Ducati rather than the new ones set by the magnificent Darmah. Oh, a thoroughbred right enough, but one clothed glamorously from a cheap bargain basement. Initially everything is fine and dandy, but after the first introductory moments when all is blood hot and ennervating, the cloth shows its true quality. And that's the infuriating things about it, because at heart it is the Laverda's equal. Even more annoying from the standpoint of a potential customer is the knowledge that, in a year of production no substantial improvement has been attempted. The seat is still secured by four badly placed bolts that encourage glass fibre base cracking; the instruments are still difficult to read and are inaccurate; the exhaust system's matt black paint is as unresistant to rusting as ever; and the gearchange retains its sloppy linkages.

But the styling is magnificent and the overall performance gut churningly good, so much so that, when I rode it I was willing to forgive it everything, but *everthing*. The Laverda, on the other hand, is so damn good all round its minor faults tend to be exaggerated and, thus, it is all too easy to remember the Ducati fondly as a courageous bike fighting insuperable odds engineered-in by an uncaring maker, and the Laverda as a potentially perfect motorcycle let down by minutea.

As a matter of fact, now that Ducati have announced a new V-twin 500 designed by Taglioni, who was never very enthusiastic about the vertical twin machine anyway, the writing could well be on the wall for the 500 as it stands now. But it does have some very attractive points about it that by rights should be used as a foundation to relaunch it in improved form.

The frame is very similar in basic form to the big V-twins, although slightly let down by the adoption of Paoli suspension which lacks the Laverda's all forgiving Marzzochi system. Over severe bumps, despite a set of Michelin tyres undoubtedly much superior than the Alpino S's cheapskate original fitments, skittering can occur under extreme stress, and frequently did. The Alpino S, on the other hand, *almost* overcame its disadvantageous boots. So I tried one with a set of Dunlop TT 100s and warmly appreciated Slater Bros. (Laverda importers) claim that my previous observation about possible design flaws in Laverda's frame design were unfounded. True enough, for the TT100 equipped Alpino chopped or held a line with an ease that improved my skills beyond their natural limitations, and gave me cause to fantasise about starting a new career in GP racing.

The Alpino's frame probably weighs 30 per cent less than the Ducati 500's, being a single loop type, rather than duplex like the Ducati, and it reflects amply the difference in the two factories' design philosophy.

Ducati set out with robustness, even to the extent of slight overbuilding as their aim, so long as the motorcycle provided the performance they were aiming for. This can be seen in the enormous engine castings, heavy frame, etc., while Laverda set themselves a weight limit to which all design would be subjucated.

Effectively, the differing approaches have been manifested in the two performances. The Ducati handles with all the steady resolve of a larger motorcycle. It is probably the equal of the Laverda through a series of bends and, initially, feels superior, even with the Alpino TT100 equipped, on poor surfaces, but this is due to nothing more than apparent superiority, not actual. The Laverda is much like the older single cylinder Ducatis, or maybe a Yamaha RD400, in that, if anything, it is too sensitive for its own good, deluging its rider with such amounts of feedback that there is a definite tendency to misinterpret at least some of it as warning signals of impeding danger. The Ducati is not like

this at all and shields its rider from all but major irregularities, thus suggesting superiority. Possibly, considering the stiffer looking frame of the Ducati, in situation of extreme stress, the Ducati might prove ultimately superior, but no road rider could ever hope to reach this state of affairs.

Once the ultra-sensitivity of the Alpino is appreciated, then it becomes possible to ride it faster over anything but motorways than probably anything else made, save a few medium-weight classics such as those just mentioned. Its strength lies in line changing, something it carries out so quickly as to always preceed its riders intentions, at least it did in my case. No matter how fast the line chop was attempted I would always emerge convinced I could have made it that much quicker.

The Ducati was different, and was best handled in a steady rhythm, with more of a flow, although even in its case deliberation was unrequired thanks to its prodigous cornering abilities. Possibly due to its more

The Ducati, as befits a sports model, features rear-set footrests, which results in a rather untidy gear change pedal arrangement. The matt black silencers do not stay that colour for long.

sporting riding position I always felt a modicum more secure on a long fast line when my inside ear was beginning to feel vulnerable. The thing would drop lower and lower, faster and faster, until commonsense warned me off. Given lower handlebars and rear set footrests the Alpino might have felt the same; who can tell?

The Ducati is one man's motorcycle, although a dual seat and pillion rest model is made in Italy, but not imported into Britain. The Alpino, despite its appetite for speed, is nevertheless a remarkably useful two-up tourer, with a comfortable seat and suspension. It also enjoys the advantage of a six speed gearbox and lower gears down the box in order a rider hauling a heavy gross loading might have an easier time persuading his machine to maintain an untroubled pace.

Previously, it was debatable which of the two was better able to supply a consistently high average speed, for both could romp along seemingly indefinitely at 90 mph, but Laverda have now got the edge. Both bikes have always vibrated a little, Ducati with a lower pitched resonance than the Laverda. Neither were bad by any means, and owners of them generally overlooked it entirely, but the Alpino S now has stolen the lead by leaving the factory with a miniature balance weight in the front of its primary drive chest, which runs off the end of the crankshaft via a gear. It's a tiny thing intended to control the secondary vibrations created by the 180 degree crankshaft's determination to rock along its length. Unlike Japanese balance cranks, this one is diminutive, and absorbs no power worth the name, but it does make the engine so

The Oxford Fairings glass fibreware decorate this brand new Ducati in the Mick Walker Motorcycles' showroom — suits it too.

Ducati's instruments (above) are Italian-made and exaggerate: the Laverda employs Japanese instruments for accuracy.

SPECIFICATIONS DUCATI 500 SPORT

ENGINE
Type: Air-cooled inclined transverse parallel twin. All alloy engine with steel cylinder liners. Vertically split crankcase. Wet sump. One-piece forged crankshaft with two plain main bearings and central flywheel. Split shell big ends.
Valve operation: Two valves per combustion chamber desomdromically activated from central gearbox driven chain. Valve clearances adjusted by shims.
Capacity: 497cc.
Bore and stroke: 78 × 52mm.
Compression: 9.6:1.
Carburation: 2 × 30mm Dell Orto PHF instruments with accelerator pumps breathing through paper cartridge filter.
Lubrication: Wet sump via high pressure gear pump and paper cartridge filter in common with transmission.
Electrics: 12v × 12AH battery charged by 200w crankshaft alternator. Current controlled by transistorised regulator. Coil and contact breaker ignition.
Claimed power: N/A, but approx. 44bhp at 8,500rpm.

TRANSMISSION
Primary: Helical gear.
Clutch: Wet multi-plate.
Gear ratios: 14.30; 9.80; 7.62; 6.14; top 5.14:1. Selection by left side one down and four up foot lever.
Final drive: Exposed unlubricated chain, incorporating shock absorber in rear hub.

FRAME
All welded steel tube duplex loop open at base utilising engine as stress member.

SUSPENSION
Front: Two-way damped Paioli telefork.
Rear: Pivoted fork. Bronze bush spindle bearings. Two-way damped, load adjustable Paioli units.

WHEELS
Front: 3.25 Michelin S41 ribbed tyre around W M3 rim × 18in cast alloy artillery wheels with six duplex spokes. Duplex 10.25in cast iron discs with double acting Brembo hydraulic calipers.
Rear: As front but 3.50 tyre and single brake.

INSTRUMENTATION
Matched 140mph Veglia speedometer and rev. counter. Ignition, main beam, neutral and turn signal warning lights.

EQUIPMENT
2.6 gallon steel fuel tank inc. 2 pint reserve. Centre stand only. 6in × 60/45w tungsten bulb headlamp. Electric starting only. Lift handle. Turn signals. Mirror. Plastic side panels. Clip-on handlebars and rear seat foot controls. Single racing style seat with poppered-on padding. Tool kit in unlockable duck tail locker. Headlamp flasher.

PERFORMANCE DATA
Fuel consumption: Mild sub-60 cruising, 70mpg. Fast riding, 59mpg. Test average, 51mpg.
Fuel quality: Four star.
Speed: Top speed with 200lb rider lying prone in touring leathers, 111mph.
Gear speeds: (at recommended safe maximum revs of 8,500): 45; 65; 84; 105; top 121mph.
Speedometer accuracy: 3mph fast at 30mph. 6mph fast at 60mph.

CUSTOMER INFORMATION
Importers: Ducati Concessionaires Ltd., 21 Crawley Road, Luton, Beds.
Colours available: Red/white only.
Price: £1,699 including VAT.
Warranty: 18 months parts and labour in conjunction with Autoguard.

much sweeter. Vibration has now been virtually eliminated, save for a few mild tingles at extreme revs. The miles pass all that much more comfortably, and the engine has most definitely lost the slightly fussy manner it once had.

In construction the two models are as far apart as their respective performances. Laverda have opted for their usual bottom end of all ball and roller bearings carrying a built up crankshaft in a horizontally split crankcase, which holds the oil for both engine and transmission. Ducati have opted for a one piece forged crankshaft, plain bearings all round, and a vertically split wet sump crankcase, also lubricating the gears. Of the two engines Ducati appear to have constructed the heavier, but as Laverda durability is the equal of any around there seems little to doubt the Alpino S's long anticipated life.

The valve gear of the pair is equally unusual. Ducati employ desmodromically activated valves, although in this instance via a gearbox driven chain, rather than a crankshaft driven shaft as is their normal practice. Laverda have plumped for four valve combustion chambers, each one wiped by a lobe from one or other of the two chain driven camshafts.

Ducati employ conventional contact breaker ignition, and Laverda transitorised. Both work very efficiently indeed, something the fuel consumption figures back up. Significantly enough neither machine is equipped with a kick starter, and no bad thing, for a quick run-and-bump in second gear fired them up easily in emergencies.

In detail the Alpino scored high marks, and the Ducati Sports low ones, principally because Ducati have remained loyal to Italian-made CEV electrical ancillaries while Laverda have opted for Nippon Denso and Bosch equipment. It made all the difference, especially at night, when the powerful quartz halogen light of the Alpino blazed down the road, against which the Ducati appeared dim and yellow. Shared by both were identical Brembo braking systems, and very similar La Traconi silencers, although the distinctly individual slugs of sound issuing from the Ducati's pipes suggested a modicum more attention to environmental responsibility on Laverda's part.

Time was when the two ran pretty close, but no longer with the advent of the Alpino S. It has advanced, and the Ducati, which could have given it a hard time in the showrooms, has remained unchanged.

SPECIFICATIONS LAVERDA ALPINO

ENGINE
Type: Air-cooled transverse included parallel twin. All alloy construction with horizontally split crankcase. Built-up crankshaft with three main ball and roller bearings and caged needle roller big ends.
Valve operation: Chain driven dohc from crankshaft centre. Four valves per combustion chamber.
Capacity: 497cc.
Bore and stroke: 72 × 61mm.
Compression: 10:1.
Carburation: 2 × 32mm Dell Orto PHF instruments with accelerator pumps via paper cartridge filter.
Lubrication: Wet sump via low pressure high volume pump incorporating transmission. Wire gauze filter.
Electrics: 12v × 18a/hr battery charged by crankshaft mounted Bosch alternator with fully transistorised voltage control and ignition.
Claimed power: N/A but unofficially 48bhp at 8,000rpm.

TRANSMISSION
Primary: Helical gear. 2.65:1 reduction.
Clutch: Wet multi-plate.
Gear ratios: 17.89; 12.13; 9.13; 8.16; 6.46; top 6.032:1. Selection by left side one down and five up foot lever.
Final drive: Exposed unlubricated chain. Adjustment by sliding wheel spindle.

FRAME
All welded single full loop with duplex engine cradle and rear sub frame, and triangle braced spine.

SUSPENSION
Front: Marzzochi tele fork with two way damping.
Rear: Pivoted fork with Marzzochi two way damped, load adjustable units.

WHEELS
Front: 18in cast alloy five spoked artillery with WM3 rim. 3.25in Pirelli Mandrake tyre, Duplex 10.25in cast iron discs with double acting Brembo hydraulic calipers.
Rear: As front but with single disc brake.

INSTRUMENTATION
Nippon Densa 140mph speedometer, rev. counter. Ignition, main beam, neutral and turn signal warning lights.

EQUIPMENT
3 gallon steel fuel tank inc. 2 pint reserve. Hinged and lockable dual seat over ducktail locker holding tool roll. Steering lock. Pillion grab rail. 6in 60/45w q/h Bosch headlamp. Turn signals. Centre and prop stands. Electric starter only. Headlamp flasher. Plastic side panels.

PERFORMANCE DATA
Fuel consumption: Mild sub-70mph cruising, 56mpg. Fast riding, 48mpg.
Fuel quality: Two star.
Speed: Top speed with 200lb rider prone in touring leathers, 105mph.
Gear speeds: (at recommended bhp optimum 8,000rpm): 30; 47; 63; 72; 90; top 93mph.
Speedometer accuracy: 1mph fast at 30mph. 3mph fast at 60mph.

CUSTOMER INFORMATION
Importers: Slater Brothers Limited, Collington, near Bromyard, Herefordshire.
Colours available: Black with gold striping.
Price: £1,675 inc. VAT. Delivery charge additional £20.00.
Warranty: Six months or 6,000 miles, parts and labour.

In The Family Way

IT FIRST APPEARED AT THE COLOGNE SHOW last October. A vision of blue and white, it stood out from the megabike mediocrity. A promise of forbidden delights oozed from its small frame. Grown men and women wilted with lust as soon as they beheld its ethereal beauty. The Ducati men stood around on their stand proud of themselves, as if it wasn't a bike they were showing, but the Second Coming of some two-wheeled Messiah, a fresh interpretation of the physics of motorcycling. Nobody's ever done *quite* the same before . . .

Of course, it's only logical. With the name that Ducati have made out of big-bore ninety degree V-twins, it was an odds-on bet that somewhere in the Bologna pipeline a middleweight version of the same theme existed. But with a difference. The 500cc desmo V has belt-driven overhead cams replacing the shaft drive to the heads found on the bigger Ducatis.

The very concept of a 500cc V-twin conjures images of sweetness, of pleasure, perhaps the ultimate hedonist trip for the true connoisseur of fine motorcycles.

The unveiling of the six-cylinder Kawasaki Z1300 at the same show served only to underline the beauty and sheer commonsense displayed in this little machine. It was a new variation of David and Goliath, the blue bomber versus the green meanie, and I know which one I'd take if they were offered.

Yes, the promise. Everybody imagined what the new Duke must be like to ride. They discussed how the power delivery would differ from that of its bigger brothers. They conjectured as to how the smaller, lighter machine would handle. For God's Sake, could it be better than the 900SS? They asked each

When Ducati announced that their latest baby was to be a V-twin, enthusiasts around the globe raised a hearty cheer. Steve Brennan took a trip to the factory to find out for himself if the smallest Duke V-twin maintains the standards everybody expects from the Italian nobility.

other, and clapped palms to foreheads in amazement.

Yes, it is possible. The promise was fulfilled for this particular hedonist in March, when *Bike* magazine decided we'd waited long enough for a ride on this particular cycle. The highlight of a week-long visit to Italy was to swing a leg over the Pantah in Ducati Meccanica's own backyard in Bologna. Not only were we the first British magazine to sample the bike, but possibly the first European magazine to do so. Certainly no American rag has been there yet . . .

In between cloud-bursts my visual impressions of the Pantah were translated into hard-riding fact. The Ducati Pantah *was* the star of the Cologne Show. In the same way that Muhammed Ali could outpoint The Incredible Hulk — if the ring was large enough, of course — then the Pantah's irrepressible sporting spirit kills stone dead the current rationale behind the Japanese megabike race.

Signore Valentine, export manager for the Ducati concern, led me down from the offices of the Duke HQ and across the factory floor into the prototype shop. There the bike was, but it didn't look much. Gone was the glass-fibre suit it had been wearing at the Cologne Show. I'd been warned that the bike was barely out of testing stage, and was consequently a lash-up cosmetically. A

dingy fairing was curled around the front end, completely obscuring that ace looking motor. An ally tank completed the impession of a back-yard Triton bodge-up while a blue glass fibre seat unit evoked only a marginal aura of racing chic. Campagnolo mag wheels — anodised gold — were the only apparent indication of real class. Tomaselli clip-ons and high foot pegs told the rest of the story. It was almost as if the entire machine had been deliberately finished to look rough: the street sleeper *par excellence*.

Unfortunately, the street was the one place where I wasn't going with this machine. Italian insurance hassles (worse than Britain's, would you believe) dictated that I could only evaluate the latest Duke on the Ducati test track, which isn't renowned for its length. The Nurburgring it isn't. The track just wasn't designed for high-speed kamikaze boy-racer stunts.

But it had to do. Production line workers downed tools and spilled out into the Italian sunshine to witness the *crazi Inglese* hacking around the diminutive circuit. But that's another story.

Sitting on the bike I received that impression that every full-blooded, pedigree sporting machine instils in its rider — that is, of being in balance with the dynamic forces of the bike. It's a sensation of being *in*, rather than *on*. A better rapport between human and machine couldn't be achieved without manufacturing some kind of sci-fi device that plugs the rider's nervous system directly into the electrics.

A further reminder that the Pantah was straight out of the prototype department was given by the competition tachometer, white with black numerals, wired up to the bars.

Above: The Pantah looks scruffy in prototype stage, but the Ducati meanness shines through. Note the latest Marzocchi shock absorbers.

Below: Going around corners on the Duke was bliss. Stacks of low down torque meant that minimum box stirring was needed.

Ducati Darmah

THE Italian motorcycle industry established a reputation on the world's Grand Prix circuits equal to any competing for World Championship honours. Moto Guzzi, Gilera, MV Agusta, Morini, Morbidelli and Aermacchi (Harley-Davidson) accepted the challenge and, in doing so, made their mark in motorcycle racing history.

Ducati too have played their part in the road racing scene with the brilliant engineer, Taglioni, producing the desmodromic four-stroke twins which challenged the world in the late 1950s and 60s.

Although they have long since given up the hectic and costly battle for Grand Prix honours they also supported Mike 'the Bike' Hailwood on his winning return to the Isle of Man this year.

Ducati's last outstanding victories were in the Formula 750 races at Imola and Ontario, when Paul Smart rode the magnificent silver and blue desmodromic V-twins from the Bologna factory into number one spot.

But the advent of the Japanese multi-cylinder two-stroke racers, that used FIM regulations to oust the big-bore four-strokes from the top of F750 racing class, originally conceived for production class bikes, meant that Ducati again gracefully retired from the road racing scene.

However, with a reputation established, the factory used all the knowledge gleaned on the race tracks to create a series of roadster designs incorporating their powerful in-line V-twin, overhead-camshaft motor.

First came the sports 750 using conventional overhead cam gear and next, the desmodromic valve super sports model based on their Imola race winner.

Unfortunately, like most other manufacturers in the late 1960s, Ducati became involved in the 'power game' which meant six-fifties grew into seven-fifties and seven-fifties into nine hundreds.

Ducati produced the ultimate sportster with their Super Sports Desmo 900 machine; a rip-snorting 130mph road-burner capable of competing with any oriental superbike.

However, not everybody is impressed by pseudo-racing roadsters with clip-ons, rear-sets and capacity for solo riding only. Consequently, the Ducati designers returned to their drawing boards and came up with the Darmah, a sports tourer, just about capable of carrying two people and incorporating the 90-degree desmodromic valve big-bore V-twin similar to that used in the Super Sports model.

Higher and wider bars replaced the clip-ons, a stylish but miniscule dual-seat slotted in place of the humped back racing pan and all the trimmings expected of a modern, superbike tourer, including mag wheels, dual disc hydraulic front brake and single disc rear were fitted.

The Darmah is an eye stopping crowd puller of no mean degree. Its red and white livery, gold sprayed wheels and massive motor bring out the beast in the mildest mannered moped riders dreaming of power in, the twistgrip hand.

Turn the twin fuel taps on, operate the ignition key, raise the choke (flood) lever alongside the left headlamp bracket, stab the starter button on the right-hand handlebar and the 846ccs throb gently into life. That is unless you withdrew the ignition key last time you used it, one turn past off, which leaves the parking lights on and overnight flattens the battery.

The emergency kickstart may be used and, as we discovered, it will start the motor when warm with a fully charged battery on the second or third kick. But the kickstart is so low geared, that it only turns the motor over one cylinder per prod and even then, the rider knocks his shin against the foot rest. Starting from cold with a flat battery is virtually impossible using the kickstart.

Mechanically, the big V-twin and its desmodromic valve gear is quite clattery and, when cold, a fair amount of piston slap can be heard emitting from the heavily finned barrels.

If you can't beat them, join them and Ducati have gone Nippon Denso Japanese instrumentation and control switches for the electrics.

A check on the warning light console indicates that the generator is functioning, the lights are on but not on main beam, while the prop stand light glows to indicate that the rest hasn't been tucked up out of harms way. The only comment we have to make here is that although the warning light system is quite comprehensive, it doesn't include an oil pressure warning light. This we consider is far more important than having a prop stand warning light.

The handlebar switches for pilot, and headlight are fairly easily operated, while the dip switch also includes a main beam flash position. The horn button is located below both switches and is easily reached with the left thumb as is the sideways moving indicator switch.

On the right-hand handlebar is the starter button and engine 'kill' switch. Both function perfectly for the purpose for which they were intended.

Within a minute or so, the choke lever can be released and the motor is warm enough to respond to gentle throttle openings without hesitation.

Operation of the clutch is medium to heavy and first gear is selected with a slight clonk. Take up of drive is smooth without snatch or judder and at just over 10mph, the clutch can be fully released as the big four-stroke thumps into its stride.

At 2500rpm it is almost possible to feel each piston being powered up and down its cylinder. A chuffing from the carburetters indicates every breath the motor takes. There is very little vibration from the big V-twin, just a healthy thump accompanied by the normal mech nical noises.

As the throttle is opened, the power comes flooding in and with a mere 3500rpm on the tachometer, an extra firm grip has to be taken on the handlebars as the Darmah takes off. The power band is wide, wide, wide and although the Darmah has a five-speed gearbox, it hardly seems necessary with top gear giving a speed range from just over 30mph to 114mph.

Once on the move, clutchless gear changes between the well-spaced ratios are the norm with perfect and positive selection of gears at all times. The lever movement is light and no false neutrals were found in the box. The only disconcerting problem was a neutral light that came on when neutral or first gear was selected.

After stalling the motor a couple of times, we learned not to trust the indicator and reverted back to the old select it and see method of stopping and checking by gingerly releasing the clutch.

Acceleration on the Darmah wasn't extra exciting; it just happened. There is no precise point at which the V-twin takes off, it

Technically Speaking

ENGINE

A gutsy, thumping 90-degree V-twin four-stroke with desmodromic valve operation which produces power like a steam train is the heart of this Italian super-tourer. Mechanically, the engine is quite noisy with the wide aluminium barrel finning amplifying overhead cam gear noise and piston slap when cold.

Oil consumption throughout the test was negligible and fuel consumption was equal to many motorcycles half the capacity.

Carburetters allowed a certain amount of induction noise, although the exhaust system was adequately muted by the large silencers.

Electric starting was instantaneous, hot or cold, although the auxilliary kick-start required considerable effort to operate when the motor was cold.

Air-cooled, 90-degree, in-line V-twin four-stroke motor with single-overhead cam-shafts to desmodromic operated valves. Bore: 86mm x 74.4mm stroke. Capacity, 864cc. Compression ratio,

just builds up momentum like a steam train. A best standing quarter mile time of 13.35 seconds demonstrates that the bike is no sluggard. But it is plain that the Darmah is a tourer and not a cafe racer. Also, after hard use, we found the multiplate, oil bath clutch started to slip.

Obviously, the hard road test use and abuse by previous motorcycle journalists had taken its toll. This also applied to the rear chain and sprocket, which had reached the end of their useful life after only 4800 miles.

Thanks to Ducati/Moto Guzzi/Harley main agent, Graham Miles, who runs Three Cross Garage, West Moors down here in Dorset, both the clutch, chain and rear sprocket were renewed ready for performance testing at MIRA.

One of the outstanding points about the 900 Darmah, which we discovered during our run from Dorset to the Midlands, was the way in which it loped along at the legal limit on a mere whiff of throttle.

With just under 5000rpm indicated on the tachometer, the Darmah maintained a steady 70mph and, in spite of only having a small three-and-a-half gallon fuel tank, stops to take on petrol only occurred every 145 miles.

Fuel economy and the effortless performance of the big V-twin motor would appear to be the major advantages of owning a Darmah. Couple this with the ability to tackle swervery in a manner approaching that of a motorcycle half its capacity and it is easy to understand why the most repeated

comment heard about the machine is: 'It's a real rider's motorcycle!'

Consequently, after the drag up the A34 from Poole, through Winchester, Newbury, Stratford and Coventry to Atherstone, we were looking forward to testing the big Duke to the limit on our special MIRA test track. The high-speed banked circuit, mile long straights and timing lights, as well as a special handling course allow us to test bikes capable of speeds up to 150mph; more than fast enough for the quickest of roadster machines.

Our first check is on the instrumentation of the motorcycle for accuracy. At 20 and 30mph, the speedometer was three to four miles-an-hour fast and outside the 10 per cent legal limit. But as speeds increased, so the discrepancy reduced.

Then we encountered our second problem. When attempting to test speedo accuracy at over 90mph, the Darmah started a straightline, high-speed weave.

Following the Dunlop tyre testers advice, we attempted the high-speed runs in a semi-prone riding position and the weave disappeared.

Obviously, the combination of high and wide handlebars, low profile Avon Road Runners and rider weight distribution upset the stability of the Darmah. We changed tyre pressures to attempt to solve the weaving problem, but to no avail. Unfortunately, we didn't have a pair of straight bars to discover if a handlebar swap would provide the solution.

Following speedo checks, we continued with the

acceleration and maximum speed tests. A claimed 130mph maximum by the manufacturer is extremely optimistic. We obtained a maximum one way figure, with rider prone, of 114.14mph and at that point, the tachometer was just about to enter the 'red' 7,500rpm danger zone.

Braking proved to be one of the outstanding features of the Darmah. The twin disc, dual piston callipers of the Brembo system proved highly effective and very controllable at all speeds. Even when riding in the wet, we discovered no serious hesitation in operation, although the cast iron discs soon turned bright red with rust if the machine was left standing for any length of time.

In fact, looking around the Darmah it was possible to find a number of points where poor finish had allowed rust to take a hold; something which the Italian manufacturers in general need to tighten up on in the quality control department.

After concluding the performance testing at MIRA, there came the 180-mile haul back to Dorset. A very enjoyable run, except that the dual-seat strap cuts straight across the rider's back-side when in a natural riding position.

As the strap serves no useful purpose, riding comfort would be improved considerably if it was removed. In fact, considering that the Darmah is a sports tourer, the small, thinly padded dual seat is quite a pain in the posterior over reasonable distances and makes it almost impossible to carry two average sized indivi-

duals for more than a few miles in comfort.

Apart from the high-speed, straightline weaving, the criticisms of the Darmah are all comparatively minor.

The Italian motorcycle industry has learned a great deal over the last decade and are beginning to produce motorcycles which not only have a distinct affinity with their racing heritage, but have many of the trimmings originally conceived in Japan to make motorcycling safer, more reliable and less physical to operate.

Japanese instruments improve the Darmah without a doubt. Control switches are easily and positively used. Also, the H4 quartz-halogen headlight provides a really superb beam for night riding with a precise cut-off on dipped beam to avoid dazzling oncoming traffic.

Pound for pound, the Ducati Darmah still remains a few hundred pounds more expensive than some of its Japanese competitors of equal performance. But if you want a bike of character, a 'motorcycle for the motorcyclist', which offers fuel economy equal to Japanese bikes half its capacity, then the Darmah could be your type of machine.

Who needs screaming, high-revving fours when a lusty V-twin does the job more economically and just as well? And that exhaust note! It's not too loud, but it has that exciting thump of a big twin reminiscent of Castrol 'R' and those long past thrashes from Brands Hatch to Johnson's cafe. Those were the days and we could almost relive them on a bike like the big Duke.

Charles E. Deane

Technically Speaking

9.4:1. Maximum brake horse power (at rear wheel) 54 @ 6500rpm. CDI ignition. Dell 'Orto PHF 32mm carburetters. Wet sump lubrication.

TRANSMISSION

The five-speed, constant mesh gearbox is operated by a left-foot lever with conventional one down, four up selection. The movement is positive and neutral easily selected. In prone riding position, the gear ratios proved ideal for maximum performance, although in normal riding position, fifth

gear acted more as an overdrive gear giving exceptional fuel consumption at high cruising speeds. Only the neutral warning light gave problems by illuminating when the machine was in first gear. The clutch did show signs of slipping after heavy use during numerous standing starts.
Primary drive by gear to multi-plate, oil bath clutch and five-speed gearbox. Final drive ⅝ x ⅜in. chain. Final drive ratio, optional. Gearbox internal ratios: 1st, 2.237:1; 2nd, 1.562:1; 3rd, 1.204:1; 4th, 1.000:1; 5th, 0.887:1.

FRAME & FORKS

Ceriani telescopic front forks which are two-way damped, plus five position preload rear suspension units on the swinging arm give a fairly firm ride with the rider taking a fair amount of road shocks over bumpy roads. The massive V-twin motor forms part of the lower frame to hold everything rigid, but in spite of good low and medium speed handling, a weave set in at 90mph plus unless the rider was in prone riding position. Campagnola wheels and Brembo brakes

complete the cycle component specification and apart from discs that rust rapidly the brakes work extremely well in wet or dry conditions.
Open cradle frame incorporating crankcases as stressed lower frame member. Two-way damped telescopic front forks and five-position adjustable rear suspension legs on swinging arm fork. Double disc hydraulic front brakes, 280mm discs. Single hydraulic disc rear brake,

280mm disc. Cast alloy wheels, 3.50 x 18in. front; 4.25 x 18in. rear.

ELECTRICS

The electrical systems have been improved by the use of Japanese made components, especially with regard to control switches. The quartz-halogen headlight gives very good illumination for night riding with a piercing main beam and an excellent cut-off on dipped position.

Electric starting was virtually foolproof with the heavy duty starter motor and electronic ignition provided a maintenance free spark system. Apart from a headlamp which literally dropped out of its shell (it's only a press fit) no electrical troubles were encountered throughout the test.

12 volt 32 amp/hour battery fed by a 200 watt alternator. Electronic ignition triggered by magnetic flywheel. Quartz halogen headlight. Standard equipment includes warning light console for prop stand, main beam, generator, neutral indicator, trafficators and lights. Three position ignition switch has on/off and parking light locations. All other electrical controls are handlebar mounted.

DIMENSIONS

The Darmah is classified as a sports touring machine and although long and narrow, the actual accommodation for two riders is very limited on a thinly padded seat. The riding position over long distances is not too comfortable even when riding solo. The high and wide handlebars and a forward footrest position cause fatigue when riding at cruising speeds in excess of 70mph and as the Darmah can lope along effortlessly at 90mph, it is the rider who tires before the machine.

Overall length, 89in (2280mm); Overall width, 30.5in (680mm); Wheelbase, 61in (1540mm); Saddle height, 31in (700mm); Dryweight, 476lb (210kg); Fuel tank capacity, 3.3 gals (inc. 0.3 gal reserve), (16 litrs inc. 1.9 litrs reserve); Oil sump capacity, 8.5 pints, (4.5 litrs).

EQUIPMENT

The Darmah comes as standard with all the trimmings expected of a modern, present day motorcycle. Wing mirrors, centre and prop stands, pillion footrests, speedo and tachometer as well as lockable steering, ignition and tool compartment beneath/behind the dual-seat. Unfortunately, the toolkit was missing, so we are unable to comment upon its quality. Also the tachometer packed up due to cable failure.

GENERAL

Price: £1,999.00p inc. VAT. (On the road price, inc. delivery charge, number plates and road tax: £2,064.00p.)

Test machine supplied by importers; Coburn & Hughes, Ltd., 21, Crawley Road, Luton, Beds.

Test figures obtained at the Motor Industries Research Association track at Lindley, Warks.

Timing by fully automatic Hird-Brown photo-electric equipment controlling Heuer 1/100th second stop watches.

Terminal speed readouts by fully automatic speed sensing equipment accurate to 1/100th of a mile-an-hour.

Test rider, Neil Millen.

Weather conditions — 10mph sidewind. Cool, overcast day but dry track.

MAXIMUM & MINIMUM SPEEDS

GEAR	Solo max.	Prone max.	Min.
1	49.40	49.61	9.85
2	70.40	71.17	16.50
3	93.39	96.17	20.85
4	106.54	109.47	26.92
5	106.74	112.20	30.34
6	—	—	—

SPEEDO CORRECTIONS

Indicated mph	30	40	50	60	70
Actual mph	26.93	37.14	46.40	57.46	68.81

Speed at end of standing 400m.

Max. Prone 112.20mph in 29.0 sec.

Max. Solo 106.74mph in 22.85 sec.

Change 4th/5th

Change 3rd/4th

Change 2nd/3rd

Change 1st/2nd

Riders: Neil Millen & Geoff Carless.
Weather Conditions:
10mph Sidewind. Overcast. Dry Track.

DUCATI DARMAH

BRAKING (Both Brakes)

mph	feet
30	28
40	57
50	95
60	138
70	186

ACCELERATION FROM REST (secs)

0mph to	20	30	40	50	60	70	80	90	100	110	120	Max.	400m
Solo	—	1.89	2.57	3.92	5.49	6.95	8.50	11.61	14.65	—	—	22.85	13.54
Prone	—	1.88	2.55	3.91	5.37	6.91	8.29	11.10	14.65	23.20	—	29.00	13.32

FLEXIBILITY, Top Gear

mph	20-40	40-60	60-80	30-50	50-70
Solo	—	6.00	6.79	6.94	7.65
Prone	—	6.18	6.84	6.64	7.38

FUEL CONSUMPTION

mph	30	40	50	60	70	80
mpg	98	73	62.5	52.6	48.8	—
Overall consumption					49 mpg	

MCM ROAD TEST

DUCATI'S LITTLE DICTATOR

Ducati Desmo Sport 500

by John Robinson

THE UNDENIABLE good looks of Ducati's 500 Sport have all the finely-styled contours you'd expect of a thoroughbred. It's sleek, slightly aloof, and nothing quite so vulgar as a cafe racer . . . and that's the first hint you get of the character locked up inside the closely-finned engine.

It most certainly isn't a cafe racer in the sense of a street bike dressed up to look like a refugee from some grand prix. In fact, the engine behaves more like a real racer tuned to a fine pitch and it doesn't miss a chance to let you know that it isn't an ordinary roadster.

When things go well, the desmo twin howls along perfectly with a crisp response which makes you want to ride along with one hand protectively clutching your driving licence. When it's good, it's very, very good . . . But push the 500 into doing something it doesn't want to do and the highly-strung engine will throw an instant tantrum.

It dictates its own terms. Play along with it and the Ducati co-operates; go against the grain and it behaves like it's ready for a new owner. The logo on the side panel should read "Ducati rules, OK?"

The uneven firing of the 180-degree twin makes it sound lumpy and rough at low speed, turning into a hard snarl as the motor picks up. Passing through a sharp spell of vibration the 500 gets into its power band at 7,000, packing in a hard wedge of horsepower before it peaks out at 8,500. The performance is there all right, but that is a narrow rev range even for a racer and explains why the Ducati demands a sympathetic rider. Keep it in this narrow band and the motor thrives, delivering exciting surges of performance which have made people addicted to big twins. Grab an arbitrary handful of throttle at lower speeds and it will just gasp and die. On the 500 Sport you don't just open the throttle when you want to go faster.

29

Powerful Brembo brakes kept up their performance in the wet.

Soggy rear brake, firm suspension but excellent damping.

The neat lines of the 500 were marred by the rapidly-corroding exhausts.

MCM ROAD TEST
DUCATI SPORT 500

Like the motor, the chassis is set up for high speed. The bike feels slow at 70mph and like it has almost stopped at 30mph; everywhere you go the Ducati wants to go faster. Dual carriageways become more boring than ever. Anywhere else the buzzy motor, the tight handling and the nice exhaust note blend perfectly to make you want to keep on riding.

The 500 Sport could have any number of faults but they'd be pushed aside by the bike's overwhelming ability to get where it's at. It focuses your attention sharply on just why you're riding a bike and not travelling on the bus. You're out on your own, making your own choices and the Ducati makes you live it to the full. It lets you turn ordinary road riding into a craft, the level of which I've only experienced on competition bikes.

If all this makes the 500 a bit special, it also makes it specialised. When you make the effort to appreciate the bike, it rewards you; if you don't want to make the effort, it's the wrong bike for you.

The philosophy behind the bike is single-minded, its scope about as narrow as the engine's power band. Handling and roadholding are the bike's strongest features and the harder you go the better it gets.

Low-speed steering is pretty heavy, emphasised by the low bars which put a lot of weight on the rider's arms. This doesn't get balanced out until the bike is up around 60mph, cutting down on agility and comfort in heavy traffic.

We found the 500 had a long, rolling weave at very low speeds and felt edgy in slow turns, especially in the wet. Later, when the back wheel was removed for the dyno test, we discovered that although there was no play in the swing-arm, there was about 1.3mm end float between the arm and the frame. This may have let the wheel move enough to affect low-speed handling, while at higher speeds the greater wheel

loading would keep it pushed across to one side. There wasn't any adjustment provided at the spindle, although it could presumably be shimmed.

But as the speed went up, the handling and the ride got better and better. Front and rear the suspension is a bit hard, giving a fairly rough ride at low speeds although the dampers made a good job of keeping the bike stable and on line. As the Ducati hit bumps, the first shock could be felt but instead of the pitching or skipping that usually follows, it felt like the dampers had just locked on to the forks, holding the Ducati firmly down.

Over 50mph the bumps and ripples started hitting the wheels hard enough to encourage the springs to play their part and the ride smoothed out. The 500 could be cranked through long fast turns, flicked through S-bends or laid down hard into sharp corners and it stayed as steady as a rock. The steering was heavy, but it responded instantly to the lightest pull on the bars, the heaviness only being a resistance to anything that wanted to get the bike weaving. The rider could make the Ducati change course, but nothing else would. In a straight line, at top speed, the Ducati wouldn't weave or wobble even when I tried pushing and pulling on the handlebars — it would go where and when I pushed and as soon as I stopped, it straightened up.

And every time it came out of a bend, the 500 felt like it could have gone through just a bit faster. It certainly demands tyres as good as the Red Arrows which were fitted — the only feel they transmit is one of grip, no twitching or slipping, no insecurity of any kind. The combination worked so well that I frequently found ways of making my journeys longer than necessary.

In the wet the only problems were on very slow corners, at junctions or in-town roundabouts — possibly caused by the strange endfloat in the swing-arm. At open road speeds and again at the track, where it rained, and it rained . . . the Ducati felt as stable as many other bikes do in the dry.

Braking was barely affected by rain — there was enough of a lag to be perceptible but neither front or rear brakes lost any

appreciable power. The twin front discs had a heavy operation but there was ample power and my only criticism is that the span from twistgrip to lever was too large. The rear brake, in contrast, was soggy and insensitive but at least it wasn't prone to lock up the wheel or make the back end hop under heavy braking.

We didn't take any braking figures at the test strip, because of the bad conditions, but I don't think the Ducati would have given much better than average figures, from our usual 30mph. Like the rest of the bike, the brakes didn't come into their own until it was being used at speed — there was nothing startling about its performance in the 30mph bracket. Double this speed, or treble it, and the brakes were just what was needed; strong and reliable, with plenty of feedback to the rider.

No matter what the road conditions, the Ducati needed to be worked up and down through the gears, buzzing the motor for the odd burst of acceleration. Pushing it through to a higher gear usually made life more difficult — the twin didn't like plonking along and wouldn't respond to the throttle. In traffic it was easy to be caught out in the wrong gear, with a spluttering motor that was about to bog down. Just before it gets into its power band, between six and seven thousand, it runs through a patch of vibration but you don't really notice it, in the same way that you don't notice the hard seat or the riding position, which could get uncomfortable in slow traffic.

Obviously it's not a bike for trotting around the West End all day — once you're on the open road it all clicks into place, the wind takes the weight off your arms and you forget the minor discomforts.

The motor is something else. It demands sympathy and concentration. All the time. It comes down to the twin's inability to pull full throttle below 7000rpm. You can accept this as something which goes with the nature of the bike and trade the inflexibility for the power that kicks in at the top end. Or, you may think it's the result of cams and carbs that are a couple of sizes too big for the engine. It's two ways of spelling out the

Sporty riding position was fine for the open road, less so in town.

The unusually-styled desmo engine had very peaky power delivery.

Performance & specification

ENGINE
180-degree parallel twin, SOHC desmodromic valve gear, twin Dell'Orto PHF30 carbs, cb and coil ignition, 12V lighting, wet sump lubrication.
displacement.................... 496.9ccm
bore × stroke.................. 78 × 52mm
compression ratio..................... 9.6:1

TRANSMISSION
Helical gear primary drive to five-speed gearbox, final drive by chain.
primary reduction 2.125
final reduction 38/13
gearbox ratios: 2.50; 1.714; 1.333; 1.074 and 0.90

CHASSIS
Double damped Paioli front forks, Paioli rear dampers with 5 pre-loads, twin Brembo front discs, single rear disc.
front tyre
  (standard Michelin S41) 3.25 × 18
    (fitted Dunlop Red Arrow)
rear tyre
  standard Michelin M45 3.50 × 18
    (fitted Dunlop Red Arrow)
wheelbase 55.2in
castor .... 62 deg
trail .... n/a
overall length 81in
overall width.............................. 26.4in
dry weight................................. 408lb
test weight 432lb
fuel tank 2.6gal
oil tank 4.3pint

PARTS PRICES inc VAT
	£
handlebar	20.02
front mudguard	13.24
speedo cable	1.60
cb points	2.31
exhaust system	47.02
set of pistons/rings	29.59
list price, inc delivery	1,699.00

warranty: 6 months or 6,000 miles, plus further 12-month Autoguard warranty.
Importer: Coburn & Hughes, 21 Crawley Road, Luton, Beds.

MAX SPEED	SS ¼-mile	Max speed in gears (at 8,500rpm, computed)				
		1st 44	2nd 69	3rd 86	4th 96	5th 109
103mph	n/a					

Fuel consumption				Oil used	Brakes from 30mph
best 49mpg	worst 33mpg	average 44 mpg	range to reserve 70-90 miles	nil	n/a

TRACK CONDITIONS; no wind, heavy rain, ambient temp 44 deg F.

HOW IT COMPARES
Model	price	max. speed	av. mpg	ss-¼	bhp*
Ducati500S	1699	103	44	n/a	40
Honda CX500		106		14.4	42
Suzuki GS550		112	51	14.2	44
Mocheck Harrier	1613.61	112	47	14.5	41
Yamaha XS750		112	39.4	13.9	57.5

*At the back wheel, measured on a Heenan Froude DPX3 chassis dynamometer.

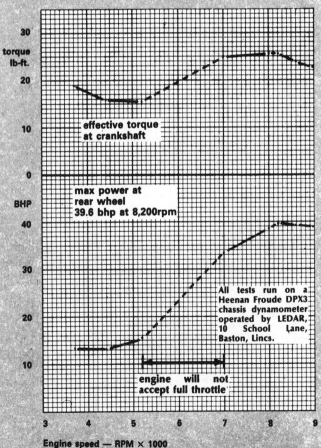

effective torque at crankshaft

max power at rear wheel 39.6 bhp at 8,200rpm

All tests run on a Heenan Froude DPX3 chassis dynamometer operated by LEDAR, 10 School Lane, Baston, Lincs.

engine will not accept full throttle

Engine speed — RPM × 1000

MCM ROAD TEST
DUCATI SPORT 500

same thing, depending on whether you are likely to become a Ducati owner, or not.

The motor fires up and idles quite reliably, helped by an air control lever on the handlebar (which is quite a relief in itself compared to the fiddly levers worn by some Dell'Orto carbs, plus the fact that all you see of the carbs is the fuel lines disappearing from the twin taps).

As you pull away, balancing the clutch against the high bottom gear, the motor still feels tractable enough. But once you're through second gear you need either the rev counter or a very sensitive seat to your pants. If you want the 500 Sport to go faster, you don't just open the throttle.

Cruising at 60mph, the natural thing to combat headwinds or hills or to overtake is to lean on the throttle. In top gear the 500 would usually slow down, give it still more throttle and the twin would run rough and start to misfire. Often, just holding a steady speed, I found I'd used more throttle than necessary and as I backed it off the bike would gently accelerate. The only way to get performance would be to drop down a gear or two and as soon as the motor got close to 7000, the throttle could be cracked open and the motor would fly up to its 8500 redline. It would rush up to a true 100mph with indecent haste and, then at the top the power disappeared as quickly as it had come in.

The motor was very sensitive to part-throttle at low speeds — a point which was exaggerated by the full-throttle dynamometer tests. There was a region around 3000 rpm where it would hold full throttle under protest, and then nothing but misfires until just below 7000 where it came in with a vicious pick-up. Between here and 8500, the motor shot up to 40 bhp — enough power to make 110mph a feasible proposition. At the track, we ran a fraction over 100mph, easily and quickly. But despite experiments with gearshift points and so on, the best we managed was 103mph. This is because the gearing is about as wrong as it could be for top speed — in top gear the motor is not far enough into its stride to pull the bike any faster, in fourth gear it's stretched out to beyond the power peak.

The motor really needs a six-speed box, with a ratio in between the present fourth and fifth. Just lowering the overall gearing would solve the top speed problem, but would spoil the bike's high-speed cruising.

On the existing gearing it will hold 70 to 90mph with a long-legged easiness and without the feeling that the engine is screaming its heart out.

This sensitivity to gearing and low speed reaction to throttle is typical of the Ducati's behaviour but there's no getting away from the fact that it is great fun to ride. The biggest drawback, for a bike which encourages you to ride it so much, is the tiny fuel tank. With two gallons between reserve and full, its useful range is about 80 miles. I dragged out a further 25 miles on reserve once, which got the 500 up to around 50 mpg. Normally it would run in the low 40s, and dropped to 34mpg at the track. The fuel consumption is not particularly impressive but it would be tolerable if the tank gave

anything like a decent range.

In other aspects of its detail design, the Ducati is an improvement over other Italian models. The electrics seem improved and more reliable. There's a powerful headlamp, steady indicators and an electronic voltage regulator built in to the circuitry. The switches, particularly the tumbler type used on the dipswitch and indicators could be better.

The Italians still seem to have a lot to learn about basic preparation — especially for our climate. The importers, Coburn and Hughes, are trying to do something about the exhaust finish — the matt painted pipes were rusting after one week. The throttle cable also started sticking after our wet

session at the track. Basically I think the bike just needs a thorough going-over before it is used, adjusting and routing cables, tailoring the riding position and controls, lubricating linkages, and so on. I found the fat handlebar grips didn't add to the comfort, and made the brake-span problem worse, and there would probably be a few other detail changes individual owners would want.

The only work we had to do on the bike — removing the rear wheel and adjusting the chain — was straightforward enough, although the engine looks as if it might be less accessible.

You could go through the machine and produce a list of faults and imperfections which wouldn't look good at all. On one of the bland Japanese models they would attract far more criticism than i've aimed at the Ducati. This is solely because the Ducati isn't bland and isn't aimed at a rider whose sole contribution is to wind open the twistgrip. It contrives to put character into both the motor cycle and into motor cycling, which, in my view, is worth a lot.

Apart from saying that the 500 Sport is far from an everyday workhorse, I see little point in criticising the machine. You can be fully aware of its problems and still think it's a great bike.

DUCATI DESMO 900 SUPER SPORT

● YOU CAN HEAR YOURSELF laughing inside your helmet. It's not a boiling laugh of some rattle-brained loony who's cooking along a high mountain road at 80-plus; it's a laugh of surprise and delight from someone who has discovered for the first time, or rediscovered for the hundredth time, how secure and stable and fun a Ducati V-twin can be in its territorial preserve.

When the Ducati in question is a 900cc Super Sport—with desmodromic valve gear, half-fairing, clip-on bars, solo seat and rear-set pegs—the bailiwick is narrow and deep: it's Curve Country, and nowhere else. Forget in-town trolling; any Japanese motorcycle is better than the Desmo there. Pass on freeway riding. Stretched torsos and coiled legs don't make it; besides, the Desmo delivers short jabs to the body through the seat and bars. Showboating at the local drive-in could be dangerous; a Honda six-cylinder will have a higher, or at least wider, profile.

Even Curve Country isn't entirely safe these days. The Japanese have made swift progress in frame and suspension technology, and Suzuki has been getting close to the heart of Ducati territory. Still, Japanese motorcycles are wide-spectrum motorcycles; a GS1000 must have an electric starter and all those other components that make for civilized riding. The Desmo has no pretense as a Do-Everything motorcycle. Comfort? Convenience? No way. In order to work well, the Ducati Desmo can't afford another 75 or 100 pounds.

To be sure, some one-liter Japanese motorcycles make the Super Sport's quarter-mile performance seem unimpressive. For that matter, both the Honda 750F and Suzuki 750 fours will leave the 900SS about two-tenths behind in a quarter-mile

sprint. But mountain roads know nothing of drag strips. Without shifting gears or screaming the engine, the Desmo will rush out of corners with the same steady, implacable, thunderous torque of an Ohio State backfield. Like a superb fullback, the Ducati can do more than power straight ahead; it can stop, cut-and-spin, change pace and direction, and run free and hard.

However limited the Ducati Desmo's territory, that special preserve still exists in 1978. At its vital center the Desmo's attraction is simple: it's easy to go fast on the Ducati, and going fast on winding roads is fun. If someone doesn't enjoy riding briskly on such terms, he will never understand the Ducati and should not trouble himself to own one.

By no means do you have to be an expert-level rider to appreciate the Desmo. The Ducati faithful will probably be aghast to learn that an expert-caliber racer can wheel the latest 550- to 600-pound Japanese Superbikes point-to-point across a mountain range more quickly than a 900SS. If a GS1000 Suzuki

has ground-clearance problems, he will work around it; if a Honda six-cylinder weighs in at 600 pounds, he can cope. His ability to deal with disconcerting behavior far surpasses those of a normal street rider. On the other hand, Mr. Average Funday Brisker can ride the Ducati point-to-point more quickly than a super-power multi. On board the Ducati, Mr. Funday's threshold of terror will be elevated to a higher road speed. The distance between Real Speed and Big-Trouble Speed will open up. He'll be going faster and still feel safer, more confident and more relaxed. And he'll be laughing hard inside his helmet.

Cycle has not examined the Desmo Super Sport since 1974; at that time the bike was a pure 750cc sports motorcycle with monster 40mm carburetors and booming exhausts. It had a gorgeous tank, rounded in purposeful curves and built with some of the worst fiberglass known to man. The motorcycle was unencumbered by directional signals or other dead-weight devices; the control switches belonged to the Italian school of Grand-Turismo-High-Tack. The ignition points could present a day-long challenge to those who took ignition timing seriously, and the front Scarab master cylinder and calipers were far below the Lockheed standard. The paint was dusty silver and institutional aquamarine. Assuming you didn't like the silvery color, you merely left the motorcycle out in the sun and the color would change to a pale olive drab. Of course, the fade-down was unequal and inconsistent. But what the hell, it was still the best sporting street motorcycle money could buy in 1974.

Changes come slowly in Italy; but if you wait long enough, substantial changes will occur. The 1978 Ducati Super Sport is

DUCATI DESMO 900

a far more presentable motorcycle than its 750cc forerunner. The paintwork has risen to an acceptable level, and the new blue-and-silver scheme is quite handsome, though the stripes on the front fender, tank, and seat still don't align properly. The windscreen has a protective molding on its trailing edge, and the fairing has been notched in the handlebar area to make room for the federally mandated directional signals. New control switches are light years ahead of the old ones; the ignition key has been moved to the instrument console; and a steel tank replaces the fiberglass creation of the 750. Those who savor the patina of real Italian fiberglass should not get teary-eyed; the fenders, fairing, side-panels and seat are glass, though the stuff is far better crafted than some of the early 750 components.

Significant changes have been made in Ducati V-twin Desmos. From the top, the bore has been increased from 80mm to 86mm, jumping the actual displacement of the 900-series engine to 864cc.

The factory still builds a square-cased 750cc Super Sport, and both the 750 and 900 have identical valve timing: inlet valves open at 63 degrees BTC and close 83 degrees ABC, while the exhaust opens at 80 degrees before bottom center and 58 degrees after top center. There's nothing all that remarkable in the timing figures; more notable is the fact that the valves are both opened and closed by mechanical means.

Crankshaft drives the clutch by means of helical-cut gears. Under crank gear is rotor for the CDI ignition.

Alternator's permanent-magnet rotor runs on crank outboard of support plate for towershaft-drive gears.

Gearshift lever has groove into which fits the peg of the actuating arm for the crossover shaft.

Brembo calipers work with huge cast iron discs to produce positive and powerful braking.

The elemental Desmo carries little excess baggage; 479-pound wet weight explains much of its performance.

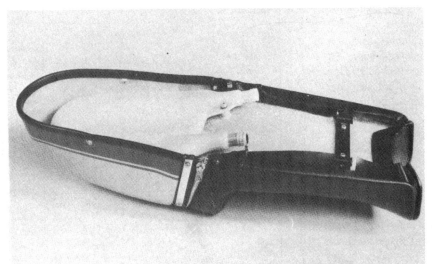

A plastic chamber for the closed crankcase-breathing system is bolted to the underside of Desmo's seat.

The wiring junctures in the 900SS are made with multi-prong plastic plugs that make quick disconnects easy.

Whatever the traditional arguments may be for a desmo system, such as drop-proof/crash-proof valves in a high-rpm engine, more practical considerations likely propelled Ducati toward the peculiar valve gear. First, Ducati has long experience with a desmo system; it's easier to get performance through familiar means than pursuing other avenues. Second, the cramped cylinder heads do not lend themselves to contemporary high-technology valve-spring systems, but this becomes a chicken-and-egg argument. It's likely that the cylinder heads are cramped because Ducati had the option to do a desmo performance system; another factory might have designed the heads to take advantage of the latest in springs and cams technology.

Because Ducati cylinder heads are built in such a way that only fairly short valve springs can be accommodated, there just isn't room for relatively long valve springs which could provide reasonable seat pressure, accurate valve control, and

Make and model .... Ducati Desmo 900 Super Sport
Price, suggested retail .... $3600, POE West Coast

PERFORMANCE
Standing start ¼-mile .... 12.91 sec @ 104.16 mph
      (with 32mm carburetors and LaFranconi mufflers)
Engine rpm @ 60 mph, top gear 3841
Average fuel consumption rate 40.4
Cruising range, main/reserve 110/75
Load capacity (GVWR less curb weight) .. 217.7 kg (477.8 lbs.)
Maximum speed in gears @ engine redline .... (1) 49.5
      (2) 70.9 (3) 92.0 (4) 110.8 (5) 125

ENGINE
Type ....Four-stroke, 90-degree twin, air-cooled,
    overhead valves actuated by desmodromic camshafts
       driven by towershafts and bevel gears.
Bore and stroke .... 86mm x 80mm (3.39 in. x 74.4 in.)
Piston displacement ....863.9cc (52.698 cu. in.)
Compression ratio 9.5:1
Carburetion ... (2) 32mm Dell'Orto throttle-slide carburetors
    with accelerator pumps. Sports kit: (2) 40mm Dell'Orto
      slide-type carburetors with accelerator pumps;
      matching manifolds and appropriate
      throttle cables included.
Exhaust system.............. Two-into-two with crossover pipe,
    La Franconi street mufflers; Sports Kit:
      two-into-two with crossover pipe,
      Conti silencers.
Ignition .... Magnetically triggered
Air filtration .... Dry felt element
Oil filtration ....Pleated paper element
Oil capacity .... 4.75 liters (5 qt)
Bhp @ rpm.. 56.33 @ 7000
Torque @ rpm .... 47.01 @ 5500

TRANSMISSION
Type .... Five-speed, constant mesh, direct-drive type,
    with wet multiplate clutch
Primary drive..Helical gear; 2.19
Final drive .... ½ x ⅝-inch chain 2.53 (15/38)
Gear ratios, overall .... (1) 12.39 (2) 8.65 (3) 6.67
    (4) 5.54 (5) 4.91

CHASSIS
Type ....Mild-steel tubular-backbone truss
    with crankcase as stressed member;
    telescopic front fork and dual-shock
    swing-arm rear suspension
Wheelbase ....1346mm (59 in.)
Rake/Trail.................................. 30.5°/120.6mm (4.75 in.)
Brake, front .... Hydraulic, two 280mm (11.02 in.)
    disc with double piston calipers
    rear..........................Hydraulic, one 230mm (9.06 in.)
    disc with double piston caliper
Wheel, front .... Wire, 18 x 2.15 in.
    rear...Wire, 18 x 2.15 in.
Tire, front .... Michelin, 3.50V18 M45
    rear..Michelin, 4.25V18 M45

Seat height.. 760mm (30 in.)
Ground clearance...................................... 135mm (5.3 in.)
Fuel capacity, main/reserve .... 18 liters (4.7 gal.)
Curb weight, full tank .... 216.3 kg (477 lbs)
Test weight .... 313.8 kg (652 lbs)

ELECTRICAL
Power source ....Permanent Magnet Alternator
Charge control... Xener Shunt
Headlight beams, high/low 12V 50/60W
Tail/stop lights 12V 5/21W
Battery... 12V 12AH

INSTRUMENTS
Includes.................... tachometer, speedometer, tripmeter,
    ignition pilot light, directional signal pilot light,
    headlight circuit, neutral and hi-beam indicators
Speedometer error, 30 mph indicated, actual 27.97
    60 mph indicated, actual.............54.54
Odometer error... Plus 2.7%
Tachometer error .... NA

Ducati Desmo 900 SS
Test Conditions:
Barometer 30.00/*30.00*
Temperature
74°F/*76°F* Wet
93°F/*110°F* Dry
Correction Factor
1.060/*1.072*
Date of Tests: 5/10/78
As Tested on the
Webco Dyno
*Race Kit

BHP* (60.40 max.)
BHP (56.33 max.)
TORQUE* (51.37 max.)
TORQUE (47.01 max.)

CORRECTED REAR WHEEL HORSEPOWER

TORQUE IN FOOT POUNDS

Engine Speed	BHP	Torque
3000	25.23	44.17
3500	30.07/31.26*	45.13/46.92*
4000	34.83/35.22*	45.73/46.24*
4500	38.91/43.18*	45.42/50.39*
5000	44.15/48.90*	46.37/51.36*
5500	49.23/53.80*	47.01/51.37*
6000	52.60/57.57*	46.03/50.39*
6500	54.65/60.40*	44.15/48.80*
7000	56.33/59.10*	42.27/44.34*
7500	54.06/59.23*	37.85/41.47*
8000	50.46/58.32*	33.13/38.29*

RPMx100   20   40   60   80   100

DUCATI DESMO 900

generous lift. Radical camshafts, buttressed by 9000-rpm-type springs, can raise hell with Ducati valve guides. The valve guides in the Ducati 750/900 series cylinder heads are short and not especially well supported. Most of the time, this presents no problem for normal valve-spring Ducatis. But high-performance cams and heavy-duty valve springs can wear out valve guides prematurely.

What's really new on the 900 Desmo is a long way from the showy valve gear. Downstairs, there's a new crankshaft assembly. The connecting rods do not appear as blocky as the original 750SS rods because the current rods carry 20mm

wrist pins rather than the 22mm pins found in early 750SS Ducatis. The neck of the 900 rod, the area immediately below the wrist pin eye, is smaller than in the early-style rods. Since the piston diameter grew six millimeters going from 748cc to 864cc, the factory has tried to contain the weight of the reciprocating mass, and smaller piston pins were a way to cut weight.

The big ends remain the same, but the biggest change can be found in the right side of the crankshaft assembly. Like the 750, the 900 drives both camshaft towers via a gear chest on the engine's starboard side. In the old 750 a bevel gear on the crankshaft drove a matching bevel gear on a central timing shaft which was dis-

posed perpendicular to the crankshaft and ran up the right side of the crankcase. This central timing gear drove the bevel gears for each camshaft as well as the ignition points drive-gear.

The 900 utilizes a different system because the oil filter now occupies the area that formerly housed the ignition points. In the 900 engine there's a support plate immediately outside the towershaft bevel gears. The crankshaft drives a straight-cut pinion gear which in turn moves two larger straight-cut gears, one on each side of the pinion, and ball bearings in the plate support the outboard ends of the crankshaft and the shafts on which the two driven gears turn. On their respective

Continued on next page

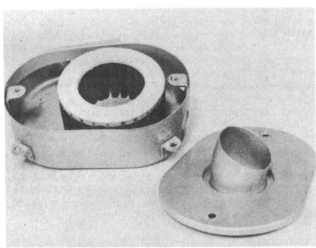

Individual pressed steel air-boxes house marginal looking fibrous felt elements.

Crankshaft is well supported; far left end runs on ball bearing in left outer case.

Permanent magnet rotor runs inside alternator stator. Alternator generates 200 watts, new high for Ducati.

Hung from the top frame tube are Ducati's "transducers" which replace conventional coils.

shafts these two driven gears key directly on their shafts to helical-cut bevel gears which then engage their match-mates that turn the towershafts. The whirring gearsets in the 900 series are simply better supported than the 750 predecessors, and—though we didn't investigate first-hand—reshimming the 900 gearchest would be less a hassle than the early 750s. Finally, outside the support plate at the far end of the crankshaft, a permanent magnet rotor for the 200-watt alternator can be found.

On the left end of the crankshaft there's the familiar helical-cut primary gear, under which is the Ducati version of the magnetically triggered ignition system. The timing is set at the factory (35 degrees BTC) and further adjustment isn't necessary. Although Italian electrics are often considered inferior, and although early Ducati electronic ignitions had their share of problems, these latest units have a good record. There's a fair amount of energy available, witness the 0.032-inch gap specified for the plugs. More persuasive testimony comes from the racetrack, where those who have compared high-energy battery/coil systems and the electronic CDI unit could determine no difference in straightaway speeds or lap times after switching ignitions.

When Ducati made the change to the square-cased 900s, the shift lever was moved to the left side, and the brake to the right. Revising the brake system was no big deal, but switching over the gearshift lever involved bell-cranks, Johnson rods, and a cross-over shaft with slide-pin and groove engagement. Some—but not much—precision has been lost in the transfer mechanism; the lever movement of the left-shift Ducati can't quite match the one-to-one mechanical feel the right-side shifters had.

The 32mm Dell'Orto carburetors draw air through metal filter-boxes with dry felt elements; pleated rubber hoses connect with the carburetors. Old Ducati Super Sports dealt with the atmosphere directly through gigantic intake trumpets which were effective but dirty. In truth, the fibrous felt elements on the 900 are underwhelming; the naked eye can see daylight through the fiber. The Italian filters are better than drawing dust and floating debris straight into the carburetors, though were the 900SS ours, we would opt for American accessory filters.

In order to meet federal regulations, Ducati has fit 32mm carburetors and LaFranconi mufflers to Super Sports destined for American highways. Current 900SS models have been sanitized in yet another way: the crankcase breathes into a molded plastic chamber, mounted under the seat, via a plastic hose; another hose leads out of the chamber and forward into the front air cleaner box. Gone are the days of the Ducati 750SS and its direct and open crankcase ventilation to the atmosphere.

The frame has been carried over directly from the earlier Super Sport. To be sure, mounting bracketry for the tank, brake systems and other items has been changed and improved, but the fundamental frame—the running frame that made Ducati famous for handling—remains the same. When Ducati introduced the square-cased 860/900 series three years ago, the running gear was redone. The new frame was characterized by a swing-arm pivot mounted in eccentrics that provided for chain adjustment and by front downtubes that were mashed flat at the engine mounting points. There were other differences, including revised tubework in the steering head area; but despite the changes, the Ducati handling survived. The Super Sport frame is the original running gear, and we suspect it's lighter, stronger, and blessed with finer touches than the now-standard Ducati 860 piece.

While the Ducati Super Sport is light, its frame is not. The Italians build frames out of stuff suitable for water pipe, and that's a good thing. Too many motorcycles do too much skimping on tubes, and the result are frames that bend too readily and produce handling that's all too rubbery. The Ducati frame, which uses the crankcase as a stressed member, ties the steering head and swing-arm pivot together

rigidly. The swing-arm pivot pin has an outside diameter measuring 29 millimeters, and it rides snugly in the swing arm's bronze bushings. It's quite unlike some Japanese motorcycles with 14mm pivot pins and plastic bushings—and so much slop in the mounting that the swing arm can be laterally deflected by hand at the rear axle. The main tubes of the Ducati swing arm are 40mm in outside diameter, and the wall thickness is 2.5 millimeters.

There's nothing outrageously trick about the Ducati chassis. It's simply an excellent design that's executed with materials equal to the task, and then some.

While it's true that horsepower and weight are the enemies of good handling, the 900SS has enough horsepower to make most chassis get weird—if they were going to. But the Ducati Super Sport chassis, to the staff's certain knowledge at *Cycle*, can withstand a 90-plus horsepower engine without producing funny handling characteristics.

Ducati is beginning to lag behind the times in the suspension department. Marzocchi rear shocks with limp-wrist damping have never been our favorites, and it's a tribute to the chassis that the bike handles as well as it does with the stock pieces. Under some circumstances you can hit an ugly bump in a corner and have the clip-ons slap side-to-side once or twice before going dead center again.

The Marzocchi front fork, with its massive 38mm tubes, offers less room for complaint. It lacks the versatility of the GS1000's air fork or the stiction-free operation of the Yamaha XS11 fork. Still, there's been progress; the 900SS fork works better on the street, thanks to softer springing, than the first 750SS Marzocchis. For racing purposes you can't quarrel with the front end, once its setup reflects the preferences of an individual rider. The rear shocks, on the other hand, should be replaced with premium grade units suitable for racing.

Since the frame and swing arm rank in the Forrestal class for strength, Ducati could afford to soften the suspension springing for street riding. Assuming the bike had first-rate damping, there would be no great degradation in mountain road handling, and real gains in ride comfort. In any event, the comfort index isn't an important consideration on the clip-on/rearset equipped Desmo anyway. Customers buy a Desmo because they intend to go production racing, or because they want to look like they intend to go racing, or because they want a very light, short-range high-performance roadster.

As a serious motorcycle for production racing, the Super Sport does not have the Campagnola magnesium wheels fitted to the style-king of Ducatis, the electric-start Darmah. Ducati has an explanation for this strange situation. Rim width is a matter of rider choice, specific tire require-ments, type of racing, and rules of the sanctioning organization. You might need different rim widths for an AMA Superbike Production event at Daytona than those required for a 24-hour club event on a slow, tight circuit. It's far less expensive to change the stock 2.15-inch rims than to buy a whole new set of wheels and shelve the street-going Campagnolas. Nonetheless, serious racers will be fitting magnesium rims to the Desmo, WM3s or WM4s on the front, and WM5s or WM6s on the rear of the bike.

Whether used on the street or on the track, the Brembo disc brakes are impressive. The first generation of Italian disc brakes (specifically Scarab calipers and master cylinders) were spotty in quality, but the latest Italian equipment, Brembo in particular, is very good indeed. Of course, a manufacturer can foul up any brake by specifying inappropriate material or the wrong master-cylinder piston size, but Ducati has got it right. The Brembos provide strong, progressive retardation without any spongy softness.

When the rider clamps the binders on hard, he must brace himself with his arms and try to dig his knees into the steel tank; otherwise he and his belt buckle could take a trip up the gas tank. Compared to the old fiberglass tank, the 900SS steel tank is sleeker and certainly safer (it doesn't leak), but the new tank doesn't look as mean and purposeful as its predecessor. Functionally, the new tank has one drawback: there are no recesses in the area of the clip-ons, so it's impossible for some riders to pull the bars back far enough back to take the twist out of their wrists. But given the uncomfortable riding position, and the hard-edged seat, who'll notice an extra little contortion?

On other fronts, street riding has never been so civilized on a Desmo. The ignition key has been moved up to the control console that's now complete with winkers and blinkers. On the left handlebar, a black box (literally) operates lights, horn and directional signals. If you thought all those twinky Italian switches were history, you have only to look to the right bar to find one still in business. And old-timey-Italian switch—a first cousin to the traditional horn/dimmer apparatus—serves as an emergency on/off switch.

In its street-legal trim, the Ducati 900SS provides 12-second street performance. That's more than a second away from the newest one-liter Japanese bikes, but Ducati has never been the straight-line champion of Superbikes. On a road that insists upon dodging left and right, for most people the differences between an 11-second and 12-second motorcycle tend to blur, and other considerations, such as light weight, low-end responsiveness and rock-steady handling become far more important.

The Michelin tires fitted to our test bike were not PZ2-compound tires; those are illegal for street use. The test-bike Michelins may stick better than the Metzelers we've encountered on Desmos before—though it's difficult to say without making a back-to-back comparison. Suffice to say that the Desmo is likely to run out of ground clearance, particularly on the right side, before the tires run out of adhesion. The low-routing of the exhaust pipes has always been a problem. While exhaust headers with more ground clearance could be built, sneak-and-dodge pipes would be more expensive. High pipes, however racy-looking, aren't practical for everyday street use.

Since Ducati offers an optional $400 production-racing kit comprised of 40mm carburetors with cables and manifolds, Conti mufflers and a 36-tooth rear sprocket, a high-road exhaust system is a logical next step. In kitted form the quarter-mile dropped to 12.4 seconds with a terminal speed of 109. That's a half-second quicker and 4.5 mph faster than the street-legal version.

Running the kit on the street makes no sense. The engine has no protection against dirt, the exhaust is noisy, and the increased straightline performance isn't enough to go hunting for certain one-liter Japanese motorcycles. We imagine that most Desmo owners will have to have a kit, just to have it—in spite of the price tag.

Playing by the numbers, you could talk yourself right out of a Desmo. You can buy better quarter-miles figures for a lot less. The Super Sport is a monoposto machine, while Honda's six-cylinder and Suzuki's GS1000 provide for two. While these Japanese motorcycles have 10 cylinders and 32 valves between them, they still don't present service personnel with the chore of desmodromic valve adjustment. There are more dealers for Honda and Suzuki than Ducati, and therefore more knowledgeable mechanics. That's a consideration when you must find *the man* among men to trust with your shims and winkler caps. Indisputably, the 1000cc Japanese bikes are better finished, with more attention to detail, than the Super Sport. The Honda six-cylinder even has more ground clearance than the Desmo.

Ironically, in these days when dealers regard a test ride as something bordering on moral perversion, the only way for anyone to know whether he's Desmo material is to ride one. Frankly, a lot of people will ride the Desmo, and they will find it an interesting novelty, and nothing more. Others will cruise it around the block, trying to outmuscle the Desmo's in-town truckiness and heavy handling. Still others will sample roads that travel uphill and downhill like a sidewinding rattler. They will sense the Ducati's stability, feel its agility, marvel at its almost hydraulic power—and come back laughing as only a True Believer can. ◉

A Duke in the Family

Mike Scott bestrides an aristocrat

It's not easy to remember the exact moment at which an obsession begins. It is possible, though, to look back into the remains of one's memory, and mark the slow build-up: from mild interest, to enthusiasm, to fascination and thence to fierce longing. Fleeting early encounters quicken the interest: then enforced separation from the object of desire etches a rosy and ever-brightening glow on the subconscious.

I'm talking about motorbikes. Mainly. Ducatis – especially V-twin Ducatis with desmodromic valve gear.

I suffer acutely from this obsession. To me, two is the correct number of cylinders for a motorcycle: excess only leads to excessive width and weight. A V is the correct way to arrange these cylinders, provided it is at 90 degrees. And, the Ducati engine is the most melodious and aesthetically perfect of all the V-twins. Add superior brakes and roadholding, and sheer physical beauty, and you have by extension the most perfect of all motorcycles.

As you can see, I've got it bad. So it was entirely my responsibility when the *SuperBike* hack BMW was lunched by a mentally defective car driver (he turned right without indicating or slowing, and knocked the R100/7 sideways into a lamp-post, ten feet off the ground), that it was replaced by the just-launched and totally seductive Ducati Darmah Sport Desmo 900.

Having a Duke in the family hasn't always been a happy experience, though it has also been marked with moments of sheer ecstasy. I'll try to be brutally frank in describing its faults, as well as glorifying its nobility. Be warned, though, I am such a desmophile that when the Darmah gives trouble, I blame myself and not the bike.

Further: so urgent and hasty was my desire to put a Darmah into the company car park that we got a very early production model. Many of the faults – such as exhausts which rust up redder than the original paintwork – have since been corrected.

Ancestry first. The Darmah represents, I suppose, a new generation of Ducatis, using the engine from the previous generation in a lowered version of the familiar semi-spine frame. The desmodromic engine is virtually identical to that in the SS900, reviewed elsewhere, but for milder camshafts, smaller carburettors, fractionally lower compression and more restrictive exhausts. And much lower gearing – which changes the Ducati character considerably.

The frame is identical in layout to the GTS, but all new, designed to cure Ducati quirks that some people might have considered faults. Seat height, for instance: the GTS (valve-spring model), and even the supersports SS Desmo, are both tall bikes. By stretching the wheelbase some two inches, and lowering the frame tubes behind the engine, the Darmah has dropped to a weeny 29 inches at the seat. And it feels as low, light and wieldy as a 350.

Previous (and still current) Dukes have also always been known for slow steering. Steeper than usual head rake and long trail leads to superior stability in a straight line, but makes the bike slightly ponderous and more demanding to place accurately in corners. Not so the Darmah: raked 1.5 degrees less than the SS, the steering is quick and light: to the extent of making the bike slightly weave-prone at higher speeds. In the twisties, it means the Darmah can be flung from one angle of lean to another with joyful abandon, and can be placed accurately and easily. Once again, it makes it feel more like a sporting 350 than a full-scale 864cc biggie. And that is nice.

The basic frame layout is classic Ducati, with a single spine tube, braced steering head and the down-tubes stopping at the engine. There's no completed cradle and the engine forms a stress-bearing frame member. Much like Mr Honda's new frames, in fact.

Further improvements run to Japanese (Nippon Denso) switchgear and instruments, and an equally Oriental Yuasa battery. And if the switches look like Suzuki cast-offs, they remain a good thing. There are also Bosch electrics throughout, including a big BM-style H4 headlamp. Hoorah – a Duke, but with the finest electrics money can buy.

It was unavoidable, I suppose, that the Italians should get mixed up in actually *installing* the electrics. That lead to one major weak spot, which first showed up when the bike had done only seven miles, and has been an intermittent problem ever since. The bloody fusebox, right. Not only did Ducati mount it just below and behind the headstock, where it receives the full force of overspill water from the front of the mudguard, they also mounted it upside down. Apart from moisture problems, this means that the fuses are very prone to fall out. Especially since the standard EEC fuse changed from a ceramic to a plastic body. Now, if a poor contact causes a spot of sparking, the resultant heat melts the plastic fuse body, shortening the fuse and causing it to drop.

Our original approach was to try to water-proof the fuse box. A dud idea, which ultimately lead to the first major problem. A starter fault caused the main ignition switch wire to burn out *and through* the fuse box. The fuse failed to blow: we were lucky to avoid a fire. Luckily, only the one wire was affected and Cloud Engineeering of Brentford soon had the Duke chortling along again. Ducati importers, Coburn and Hughes subsequently replaced the fuse box altogether, since it was badly corroded. Their solution is not to try to keep the water out, a hopeless task, but to drill large drain holes so that it can run out faster than it gets in. So far, so good. Any more problems, and we'll relocate the fuse box within the headlamp shell, where it should have been all along.

Enough of the bad news. Let us turn to that divine desmodromic engine, where only a failed starter motor has marred almost 5000 miles of sweet running. When the Duke was new, running in, I was perturbed because the motor felt *too* sweet, *too* crisp. Hell, it should rather have been tight and temperamental. Knocking up the miles hasn't yet borne out my fears, it is still the sweetest, smoothest and most alluring big twin in the world.

In terms of performance, it takes a ride on an SS900 to make the Darmah feel disappointing, in exactly the same way that the desmo Darmah makes the valve-spring Ducati engine feel crude by comparison. What that Darmah needs (and what the new Darmah Sports has got) is bigger carbs and the deliciously bass open Conti exhausts.

One thing common to all Duke V-twins, and stronger in the desmodromic version than the others, is the widest range of expression in motorcycling. At different throttle openings and revs, the big twin is alternatively docile and gentle, then soulful, then raunchy as seven schoolboys from Portsmouth. At lower revs, it is quite astonishingly smooth, and it will pull from around idling speed. As the revs rise towards the 8000rpm redline, a tingle sets in, but it is never more than a tingle. Although it certainly honks along with more enthusiasm beyond 6000, there isn't a power band as such. Just an almost infinite choice of revs. There's a dialogue between rider and engine, communicated through the throttle cable. When an engine has such a wide vocabulary as

does the desmo Duke, the conversation is satisfying indeed.

At least partly responsible for this even sweeter than usual Duke engine is the new electronic ignition system developed jointly by Ducati and Bosch. This has no less than four separate stages of ignition timing advance built into it (it says here), which offers a full working rev range of over 6000rpm, from below 2000 (with a light hand) to above 8000 (if you ignore the red line).

And the only limit to revs is the sheer size of the 432cc slipper pistons. Desmodromic valve gear, as if you didn't know, means that valves are opened *and closed* by the single overhead cams, instead of being closed by conventional valve springs. Valves that cannot bounce, in short.

It's impossible to discuss the sweetest V-twin without mentioning its sound. It can be very whirry, if the bevel-drive to the overhead cams isn't shimmed to perfection. But it's exhaust noise I mean: the deep throbbing off-beat thump that is bassly plaintive and exclusively Ducati. And the sad-angry snarl on the over-run It sounds like a real motorcycle . . . and then some more besides.

Up to now, Ducati have exploited the low-rev guts of their engines by installing relatively high gearing. All this changed with two extra teeth on the rear-wheel sprocket. It helps standing quarter-mile times: our bike clocked the mid-12s after it was run in. But it also turns it into a bit of a buzzy bike . . . you're always running out of gears, and it was altogether too easy to redline it in top, at around 115mph. It's about the worst thing that can happen to a Duke We swopped the 38-tooth back sprocket for a 37-toother, which has knocked acceleration to 13.1 seconds for the quarter, but made the Darmah considerably more relaxed and enjoyable to ride. Now it is closer to the Ducati ideal . . . the ability to go very fast without ever needing revs or even much throttle. Unostentatious high average speed.

The gearbox itself has been revised internally, to complete the conversion to left-hand change. It too has been a source of some bother to our bike; again because we missed out on some modifications made to the linkage early in the production run but after our bike was built. Even as I write, we are waiting to discover just why the bike is now by-passing second gear into a false neutral and jumping out of fourth.

However, the handling and roadholding make up for an awful lot of niggling problems. Like all Italian bikes, when it was new, the Ducati had the ride of a hard-edged plank. As the miles ticked by, it has softened up considerably. Yet it's still firm enough to jolt your kidneys if you don't steer clear of the bumps and to remain perfectly stable in the most adverse of conditions. Linked with this is its low centre of gravity, largely due to the low-slung front pot, and relatively light weight. The happy result is that when things do get out of hand, it's amazingly easy to regain control.

Ducati's have long been revered for this forgiving capacity: almost thinking for the rider and covering up for his mistakes or misjudgements. The low slung, quick-steering Darmah, in my opinion, takes Ducati safety and security a stage further.

Some writers, me included, complained of slow steering and a front-end wander when the Darmah was first launched. Felt like an over-tight steering damper, I said. In fact, the Duke comes with a hydraulic steering damper installed. A fine piece of conceit in a bike that handles superbly. Throw it away, and the ponderous feel disappears along with the wobble: at the quite acceptable expense of some

40

straight-line stability at speed.

With that gone, you have a low-slung machine with which you can truly feel at one as you swing through the bends. The Darmah responds so well to being flung about you begin to feel invulnerable.

Riding at the sort of pitch the bike encourages, especially on a circuit, soon leads you to discover a serious lack of ground clearance on the left. It's the side and centrestand foot-tangs which hit the ground when you still have several miles an hour up your sleeve. For serious cornering nearer the Duke's considerable limit, they simply have to go.

One thing mars the bike's quick handling, and then only in traffic. For some obscure reason, styling was allowed to compromise the steering lock. Because the tank is so far forward and because the steering triple clamps are almost flat (the fork legs are nearly side by side with the steering head, instead of being well in front), the Ducati runs out of steering lock alarmingly early and at the most awkward moments. Usually when you're filtering through traffic feet up, and swerving to avoid a taxi. At best, you hit full lock and have to put a foot down to compensate. At worst, you drop the bike, in the most embarrassing way.

Braking is simply superb, despite a rather awkward-looking bent rod linkage to the back master cylinder. The three cast-iron discs are Brembos. They are truly excellent — sensitive, powerful and trustworthy in wet or dry.

I have deliberately given priority to engine performance and roadholding, because they're more important to me than appearance. Stylist Leo Tartarini may not agree, and the Italjet tart-up artist certainly gave his best shot to the Darmah. The bold white styling stripe on vivid Italian red echoes the diabolically pretty Ducati Desmo 500 twin.

It seems to me, though, that too much has been sacrificed to appearances. Unnecessarily restricted steering lock I've mentioned: and that smacks of bodgery. Seating is another problem. Terminal pains in the bum have given way to a slightly less acute condition as the suspension has softened, but the seat on its glassfibre base is simply too narrow and too hard. Perhaps the medical word for piles should be Darmarrhoids. Or perhaps Ducataracts.

Beneath the not-so-soft black bit is a one-piece 'glass moulding, cuddling the frame tubes up front and broadening to the ducks tail mit rudimentary aerofoil at the rear. The styling rules out carrying any luggage behind the pillion (no bad thing, provided you have somewhere else for it), and there is a small stash-space within the hump. This is reached by removing the seat itself, which is secured (joke) with a lock. Finish is all mildly shoddy, and the stash space gets very wet. Two out of four locating pegs for the seat broke within the first month of ownership: replacements are still not available.

There's no denying, though, that the Darmah does look superb. Tartorini's bit sits atop the crowded and functional engine room, with its two round single cylinders. Despite the stretch in wheelbase, it looks squat and stubby. The gold lacquered Campagnola magnesium alloy wheels are expensive and handsome. The Duke is a visual feast.

Along with the new styling comes a real attempt to turn the Duke into a convenience bike. This is the first Ducati with a side-stand. And a warning light; to stop you riding off with the stand deployed. (There's also a light to tell you when you're in first gear. It says "Neutral".) In fact, the stand was rather too long to be of any use except on steep cambers. Coburn and Hughes added spacers to the springs in the front forks to improve ride height and thence cornering clearance; the sidestand became usable at the same time.

Another contribution to the easy life is established Ducati practice, and has more to do with good handling than marketing. It's chain adjustment, which is achieved by an eccentric mounting for the swing-arm spindle. Slacken two pinch-bolts at the point where the swingarm meets the frame, use a special tool to rotate the eccentrics, and the entire back sus-

pension assembly moves backwards to take up the chain slack. The spin-off is that wheel alignment remains spot on, and the wheel spindle is more rigidly mounted.

The overall picture is clear. In a world over-populated with overweight multi-cylinder superbikes, here is one that makes up for less impressive sheer power output and standing quarter-mile times with an amalgam of agility, light weight, artistic engineering and sheer excitement. The Darmah knows few rivals on a twisting road. To anyone looking for a deeper relationship with his motorcycle than just showing off in a straight line, it represents an entrancing alternative.

But how has it been as an office hack? What is it like actually living with it? Have Ducati succeeded in laying to rest the ghosts of poor finish and dodgy electrics?

Pause for reflection.

Then, taking *SuperBike's* Ducati Darmah (soon nicknamed the Drama after its umpteenth early problem) in isolation, I'd have to answer "not really" to that final question. Of course, it's not as clear cut as that, and I'm beginning to think that our very early bike was just a bit

of a dog, a Friday Afternoon bodge-up.

It already had paint chips on the seat unit when we got it. These have been added to in number and size with every disassembly. The exhausts have rusted badly. Since then, new Darmahs have improved chrome quality, which should ease the problem. The handlebars are prone to rust, though easy enough to shine up again. One indicator stalk rusted so badly we junked it. The chrome headlamp supports are **prone to corrosion: why did Ducati drop those** simple and sensible bent-wire supports? On the other hand, the stainless steel mudguards are as good as new, the paintwork on the tank still takes a deep-gloss shine, the chrome tank-cap is immaculate, the switches all work.

I'll list the Duke's worst failings, but first let me describe the minor nightmare I believe was ultimately responsible for most of the problems. The dealership from whom we got the bike went into liquidation soon afterwards. This followed a period of shoddy service: all during the crucial first 2000 miles of our machine. We suspected as much, for the bike more than once came back to us with the same faults that we'd asked to be repaired under

guarantee, along with an assurance that "Everything's fine".

One example was the starter motor. The mechanism performed erratically for some time, though we were assured there was no problem. Then the ratchet mechanism in the chain drive seized up during operation. The result was that the starter didn't free, and when the engine fired (as it always does first time) the starter spun with it. It spun at perhaps five times the revs it was designed to do, and within a second had lathed itself to internal destruction, causing the main ignition-switch wire to burn out at the same time.

This was at just over 3000 miles, and the new bike was looking very sad. The desmo valve gear was noisy. The swingarm was flopping about in its bearing, leading to swoopy and scary handling. Electrical continuity was becoming harder and harder to maintain in the by-now heavily corroded fuse box. We removed the starter mechanism completely in order to ride the bike to be repaired. Then the gearchange mechanism jammed. It was on to a trailer and up to Luton, where importers Coburn and Hughes had generously agreed to step into the hole left by the now defunct dealership who had "looked after" (another joke) our prize possession. I won't name the dealers, there's no point. It's there in a past issue, if you care to look.

Coburn and Hughes men Pat Slinn and Vic Holliday worked wonders with the Darmah. I'd virtually given up hope. Within a week, the bike was back, running as crisply and sweetly as it ever had in all its life. Nearly every problem was attributable to bad or neglectful servicing, too. The valve gear simply needed normal adjustment — which should have been done. The floppy swingarm was dry — it just needed greasing. The fuse box was replaced. The starter mechanism could have been saved if our early reports of erratic behaviour hadn't been ignored: it was replaced. The gearchange mechanism needed adjustment. And our Duke was once again a thing of joy.

Almost 1500 miles later, it again needs attention. This is the regular service interval — the desmo mill is finicky, and needs constant setting up. But more problems have cropped up: the second gear-shift problem I described earlier; and a slipping clutch. Both, I think, are matters of adjustment rather than replacement or repair. We shall see.

I must answer no again to the question of whether it's been or ever going to be a good office hack. No way. It's not that kind of bike, and it's a pity in a way to treat it as such (it's also the only way I could think of to get a Darmah between my knees on a regular basis, so it's a necessary compromise). A hack goes long distances at short notice; it also does a lot of fretful town work. It gets passed from one rider to another, often for short periods of time. Cleaning and minor routine servicing tend to get neglected. And the Duke doesn't like that much.

Rather, it's a one-man bike. It should belong to an owner who is prepared to spend a little time keeping it fettled and preserving the finish: **who's capable of giving it the highly-skilled** attention that desmo valve gear needs himself, without relying on faceless mechanics to perform this time-consuming task. Or he needs a dealer he can trust.

His efforts will be rewarded with a motorcycle so satisfying to ride, so inherently safe and so damn enjoyable that he will consider his time well spent. A well-trimmed Darmah has an authority in motion that way surpasses any niggly problems.

So, the final question. What is it like to live with? As a confessed desmophile, I find it mildly, almost amusingly irritating in its worst moments, and perfectly ecstatic in its finer hours. It's fast. It's exciting. It's beautiful. It's a bike you can relate to, with which you can be one. A bike with a soul, a character. And, if you're prepared to look for it, a big, big heart.

I'm happy. I never asked the Darmah to be the best bike on the road, nor the most dependable. Just the nicest — and it is.

DUCATI DARMAH SD 900
£1999

PERFORMANCE
Maximum Speed — 113mph
Standing Quarter Mile — 12.6sec
Fuel Consumption — Hard Riding — 39mpg
Cruising — 46mpg
Best Full-Tank Range — 160 miles

ENGINE
Type — 90 degree V-twin, air-cooled, single overhead camshaft, desmodromic valve gear
Displacement — 863.9cc
Bore & Stroke — 86 x 74.4mm
Compression Ratio — 9.4:1
Induction — two Dell 'Orto P4F 32mm carburettors with accelerator pumps
Exhaust — two-into-two with balance pipe
Oil System — wet sump
Ignition — Bosch/Ducati four-stage electronic

TRANSMISSION
Clutch — multi-plate wet type
Primary Drive — helical gears
Final Drive — chain
Gears — five-speed left-hand change

CHASSIS
Frame — open-cradle spine type
Front Suspension — telescopic hydraulic fork
Rear Suspension — swinging arm with eccentric spindle chain adjuster and five-way shocks
Wheelbase — 60.6in
Castor — 31 degrees
Seat Height — 29in
Weight — 460lb (dry)
Fuel Capacity — 3.5gall
Tyres — 3.50 H18 front, 4.25 H18 rear
Brakes — triple Brembo discs

INSTRUMENTS
150mph speedo with trip; 11000rpm rev counter, red line at 8000rpm, warning lights for stand, lights, main beam, neutral, generator and indicators

EQUIPMENT
Electrical — 12V 36Ah battery, 200W alternator
Lighting — Bosch H4 headlamp

Vee haff vays of making you torque

First Magazine Test

Ducati's 900SS Is The Arch-Duke Of The Twisty Road. Dave Hamill Explores The Limits

"Form follows function," is a hoary old adage which is much beloved of the art and design fraternity. Hoary it may be, but the basic precept holds true. In other words it means that, say, Concorde is shaped the way it is because of the job it has to do, and this fact makes it an aesthetically pleasing object. Mind you, some cynics might say that in order to perform its true function, *that* particular example of Anglo-French extravagance should come equipped with a high capacity mechanical shredder capable of ingesting £10 notes at one end, and expelling the odd whiff of expensive smoke at the other. Anyhow, to get back to our little treatise on aesthetics, if you start to clutter up a design with unnecessary adornment – so the theory goes – it ceases to reflect its true function and looks grotty as a result. OK the lesson's over, but ponder on that truism the next time you have the pleasure of casting your eyes over the lean, economic, purposeful lines of a Ducati 900SS.

If ever a bike reflected its purpose visually, that bike has to be Ducati's muscular flagship. Parked in a row of Joe Average Japbikes, the SS looks about as incongruous as a great white shark in the municipal goldfish pond. It's single minded in a way that makes even a Jota look like a compromise. From skinny glassfibre front mudguard to tail light, everything's there for a purpose and there ain't any frills. It would be an injustice to call the SS a cafe racer. Nope, it's just a thoroughbred racer pure and simple – and the fact that Ducati have chosen to embellish it this year with civilising touches like a dual seat which looks as out of place as an olive branch in the barrel of a howitzer, can't disguise that fact.

The SS is one hell of a lot of engine hung in a rolling chassis that's about as vestigial as a stripper's G-string. The astounding thing is that this scanty little collection of tubes, aided by the crankcase which is a fully structural member, knit together into one of the most rigid frames ever. Sure this is nothing new – Ducati frame technology must've received enough compliments in print to fill a book – but the formula's so successful that it's got to be worth mentioning yet again.

The engine is the clincher in this setup. With such a large and rigid lump of metal forming the lower component of the frame, it's little wonder that the steering head and swing arm are locked together in the sort of eternal embrace that must have Japanese chassis engineers crying into their saki and wondering just where they went wrong. Keep these two crucial points accurately aligned in relation to each other, and you're well on the way to locating that elusive holy grail of biking, The Perfect Chassis.

Alas, Ducati have fallen a bit short of this objective on the SS by hanging some slightly suspect suspension components off this wondrously tough assemblage. No complaints about the front forks – massively constructed Marzocchi units which make the beanpole-like items fitted to many contemporary bikes seem pretty puny in comparison. No complaints for that matter about the swing arm which is sturdy, to say the least, and rides on a *very* heavy duty pivot no less than 29mm in diameter. Nope, the fly in the ointment appears to be the Marzocchi five position rear shox which the big Duke is fitted with.

For normal road use these were adequate, if a trifle mushy. On the track though they gave rise to a whole clutch of inter-related handling problems. After eliminating every other conceivable culprit, it's a fair certainty that they were the cause of some alarming and very un-Ducati-like excursions on bumpy corners, riding one-up on the softest setting. Cranked over, the front end stepped out on anything other than the smoothest surface and, possibly due to the Michelin M45 tyres fitted as standard components, the SS weaved badly on white lines and manhole covers – even in dry weather.

As if that lot wasn't enough on a bike which, after all, is supposed to be a street-legal racer, the centrestand made its presence felt with embarrassing regularity on corners, to the extent that a day at the test track ground off a sizeable chunk of metal. Oh yes . . . while I'm breaking bad news, the springs on the centrestand could've done with being beefier too, because the whole assembly was free to bounce up and down to its heart's content on our machine. This was especially apparent when the suspension bottomed (a surprisingly frequent event on-track, although not, thankfully, a common occurence on the road), which led the stand in turn to hit terra firma with a sound not unlike the suspension noises you get in the back of an empty Transit van on a rough road.

Pitted against our Darmah (of which you can read more elsewhere in this issue) on a tight, twisty handling course with some sneakily treacherous cambered downhill bends, the SS came off surprisingly badly. Maybe it was the Darmah's extra weight, maybe it was the psychological advantage of an upright seating position, or maybe it was the fact that the Darmah was shod with Roadrunners; it certainly had the edge over its much sportier brother.

OK, the foregoing might seem like an unrelenting condemnation of the 900's rolling chassis, but having highlighted the bad bits, it's only fair to point out that despite my previous utterances the SS can still outhandle all but a few of its contemporaries by a handsome margin. On our bike we were able to effect some significant improvements by simply jacking up the rear shox a couple of notches (at the expense of a boneshaking ride admittedly) and juggling around with tyre pressures until we reached what appeared to be an optimum of 30lb at the front and 33 at the back. Chances are that a pair of Red Arrows, Roadrunners

or, even better, endurance racing covers plus some air shox would improve matters even more.

As a rock-steady straight line projectile, the SS was second to none. 100mph, 110mph, 120mph; it took them all in its stride and stuck to terra firma tenaciously. Even the M1's notorious sidewinds failed to deflect it on a memorably nasty day when other bikes were visibly performing a sort of drunken side to side roll and struggling to keep in contact with the carriageway. After a while I even managed to overcome the temptation to throttle back on corners as the handlebars tried to tie knots in themselves because, despite the pyrotechnics, the SS kept its line immaculately. For a bike that only weighs in at a skinny 415lb, this isn't bad going.

Talking about weight, or rather lack of same, it's very apparent that Ducati's engineers have taken great pains to trim any excess flab off the SS, with the result that it's a full 64lb lighter than the Darmah (which is no heavyweight itself). Even the calipers on the Brembo discs have been denuded of their protective covers plastic intake trumpets for the carbs and skeleton footrests all help to keep overall weight lower than many Japanese 500s. The benefits for would be racers are obvious, and for road

riding the SS's lightness pays dividends in braking performance and agility.

I don't really need to write you a treatise on Ducati's Desmo 900 engine cos it's a legend in its own time, innit, so I'll confine myself to the multifarious mechanoid details which distinguish this year's *oeuvre* from its predecessors. First and foremost among these are a pair of monstrous 40mm Dell'Orto PHM40 carbs, which replace last season's more modest 32mm units. These giants of the carburettor world are equipped with the aforementioned low restriction bellmouths, and while I appreciate the need to keep their voracious appetite for air satiated, I'm just a tiny bit worried about the absence of any form of air filtration. Unless, that is, you count the coarse mesh bellmouth covers which would be just about capable of preventing an elephant from entering the inlet tract. Whatever, the intake trumpet for the forward cylinder would benefit from resiting, because it's ideally angled to collect rainwater at present.

With all this finery on the inlet side of the engine, the exhaust department doesn't get left out either. The action here comes courtesy of

a pair of Conti silencers which don't seem to put many obstacles 'twixt exhaust ports and outside air. Or to put it another way, they're loud. Boy are they loud. Still, who's complaining when the sound which issues forth from them is about the closest thing to heaven you're likely to hear in a London traffic jam. It's a crisp, aggressive bark that's reminiscent of days gone by and bikes long since departed; so what if it isn't 100 per cent legal on full song.

Surprisingly, the 40mm carbs and Contis managed to account for the lion's share of the SS's considerable performance advantage over the Darmah between them. According to Pat

Slinn — resident technical supremo at importers Coburn and Hughes — both motors use identical cams and pistons, although the SS is fitted with polished strengthened conrods to cope with the extra loads likely to be imposed on it. Both now also share the same Bosch magnetically triggered electronic ignition system, which will come as good news indeed to those unfortunates who've tangled with the highly erratic conventional systems on previous SSs.

We've already established that the big Duke is but a racer lurking under the thinnest of disguises, so it should come as no surprise to learn that an electric start isn't part of the SS scheme of things. Nope, there's just a good old break yer ankle kickstart, which is as it should be on such a performance orientated machine. I can already hear choruses of biking poseurs splitting the crotches of their one piece leathers with indignation. However, the said poseurs might do well to reflect on the fact that they are carrying many pounds of excess weight on their bikes for the dubious pleasure of pushing a button to start their engines, rather than simply exerting a bit of muscle power.

As it happens, the 900's kickstart gets the engine running first jab once you've got the knack. Ah yes ... getting the knack. Well first off there ain't no choke, so you've got to gas up those monstro carbs good 'n' proper. The approved method is to give the ticklers which Dell'Orto thoughtfully provide, a good tickle. Because the rear one's virtually inaccessible, I found a better alternative was to pump the throttle a few times to get the petrol flowing, and then hold it about a quarter open while giving the kickstart a death or glory swing. Seemed to work nine times out of ten, thanks to the wondrous cold starting characteristics of electronic ignition, which also kept the engine idling nicely despite the lack of a choke. Time ten was something else though, as my ankle will testify.

Incidentally, the actual crank is a whole lot cleverer than the unfortunate contraption which Darmah owners are lumbered with, plus it's suitably geared to turn the engine over without prodigious amounts of effort. Wish I could be as keen on Ducati clutches though. The long and short of it is that Duke clutches and me just don't seem to get on, and I've yet to come across one which didn't display signs of slipping after a very short time. The SS was no exception, and it soon displayed all the dreaded symptoms of the malaise which seems endemic to the breed, to coin a medical phrase or three.

Enough of this petty techno talk, and on to the real *raison d'etre* of the SS. Yes folks, this here's the bit where the first pale shafts of sunlight are filtering in over the drab rooftops of London and the early morning sounds of the milkman on his round disturb the tranquillity of the still misty streets. A man and his bike are about to set off on a long, long journey and the calm is suddenly shattered by the staccato growl of twin Conti exhausts and the mighty sucking of Dell'Orto 40mm.

OK, I know it sounds soppy, but that's the sort of scenario the SS was built for. Shame then that Ducati have shattered the image ever so slightly by replacing last year's magnificent, swoopy single seat with a limp wristed dual seat. No way is the SS a two-up bike, and travelling with a pillion ruins the entire feel of the machine. Never fear though, a single seat option is still available, and in view of the fact that changing seats is a simple two bolt job, prospective purchasers could easily get the best of both worlds by buying one of each. Visually the single seater looks a whole lot better too, while the dual option looks distinctly afterthoughtish.

You'd better believe that the Desmo 900 engine churns out the stuff like it's going out of style, because it sure as hell isn't the diminutive high geared rear sprocket that drags you off the line as if you're rocket assisted.

Change into second and the bike's coming into its element. No clutch slipping now, just solid power right up into the blurred horizon where you're redlining in top at not far off double the legal speed limit. The whole setup is taut and responsive in a way that, say, the Darmah never could be. Things happen when *you* want them to; not when the bike feels like it. Take braking for instance. Three drilled cast iron discs and Brembo calipers is a good setup in my book, and with a bike as light as the SS, stopping becomes a high-precision high-G affair and you get the feeling that you'd be over the handlebars long before anything would start locking up.

One of two things can happen now. You can either have a fuse go or pull into a local cafe to become the centre of attention and indulge in a little ego bolstering. In the first case it's a few seconds work to take the seat off and replace the offending fuse in the excellently located under-seat fusebox. In the second case, just sit back and be a hero. A set of superbly cast and finished Campagnolo mags, a beefcake pinup of an engine just oozing muscle, those wake-the-dead Conti exhausts and that ultra smooth black and gold paint scheme: they're the definitive work on How to Win Friends and Influence People (Motorcycle Division).

You've got to hand it to Ducati; they sure know how to make a good looking bike. About the only reservation I have on that score is whether the SS will stay looking that way. If our experiences with a Darmah are anything to go by this will require constant loving attention, many hours of patient polishing and, preferably,

a garage. Other niggles? Well I'll be charitable about the Smiths instrumentation which at least didn't fail, although the speedo was inclined towards gross optimism. I'd have preferred Nippon Denso clocks à la Darmah, but tucked away on a neat little panel in the fairing along with a centrally mounted ignition switch, they didn't look *too* downmarket. I'll extend my charity to the rear light which tended to blow almost as often as fuses, assuming that our bike's slightly damaged rear mudguard was setting up too many vibrations. Can't be as sympathetic towards the incredibly cramped steering arc though, and the only thing I managed to extend towards the almost inaccessible oil filler was a cut-down washing up liquid bottle which served as a makeshift funnel. Even this tended to drip oil all over the place and with the SS burning a pint of the precious black stuff every 350 miles or so, topping up was a regular and messy operation.

Plus points include a high standard of finish throughout – with the reservations I've expressed previously–and quartz halogen lighting which makes riding at night considerably less of a hit and miss affair.

A bike for every man? A sportster for the masses? A walk on the wild side for Joe Average? Nope, the 900SS is none of these. It's a bike for the few, and this isn't really due to its £2499 price tag which places it fairly and squarely in Laverda country. The reason lies more with the uncompromising philosophy of the machine. It's built to travel fast and light, and to put it to any other use would be a complete and utter waste. In this it joins a very short, very exclusive list of bikes, following in the tyre treads of immortals such as the Black Shadow. It won't be everyone's cup of tea, especially so when the Darmah has a far better all round specification, on paper at least, and

costs hundreds of pounds less.

The SS is an ultimate, the outer fringe of road biking where the distinctions between street and track break down and blur. There'll always be a steady stream of customers who want that sort of excitement and don't mind paying the penalty in terms of initial cost and upkeep (for a bike as tautly stretched as the 900SS will surely require regular attention.) For most of us though, the SS will stay firmly rooted in the realms of fantasy; a black and gold blur vanishing into the middle distance, somebody else's bike, the bike we'd buy if.....

DUCATI 900SS
£2499

PERFORMANCE
Maximum Speed – 129mph
Fuel Consumption – Hard Riding – 38mpg
Cruising – 46mpg
Best Full-Tank Range – 184 miles

ENGINE
Type – 90deg V-twin, air cooled, single overhead camshaft, desmodromic valve gear
Displacement – 863.9cc
Power – 80bhp at 7000rpm
Torque – 64lb/ft
Bore & Stroke – 86 x 74.4mm
Compression Ratio – 9.5:1
Induction – two Dell'Orto PHM 40 carburettors with accelerator pumps
Exhaust – two-into-two with balance pipe and Conti silencers
Oil System (type & capacity) – wet sump, 8.8 pint capacity
Ignition – Bosch/Ducati four stage electronic

TRANSMISSION
Clutch – wet, multi-plate
Primary Drive – helical gears
Final Drive – chain

CHASSIS
Frame – open cradle spine type using engine crankcase as structural member
Front Suspension – Marzocchi telehydraulic fork
Rear Suspension – swinging arm with five position Marzocchi shocks
Wheelbase – 59.5in
Ground clearance – 6.5in
Castor – 29.5deg
Seat Height – 31in
Weight (wet) – 454.7lb
Fuel Capacity – 3.9gall
Tyres – Michelin, 3.50 V18: front, 4.25 V18: rear
Brakes – triple Brembo with drilled cast iron discs

INSTRUMENTS
150mph speedo with trip; 11000rpm rev counter redlined at 8000rpm, warning lights for generator, main beam, neutral, lights and indicators

EQUIPMENT
Electrical – 12V 12Ah battery, 200W alternator
Lighting – Bosch H4 55/60W headlamp

OPTIONS
Single seat with toolbox, fairing, Imola racing cams, racing kit consisting of full fairing, oil cooler, racing exhaust system and cams

Test bike supplied by Coburn and Hughes Limited

Open up the fast action throttle and a single, powerful message wends its tortuous way up from the nerve endings of your right hand, does a slight detour across to the part of your body that manufactures the odd job lot of adrenalin and then turns on to the expressway to your cerebellum. Torque, it says. T-O-R-Q-U-E.

Winning Formula

Hailwood's Ducati on the dynamometer

WE HAVE all read the claims about 120bhp race bikes. Each year the figure goes up for the latest machines from the major factories. And so much emphasis is placed on horsepower that the bhp figure seems to be the main criterion on which a bike is judged.

To discover some of the truth and attempt to get a better perspective on the

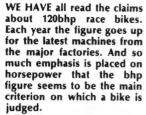

balance of power and handling we put Mike Hailwood's formula One TT winning Ducati on the MCM dynamometer. You may remember we did a full feature in our June issue on how the engine was prepared and tuned by Sports Motor Cycles of Manchester. Dave Walker now tells the story of the first road racing bike to be run on our dynamometer.

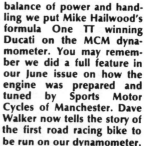

STEVE WYNNE threw open the doors of his Transit van and said: "I haven't got a ramp, but it's very light." Wedged between a small sink and a gas cooker sat the Hailwood Ducati. The damage from Mike's Donington fall was still very much in evidence. The familiar red, green and white tank and seat had been replaced with a new unit which was still in an unpainted state. Some of the frame was still scuffed but overall the damage did not look as if it had been bad.

The purpose of Steve's visit was to run the Hailwood Ducati on the dynamometer which we use for all our road test machines. Since our feature on the Ducati in the June '78 issue, a lot of people, other magazines and rival race camps, have said that the engine we covered was not the one Mike raced. They claimed that the IOM race motor was a special factory job with re-angled valves and lots of secret goodies.

Steve Wynne assured us that the motor we saw was raced by Mike in the Island, and he was only too willing to run it on our "brake". Steve says that when a motor cycle is raced, you race the whole bike, not just the engine. Handling and braking are much more important than a massive power output you can't use. In this way the power you

Winning Formula

do have can be put to better use. Keeping the weight down, and having a small frontal area were essential requirements for a successful racing motor cycle.

Lifting the machine from the back of the Transit certainly proved Steve's point. The bike *was* very light. We sometimes have problems hooking up larger machines on to the brake but the Ducati was a piece of cake, even though it didn't have a centre stand.

With no kickstart or electric motor to bring the engine to life, dynamometer operator Leon Moss adapted an electric motor to drive the brake via a rubber belt.

Steve Wynne keeps a careful eye on the rev-counter as the Ducati is warmed up.

Steve took one look at the oversized elastic band and laughed: "Do you think that thing is going to start my Ducati?" . . . it did.

When the unsilenced motor burst into life for the first time it sounded just like a Manx Norton — and so it should have: only one of the cylinders was firing! Steve explained that when the bike had left the road at Donington it went off into the catch pit. With the motor going full song at 9000rpm it had gulped in an awful lot of sand. The cylinder bores and pistons had been ruined, and a lot of grit had found its way into the carbs, blocking the jets and drillings. Since Steve had no more 11 to 1 compression ratio pistons the engine now runs on a 9.5 to 1 compression ratio.

Incidentally, for graph studiers, the power output is for the motor with 9.5 to 1 pistons. We did some quick calculations and estimate that with an 11 to 1 compression ratio the maximum output would rise to around 86 bhp.

A quick check on the exhaust pipes revealed no heat from the front pot, so its carb was pulled off. A blocked idle jet was discovered and cleared. This time the engine fired up and the noise was beautiful. In the confined area of the test house you could feel the motor breathing in and out as the throttle was blipped. Steve explained that the fabulous oooh-aaah sound was not known as "noise". It was something called "music".

As the engine neared its working temperature the familiar smell of Castrol "R" became apparent. Here was a machine which appealed to all the senses. It even felt good to open and close the twistgrip — you could almost feel the power.

When I passed comment on the lovely aroma it was patiently explained to me that these were not oil fumes, but "perfumes" which filled the air.

It would have been all too easy to get carried away with the nostalgic talk of Manx Nortons, Castrol R and the good old days, but we were there to record the power output of the fastest four-stroke machine that had ever lapped the Isle of Man. Yes, Hailwood went even faster on the Ducati than he did on the famous 500 Honda four.

With ear defenders in place — you really can have too much of a good thing — we tried the motor at full throttle with the brake holding the revs at 4,000. We managed a steady reading and then let the motor sing up to 6,000 where a healthy 66 plus bhp reading was recorded. Things seemed to be going well until we reached 7,000. The motor was pulling like a traction engine when suddenly the power evaporated. I closed down and pulled in the clutch — the engine died. I thought we had blown it, and Steve Wynne was looking more than just a little worried.

The only man not disturbed by the apparent disaster was the dynamometer king, Leon Moss. His philosophy is: "They shouldn't make them if they won't hold together". Clearly he had blown up bigger and better engines than this one.

For the next ten minutes worried heads were put together. It was definitely the front cylinder. The spark proved okay and there was still plenty of compression. Once more the front carb was stripped and once more a grain of sand was extracted from one of the jets.

The healthy bark of the Ducati again filled the test house — I doubt if the neighbours called it music — and we continued the power runs. The motor was very smooth from 7,000 up to 8,500rpm where it gave peak power. Of course we didn't know that this was the peak until we ran it at 9,000. At these revs vibration was quite severe and I had some trouble keeping the thing on full bore because the fine dimples on the twistgrip rubber slipped through my fingers. Since the motor had now "gone over the top" we decided not to push the engine any further. There would be nothing to gain and everything to lose. As you can see from the power curve, the maximum output of 80.5 bhp is not dramatic, but there is a really good spread of power.

When we covered the engine in the June issue Steve Wynne was good enough to pass on some of his tips from tuning his production racers. One of these was cutting the bellmouths down, to shorten the overall inlet tract lengths. Steve didn't think that this helped the top end but said it had a real bearing on the point where the power came in.

While we had the bike on the brake, we decided to check this out by loading the motor on full noise, at 4,000rpm, and then letting off the brake and checking where the power came in, and how much of it there was. As the brake load was eased off, the tacho crept up the scale. When it reached 5,000 rpm, it shot up to 7,000.

After cutting the engine we removed the bellmouths from the carbs and tried the same test again. This time the engine reached 5,000 rpm and stayed there. The power eventually came in at 5,500, but the jump was only as far as 6,800 rpm

Winning Formula

Obviously the inlet length with the little plastic trumpets in place was about right for mid-range power. A quick calculation with the slide-rule showed an improvement of around 3 bhp — just from fitting the bellmouths.

Since the motor pulled quite cleanly at peak power it was generally thought that the mixture was about right. Just to make sure we decided to try some larger main jets. If there was any extra urge to be had, Steve wanted it. The carbs were removed once more and the main jets swopped for a couple of 170s.

We didn't bother with a full power curve, but simply ran the engine straight up to 8,500. The power was exactly the same as before but the mixture was well over rich. The fumes in the test house were now so strong our eyes were watering.

The mixture wasn't over rich to the point where power was wasted, but a lot of the fuel was being chucked out of the exhaust pipes without contributing to the useful work load.

At last! Dave Walker gets on the Hailwood Duke for an all-too-brief test ride.

Looking at the power curve you can [...] that the power really came in arou[...] 6,000rpm and did not drop off after p[...] revs. It would have been interesting to [...] the motor up to 9,500 but we felt it would [...] pushing our luck too far.

The power was spread thickly over the [...] range, which should make it a very easy b[...] to ride. I know that top-class riders of t[...] stroke machines have to cope with v[...] narrow power bands, but they must h[...] problems with certain tracks in getting [...] gearing spot on for every corner — [...] there are quite a few corners in the Isle [...] Man.

Ultimately, power output from the cra[...] shaft is related to performance only in te[...] of power-to-weight ratio. Lots of pow[...] pushing along lots of weight means p[...] performance. And you have to stop the b[...] once you have attained that performanc[...]

What did the Ducati weigh? Steve did[...] know but various people had made vari[...] estimates. We decided to put the bike [...] our scales and find out exactly. The b[...] topped the scales at 360lbs ready to race[...] but without petrol. A five gallon load in [...] tank would add a further 40lbs to the all-[...] weight. It's not surprising that lap reco[...] tend to be broken towards the end of a r[...] rather than at the start!

Riding

If races were won on a power-to-wei[...] ratio scale, we could just compare machi[...] on the start line and not actually bother w[...] the business of rushing around the tra[...] However, when it comes to scratch[...] round a circuit, handling is the name of [...] game. Unfortunately this is something y[...] just can't measure. What fills the bill for o[...] rider can be very wrong for another. T[...] only way to evaluate handling is to ride [...] machine in question and see if you like[...]

Getting a ride on the Hailwood Ducati [...] little like arranging an audience with [...] Queen. Quite a few road racers have ridd[...] the bike, and passed on their commen[...] but as far as I know I am the only scribe w[...] was allowed to plant his backside in Mik[...] saddle.

Sports Motorcycles had arranged fo[...] tyre testing session with Dunlop so t[...] Mike could try out a slick tyre on the fr[...] wheel. Special wide wheels were order[...] from Italy and arrangements were made [...] Mike, Dunlop, and the new wheels, [...] arrive at Silverstone at the same tir[...] Unfortunately the wheels didn't arr[...] because of the strike by French air tra[...] controllers.

When Mike had finished his initial test[...] the bike was made ready for a test rid[...] made my way to the pits and arrived jus[...] time to see a certain road racer climb[...] aboard the Ducati. Since he was bigger t[...] me I decided to keep quiet and wait [...] turn. What I didn't know at the time was [...] he was going to hog the bike for most of [...] track session and only leave me time fo[...] very brief spin at the end.

Up to that point I had only been think[...] about riding the bike. Now I had time to [...] back and contemplate the prospect of ru[...] ing around a circuit that I had never se[...] before, on a bike that was quicker t[...] anything I had ridden before, and in so[...] very fast company. By the time Mr Gre[...] came in I was one very psyched-[...] journalist.

I began to think of lots of reasons why I really shouldn't be riding the bike. What if I dropped it, for example? Before I had time to voice these objections, Steve Wynne had shoved me on to the bike and was pushing me up the pit road. I cruised down the pits in first gear with just a couple of thousand rpm on the tacho.

As I gingerly opened the throttle the bike gently eased its way up the slip road. Getting braver I found second gear and opened the taps half way.

The carburation was really clean: the engine would pull from nothing on part throttle and the high gearing made it quite docile. This two wheeled tiger was nothing more than a great big pussy-cat. The big power jump we had recorded on the brake just wasn't apparent when riding. Obviously it was damn fast but not at all frightening. The close ratio gears gave acceleration the feeling of one continuous rush, rather than that kick-in-the-pants feeling which you get from a really big road bike.

A road racer probably wouldn't even notice these things but for me the experience was totally new. Even the "music" from the exhaust was exciting. I am just about the same height and build as Mike Hailwood and the riding position fitted me like a well-worn glove. It was this very "balanced" riding position that made the bike so deceptive. The hump in the seat and the forward lean cancelled out the feeling of being left behind as the bike surged forward, but the footrest positioned the legs so that they could take the weight under braking.

This meant you didn't feel as if you were going very quick until you arrived at the bend, when your pulse rate doubled. Squeezing the brakes didn't appear to slow the bike very rapidly, but you could end up almost at a standstill at the approach to the turn.

For me, the curves in the road are what motor cycles are all about. If a bike didn't lean over through a corner, but stayed upright like a car, I wouldn't ride one. The Hailwood Ducati was the best handling bike I have ever ridden — why can't road bikes handle like that? It was rock solid. Having said that, the suspension did feel a little on the hard side, but I am used to a soft dual seat under my backside, not a thin slice of foam rubber.

The corners at Silverstone are near constant radius curves. Several times I went into the bend much too slowly — those deceptive brakes — and opened the taps, bringing the speed up to the point where I scared myself. Closing the throttle slightly produced no change in line, or other antics. Not having a clue where the road went I tended to take the curves all wrong, but the Ducati is such an easy bike to ride you could pick it up and lay it down again without any conscious effort.

To sum up the whole machine I think you could describe it in one word: effortless. I would have been quite happy to stick a number plate on it and take to the road, and that's saying something about a machine which has won so much in such a short time.

I really shouldn't have been so surprised because the bike is, after all, only a modified road machine. One of the most interesting points to come to light about the whole test concerned the man who put the bike together: Steve Wynne. He has proved

Mike Hailwood joins in the preparation at Silverstone

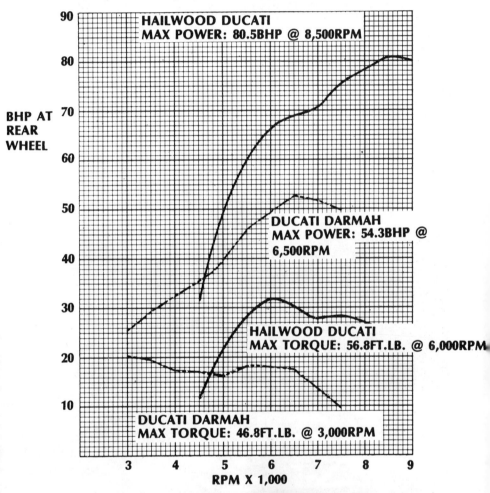

that you do not have to own a dynamometer to develop a race winner. Steve's development was done on a "suck it and see" basis. He made his modifications one at a time and track tested each until he was happy with the result. He had no way of knowing if they worked other than that they felt right. The tuning of the inlet tract lengths was spot on, as was the mixture.

It just goes to prove that if you know what you are doing you can "tune by ear".

Right: Carburetter checks found sand in the works after Mike Hailwood's Donington crash.

Street Racing For Real

GO INTO any High Street shopping area and wander past the shops, not buying but merely looking. At the bank you'll see signs of money-anxiety: Take Out A Budget Account And We'll Look After Your Bills, or Open An Account For Your Child — Now. Carry on through the supermarket, ignoring the four wheeled trolley that'll help you carry all the convenience foods you could buy there. You'll spot the dirt-anxiety: Double Wrapped For Your Hygiene, or Helps Protect Your Home. Buy a disinfected, cling-film-covered pack of apples and get a lemon free — yourself.

Anxiety in the face of the facts of living even spreads to the local bikeshop. Think Bike and Wear Bright Yellow And Be Spotted Like A Pansy hit you in the eye as you slip on the wet lino where some slavering lackey has persuaded another sucker to part with ten quid down and a fiver for the rest of his natural — the Can't Be Without One Like The Rest anxiety. How does a motorcycle so unashamedly functional as Ducati's Desmo 900 Super Sport fit into this pseudo-life where cringing blockheads worry themselves sick at every turn?

Well the simple and sad fact is that it doesn't, or at least is unlikely to for very much longer. We've seen it happen in America where paranoia over lead fumes, carbohydrates, back pressure, air pressure, noise,

being noticed, not being noticed and the rest has resulted in as pure a sporting bike as the 900SS being muzzled. It almost happened here, but fortunately importers Coburn and Hughes heeded the outcry from potential Desmo owners and the '78 Super Sport is back to original spec with its gulping great 40mm carbs and blaring Conti silencers. How long they'll be permitted to import the 900SS in this form is anybody's guess. Mine is until The Man Who Is Ultra-Paranoid About Bikers at the DoT is blown off by a fit combination of Desmo and rider.

And the most ironic thing of all is that the Super Sport is probably the safest bike I've ever ridden. Sure it's fast, but you haven't got to go one hundred per all the time. Sure it's lean, low and hungry-looking but since when have racy lines made a racer (remember the Suzuki F500)? Those clip-on bars, rear sets and a small firm seat may not be ideal for everyday biking, but they are right for utmost control in all conditions. The riding position takes getting used to, with the semi-racing crouch punishing wrists and necks cruelly for the first few rides. But whether you're zamming along a twisty lane or poodling around looking for chicks, you've got control that's so finely tuned and uninhibited by dead weight that all motorcycle designers should be made to ride one.

We had the 900SS for test during that

period when the weather was in a contrary, foul mood, when you'd suddenly find a wet patch on your favourite line through switchback esses, necessitating instant action. Time and again I'd slink into the office slyly grinning yet reluctant to tell the tale of that morning's excitement. No-one ever really believes such stories. Eventually the simmering in my stomach would die down, the trembling in hands and knees stop and I'd be able to look up and face the others with a slightly less gormless expression.

It wasn't that I scared myself on the Ducati, but more the awe I felt as I grew more aware of the capabilities of that almost faultless chassis and the easy-going characteristics of its thundering engine. My best moment came when I touched down the nut on the clip which tightens the silencer to the right hand exhaust pipe. Bravado had little to do with that incident though it was a surprise that the bike did have physical limitations after all. No, it was more the culmination of a day's riding that was in no way unsafe but merely a reminder that I wasn't on a race track but instead a roundabout on Peterborough's bypass.

That's the real problem with the 900SS — you keep forgetting that you're part of the outside world and that you're supposed to obey such mundane things as speed limits, laws, staying on the left side of the road and

so on. As your mind dials into the super awareness that high speed riding demands, you also lose contact with reality around you, apart from the tarmac in front. The Ducati sits on the road like a stomach full of stout with its 60 inch wheelbase giving leech-like qualities. Even with the highly inaccurate speedometer flailing around at 10-15 per cent above the true figure, it still comes as a shock when your eyes flicker long enough on to the clock to register what it says. It's as though the whole bike is conspiring to lose you your licence in the most spectacular way possible, short of chemical or liquid meditation. Tucked in behind that useful half-fairing, you haven't even got the wind pressure to remind you of the possibly illegal speed at which you may be travelling. Take a look at the top speed figures and you'll notice that the prone speed of 131.5mph is a full 8mph quicker than the sitting-up speed — a position in which no sane person would find himself at those speeds. At 131.5mph, the revcounter was indicating 7,500rpm — though there's no guarantee it was any more accurate than the speedometer — and the bike would seem to be slightly overgeared for it would rev far higher in fourth gear. This high gearing would account for the incredible fuel consumption figure of 50mpg overall which dropped to only 48mpg when ridden maniacally . . . sorry, hard. On one rain-soaked trip along the

beautiful, winding A15 to Lincoln and back I even recorded 54mpg — quite incredible for a bike that spends most of its time on hard acceleration.

The reasons for this frugality are, of course, the efficiency of the engine and the light weight it has to propel. Indicators and a dualseat are the only concessions made to civilisation by the 900SS; the indicators by Federal law in the States and the dualseat by popular demand. It's no good looking mean and purposeful if you don't do it to any purpose. Elsewhere the chassis is just dedicated to function. The mild steel tubular frame uses the crankcase as a stressed member with the two front down tubes bolting on either side of the front cylinder.

The steering head has another three frame tubes running rearwards to a triangulated rear subframe, providing absolute rigidity that goes a long way to disguising the activities of poor rear shock absorbers. Marzocchi supply front and rear suspension and, while the forks are supple, bump-absorbing and well damped, the rear units are rebound damped only and over-sprung. Consequently the rear end tends to jump around a bit if you hit a particularly nasty pothole while cornering. These units are so out of character with the rest of the bike's superior qualities that they're worth junking straight away. The weave that can emanate from the rear end is

kept to a minimum by the strength with which the swing arm is endowed. The 900SS hasn't got the eccentric swing arm bushes fitted to the Darmah (and for which a special tool and often a hammer are needed to adjust the chain), but instead it's got a conventional bronze-bushed swing arm pivot with an unusual but clever method of chain adjustment. The closed swing arm ends have the adjusting bolt through the centre of the tubes and pull back directly on the spindle.

The brilliance of those front forks shows not only in their ability to handle bumps with hardly a twitch but also with a progressive action when braking fiercely, a habit which I tended to slip into during the test and which had absolutely nothing to do with the anatomy of my passenger. This was the only time you really realised how fast you had been motoring — when, with arms locked against the bars, you'd squeeze the front brake lever harder and harder until it seemed certain the tyre would be ripped to shreds. Those brakes, two 11in diameter twin piston discs up front and a 9in disc at the rear, must rank as the ultimate system fitted as standard to any production bike, with the possible exception of Moto Guzzi. While I applaud the Guzzi integral braking system, I must admit I've never got quite used to relying on foot pressure alone, though no doubt it merely takes time and a few thousand miles. Not only

Above: lying flat on the tank your nose is just four feet from the ground — we measured it! The straight-across fork yoke helps to keep the steering easy by reducing inertia about the steering head.

Above left: that gaping mesh covered instrument is the 40mm Dell Orto carb and given half a chance will have your leg as a petrol substitute.

Below left: note how the crankcase forms part of the frame, offering great rigidity. Oil only goes in one hole — on the finned sump. The aluminium dipstick/filler plug needs a spanner.

Street Racing For Real

are the Brembo discs made from cast iron but they're drilled as well and remain effective and grab-free in the worst wet conditions.

The succinct description of the Ducati engine in our Checkout panel will bring tears to the eyes of anyone who has ever rebuilt one of the 90 degree V-twins. Those nine characters of 8/8½ Optima Bold belie the expertise which goes into correctly setting up a Desmo engine. The desmodromic principle has been explained many times before and it suffices to say that it is a means of mechanically closing the valves rather than relying upon mere spring pressure. The improvements made in recent years to conventional spring-returned valve gear, notably by Kawasaki with the Z900 and followed by Suzuki with the GS range, has meant that the Desmo method of precise valve control at high rpm no longer holds exclusive territory. However, it is highly efficient when tolerances are perfect, but this is a difficult job for anyone to do, let alone the DIY rider. The clearance between the 'top hat' on the top of the valve stem and the forked ends of the return rocker arm must be set at a maximum of two thou otherwise the rocker will be battered or, if it's too tight, the cam lobe will wear.

The advantage of the desmo valve gear is at high rpm, but the real joy of riding the 900SS is the massive torque that floods in from 2,000rpm giving the bike a most un-racer-like tractability and the rider a most-racer-like ability. It's difficult to be caught in the wrong gear on the 900SS, which goes a long way to explaining its rapidity through the twisty bits. And yet when you come to the straights and zap open the Tommaselli quick action throttle, the Conti exhausts take on a hard edged *blat* that seems to hang around your ears and the tacho needle spins very quickly to the red zone. A maximum power output at the rear wheel of around 60bhp doesn't sound a lot these days and, indeed, in a straight line race the 900SS would lose out to most of the megabike multis. But that's not where the real fun of biking lies anyway, and I suspect that owners of the 900SS take a perverse pleasure in letting Jap bike riders steam into the distance and then outbraking and leading

them into all sorts of cornering acrobatics.

Starting the Desmo was surprisingly easy after all the warnings I'd had. It had one of those old-fashioned lever things sticking out the right side, a kickstarter I believe they're called. There's no choke and from cold it's necessary to tickle the Dell Orto carbs (reaching behind the left side panel for the rear cylinder), open the throttle a fraction and swing firmly. Occasionally it would spit back through the open mesh of the carbs.

The standard of finish is largely irrelevant on a bike of this sort, but some irritating details have improved over the years since the days of the earlier 750 Super Sports. Switchgear is by the Italian CEV company (unlike the Nippon Denso equipment fitted to the Darmah) and almost acceptable. It is at least accurate in its decisions, unlike the tin box affairs of the past, but still a little clumsy to operate. By contrast the CEV 60/50 watt headlamp is superb, receiving its power from a small battery wedged between the side panels via a Ducati Electronica 200 watt alternator. Bosch supply the coil ignition which is magnetically triggered. An array of idiot lights between the Smiths instruments could dismay an unsuspecting rider for there's always at least one light on.

The swapover of sides for the gearchange linkage has worked well despite the complicated internals constructed to achieve it. The gears snick in quickly and the clutch action is light and smooth even if it did get a little soggy during the standing start quarter-mile tests. That wasn't surprising, for, with such a tall first gear (overall 11.95:1) the clutch had to be slipped off the line and second gear not engaged until 50mph was reached. I'd only just got into third gear by the end of the quarter — and then we found the lights weren't working. The Checkout figure is an estimation based upon Simon Grey counting his fingers.

The Ducati 900SS is possibly the purest form of motorcycling there is, a kind of Nirvana of the thrills and sensations that makes it all worthwhile. But it wouldn't suit everyone, or even most bikers, so be careful before committing yourself. Street Racing For Real? Well, maybe.

900ss: The Truth

R. P. McMurphy on a year with his 900SS.

'WELL, DOCTOR, it all started when I was about fourteen.'

'Would it be true to say you have suffered a steady decline since then?'

'Yes, it nearly cost me my exams and definitely stopped me from going to university, gave me haemorrhoids, arthritis of the lower spine, alienated my family and friends and has had me on the verge of bankruptcy for years.'

'Have you ever tried to do anything about it?'

'Oh yes, I've tried several of the latest Oriental remedies and even some of the ancient British cures, but all to no avail.'

'I see, this is a very serious case, already. Did any traumatic event cause you to come and seek psychiatric help?'

'Y . . . Ye . . . yes, sorry, I begin to . . to stutter when I have to t . . . ta . . . talk about it.'

'Well tell me about it.'

'I've j . . . just paid two thousand pounds f . . . for a se . . . sec . . . secondhand D . . . De . . . De . . . Desmo.'

'What! Nurse, certify this patient immediately, give him 500 milligrams of chlor-promazine and a course of electro-convulsive therapy!'

It's not really like that, but I sometimes wonder. I saw my first Ducati when I was fourteen, a 250 Mach I complete with jelly-mould tank, clip-ons, great big alloy drum brakes and that amazing, shaft driven over-head cam, beetle-browed engine. It was bright red and had an open mega, and when the guy riding it gave it some stick I thought the high street was going to cave in. The visual and sonic impact of that thing was more than a kid just getting into bikes could stand.

With an income of less than zero at this time, the hot setup for obtaining one's first motorcycle was to wander around suburban streets peering into front and back gardens for heaps of rotting tarpaulin, where, very often, lurking thereunder was an abandoned Fanny Barnett, James Captain or even a BSA CIIG. They'd been thrown there after the master of the household had finally saved up the deposit on a Ford Anglia. This up and coming socialite would then be approached with an offer not exceeding thirty bob and if successful one would half wheel, half carry, this heap of junk triumphantly off for rebuilding in the bedroom.

Trouble was, the tarpaulin I discovered hid not a girder-forked two-stroke bicycle, but a squat, open-carbed, open-megaphoned bright red Ducati 200cc Super Sport. It took a month to borrow, from eighteen separate sources, the asking price of thirty quid. On enquiring why it had no lights or number plates I was informed that the previous owner had raced it at Brands Hatch in club meetings against Tiger Cubs and the like. I was then given the box containing mudguards, lights and so on and told to get on with it.

To cut a long story short, I passed my test on a bike with a 10.5:1 piston, 32mm carb, 15 degrees of lock and a clutch which needed slipping up to 15mph in bottom. On a good day it would get within sniffing distance of the ton in top.

It was the best bike I have ever owned and if anybody has still got FTD 87B, get in touch. I'll buy you a pint and make you an offer.

All this nostalgia crap is to explain why, when they appeared, I had to have a V-twin Ducati and why, when it was finally produced, I could not sustain a meaningful existence without owning a 900 Desmo. I had to wait some time before I could afford one (I still can't) and, of course, during this period Ducati diluted the specification by fitting air cleaners, reducing carb size, bodging a left hand gearchange, fitting enormous absorbent silencers and other garbage. Gloom and doom pervaded the atmosphere until I found, in deepest Kent, an early spec model complete with curvaceous fibre tank, 40mm bell-mouthed carbs, open Conti megas and brake and gearchange on the correct side.

Riding it confirmed my worst fears. I had to have it; there was no way out.

Do you remember the first time you rode a big bike — say a 650 — after pootling about on a 250? The eyeball-popping power of the thing, the panic braking before the first bend just in case you were going too fast, the sphincter-loosening acceleration when you plucked up the courage to open the throttle more than an eighth? Well, that's what the Desmo did to me and that was straight after getting off another 900cc bike. Mr. Daryn, purveyor of motorcycles to the Gentry, and me, had no trouble in taking all my money after that test ride.

Living with a Desmo is a very character-forming experience, on a par with transcendental meditation and staying with your mother-in-law. You have to stand there and take it while those that don't know take the piss out of the rust and the paintwork. You have to think up ever more extravagant excuses to prevent those who do know from cadging rides. You have to bite your lip as you sign over your personal fortune to an establishment in Wisbech and receive a size 000 Jiffy bag containing some shims in return. You have to develop parasympathetic nervous control to remain cool, calm and collected as the restricted steering lock finally gets you and you crash to the ground trying to turn round in the pub car park.

Then again how can I explain the pleasure of getting back from a ride on a warm summer evening, letting the adrenalin subside by sitting on the step and just eyeballing the bike, taking in the special alloy Brembo calipers, the intricate radial webbing on the wheel bearing carriers, the front engine mount, the carved dural plate that supports the rear caliper. The failing light takes away the warts of the finish and makes you realise that you haven't bought a motorcycle, a machine, but a person's — a human being's — expression of what the act of motorcycling should be performed upon.

Mr Ducati has built a bike which will show you The Truth. If you can live with that, have a well-equipped workshop and a sense of humour, buy one.

Below: left is R. P. McMurphy's 900SS (with Campbray wheels) and right our test bike.

Ducati 900 SS

Faster than we expected, Ducati's desmodromic twin turns on real performance — but at a price.

£2500 will buy sports motorcycling in the traditional mould, and more muscle than most roadsters can use. That includes one or two rough edges, but ironically the big Ducati was easy to manage and even sprang one or two surprises, like 60 mpg fuel consumption. ▶

Ducati 900 SS

More at home on the track than on the road, the 900SS puts all its energy into going quickly.

No compromise, no unnecessary trimmings — Ducati's 900SS only offers plain, raw performance. But it is real performance, not imaginary or accentuated by the frame's misbehaviour.

Perhaps the bike's attraction is that each part of the machine is tuned in to deal with the engine's full output. Even 70-odd horsepower isn't excessive, compared to the CBX for example, but the Ducati is light and low. Its sleek lack of air resistance is worth many hard-won horse-power. The lack of weight and width make the tenacious road-holding easy to use.

Admittedly, the big V-twin has a narrow range of appeal; it focusses on a very limited stretch of the motorcycling spectrum — but it focusses very sharply indeed.

It demonstrated its abilities amply at the test track, going through the radar beam at 129 mph. That's not bad in itself, except the Ducati went through on a rolled-off throttle because the clutch had started to slip during the run-up! The clutch problem was something else, which we'll get to later. The relevant point at this stage was that the Ducati wouldn't take full power and couldn't be run much above 6000 rpm. Because of this we didn't risk taking standing start tests but, in this state, the Ducati lapped Snetterton only two seconds slower than we'd managed on a CBX and was holding its own against a 1200 Laverda Mirage which we were running at the same time.

That sums up how well the various component part of the Ducati work together. Even with the engine effectively governed by the clutch, the blend of handling, braking, lightness and so on could compensate for the lack of power. It was using only 50 or 60 bhp to do what the big Honda needed 90 bhp for.

If that's good for performance, it's good for the rider too. It's a lot easier to use 50 horsepower than 90 and the end result has to be a bike which is more manageable and safer.

These conclusions seem pretty inevitable after riding the 900 but they are a long way from what I was expecting. I'd assumed it would simply be a noisier and less comfortable version of the 860. The cafe racer riding position can be very comfortable but in practice it has to be tailored very carefully for it to work. Trying to build a bike in this style to suit all sizes of people usually makes it worse than the conventional layout which is nearly right for everybody. And when I learnt that the huge 40 mm carbs had no choke. I just accepted it with resignation. They also have accelerator pumps which can squirt in enough fuel to richen the mixture for cold starting. But my first attempt resulted in a couple of smokey blow-backs and one ankle-wrenching backfire when I took my weight off the lever before the engine had decided whether it was going to fire forwards or backwards.

Then the motor roared into life with a staccato bark from the Conti silencers and from there on it took about five seconds to convince me that this was a bike I could get to like.

I still wasn't expecting a lot of performance but the Ducati has, if anything, too much performance. It is frustringly unsettled at anything much below 80 mph; virtually every aspect of the bike had mediocre low-speed characteristics which improved considerably as the speed went up.

At low rpm the engine was flat and noisy, in the top half of the rev band it became crisp and only the exhaust was noisy. The torque curve is flat, peaking at 4500 and then slowly tailing off to the 7900 redline, but the engine doesn't like taking full throttle below 4000 rpm. It has, compared to the flexible four-cylinder bikes, a very narrow power band.

It can be run around at low rpm, and ridden virtually down to idle speed, but it won't respond to the throttle. The gearshift is also ponderous and chunky if the gears are casually pushed through at low revs. Once the engine is spinning at a happy speed, the selector action becomes slick and accurate — the Ducati just doesn't like being pottered around.

There are ten rear wheel sprockets available and two or three gearbox sprockets, giving an ample choice of overall gearing. Our model had just about the highest gearing available, which aimed for 152 mph at peak revs in top. That is a bit ambitious but it gave the bike superb high-speed cruising; 75 mph at 4000 rpm, in top, and nearly 90 mph available in second gear. The motor had no trouble pulling this and still gave pretty exciting acceleration. We didn't risk destroying the clutch by running standing starts but before we tried the high-speed runs and noticed the clutch slip, we'd been playing around running the bike up to the radar to check the instruments. Without any attempt at a rapid take-off, just squirting the power on from a 5 mph rolling start, the Ducati was hitting over 80 mph inside about 200 yards.

Harsh suspension and heavy brakes only start to work well at high speeds.

The clutch slip problem didn't affect the bike in normal road use and only happened when we asked it to pass a lot of power. It was as if the clutch had decided it was going to transmit 59 horse-power and no more.

It didn't seem possible to get a full power curve from the engine but when we ran it on the brake it didn't show the same characteristics as on the road. it gave full power up to around 5000 rpm, and above this, as the dynamometer load changed, the clutch began to slip. But instead of going wild like it had on the road, the revs went up to 8000 rpm and stayed there. It could have been because the power drops off so sharply that it got down to a level which the clutch found acceptable. Anyway we found we could then use the dynamometer to wind the engine back down from 8000 rpm and get power readings through the full rev range. Once it had slipped and gripped again, the

The desmo engine looks big but its slim lines allow a simple and rigid frame assembly, which, in turn, allow the best use to be made of the power.

Source of the Ducati's muscle — the huge 40mm Dell 'Orto carburettors.

clutch seemed perfectly stable.

Back on the road once again, we couldn't duplicate the clutch's test-bed behaviour. We took it over to Mick Walker's shop at Wisbech to have new plates fitted. The lined plates were worn down — we have no way of knowing whether the clutch had been damaged by previous abuse or whether it is simply the weak link in the Ducati's transmission.

It's worth noting that Steve Wynne, of Sports Motorcycles, fits the stronger clutch springs from the 450 Ducati into his V-twin racers. On reflection maybe we should have asked for new springs to be fitted when the plates were changed — it is possible that the heat generated by the slipping clutch could have weakened them.

With the new plates fitted I took it easy for a couple of hundred miles to give them a chance to bed in. Then we went to Snetter-

ton. For the first half a dozen laps the bike was OK and pulled enough revs down the straight to give a speed of 130 mph. Then the clutch began to give up in exactly the same way as before — the bike was still rideable but wouldn't take full power for acceleration and top speed was limited to 120 mph.

Had it been a normal clutch failure we would have expected it to get worse — but it didn't. It simply cropped off peak performance and left it at that.

The bike itself felt really at home on the track. Everyone who rode it got enthusiastic about the big Ducati's style. A Michelin on the front and an Avon on the back gave the bike a heavy feel but it stuck to the road and could be flicked through corners like a lightweight. The only criticisms were that the machine felt too rigid to give any feedback to the rider and that the throttle had slightly too much movement.

At these speeds everything on the Ducati got into its working range. The suspension, which is hard for road use, started to work over the bumps and ripples. While the rider could still feel the bumps they didn't put the bike off line or cause any sudden grounding. The brakes which normally were heavy to use with a hard feel to the lever, suddenly became powerful, controllable and didn't need a particularly high pressure.

As the bike was heeled into corners the stand would chatter up and down on the road surface. But, deep into one right-hander, I felt something touch down which was obviously a lot more solid. It pushed the whole machine to the side before I could lift the bike. This happened a couple of times and was really the limiting factor on the Ducati's cornering — it turned out to be the bottom of the kick-start lever.

The best thing about the Ducati was that it remained completely stable. It would rattle over bumps without changing line, you could throttle back, brake or change gear while it was cranked into a long fast bend and it wouldn't even twitch the handlebars. It didn't move around under heavy breaking — this general steadiness tended to remove

the impression of speed so that at 100mph the Ducati felt like most other bikes do at 70 or 80.

The 900 conserves its energy, concentrating all its efforts into the job in hand. The way it eliminates waste effort could even be measured — it was lapping at roughly the same speed as the CBX we tested, yet it had far less power available. And where the CBX averaged 21 to 22mpg, the Ducati gave 38mpg. It emphasises the point that everything on a bike can be equated to horsepower — that the slim profile, the low riding position, the fairing, the braking and the handling can more than make up for a bigger, more powerful engine.

This single-minded function also means there can be no compromises. The Ducati isn't difficult to ride — in fact most people would find it one of the easiest machines on which to travel quickly and safely. But it means that the bike is not so good at low speeds. Everything is heavy and harsh. The suspension is too hard for any pretence of comfort along country lanes at 50mph. Attacking the same bumps at 70mph would probably give a smoother ride. The seat is also hard, the side panels foul your legs and the riding position puts a lot of weight on your wrists at town speeds. The steering is restricted by a tight lock which cuts down low-speed manoeuvrabilty.

Up to 50mph the steering is heavy and so are the brakes. The only aspect which does improve as the speed goes down is the fuel consumption. The Ducati averaged 47mpg over the test period but it also gave 60mpg when it was treated fairly gently.

A bike with this kind of character could be expected to be very crude in its accessories, particularly as it is Italian. In fact the Ducati was surprisingly good. Even though it had no cold-start control, it usually fired up within two or three kicks. The lighting was powerful enough, with a 55/60W H4 headlamp, although dipped beam had a cut-off which was way too sharp for the Ducati's performance. The switches themselves aren't too inspiring and it is still possible, with heavy gloves, to turn off the main lighting switch while operating the dip switch.

It lost its front left-hand indicator early in the test and, towards the end of the test the whole lighting circuit failed. This was not an electrical failure but seemed to be caused by the tank rubber mounts working out of position and allowing the tank to chatter up and down on the wiring harness. The rubber pads were coming away from the frame when the clutch was first stripped and were put back, but they obviously didn't stay in place. The precise cause of failure wasn't found, but the tank succeeded in chafing through one of the plastic loops which holds the wiring to the frame, so presumably it could do the same thing to the wiring.

Fortunately it didn't affect the electronic ignition which uses two small coil transducers to trigger a capacitor discharge circuit which is supplied direct from the alternator. The system can even be run without the battery, for competition use or in an emergency. To do this you have to disconnect the wires from the transducers to the engine-stop relay under the tank. The lights and other electrical accessories must not be used in this condition.

Based on the earlier 750SS, the 900 comes in a variety of guises, with different car-

Ducati 900 SS

burettors, exhausts, cams and even a full race kit available. Our model had the 40mm carbs, with no air cleaners, and the less restrictive (for want of a better term) exhausts. Smaller carbs (32mm), air filters and quieter silencers are available, or, going the other way, Ducati have high performance cams and high level exhausts which come as part of their race kit.

The rest of the kit includes a full fairing, 24 litre tank, chain, and an oil cooler. The standard fuel tank is supposed to hold 18 litres — 4.4 gallons — but after our machine had gone on to reserve it only took 2.8

Sleek and low — the cycle parts also work to turn horse-power into performance.

gallons to top it up. This gave a useful range of about 140 miles, compared to something like 200 miles had there been 4 gallons available.

Ducati's chassis is neat, simple and demonstrably rigid enough. The castor angle is quite steep and, with the bike's obstinate refusal to wobble or weave, it could use forks with softer springs. More wheel movement is not likely to upset the Ducati's handling but it could really improve the ride comfort. There is a friction damper on the steering which is about the the last thing the Ducati actually needs. At the back end they've obviously made an effort to keep the swing arm assembly as stiff as possible. The pivot bolts up solidly to the frame and carries the swing-arm on bushes. This is shimmed for zero endfloat. The wheel's axle is carried on sliding adjusters inside the fork legs, with external clamps.

Overall, the Ducati is a difficult bike to sum up. It is built like a racer and is obviously intended for the hardened enthusiast. But it is well made and functional, as opposed to just looking like a racer. What it does, it does very well; it economises on power and somehow gets the utmost performance from the available tractive effort. And that's more or less where it ends. The Ducati has no other pretensions. There are other bikes with more power, more manoeuvrability and certainly more comfort. In the hands of an expert rider many of these machines will out-perform the Ducati. Where the V-twin wins is that it is less demanding and less tiring to ride at high speed.

John Robinson

Performance & specification

ENGINE

SOHC, 90 deg V twin with desmodromic valve gear. Magnetic transducer/CDI ignition, two 40 mm Dell 'Orto carburettors, wet sump lubrication, 12V alternator, 12 Ah battery.

displacement	863.9 ccm
bore x stroke	86 x 74.4 mm
compression ratio	9.5:1

GEARBOX

Helical gear primary drive to multiplate clutch, five speed gearbox and final drive by chain.

primary reduction	70/32
final reduction	33/15
gearbox ratios:	2.237; 1.562; 1.204; 1.00 and 0.887

CHASSIS

front tyre	3.50V18
rear tyre	4.25/85V18
wheelbase	59 inch
castor	60.5 deg
trail	n/a
overall length	87.4 inch
overall width	26.6 inch
dry weight	415 lb

fuel tank capacity	4.4 gal

List price inc. VAT and delivery £2,519.
Warranty: 6 months/6,000 miles plus 1 year Auto-guard (engine and gearbox only).

PERFORMANCE

maximum speed	129 mph*
standing ¼-mile	n/a*
braking from 30 mph	28 feet

speeds in gears at 7,900 rpm
(note: wide range of optional sprockets available.)

1st	60 mph
2nd	87 mph
3rd	115 mph
4th	133 mph
5th	152 mph

FUEL CONSUMPTION:

best	60 mpg
worst	38.1 mpg
average over test	47.3 mpg
fuel tank range to reserve	106 to 168 miles

* test runs aborted because of clutch slip.

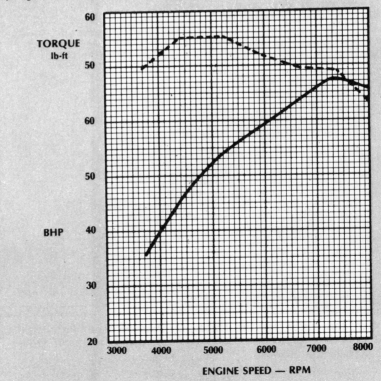

Simple Service

Ducati Darmah

FOR a Ducati Simple Service it seemed only natural to approach Sports Motorcycles. After all, they prepared Mike Hailwood's winning TT machine. Roy Armstrong, who did our service work and passed on his experience of the big V twins, didn't actually prepare Mike's bike, but he has serviced more Ducati Desmos than most.

Roy's first tip concerned draining the oil. After removing the drain plug — with a six-sided spanner — the bike should be tipped to one side so that all the old oil is drained. Some oil can be trapped in the bottom of the sump because the drain plug is set to one side. Take great care of the alloy washer on the sump plug. If it's left off, the plug will be near impossible to remove the next time you want to drain the oil.

When topping up, there are another couple of points to look out for. Roy says that the plug has to be held dead level in the hole or the dip stick gives a false reading. Also, when checking the level, the bike has to be left standing for at least a couple of hours. It takes this long for all the oil to drain down into the sump. The cylinder heads actually retain 1½ pints! The "book" tells you to change the oil every 1,800 miles, but Roy says that every 1,000 is a better bet unless you do a lot of long runs.

The oil filter was tackled next, and again there is an alloy washer under the bolt head to look out for. Before the bowl can be removed, however, you have to loosen the front carb and rotate it on the head stub. There is a rubber washer under the cover and also a steel one that more often than not sticks to the filter element. When the old element gets thrown into the bin, the steel washer often goes with it.

Fitting the new element is straight-forward, but after twisting the front carb straight, tighten it up! More than one Ducati owner has had his carb fall off after a service! Staying with lubrication, the swinging arm should be greased at least once a month. All you need are a couple of strokes from a decent grease gun. This is important because, without this attention, the adjusters will seize solid.

To adjust the final drive chain you simply release the clamps and turn the eccentric with the tool provided in the bike's kit. When tightening the clamps keep the gap even. It is possible, if you use excessive force, to make the ends meet. This will mean that you have crushed the frame. The chain should be set off the stand, with around 20mm of free play at the slackest point. A final word of warning: if you can't turn the adjusting spanner by hand pressure alone, the adjuster is seized. Don't resort to a hammer. The thing will have to be stripped out and greased.

Unless you are prepared to fork out for the special tools, ignition timing is a dealer's job. Roy insists that the timing NEVER alters, and if you leave the ignition pick-ups alone all will be well. If you do remove the clutch cover for any reason, the pick-up screw is paint marked — and that's the one to leave alone.

If you have the special tool, shown in the pictures, it's simply a question of removing the cover plug and fitting up the wicked-looking knife blade into the end of the crank. A strobe light is then used to check the "blade" against the marks on the cover. One is idle, the other full advance. The electronic ignition feeds two Champion spark plugs, grade L88A, and gapped at

Super-stylish and super-fast, the Ducati Darmah SS is an enthusiast's dream. Dave Walker goes through the servicing routine at Sports Motorcycles of Manchester.

60

.6mm or 25 thou.

The clutch adjustment is quite simple although many owners seem to make a hash of it. Remove the little clutch adjuster window from the cover, then unlock, and screw in, the adjuster until the clutch arm on the other side of the casing just touches the end of its slot. Now back off the adjuster until you can feel one mm of free play in the arm. This can be anywhere in the clutch arm slot as long as you have the correct free play — and the arm does not foul the end of its slot on full lift. Naturally you slacken the cable right off, or unhook it to make these adjustments.

To get to the air filters and battery, you have to remove the side panels. These should be pulled off square. If you yank them away from the bottom, the paintwork on the seat unit gets damaged. The battery level can be checked visually, but if you have to remove the battery for any reason it MUST go back the same way around.

If the battery is refitted the wrong way around, the leads are still long enough to connect up. However, when working on the back carb, ie twisting it to get at the main jet, the main body will short out on the battery terminal. This has actually happened in the Sports Motorcycles workshop — the battery exploded, and apart from the not inconsiderable damage to the bike, the luckless lad working on the bike was taken to hospital.

To gain access to the rear filter the seat has to be removed. You have to remove the petrol tank to get to the front filter and it all gets to be a bit of a hassle. There is quite a temptation to chuck the filters out and thus eliminate this part of the service. If you do just that you will have to jet up the carbs to suit — the motor runs weak without filters and the engine will overheat.

Another common mistake is to overtighten the carb mountings. The intake gasket is a special steel plate set in bonded rubber. If you tweak up the mounting nuts on the carbs, the rubber splits and the steel shows through. This results in the motor breathing through the gasket instead of the carb! As a part of the service, the float bowls should be drained and cleaned, along with the filter in the fuel line.

Roy doesn't use any special tools for balancing the carbs. He starts by backing off the throttle idle stops and checking the cables for free play. There should be 1 to 2mm in each cable. Next, the throttles are opened fully, checking that they clear the top of the bore. To balance the slides, Roy feels the back carb while watching the front one. The cables are then altered until both slides open at the same time.

Next, set the mixture screws to 1½ turns out from fully home, and you are ready to tackle the throttle stop balance. Roy does this by "ear" listening to the exhaust note and adjusting the stops until the tickover is smooth and even. Mere mortals would probably prefer to use a car type balancer over the inlets, or a piece of hose to listen to the intake hiss.

Please note that the choke cables MUST have at least 3mm of free play. This is to prevent the choke plunger being held off its seating, thus upsetting the carburation.

While the tank is off you can check out the electrics at the front of the machine. Roy says you can spray all the wiring with WD40 or similar, to good effect. He also advises filling all electrical connections with silicon

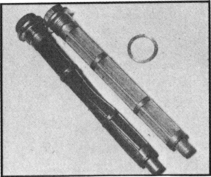

1 The drain plug also contains this strainer. You have to replace the lot if the gauze is damaged in any way.

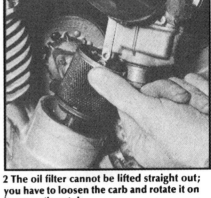

2 The oil filter cannot be lifted straight out; you have to loosen the carb and rotate it on its mounting stub.

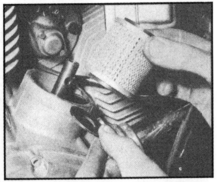

3 The new oil filter comes complete with rubber sealing rings. Don't forget this steel washer under the filter base.

4 The carb float bowls should be removed and cleaned out. Don't forget to re-tighten after fitting the filter.

5 This fuel line filter should trap most of the rubbish carried in the fuel. It can be cleaned out in neat petrol.

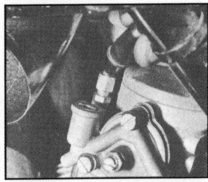

6 The choke operating cable MUST have at least three millimetres of free play to allow the choke plunger to seat home.

7 The front air filter element is quite a job to remove; if you leave them out you have to jet up — see text.

8 After loosening the clamps the chain adjuster spindle should turn under hand pressure only — see text.

9 Regular greasing is essential, not just for lubrication, but to prevent the adjusters from seizing.

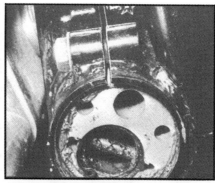

10 When retightening the clamps, only "nip" them up. The sides of the slot should remain parallel or the frame will crush.

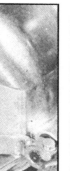

11 The clutch carries a conventional push rod adjuster in its centre but its setting can be confusing.

12 With the cable removed from the arm it will fall to the back of the slot, see text for adjustment details.

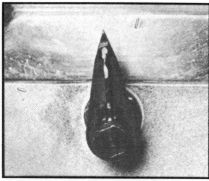

13 You need this special tool for checking the ignition timing. However, it rarely needs altering.

14 The warning light bulbs are actually the warning light itself. Sports Motorcycles have them all in stock.

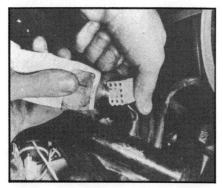

15 Silicon grease should be pumped into all electrical connectors and multi pin plugs. Ordinary grease will NOT do.

16 The fuse cover should have these drain holes to allow the rainwater to drain away, you might have to drill your own.

grease. Silicon grease is a little like WD40 in a solid, rather than a liquid, form. It is *not* an expensive substitute for normal grease.

The multi-pin connectors are not treated at the factory and tend to corrode quite quickly — once exposed to the British climate. You should pull all connectors apart and clean off all signs of "growth" then pump in plenty of silicon grease. This also applies to the ignition switch and the switch on the prop stand. If you bought your Ducati from Sports Motorcycles, this treatment will have been carried out for you before you took delivery.

Another important point to look out for concerns the fuse box. The lid of the box fits up under the tank, just where rain water can drain into it. There should be a drain hole in the cover, but the chances are it will be missing. It takes only a second or two to drill a couple of holes which will let the water out again. It's a small point but one which can produce a lot of headaches if neglected.

Warning light failure is another small, but irritating, fault with the Ducati. A lot of owners ask for these to be replaced when their bike is being serviced, not realising that the labour amounts to nearly a full hour. You have to pull most of the headlamp assembly apart to get to the warning lights. The confusion arises when you try to locate the bulb. Strictly speaking there isn't one! The coloured lamp glass IS the bulb. The picture will make this clear.

Although you may have Marzocchi or Ceriani front forks, they both take 185cc of oil after draining. The actual grade is AGIP "OSO25", but most owners experiment to find the weight best suited to their riding technique; AFT fluid makes a fair starting point.

The brake pads can be inspected after removing the cover over the caliper. The minimum wear limit is 4mm. When you consider that the pad starts life with only 7mm of material this does seem an awful lot of brake pad to throw away. Don't be tempted to let them go any further. Roy assures us that once under 4mm the friction material starts to break up.

There are more than just one or two points to look out for when setting up the clearances on the Desmodromic valve gear. However, Roy says that any owner with average intelligence and a little patience can tackle the job. Checking the clearance is fairly straight-forward, but watch out for oil spillage when you remove the lower cylinder's cam cover.

With the valve gear exposed, set the crankshaft to TDC, on compression, and measure the clearance under the top rocker. This should be 4 thou. To check the lower clearance you have to force a feeler gauge under the "top hat". You will be working against the pressure of the "helper" spring on the bottom (closing) rocker arm. This does complicate matters, and to add to the confusion Roy says it is a good idea to turn the motor over and check the clearance over the whole base circle of the cam — the clearance will vary. Anything from zero to two thou is within tolerance, although Roy does re-adjust at two thou because he says it will need doing shortly once it reaches this clearance.

If the valves need attention you are going to have to replace the shims to alter the clearance. Start by removing the side cover on the head and this will reveal the end of the rocker spindle. The end of this spindle should have a threaded hole in its centre. If it hasn't, then some clown has done the tappets before and put the spindle back the wrong way around. Take care you don't make that mistake.

The spindle can be withdrawn using the Ducati special tool, or a 5mm screw clamped with some Mole grips. As the spindle comes out, watch out for the shims fitted either side of the rocker. They MUST go back on their respective sides. The rocker is shimmed side to side so that the arm clears the closing rocker. Get them back the wrong way around and the two rockers clash.

Having laid out the rocker and its shims in their correct order, you can remove the valve clearance collars. You now need a micrometer to measure the thickness of the two collars. The top is simply measured with the micrometer sitting as the valve would. The second "top hat" has to be mike'd from its base to the ridge on its inside.

Once you have determined the thickness of the present collars, or shims, you have to select a shim that much thicker, or thinner, to give the required clearance. After refitting recheck the clearance to make sure it is within limits. If you haven't got a supply of shims — and who will have? — you can simply measure the clearances, strip out the shims, and send them to Sports Motorcycles, Liverpool Road, Manchester. These kind souls will then mike up the shims, compare these to your present valve clearance, and then send you the correct replacement.

Please note that when measuring the valve clearance you must have the side covers fitted in place. These support the outer end of the rocker shaft and affect the reading of your feeler gauge. You may also find that when you get the new shims back they will not be spot on for clearance. The range of shims is limited and you just might have to resort to a little "grinding" of the faces to get them spot on. If all this bothers your brain more than just somewhat, you might be better advised to let a dealer do the job for you, but at least you know what you are letting yourself in for.

Our thanks to Sports Motorcycles, and Roy Armstrong, for their help with this feature.

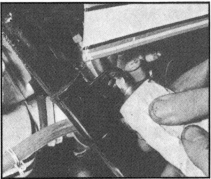
17 Silicon grease can also be used on the side panel rubbers; it doesn't corrode the grommet like normal grease.

18 Four millimetres is the minimum wear limit for the brake pads. Much below this and they start to break up.

19 Tappet clearance is measured here, the bottom setting being checked over the whole duration of the base circle.

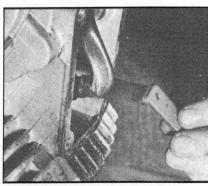
20 The bottom clearance can last up to 30,000 miles, the top one may need doing every 6,000.

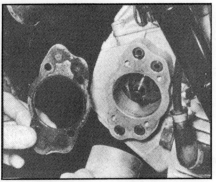
21 To remove the rocker spindle this side cover is lifted off. The gasket can be reused with a dab of grease to seal it.

22 When measuring the lowr clearance shim you have to mike from this ridge, to the base.

Service Data

Every 1000 Kms:
Check oil level in the sump
Lubricate the drive chain, check and adjust its tension
Check battery electrolyte level

Every 3000 Kms:
Change the engine oil (let the oil thoroughly drain from the sump with the engine warm). The oil filter element should be renewed every other oil change.
Check and if necessary adjust the valve clearances

Every 5000 Kms:
Remove the air filters and clean them with

compressed air
Check the carburettor float chambers, main and pilot jets for cleanliness
Adjust the clutch operating mechanism
Lubricate the swinging arm bushes
Check brake pads for wear and check the brake fluid level
Check bolts and nuts tightness
Check the spark plug conditions and the electrode gap

Every 10,000 Kms:
Renew the air filter elements
Renew the spark plugs

Every 20,000 Kms:

Change the front fork oil
Change front and rear brake system fluids.
RECOMMENDED LUBRICANTS
Engine oil: AGIP SINT 2000 — SAE 10 W 50 Multigrade oil (sump capacity: 4.5 Kg = 5 lt).
Front fork: AGIP "OSO 25" or equivalent (185 cc each leg)
Hydraulic disc brakes: AGIP F1 Brake fluid Super HD or equivalent
Drive chain: Rocol chain lube or equivalent chain lubricant
Tachometer and Rev-counter cables: AGIP F1 — Grease 30 or equivalent
Swinging arm bushes: AGIP F1 Grease 30 or equivalent.

It Took Four Dukes Before I Found A Friend...

Short-lived production and high-tune temperament regardless, 500 Desmo owner PAUL AINSWORTH reckons he's found the real Ducati. Surprisingly, this is from a man who's owned four — and that's including two V-twins. Here's his owner's report.

DUCATI'S 500 Sport Desmo hasn't broken any sales records and it's easy to see why. Japanese machinery riders might look wistfully through showroom windows but rarely buy, and many current Ducati owners don't readily accept the parallel twin as a *real* Duke. But for me the little Duke had everything I wanted in a

bike — except a $2600 price tag.

I *nearly* bought one at that price but a combination of severe new bike depreciation and patience paid off. Only 12 months after its Australian release one turned up in the classifieds for a paltry $1600: As good as new with limited use, long rego and an engine that had been tuned by one of the best Ducati tuners in Sydney.

Let me recap, though. I wasn't new to Ducatis when I bought the Sport; or even new to the 500 parallel twin. I'd owned two 860s and two 500 GTLs before the Sport, but even so I was struck with the blatant sports nature of the beast. Sure it can be toured, but it's the antithesis of the torquey, mile-gobbling V-twins.

The most immediate and striking feature of the bike is its tastefully distinctive styling, and the red and white paint scheme really turns some heads. Parking cops cast admiring eyes and forget the tickets, *(oh*

My sporting friend at rest. Michelin tyres, Brembo discs and calipers but no Ceriani forks or Marzocchi rear units. The Paioli suspension is okay but the damping should be better.

yeah? — Ed.) old timers wish for younger limbs and Italians gesticulate all over the machine *(but what are they saying? — Ed).*

The tank is superbly sculpted; a real work of art. It also fits the knees very comfortably, while the thin-but-firm ducktailed solo seat supports the backside with equal comfort and grace. On a recent 400 km blast out in the sticks, 250 km were spent banking like a jet fighter but the only casualty in the comfort stakes was my neck. The Bell Star II might be the best you can buy but it's heavy!

The engine was originally developed as a conventional sohc, two-valves-per-cylinder with springs to seat the valves. But it wasn't

long before the Desmo valvegear was grafted into the Sports engine. And she's a beauty mate! A 500 parallel twin that will propel you to the brink of 185 km/h has to have something going for it. The 860 could only just manage that speed.

The real arm-wrenching power doesn't come in until 6000 rpm. In first, second, and third gears taking the needle past the 6000 rpm mark is eye-watering stuff, but the penalty of such tune is barely enough torque for city lugging. The 500 Sport doesn't like hills, and changing down is a necessity. Around town top is simply not in sight!

Fuel consumption is economical, and just as well too because that fine-looking tank only holds 12 litres (shades of Z1-R). I can usually expect around 23 km/l (60 mpg) and the reserve has eight litres of warning.

For a parallel twin the Desmo 500's smoothness is exceptional. It proves that a well-built twin doesn't need counter-rotating junk. When the engine is not under load or hard acceleration this baby just pulsates. At high speed there is no vibration to be felt at all — except from the chain. Vibration under hard acceleration does not significantly affect comfort because of its short duration.

The gearbox ratios are a good match for the bike's power characteristics. In typical Italian fashion they're fairly tall but ideally spaced. First gear allows the bike to trickle along at 2000 rpm, but at these revs it has no power and doesn't even start running cleanly until 2600 rpm. Gearshifts are quick and positive. I have only once struck a false neutral.

The clutch is very light and has good feel, but even so I don't think the transmission package is quite as good as the old 860's; that was superb!

"You'll be glad"

Starting from cold is immediate and demands having the choke turned off straight away. Once at running temperature the bike starts easily and (to my surprise) settles immediately to a smooth idle. The electric starter is proving to be reliable and so it should — there isn't any kickstarter. On the odd occasion it has been a cranky starter, the power from the largish 18

amp/hour battery hasn't even begun to wane. But let the bike get out of tune and the easy starting disappears. I've heard of other Sport owners with starting problems but it's only a matter of maintenance guys — truly!

The old Ducati sales slogan?

It holds true for the 500 Sport.

"If you ever find yourself in a corner at the wrong speed, in the wrong gear, on the wrong line, you'll be glad you own a Ducati". After owning seven other types of black-top machine I am convinced beyond any doubt that the 500 Desmo is the best-handling road bike available. The strong frame and low seating position are bonuses on a machine both extremely sensitive to body input and quite unconcerned by velocity. If you want to lean the bike, then you lean it! It doesn't matter whether you're at maximum or barely seeing 20 km/h — it will just glide right through that corner without the slightest feeling of falling into it. But I wouldn't practise these techniques if it didn't have superb tyres. I refer to the stan-

dard Michelin rubber. Of all the tyres I've ridden on (Avon, Dunlop, Metzeler, Continental) none match this brand.

Unfortunately the little red Saturn V rocket in disguise hasn't the same fine quality suspension components that grace all other Ducati models. No Ceriani and Marzocchi bits. It is fitted with Paioli suspension front and rear. The forks originally didn't perform to the same fine Ducati standard — and still don't — but a change of oil worked miracles. What came out of the forks during the change had best be left unmentioned. But it was gunky.

The rear shocks give their best at the stiffest preload setting, giving the bike a more responsive feel. Sure it makes riding a little more uncomfortable but it is a sports bike and shouldn't have been fitted with such soft suspension (relative to the average Ducati) in the first place. Overall the suspension is very good but it doesn't have the same quality damping the other models enjoy.

The brakes are Brembo triple discs, and are still the best in the business. The quality and safety I've become so accustomed to was really driven home after a ride on my brother's Suzuki GS550. The brakes were certainly powerful, but were also harsh and insensitive. When you are *really moving* on the Duke (and the greater the speed the more pronounced the effect), very moderate pressure on the lever and pedal will get your speed scrubbed off so quickly and smoothly you'll wonder if it's possible for brakes to be so good. They are, and they work in the wet too. At slower speeds the characteristics of the brakes change. Much greater pressure is required to get results but the same sure feel remains at your fingertips. The discs are bolted onto the nicest looking mag wheels available. Finished in silver, they match the overall styling impeccably.

The biggest hassle with the Sport is *not* the switchgear (which is new) nor any of the electrics, but rather the need to have the bike tuned professionally because the tappets are the shim-type and the ignition timing goes off fairly quickly. Desmo valve gear needs to be kept within working tolerances at all times, which means setting at least one of the buggers every 3000 kilometres.

In 13 months and 6200 km of ownership I've discovered the Ducati 500 Sport Desmo is a Jekyll and Hyde motorcycle. You can turn it into a racing machine by flicking the tacho needle past 6000 rpm and it will love you for it, begging for the next gear and full throttle . . . or it can be as quiet as a 250 commuter without protest. Whichever way you ride it, you have to do just that — *ride* it. It is a precision machine and demands a precision rider. It isn't for the rider who likes soft-cored, mushy rice burners. It is a woman. You always have to dominate her but give her what she wants. What she gives in return will delight your senses.

Halfway
To Happiness

Ducati's '79 range is comprehensive to say the least, from the touring 900 GTS to street racer 900SS. Dave Calderwood tests the SS Darmah, the quiet one with the good looks. Photography Duncan Cubitt.

Top: Now there's a sight for sore eyes. The Taglione twin looks timeless in its beauty.

Bottom: Note neat switchgear, Nippon Denso dials and proliferation of classy ancillaries.

INSPIRATION COMES AT THE WEIRDEST times. There I was, bopping down the leafy lanes of the A10 through Cambridgeshire, when I started rationalising about the Serious Heavy Metal Biker. This line of thought was prompted by the rain, which was dribbling down the back of my neck; the cold, knifing through sodden gloves into my sensitive fingers; and the cost of the motorcycle I was riding: £2299 worth of Ducati SS Darmah. Who the hell pays that kind of loot for this kind of experience? was a rough approximation of my brain waves.

There again, I pondered, the only reason the weather is getting to me is because the rain is wet and cold and I'm getting wet and cold. Unlike many hefty large capacity bikes, I'm not actually having to concentrate any harder or even slow down a lot. The brakes work as well in the wet as in the dry, the Michelin tyres grip and don't slither around and the power delivery is so smooth that you can take it for granted that there'll always be plenty available. The rumbling motor delivers the goods in such an undramatic fashion that to a Jap-bemused biker, it can appear unexciting at first.

The SS Darmah is an oddjob within the Ducati range which begins with the now humble 900GTS. At £1749, this model looks extraordinary good value but a shade dowdy compared with its flashier brothers, derivatives of the original red and white Darmah launched in summer '77. The GTS is now the only Duke with the conventional spring-returned valve gear and the older styling; next up is the basic Darmah with desmo engine, 32mm carbs, Lanfranconi silencers and flat 'bars. A tuned version of this model, the Darmah Sport, comes in black and gold, has 40mm carbs (but retains the standard 30mm inlet ports), Conti exhausts and is generally much sharper off the mark. The SS Darmah, under test here, comes in at £2299 with the spectacular styling that's halfway between the Darmah and the top-of-the-range 900SS. The SS Darmah has 32mm carbs, Lanfranconi silencers — the Contis can't be called silencers — and the half-fairing.

The Darmah models all have desmo engines with an electric starter; the 900SS with its production racing trim has no electric start, 40mm carbs with enlarged ports, the straight-thru Contis and rushes your wallet an extra £200.

Got it? Good.

What subdued my initial enthusiasm for the SS Darmah (as it will henceforth be known) was its obvious aim of falling between two roles. The motor is in a lesser state of tune than the 900SS and extras such as the electric starter, seat moulding, etc, have made it 40lb heavier at 483lb (with one gallon of petrol). The result is that my memories of roaring round the ringroads of Peterborough, terrorising the countryside at six am when the lanes were clear of clones, upon the 900SS, were dampened by this bike. It's not as quick, on acceleration or top speed, and surprisingly, it wouldn't stomp out of turns from the lowly revs that the 900SS would.

Though it hasn't the outright performance of the 900SS, it is lumbered with the pseudo-racer clip-ons and rearset riding position. Now in my not-inconsiderable range of pseudo-racer biking friends (including several Ducati owners), it's my true knowledge that all of them want maximum stomp whether or not it's of any practical use; there's always at least one corner in any trip where everything slots together. But it's possible to get the same level of performance with one of the flat 'barred models which may not look as spectacular as the SS Darmah but which will be a darn sight more comfortable.

Having said all this, after just over 700 miles on the SS Darmah, things started to settle

66

Right: Lanfranconi silencers emit a healthy off-beat growl. Tail unit houses the toolkit.

Below: Marzocchi dampers keep the rear end in line, Brembo ensures powerful controllable halts.

down nicely and the old bad habits of late braking, early accelerating, hard leaning started to flow again. The whole biking experience for me depends upon the degree I can enjoy these basic attributes. And a Ducati is still a Ducati, which almost says it all.

Repeat after me: (softly- 'Du-catee, Ducatee . . . (rising in volume but maintaining cool) . . . Du-catee . . . '

When broaching the experience of hard riding, the name alone is my Mantra, inducing that state of sensitivity to road conditions never possible in a car, yet locked into a private world of half-fantasy and half-reality where the mundane hassles of life never intrude. Even loaded up with Swagman panniers, tank bag, tote bag and a tent, the Darmah would hold a perfect line through the bumpiest bend. It maintained stability at ton-plus speeds and would brake evenly and without panic even with a death-grip handshake on the Brembo lever.

Ducatis have always held a fascination for me in the way they'll steer into bends so much more easily and precisely than any other motorcycle. The full cradle frame has so little bulk to support compared with some other bikes that, coupled with its basic good design, there's no wonder that it handles the

plot so well. My one criticism of last year's 900SS was aimed at the poor rear shock absorbers and while the 900SS continues with those units, the Darmah range all sport the latest from Marzocchi. These have a remote reservoir and combined air/coil spring springing. Unfortunately, they're so new that little information is yet available but the air springing facility is contained with the damper body itself and adjusted via a valve atop the reservoir. The pressure should be set at around 28lb per sq in which, combined with the five position spring preload, gives a considerable range for the discerning rider to play around with.

These shocks at last match the superb performance of the Marzocchi forks to give supple absorption of bumps, ripples, caves and land slips with nary a trace of wallowing or otherwise uncontrolled movement. This proves, to me at least, that Marzocchi are the leading exponents of the suspension art at the moment, notwithstanding trick items fitted to Japanese racers or moto cross machinery.

A major difference of attitude between the Italians (and BMW) and the Japanese engineers can be detected with the latest generation of machines from each. The Japanese, because of their high turnover and

preoccupation with innovation, can afford to redesign a brand new bike every two or three years to supersede the previous best. The Europeans either cannot afford to do this or don't appreciate the need; they prefer to develop a good design along a natural path of evolution, considering each component in the light of new experience. Thus the current 900s share a great dea of common ground with early 750 V-twins yet the components on those bikes which weren't so brilliant have been modified. With the advent of the '80s, the Italians are really getting their act together.

Electrical bugs have infested Italian machinery for years and it's still true that they've still not mastered the art. So Ducati did the best thing by opting for Japanese Nippondenso switches and instruments. They're not the latest design and look dated compared with Honda's aircraft inspired equipment, but they're adequate and do the job easily.

In fact, the speedometer proved more accurate than many of the items we've tested fitted to recent Jap bikes. Front lighting is superb with the 55/60 watt Bosch H4 unit throwing a wide, penetrating beam that picks up road blemishes, cuts through the hidden night and scares shit out of car drivers who *forget* to dip when approaching you. Minor electrical hassles still afflict the bike though an afternoon spent by Joe Average could solve these. The neutral indicator came on when second gear was engaged, for instance, and the side stand warning light didn't operate. I only mention that 'cos one of our staff had the misfortune to ride off with the side-stand down and peel off into a roundabout at 60 per . . . After a couple of unrequited occasions, I gave up using the sidestand since it's a short, awkwardly-angled prop that only works on very safe road surfaces. It doesn't flick up should you ride off with it down either.

Interesting outcome of that incident was the gold anodised Campagnolo wheel having a chunk completely knocked out when the rider hit the kerb, on the other side of the road. Fortunately, other damage was minimal though I understand a contract has been sent out from Luton to deal with the offending *Biker*. Don't worry, he's already been condemned to drawing bikes rather than riding them.

No-one could deny that Ducati have given the SS Darmah an amazing styling job. The half fairing flows neatly into the tank which continues into the seat (an idea followed on Honda's 900FZ). Care needs to be taken with such a finish, however, and signs of wear and tear showed after a mere 1,400 miles. To be fair, the test bike was one of a batch that got held up because of the winter snows and/or lorry drivers' dispute at the beginning of this year. Odd signs of corrosion afflicted the bike such as the cylinder head nuts' consistent coating of rust. Surprisingly, the aluminium alloy castings were unmarked — none of the white 'fur' that Kawasakis, for instance, are so prone to.

The glass fibre seat base quickly chipped with just the natural action of thigh muscles gripping, knee marks appeared on the tank

and scratches from boots on the side panels . . . develop this line of writing and I could make a fortune in soft porn stories. (What do you do upon a motorcycle, David? Thighstretching - kneegripping - ankleturning. That half-fairing is a useful shape but wobbles under wind pressure so at high speed the screen can't be looked through with any degree of clarity.

Above all with a Ducati you feel it's a real Owners' Bike. They need careful setting up to individual preferences and constant attention to little details to maintain that high state of individuality. The rewards for this level of attention are more magnificent than a mere increase of motorcycle response. Anyone who's read Pirsig's *Zen And The Art* etc will understand this state of symbiosis. By being in touch with the components of the machine, you'll know what to do and when to do it should things not be running perfectly.

Perhaps that's why it took so long for me to get into the SS Darmah. With last year's 900SS, the bike fitted me immediately; the SS Darmah's fairing dug into my knees if I sat in the correct position. I had to sit further back to get my knees tucked in or have them poking out like taxi door ears. Whichever way I tried, it wasn't comfortable.

Then subtle things such as the throttle, link to the fastest rush in everyday life, upset me at first. The 900SS had a smooth, well-oiled quick action feel while this SS Darmah had the standard handful-and-a-half coupled with a sticking cable. Its lack of response at low revs could also be attributed to its low mileage too; Ducatis need around 5,000 on their bores before they're really run in.

I came away from the SS Darmah thinking that here was a good motorcycle spoiled, meaning the 900SS. But on reflection, if you want the styling and are prepared to sort little things out, then it's definitely a more sociable machine than the 900SS.

CHECKOUT

DUCATI 900SS DARMAH

Engine	ohc V-twin
Bore × stroke	86 × 74.4mm
Capacity	863.9cc
Compression ratio	9.3:1
Carburation	2 × 32mm DellOrto
Bhp @ rpm	56 @ 7000
Max torque	47lb/ft @ 5500
Primary drive	Gear
Clutch	Wet, multiplate
Gearbox	5 speed
Electrical system	12v 200w alternator, electronic ignition
Lighting	55/60w H4 headlamp

DIMENSIONS

Wheelbase	61in
Seat height	32in
Overall width	31in
Ground clearance	6in
Weight	482lb (with 1gal fuel)
Fuel capacity	3.3gal

EQUIPMENT

Trafficators	Yes
Electric start	Yes
Trip odometer	Yes
Steering lock	Yes
Helmet lock	No
Headlight flasher	Yes
Others	Cast wheels, sports fairing, steering damper

CYCLE PARTS

Tyres	
(front)	3.50 × 18in Michelin
(rear)	4.25 × 18in Michelin
Brakes	
(front)	2 × 11.25in discs
(rear)	11.25in disc

PERFORMANCE

Top speed	
(prone)	122mph (est)
(sitting up)	115mph (est)
Standing ¼-mile	13.2sec
Speedometer error	
(at indicated 30mph)	27.4mph
(at indicated 60mph)	57.3mph
Braking distance	
(from 30mph)	28ft
(from 60mph)	128ft
Fuel consumption	
(overall)	52mpg
(ridden hard)	46mpg
PRICE	£2,299 inc VAT
Guarantee	6 months
Supplied by	Coburn & Hughes, Park Street, Luton.

SCOOP-
FIRST FULL ROAD TEST

Ducati's Sensational Pantah
Two for Vee, and Vee for Two
by Michael Scott

Some things in life are just too good to wait for. No matter how many people tell you to wait for the correct time, for maturity, or for the right circumstances, and no matter how much you respect those people, you just can't. You have to go straight ahead and do it at the very first opportunity.

I could make a list of such things, but I'm sure you don't need it. Here is something to add to that list. Ducati's new 500cc Pantah.

I was the first British journalist to ride the Pantah. I mean really ride it – nigh on 1000 miles on road and track, night and day, rain and shine, good roads and bad. The bike I rode was a pre-production prototype, just one stage away from the final machine. Hell, they hadn't even started making them when I tweaked the controls.

The Pantah is expected to reach Britain in saleable quantities by early Spring. A few more pre-production bikes might just be here by the time you read this. As I write, though, there are just two – the bikes that were seen at Earls Court. One, a non-runner, stars in our colour pix. The other, the green and red option, is the bike I rode, sneaking right in among the troops guarding it from the Press and spiriting it away.

It couldn't have happened without Graham Miles. He's the boss at Three Cross Motor-cycles, the big southern Italian bike dealers, and he purchased the bike for himself the second he clapped eyes on it at the show.

Even he had to wait until the boffins at Coburn and Hughes and at Sports Motorcycles in Manchester had given it a thorough shake-down (and some pretty solid running-in), looking for faults that must be ironed out before production. They found a few, and so did I. It's important that you remember, as you read this, that they'll likely be gone when the bike hits the showroom floor.

Graham Miles' first act was benevolent. He lent his bike to *SuperBike* before he'd even heard it running, giving us (and you) the first full British road test of the most exciting bike of the decade.

How was it? Couldn't ever have been anything but superb. You have only to look at it for a short time, to skim through the specifications, and to consider its pedigree. A light half-litre version of a 900cc paragon is so immediately attractive that riding it could even prove an anti-climax. Almost. Except that it's as delightful on the move as it is on paper. It sets new standards of roadholding and handling. It goes as good as it looks.

The tested top speed of 109mph and a standing quarter of 14.2 seconds simply don't tell half the story (not least because they may be changed by the time it comes to production). Indeed, such arbitrary figures are a woefully inadequate yardstick of any motor-cycle. It's true that the Pantah is not out-landishly fast, nor does it accelerate like a drag bike. More to the point, though; light weight, a sufficiency rather than a surplus of power, superb brakes and handling mean that it covers ground far better than many bikes with much more impressive performance figures.

It certainly looks the part. It's dressed in the flashest glassfibre suiting I can think of on any production bike, and painted in a stunning two-tone scheme that will have punters everywhere rocking on their heels. Personally, I find it a little over-dressed. It seems to combine so many different styling themes – wedge-shapes versus soft contours; slab sides versus complex curves; razor edges versus voluptuous fleshy folds. It's a tribute to Italian styling that it does hang together as a visual entity. I'd just prefer to see more of the engine.

It was with eager anticipation that I thumbed the button of the Pantah. There'd been plenty of drama attached to the whole scoop saga. Believe me, you're only reading this exclusive test by the skin of my teeth.

It goes back further – to the time I first heard of the forthcoming half-litre Duke in some seedy Italian dive. I immediately started twitching to get my hands on one.

I love vee-twins – breathes there a Man of Iron that doesn't? – and here was a new ultra-modern vee-twin. I love the way Dukes handle, and here was a new Duke, a shorter, lighter and more agile version of the bike like Mike won the TT on. And I'm learning again to love 500s. The Z500 Kawasaki rekindled the fire, the Montjuic stoked it to furnace pitch. Now, the Pantah. . . .

Like I said, eager anticipation.

I was a bit disappointed at the puny whiffle that emerged from the pipes. Not your ballsy Ducati thunder at all, and the fact that it's only a 500 is only an excuse if you've never heard a Montjuic. I continued to curse the heavily muffled noise until, the engine thoroughly warm, I started to rev the bike. Then it sings, the same song as the big Dukes, but in descant. The distinction is indicative of the very different character of the new junior Duke.

The gearchange is rear-set, and was at first a little too high for comfort. There's adjustment on the linkage, so it's soon sorted out. The change itself is slick and smooth and quick and crisp. Just as well, because you use the five close-ratio gears a lot to keep the vee on the boil. Production bikes may well have a wider-ratio box. Which will be a pity out on the sort of magnificent roads where I spent the first 100 miles on the Pantah, and also on motorways, where fourth and fifth combine to keep you cruising close to the ton; but a boon in town, where the high first gear of the test bike imposed rather more slipping of the clutch than it seemed to enjoy. Indeed, that component was showing signs of distress on our hard-used prototype, and started slipping at high revs in the upper gears towards the end of the test. I boiled the plates in detergent, for there were no spares, and it was cured.

Oddly, the super-slim 90-degree desmo vee seems less liquid-smooth than the bigger bangers from the same stable. Not that such an advanced and intricate engine would do anything so crude as vibrate. But at high revs, there's a slight but discernible tingle, and the (non-standard) mirror was blurred. It's very smooth through the rest of the rev range though.

Power? A German magazine quotes 48bhp at 9000rpm for the Pantah; my own estimate had been slightly lower at the same revs. It's possible, even likely, that the tortuous air-filter may be revised before the bike goes into production. Cam profiles might even be changed. Best way to describe the test bike's power is that there was plenty there, but it would have been nice if there'd been even more.

As it is, the power is snappish and full of zest when the revs are up, yet still fairly well-spread through the rev range. As one might expect, the 500cc engine has little of the uncanny low-down torque of the big Dukes, and in turn revs much more freely.

But it'll pull happily from 2000rpm.

It starts to sharpen up distinctly at 6000, though there's no actual power step. The surge from 7000 to the red line at 9000 is full of bliss. Working the gears, you can keep the rev counter between 8000 and 9000 and you have one hell of a sporting 500. It's crisp and dramatic in the bottom two gears, and a little more earnest as you work your way up from third towards 100mph.

It's just past that figure that the Pantah starts panting, at least in the form tested. Carburetion ills were blamed for the unpalatable fact that it was generally quicker in fourth than in fifth, and that it would not take full throttle in top until 8000rpm had been attained, which only happened when going downhill.

I want to be sure you understand that this sort of minor tuning deficiency – for I am convinced it is just that – is exactly why people don't like the press to get hold of prototypes and road test them, for they're not necessarily perfect, and one is bound to tell the truth.

Why, then, am I so convinced it's just a minor tuning deficiency? Listen, I snooped around Sports Motorcycles in Manchester, and got some info I shouldn't have. During their testing of the bike, they revised the intake and the carburetion. Like those nasal spray ads, the junior Duke sighed with relief, uttering the immortal words: ''I can breathe again''. It started pulling properly in fifth gear, and recorded a top speed of 125mph. I expect that was in pretty good conditions, for it's very quick for a 500. But I believe it.

Sorry to dwell so long on that, for it is after all only noticeable when you break the law on a motorway or other wide open road. Certainly, there was no misfire on the less lavish A and B-roads where the Pantah showed its magnificent best.

Yes, it's very quick point to point. Not just

for a 500, for any bike. It's not just power that makes a good road bike, though the monster Japs and their legion of fans might have you believe otherwise. It's a number of ingredients – and the junior Duke has them all, in well-balanced proportions.

Throttle response, for instance, is as important as sheer poke, when the road gets twisty. Keep the Pantah humming above 6000 and it launches with dedication. The big Dukes don't feel fast – they are so relaxed at speed it takes a glance at the speedo to confirm it. The junior Duke is different: it revs hard, and you change gear a lot when you're going really quick. Even so, it retains a hint of the same vee-twin characteristic. There's little drama as it gathers high speed, and it too can give surprises with its speedo.

Good braking is a vital element. And light weight is as important to that as having the right hydraulic hardware. The Pantah has the lot. Triple Brembo discs each have twin-piston calipers and bite on cast iron discs. Both hand and foot controls have delicate feel and plenty of power. You have to be very clumsy indeed to lock up either wheel; and the Pantah is light enough to co-operate when the tyres tell it to stop. Who could ask for anything more?

Handling is the final ingredient. Glad to report, then, that the 500 Ducati has the feel, the finesse and the firmness of the legendary big Dukes. A happy balance has been struck with the steering. As with the 900SS, it's on the slow side (the newer Darmah is different), and as steady as you can imagine. I found it impossible to induce any steering weave in the Pantah, under any circumstances. It was on TT100s, still my favourite tyres. I never found the bike's limits on the road – I am grown far too wary to go that fast on the Queen's highway, populated as it is by murderous fools. I went as fast as I felt safe, and you have my word that on the Pantah, that's very fast. Such speeds would have your average big-inch multi shaking its head and using lots and lots of road. The Pantah slips through, well within its capabilities.

At the test track, I did manage to scrape the centrestand tang on the left, but it was hard work. Nothing scraped on the right. I was working on it when the rain started, which made me curse at first. Then I discovered the depth of character of this fine bike. It coped so well with the slippery track that I was soon actually enjoying mastering the difficulties.

There's nothing new about Ducatis that handle well. But here's some real progress. It's comfortable! The ride is supple, the front forks are free from stiction, the back gas shocks combine compliance with strict wheel control. Both are by Marzocchi, and well done chaps.

The riding position is as good as clip-ons are ever going to be, especially above 50mph, when enough airstream comes over the top of the screen to buoy up your head and shoulders and relieve the pressure on your wrists. Don't expect weather protection for much more than your chest, though. The fairing is more about wind-cheating, and looks.

Hmmm. Nearly finished, and I haven't mentioned the lifting handle yet. It's a whimsical touch, a sort of hinged footrest mounted upside down. Makes the trip on to the centrestand an easy hoist. Since there's no sidestand, we should be grateful.

Riding the new Pantah is an uplifting experience. Living with it, if only for a week, was a pleasure. It comes into the world with a hell of a heritage to live up to. From 450cc to 900cc, the previous generations have set the standards of road-bike roadholding.

The Pantah had to be superb even to compete. It fulfils that demand: every promise has been kept. I love it already, and they haven't even started making them yet.

Stop Press: No price has been finalised, but it seems it'll be around £2300. Very expensive. Just as well it's such a superlative machine.

Inside The Junior Duke

The specifications of the new 500cc Ducati are mouth-watering. Belt-driven overhead cams, desmodromic valves, gas suspension, a slender 90-degree vee, the swing-arm pivoting on the engine itself, a unique overhead-ladder frame, and the breeding of an aristocrat.

It has all the simple unorthodoxy that makes Ducatis great. What's more, it's modern.

Read the test, and discover that it's not just a paper Pantah. Meantime, dribble a while over the elegant anatomy of a beautiful new middleweight, a milestone in the art of building superior motorcycles.

Ducati have a tradition of doing things slightly differently. Fabio Taglioni is the reason why. He's the engineer who designs the finest Dukes: bikes of wit, delicacy and brutal purpose.

His is the 90-degree vee-twin – chosen because of its uncanny smoothness and in spite of the long wheelbase that comes with it (the more usual 60-degree vee fits better in a bike frame, but they tend to be agricultural). The new 500 is the vee's most modern expression, and it's beautiful. A pity that it's largely hidden by the heavily styled bodywork.

The usual roller-bearing crankshaft and single-pin big end are at the heart of the matter. Stroke is 58mm, while the bore is 74mm. It's a very oversquare engine, and the two valves per cylinder can thus be big. Those dimensions are step one on the road to high revs.

The pistons are substantially smaller than the big 86mm slugs of the 900 Dukes, and thus much lighter. Nor do they have nearly such a distance to travel – 74.4mm on the big bike, just 58 on the Pantah. The pistons are thus lighter, and travel at lower speeds. *Voila*, the primary limit to any big twin's ability to rev has been moved up a notch or three. Another step along High Rev Trail.

Journey's end on that road is reached by the desmo valve gear. As I'm sure you know, desmo valves are closed positively and mechanically, instead of being left by the cam to bounce back on their springs. Thus they simply cannot float: there's no way they'll linger to get clouted by a piston.

Desmo Dukes are familiar, but the Pantah is the first to exploit this unique valve gear by having pistons small enough to rev hard. Maximum power is at 9000rpm, and so was my arbitrary red line. I've no doubt that when people start racing Pantahs, they'll regularly exceed 10 000rpm.

The first major design innovation is the toothed belts that drive the single overhead cams. This method is common in cars, Gold Wings and Moto Morinis, but no other motorcycles. The benefits are manifold. It's a simple system, and very quiet in operation. They need no lubrication. They don't rattle or whine. And they're cheap. The big Dukes have shaft drive with bevel gears – expensive to make, exacting to shim correctly, and very noisy when they're not. Modern is good.

That's not the only car-inspired technology. The Pantah also boasts a cartridge-type oil filter – one of those blue things that you simply screw out and throw away. It's sunk into a cavern in the wet sump, with just enough rim protruding for you to get a finger-hold. Yet again, servicing is simplified.

Inhalation is via a single air filter. A sticker on the top proclaims it to be of the "universal" type. Certainly it's a disappointment not to

71

find a purpose-built filter on such a thoroughly engineered bike, for it means unequal-length intake plenums upstream of the carbs. They are two pumper Dell'Ortos of truly monumental size. Each is 36mm, and I thought the Montjuic's carbs monstrous at just 32mm. Yes, the twin is built to rev. Exhaust is via close-clinging pipes leading to a massive balance tube and two silencers.

The electrical system – 260 Watt alternator and electronic ignition – are by Bosch. The battery is by Yuasa, and the switches and instruments are also Japanese, from Nippon-Denso. This new Duke continues the firm's recent policy of dumping the worst Italian gear and buying the best components available, no matter where they come from. Notably, suspension is by Marzocchi, and brakes by Brembo: both Italian.

More innovations – for non-Japanese bikes – are inspection windows: large glass portholes that show oil level on the right, and crankshaft timing marks on the left.

Primary drive by gear leads to a conventional multiplate oil-bath clutch and an equally predictable five-speed constant-mesh gearbox, with torque-multiplied drive exiting on the left side.

Just behind the sprocket, less than two inches away, is the swinging-arm pivot, which is mounted on the gearbox. Yet another piece of strikingly unorthodox modern design to distinguish this milestone among middle-weights. Yes, I know the Guzzi V50 does the same thing, but that's a shaft-driver, and thus a different bag of beans. In this instance, the proximity of the swing-arm pivot and drive sprocket minimise the variation in chain tension as the suspension moves – a boon to chain life and even to handling, since power reversal can exert only minimal influence on the back end.

So that's the power unit, bang up to date and a worthy smaller cousin to the beautiful big vee-twin that caused such delight when it was launched in 1970.

Technical delights don't stop there, by any means. The Pantah's frame is a logical development of the principles of the big Duke frames, but one step further along the road to unorthodoxy.

The big-bike frames are basically cradles with the bottom loop left out. The engine braces up the structure in their place.

The Pantah frame uses the engine as a true load-bearing member, rather than as a brace. It's that swing-arm pivot on the gearbox that draws the distinction. By the way, that system rules out Ducati's eccentric swing-arm pivot method of chain adjustment, it being a bit fiddly building the necessary pinch-clamps into an oil-tight casing. They've gone back to the solid but basically conventional method of adjusting the chain at the back end, though without compromising the strength of the tube by welding a flat section to locate the axle.

Back to the frame. I suppose it's a spine type: but I prefer to call it overhead-ladder, because that's how it looks. There are two ladders, one each side, making for four top tubes. The lower pair of rails go down to the top of the crankcases, and the engine is mounted at two points by long through-bolts on these tubes: one between the vee and one at the very back. A further spur extends downward to provide a third mounting point at the bottom rear of the engine. The swinging-arm pivot is above and ahead of this point. The frame is light, and supremely rigid. And shows great originality in conception, too. A pity that some frame tubes had to be flattened to give access to the cam-belt covers.

Suspension front and rear is by Marzocchi – conventional teles up front and flashy gas-shocks at the back. A red reservoir juts up behind and parallel to the spring: a tyre valve is on top of this for fine tuning of the springing by adjusting the pressure. There are also five pre-load positions for the conventional coil that supplements the air springing.

And finally, the bodywork. Look in the test for opinions on the glassfibre, for now it's enough to describe its fitment. The fairing, along with the instruments, is mounted on a single spar coming forward from the steering head, and at the back on to lugs on the lower frame rails. The tank squashes forward on to rubber bungs at the front, and has two rubber straps at the back. Innovation's gone awry on the glassfibre-based seat: two rather silly (but very modern) expanding screw clips attempt unsuccessfully to hold it in place, and there's a small cubby for a tool kit in the shapely hump. Two side-panels are held on by a single screw each, but to gain true acces-

sibility to the engine it's best to take the entire back bodywork off. Good news. Four bolts hold it on, and it comes away without interfering with any wiring or other bits.

The end result is a motorcycle that – on paper – looks very good indeed. Some stunningly creative design has made a Pantah that shouts refinement. Its credentials are impeccable, its ancestry enviable. Rivals must go green looking at the specifications.

Ducati Pantah 500 Desmo
£2300 (to be finalised)

PERFORMANCE
Maximum Speed – 109mph (prototype bike)
Standing Quarter Mile – 14.2sec (prototype bike)
Fuel Consumption: Hard Riding – 56mpg
　　　　　　　　　　　Cruising – 64mpg
Best Full-Tank Range – 310 miles

ENGINE
Type – 90-degree air-cooled vee-twin, belt-driven SOHC, desmodromic valves
Displacement – 498.6cc
Power – 48bhp at 9000rpm
Torque – 40Nm at 63000rpm
Bore & Stroke – 74mm × 58mm
Induction – two 36mm Dell'Orto pumper carbs
Exhaust – two-into-two with balance pipe
Oil System – wet sump
Ignition – Bosch electronic

TRANSMISSION
Clutch – multiplate wet
Primary Drive – gear
Final Drive – chain
Gears – five-speed constant-mesh

CHASSIS
Frame – twin overhead ladder spine, engine locates swing-arm
Front Suspension – Marzocchi telescopic forks
Rear Suspension – Marzocchi air shocks
Wheelbase – 57.09in
Weight (wet) – 398lb
Fuel Capacity – 4.84gall
Tyres – 4.10 × 18 front, 4.25 × 18 rear;
Dunlop TT 100
Brakes – triple Brembo discs

EQUIPMENT
Electrical – 260W alternator, 12 volt battery
Sundry – fairing, clip-ons, rear set footrests, alloy wheels, tool kit

Test bike supplied by – Three Cross Motorcycles, Three Legged Cross, Verwood, Dorset 020 123 4531

To Italy on a Ducati 900 SS

FOR THE past 12 months I have had the pleasure of riding one of today's finest motorcycles. The Ducati 900 SS PR. Since delivery I have covered over 8,000 miles, the last 2,500 to Italy and back in five days; and it is on my findings during this trip that I intend to appraise the vee-twin.

Developed from the 750 series, the 900 SS has a capacity of 863.9 cc. The stroke is the same as was the 750's, at 74.4 mm; bore measurement is 86 mm. The compression ratio is 9.5 to 1. Two 40 mm Dellorto carburettors are used, without air filters. The rest of the engine design is as for the 750s, with the unique desmodromic valve mechanism operated by a single cam. A replaceable oil filter is now provided to supplement the mesh unit in the base of the crankcases. A Bosch electronic ignition system replaces previous notions, and on this model no electric start is provided. However, provided a quickly learnt sequence of operations is followed, the engine rumbles into life first kick. Rarely, however, is this followed by the delightful off-beat tickover . . .

My first year of ownership has not been without tribulations. The initial 500 miles were plagued by blown gaskets and loss of the kick-starter ratchet. Seemingly, this last item is still having to be replaced; I recently met another Ducati owner of only 700 miles standing who has had to have two new ratchets fitted. Simply bad design. At just over 4,000 miles, the six securing bolts holding the cush-drive housing on the body of the wheel sheared. Thankfully, it was replaced under warranty, as the cost would have been £260+. Ducati's are now fitting different wheels, which are not, to my eyes, in keeping with the nimble, sleek lines of their flag bikes.

And what a flag bike! When ridden for what it was designed, it is one of the very best available. At 4,000 revs in top gear, a true 70 mph can be maintained with petrol consumption at 58 mpg. It is a bike for the open road. Pottering around in towns is tiresome and irritating because of the riding position, tight steering lock and heavy brake and clutch action at low speeds.

I have made the following alterations to the original as supplied, and recommend them. . . . I found the fitted Michelin 45s excellent except on tight corners and so, at 6,000 miles, with 3 mm of tread remaining, I changed them for TT100s. Even the tightest bends can now be taken with utmost confidence. The standard Marzocchi rear shocks gave unnecessary stiffness to the rear ride which made bumpy bends at 40 or 50 mph most uncomfortable, so I replaced them with Girlings. After 3,000 miles, I had the clutch springs replaced with the stronger 450 ones, but even with these, clutch adjustment is a regular feature of maintenance, to keep full power spinning the rear wheel. Finally I fitted a Renold Grand Prix chain in place of the DID item.

And so from Bermondsey to Bologna in late October. Not the best time to travel by motorcycle, but as I made my way down the A1 and M2 a warm, ripening sun was out. A strong, gusty crosswind was blowing on the M1 but as

ever the Ducati kept its line. It never twitched or deviated from its course. I arrived at Calais at 3.30 pm, the weather perfect, and I was soon on the N43 heading towards the Autoroute. The N43 is a well-surfaced rolling A road and very familiar to my Ducati, as well as being ideally suited to the engine's power band. The 900 SS produces power in abundance throughout the range (the maximum between 4,200 and 5,500 rpm). And along these 40 or so miles it was mostly pulling in second and fourth gears, between 2,500 and 5,000 rpm. As I've said, a perfect match of road and maximum engine

power. The 900 cc desmodromic engine is such an efficient unit, and the low-down useable power it produces makes riding so effortless and such fun.

I find fifth gear unusable except on really long stretches of road (internal ratio is: 1:0.887). And although the engine will pull from 2,000 rpm in this gear to oblivion in a matter of seconds, its use is cumbersome and I tend to click up only on motorways. The rest of the gears are: 1:2.237; 1:1.562; 1:1.204 and 1:1, which all adds up to a very well-spaced set. Primary reduction is by helical gears, with a ratio of 2.187:1. Two gearbox sprockets of 15 and 16 teeth are available. And Ducati offer 12 rear sprockets, from 33 to 45 teeth. These last two items are joined by a ⅜ × ⅝in chain of 102 rollers. Which is not lubricated. My machine is standard with a 16 tooth gearbox sprocket, and the smallest rear sprocket, providing smart acceleration and a theoretical top speed of 140 mph. The rear wheel has a rubber cush drive and the wheel can be removed without disturbing the chain.

Just north of Bethune I joined the deserted A26 Autoroute with the Ducati rumbling along at 5,500 rpm, just over 100 mph. Truly what a beautiful machine it is! Up to 6,500 with just a touch of the throttle but the speed is too fast for conviviality. So back to between 5,000/5,500 for the rest of the ride to Senlis. I had intended to reach a small town south of Paris but early rush-hour traffic built up the further south I went. So I pulled in at Senlis and an excellent hotel/restaurant. I left at just after 8 am on Saturday morning, after the usual French breakfast supplemented by my own two tablespoons of honey. This item I find essential before any ride. It was a cold, misty morning and the minor roads were slippery. However the Autoroute was dry and by the time I reached Paris the mist had lifted and the day promised to be fine. The ring road around Paris is well signposted and I was quickly on the A6, heading south. Like other riders, no doubt, I found the "Raignurage" very disturbing. It is a type of road surface found only around Paris and consists of concrete laid in 1in or so strips with ¼in gaps between, running in the direction of travel. Riding over this make you feel that all your bearings have collapsed! I found it easier on the hard shoulder, but this is just as frightening. You are warned about this surface but with only 300m to the judders there are few alternatives. Apparently it helps dispel surface water. If it had rained, I would have stopped, removed a vital component and called on my £10 worth of AA 5-Star Insurance. It really was as frightening as that. (While on the subject, this 5-Star scheme seems to be excellent value. The £10 premium covers 31 days and includes full personal insurance and vehicle recovery.)

After lunch in a beautifully situated café overlooking the Yanne valley, I decided to open the Ducati up for a sustained run at high speeds. The Autoroute was deserted, the weather perfect. As I pulled back on to the motorway, I eased the power until a good 80 in second was registered, up into third to 110, and then fourth and still more power flooding in. Smith clocks are provided and although they function they're inaccurate and not up to the standard of the rest of the equipment provided. However, out of interest, at 7,500 rpm the speedometer was registering 130 with a +5 mph flicker. Later PR models have Veglia instruments. However, back to the sunshine and the empty road. I maintained these exhilarating speeds for 20 or so miles. Dropping into fourth going into the long sweeping bends, accelerating out — just what the machine was designed for.

The 900 SS is fitted with a half fairing. It is a feature that epitomises the Ducati: stylish and

"In the 900 SS Ducati have produced a motorcycle with looks to melt your heart and, more important, with superb performance, apparent reliability and fuel economy." A report based on an 8,000-mile year

ITALY ON A DUCATI 900 SS

functional, but not very useful below 75 mph. Over this speed, it wedges the air flow very effectively, giving the rider a relaxing time.

Just north of Beaune the A6 joins the A37 and as this intersection approached, I throttled back, relishing the final bends at 80 or so. An early afternoon ride to remember.

On the way down to the Alpine foot hills, a well-driven Lancia was excellent company, as much a test of the Ducatis's brakes as engine power. These are drilled cast-iron discs by Brembo, two 11in units on the front wheel and on the rear, on the left, one 9in unit. Double organic-pads are used on each caliper and each pad is provided with two anti-squeak grooves. Braking action is slightly heavy at low speeds but at speeds over 50 mph it is progressive, sure and positive. A most effective match for the speed and acceleration it has to temper. The whole set up is well designed, requires only a minimum of maintenance and functions to the highest of standards. My only crib is, why the removal of the pad covers; to save weight? A little extreme for a bike sold for the road even with a PR suffix.

As I was leaving Bourg, I came across a motorcycle demonstration. Their complaint: the orange headlight shade and proposed changes in cc regulations effecting taxation. There were about 300 bikes in all, effectively blocking a major crossroad. However, I was able to slip through and although it was good humoured at first it took a nasty turn when an impatient juggernaut driver mowed down a line of bikes, including a Moto Guzzi Le Mans — What a waste! Police were present but only as observers. I really couldn't see the point of arguing with a 40 ton lorry while the real mischief makers, the French legislators, were probably miles away. This type of protest is hardly likely to win support among the haulage contractors or anyone else caught up in the jam they caused.

After leaving my baggage in Nantura, I made my way down to Culoz via a beautiful by-road. The road back up the Valserine Valley was peaceful and scenic and although it was poorly surfaced, I thoroughly enjoyed the jaunt: — just

me, bike, wind and sunshine. I arrived back at the hotel exhausted. To be able to enjoy the scenery it was necessary to restrict speed to 50 mph, and at these speeds the Ducati is difficult to manoeuvre.

The reason for the 900 SS's peculiar handling characteristics at low speeds on tight twisty roads is to be found in the headstock. To increase the already excellent high-speed manners of the Darmah, 1½° have been shaved off the rake. This gives the SS a weave-free ride throughout its speed range but adversely affects handling when the above two features occur together. On these Alpine back roads the Ducati would have zipped along as it did on the motorway; it can take every bend in its stride provided the propulsion is there. Rake angle is 23° 30' and with a wheelbase of 59in and a seat height of 31in, it will be appreciated that something will be compromised. I left Nantua at 10 on Sunday morning. Although it was cold and had rained during the night, the sun was out. However on the B42 motorway leading to the Mount Blanc tunnel, the clouds dropped, and it was a miserable ride on damp roads with the beautiful views obscured by swirling mists. The twisty road up to the tunnel was a challenge after the motorway but surface water restricted speed. Under construction is a link motorway from the B41 to the tunnel mouth itself — what a spectacular ride that will be. The drop down into Italy was glorious. Warm sun broke through the sheets of grey; the roads beautiful in feature, long sweeping bends and, for the first time, lots of other bikes around for company.

At Aosta I joined the A5 motorway and headed south towards Turin (I prefer the Italian name, Torino). I left the motorway at Ivréa and followed a gently rolling back road to Vercelli. During lunch on the outskirts of Vercelli, two stout Italians tried to get me drunk while patting and prodding me, reciting a string of names from a motorcycle racing vocabulary. It was all good fun and I took one of them for a spin.

It was by then a beautiful afternoon, similar to a dry hot mid-August day in England, except that the sun was lower.

Vercelli is the centre of an important

rice-growing province and the flat A roads are ideal for making good time. These roads are not unlike the bog roads of Ireland with their unexpected bumps. I made a number of stops between Vercelli and Alessandria, the last time in Bosco Marengo for a brief visit to the Church of Santa Croce, a majestic building containing sculpture and paintings of the Mannerist period and a security guard who was sound asleep (Even the to-be-mentioned-later Contis didn't wake him.)

I rejoined the motorway just north of Alessandria and less than an hour later arrived at Modena. The Ducati used just over 2½ gallons of petrol to cover the 117 miles: 44 mpg at over 100 mph speaks for itself. I had not intended this to be a high-speed/petrol consumption test, but just before joining the motorway I had filled the tank brim full and as I collected a toll ticket a Simca Matisse drew up. The driver wasn't particularly good — just fast. I found his driving no more than what seemed like a hair's breadth behind irritating.

Two closely related points are worth developing from this part of the trip. I arrived at Modena in as fine fettle as I left Alessandria, but it is difficult to attribute this to any single fact. It is simply the Ducati's overall construction that makes for such relaxing, effortless cruising. Employment of the engine as a stressed member of the frame helps; it means the headstock and the swinging arm are constantly in line, allowing almost unlimited acrobatics at high speed. The swinging arm is a 29mm unit shimmed out without end-float. Front suspension is provided by Marzocchi oil-damped telescopic units. These, unlike the standard rear ones, are more than up to their task and function in unison with the already mentioned frame members in a way that instills confidence. One particular nasty pot-hole I just "glanced", at well over 100 mph, sent the bike momentarily in many directions but a split second later it was back on course. Ducatis have this reassuring habit of self-righting (which is unnerving at first). One further point: side winds, even strong, gusty ones, are simply shrugged off, but only if you allow the bike to do the work. "Don't fight it, feel it". Trite? Maybe, but also very true.

My hotel in Modena was again excellent, the bike garaged in an ante-room next to the reception. After a shower I settled down to watch Italy's equivalent of Match of the Day. I wasn't impressed by the football or its presentation. During the commercial break it was very bizarre to hear Kate Bush singing about Heathcliffe in Italian, advertising ladies' underwear. After an excellent five-course meal for less than £8 in a noisy, friendly restaurant, I made my way through the beautiful centre of the city to a concert of Vivaldi cantatas. Another interesting day! Tomorrow Bologna and the Ducati factory.

My first impressions of the factory was of its need of a coat of paint, and also its size. Ducati Meccanica are not just motorcycle engineers and assemblers, they also make a range of standing diesel engines, two-stroke outboard engines (which are very successful in off-shore sprint events) and various other engineering and electrical components. At the time of my visit intermittent strikes were disrupting production and the effect was evident throughout the shop floor. However, this is not the place to discuss the problems or the considerable achievements of Ducati SPA. Suffice to say that my day at the works has only added to my admiration of one of their products.

I left Italy via the St Bernard tunnel after spending the night in the summer resort of St. Vincent. The ride through the Alps was again spoilt by mists and wet roads. Huge car transporters from the Fiat factories added to the misery. However, coming down into Switzerland was a joy. The roads were dry and the quality of the surface together with the gentle cambers, fast bends and the lack of traffic more than compensated for the dreary morning. I stopped for an early lunch in Lausanne. I really like the Swiss newspaper sticks. Shaped like an umbrella, the newspaper is rolled around and secured with an elastic band when being carried. It flips nicely inside the classic Swiss cape-like mackintosh. Beautiful.

As I came into Lausanne on the N9 motorway it started to rain heavily, stopped while I had lunch and during the ride through the delightful suburbs, then started again as I reached the French border and continued until I stopped at Dôle, exhausted. The roads between Lausanne and Dôle, via Vallorbe and Pontalier were diabolical. The 900SS was never designed for off-the-road work, but the half-made surfaces, along with the rain, turned huge stretches into a near scramble. A great strain on me but the bike just chuntered along. I do vaguely remember crossing the Juras and thinking this must be a beautiful ride on a sunny day. The road was lined with conifers and the surface excellent . . . a great pity I wasn't feeling more receptive.

After drying out in Dôle, I set out for London. The morning was dull but by noon it was clear. Although there was a gusty cold wind it was dry and remained so for the rest of the journey. I rejoined the motorway at Beaune and made steady progress to Fontainebleau where I started my detour of Paris. This is well worth the few extra miles. The roads were well surfaced and there was little traffic. Just north of Melum I came across a column of about 100 police cavalry. Huge, majestic beasts, their riders in a distinctive royal blue uniform. As I came upon them I cut the engine. Every time I've approached a horse on the Ducati I've been apprehensive. The 900SS doesn't have silencers but is fitted with Contis. I've no complaints about these as units of engine performance, but they are a contravention of the spirit of the Noise Abatement Act and they do frighten animals. Horses aside, these silencers and the 40mm Dellorto carburettors are the only differences in the engine department from the sedate Darmah. Together they account for that marked performance difference I chose when I bought my noise machine. Confession: I do find ear plugs a help on long runs . . . which I realize is an insult to everyone I happen to pass (which usually is *everyone*!). The only consolation is that the noise very quickly passes. . . .

I rejoined the A1 motorway at Senlis and quickly found the rhythm of high-speed riding again. Smoothly, and so quickly, the engine delivered its powerful revs at just a touch of the throttle, settling down at just over 6,000 in top.

"And you're in love with all the wonder it brings,
And every muscle in your body sings,
As the highway ignites,
You work nine to five
And somehow you survive
'Til the night".

The Ducati just surged along, leaving all behind. On the congested stretches the acceleration available removes any doubts when overtaking. Easing up as dusk dropped, I pulled into the Peronne service station for my last cup of Espresso coffee. Back out into the night, the Bosch 55/60 watt headlight providing adequate illumination up to 100 mph, which is probably the safest top speed for night riding. The rear CEV unit is a 5/21 and gives adequate warning to anything behind. The alternator, housed clutch side, is a 200 watt unit passing its charge to a regulator under the right-hand side-panel.

The Electrics

The battery is a Yuasa of 12 volts, with a 12 ah A3 fuse box provided conveniently placed under the saddle. I'm aware of criticisms of the earlier 750 and 860 models, regarding the electrics in general. These must have had the desired effect. The overall standard is now very high, on close inspection; certainly the electrics have yet to fail me.

The last 100 miles back to London were completed in much the same way as all the other miles by Ducati — effortlessly. In the 900 SS Ducati have fulfilled the promise they made when they introduced the 750 series. They have produced a machine of equal performance to any other available, that handles without fault, is reliable, possesses stamina and is very economical. It also has looks to melt your heart and is a joy to ride, mile after mile. It is said that if you go to Italy and don't buy a pair of shoes, you mean restless until you return. Test ride a Ducati. . . .   A.S.

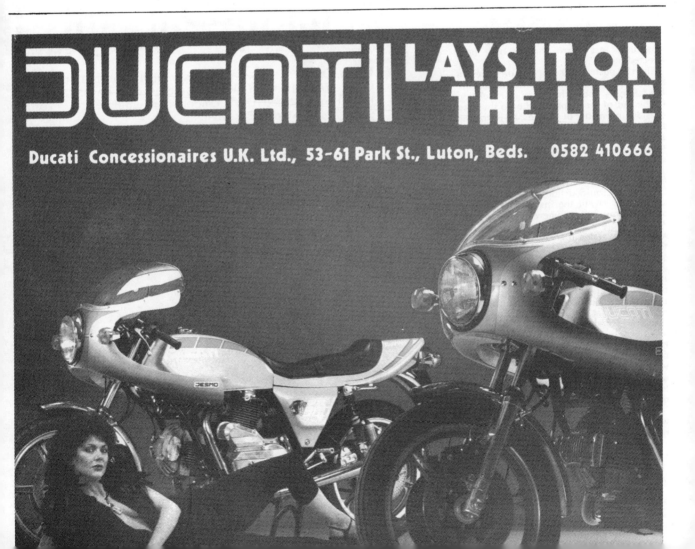

THERE'S GOOD BITS AND BAD BITS ABOUT doing this job as editor of *Bike*. The good bits are usually to do with the fact that I make most of the decisions about what we're gonna do, the bad bits are usually based around the opposing view that most of these decisions have already been made for me by fate. Thus, a few weeks ago I was en route to the West County, normally a region I visit with great pleasure, and I ended up hammering the steering wheel of the *Bike* pick-up truck with my rolled-up fists. This was frustration taking its toll at yet *another* hold-up in the traffic, and it was at the tailend of yet *another* ulcer-inducing day when everything had gone wrong, and the phones were going berserk. 'Mazing how some people think we've nothing better to do than answer phone calls all day.

This is all leading up to an admission that, had the Gods of Destiny and Luton not decided to shine upon me one day in early Feb, I might very well have taken my type-writer, telephone, desk and calculator and thrown the lot through my office window, along with a terse note indicating 'enough'. That was when the Ducati Hailwood Replica came into my daily routine . . .

That there's any *Bike* magazine at all this month is due to an incredible display of loyalty and hard work by the full-timers on this rag, and that Duke. 'Cos every time the chaos reached my nervous system's breaking point, I'd just kit up, ignore the resigned glances from the others in the office who knew by now full well what I was up to, march out of the office oblivious to the pleas of Sue, our long-suffering secretary, and kickstart the Duke.

For a couple of relaxing, soothing minutes I'd just listen to that booming, consistent deep bass exhaust note ticking out of the almost hollow Contis. Imagine a sensation like Tiger Balm being rubbed into an aching neck by the delicate hands of a Chinese Taiwa masseuse, that's how that echoing note affected me.

Then I'd push the bike forward off its centre stand — no sidestand is fitted because of the full fairing — and with a bit of manipulation I'd be out of the carpark and onto the road outside. In a matter of seconds, I'd be joining the slip-road to the dual carriageway by-pass, sneaking past the derestricted speed limit signs like a malevolent dog looking for a pristine bit of pavement to shit upon.

Ten or so minutes later, when I'd judged the oil to have started to warm up reasonably, I'd give the quick-action twistgrip a sharp snatch and savour the instant kick forward and tumultous noise somewhere behind me. A roundabout would loom up and, with the knots in my stomach at last untying, I'd flick the Duke into the attack mode with just a slight pressure to the left 'bar. If a perfect line was possible through the roundabout — and I'm very careful not to get entangled up with other road users when I'm in this mood — I'd be okay for a couple more hours with my mind no longer beset by such rubbish as budgets, planning schedules, production schedules, weather forecasts, and the other stuff which has nothing to do with bikes, journalism or a creative, positive approach to life. If the line wasn't clear then, well, I'd just have to carry on and find a roundabout or a long sweeping turn which was . . . there really wasn't any other way it could be.

Now this unprecedented confession may well clarify things for a few of you who tried to ring me during February and constantly came

⫶UPLIC⫶

While Ducati's Hailwood Replica might not conform to the Oxford Dictionary definition of an exact copy by the same artist, it certainly helped Dave Calderwood emulate the maestro's style. Pix by Martyn Barnwell.

ꓱUPLICATI

up against the phrase: 'Yes, well, Dave is in the office today but he's gone on a round-Peterborough marathon. Yes, he will be back but we're not sure in what state.'

Ducati's Hailwood Replica is one of those rare bikes which successfully achieve the two highs of owning a big bike — it poses well and it goes well. To carry off with aplomb the mere act of slinging the leg over the Replica, and making more noise than the rest of the world believes is good for the average human brain, needs a rider with a hint of an exhibitionist about him. For a start, it looks like a racer with the curvaceous fairing, long slim tank, humped seat and shorty guards. Then its colour scheme of bright red and green makes it, er, *conspicuous* to even the most myopic bobby.

The reason for the Hailwood Replica, in case you're new to the biking scene or have been dead for the last couple of years, comes from Mike's amazing return to the Isle of Man TT in 1978. The year before, Ducati had come

Above: Ducati's cunning converter for occasional pillion.

Far left: Marzocchi, Pirelli, Brembo and Campagnolo — Italy's leading co-op?

Left: Nippon into the office for a spot of clock-watching.

Below: One of the Duke's pair of sippers — a 40mm Dell 'Orto.

very near to winning the F1 TT with Roger Nicholls on a 900SS. If the race hadn't been cut short by a lap, and Phil Read on the works Honda four had made his planned fuel stop, then . . . but racing is full of ifs. The following year, however, there never seemed any doubt once Hailwood was off the line. For '79, things weren't quite so rosy with the Ducati factory producing a special frame that didn't work as well as the standard 900SS chassis, and the Sports Motorcycles team of Steve Wynne and Pat Slinn, who did all the mechanicking on the Duke (as they had the year before), worked all night to get the bike back to as near as possible to the specification of the previous year's bike. It didn't win, not surprisingly really since it was a cobbled together machine, but managed a creditable second.

The Hailwood Replica is different from the standard 900SS only in a very few details apart from the obvious cosmetic changes. It has a

different cast alloy wheel design with thinner spokes and less webbing, saving a small amount of weight. The brake calipers are a slightly different design and are reputed to be of a lighter alloy. They're anodised a nice trick looking gold now so they must be better! These changes are from last year's 900SS and are likely to be included on the 1980 SSs too.

Instrumentation is the console from the 1979 Darmah SS, with the Japanese Nippon-denso clocks and switches etc, instead of the all-Italian Veglia bits of the 900SS. There's not much to say about these other than they do their job fairly accurately and efficiently though Ducati, in their usual bizarre fashion, have decided to have the red generator warning light glowing when it's working correctly and it only extinguishes when there's either a malfunction or the ignition is killed.

This, and an abnormally bright main beam warning light, intrude a little onto night riding; the answer's simple: stick a bit of slightly translucent tape over them to dim the effect.

As soon as you sit astride the Replica, it's easy to imagine the racer role since it has that same cobbled together feel — not that it's a bitsa but every component gives the impression that it's only present to fulfill some essential function. The clip-on 'bars automatically place the rider in a semi-racing crouch, completed when you finally get tucked in behind the one-piece fairing and screen. The long, slim five gallon petrol tank forces your bum back a fair way so it's quite a stretch to the 'bars. This tank, say Ducati in their handbook, is 'Of anatomical shape specially studied for a correct racing position of rider. This styling represents a valid solution between shape and capacity requirements.'

Oh, yeah man, quite agree . . .

This riding position forces the rider to take a very objective view of his riding style. Threepenny-bitting (for all you extremely young readers, a 3d bit was a pre-decimalisation coin with eleven flats) is definitely out; only neat, consistent lines are allowed and, indeed, it's almost difficult to do anything else. Just a slight shift of rider weight to one side and the bike'll bank into the turn with no trace of over or understeer, one or other of which seems ever-present on big, multi-cylinder bikes.

It's this oh-so-secure feeling when you're going into a turn, and when you're in it, and when you're exiting, that distinguishes the Ducati from almost every other production bike available. During our test day at MIRA (Motor Industry Research Association's circuit), when we had the GSX1100 Suzuki and Replica out there together, the Ducati was no slouch through the speed taps, recording 132mph top speed and a standing quarter-mile time of 12.5 seconds, but it's fair to say that it was blown into the weeds by the GSX with its 137mph and 11.3 seconds.

What those figures conceal is that on the Replica I was tucked in behind the fairing in, for that bike, the normal riding position. On the GSX at that speed, it was necessary to lie flat on the tank, feet on the pillion footrests and clutch hand off the 'bar and onto the fork stanchion, to get as much body as possible out of the wind to avoid being blown off the bike. Coming back from MIRA along the long sweeping curves of the A47 — remember that we'd already had an adrenalin-pumped day of high-speedery — we, er, bopped along at, er, a relatively respectable pace. The Ducati, despite developing a slipping clutch from the brutal standing starts, just held the road — no drama, lots of fun, it was so safe it could have

been any speed. The GSX, fine handling motorcycle that it is, pops the rider up into such a position that he really has to fight to stay on. Whereas I could have maintained the pace for a while longer, Barry was exhausted in having to hang on.

Perhaps it's unfair to align the Replica with other big bikes; its sole purpose is high-speed motivation and it does little else with ease. Through towns, it's quite quick nipping through traffic because of the positive control of the brakes — so good that it takes a while to become accustomed to their ferocity — the precise steering, and narrow lines of the bike. But the crouched position kills your wrists, gives your neck the time-honoured crick, and your back a permanent ache. Prolonged town use gets the motor hot and bothered, giving off an aroma reminiscent of a chip pan fire. You get irritated with the gearchange — not the world's most wonderful with several short linkages — the heavy clutch action, and stiffish throttle. In fact, just a few minutes of contact with the real world is enough to send you scuttling back to your own private domain.

One of the cleverest ideas on the Replica is the seat which can be converted from a single, large-humped racer to a dual bumpad. A foot-long section of the rear hump has three screws holding it (and the seat) in place. Remove these and the rest of the seat is revealed. Replace the three screws and you're away. The only other manufacturer to come up with a better idea for these dual roles is MV Agusta who once had a sliding rear hump. Right at the very end of the seat is the Ducati's reasonable toolkit, including a long box spanner which, somehow, is supposed to reach the crankcase oil level dipstick negotiating the one-piece fairing.

Unfortunately, the fairing wraps right around underneath the bike and doesn't have quick-release catches such as Dzus fasteners. It's an effective shape, penetrating the wind with no trace of instability, well-finished and securely mounted at the front, at the sides

and at top, across the steering head nut. The tank has a small elastic strap at the back but is also bolted to the chassis at the front. Not much steering lock comes with the Replica and what there is is further restricted by the proximity of the 'bar ends to the tank when turning, pinning down your thumbs.

The lack of sidepanels (which are fitted to the 900SS) gives good access to the battery on the left, and rear carb on the right, but not a lot of security. The bike worries me with its trust in humanity since there's no protection for the toolkit and a number of parts can be got at easily. However, the front carb is tucked away inside the fairing so deeply that it requires the arm and wrist of a rose-jointed monkey to perform the necessary action of tickling the carb for cold starts.

No choke or air filters are fitted to the monster 40mm Dell 'Ortos, just a wire mesh grill to fend off inhaled leaves, jeans and legs. And with the front carb's bellmouth pointing invitingly skywards, it's advisable to carry a small polythene bag to put over it and so prevent rain entering. The bike starts easily, thanks to the electronic Bosch ignition which provides a nice progressive spark advance.

The engine, transmission and chassis are virtually identical to the 900SS apart from the rear shock absorbers being 20mm (0.78in) longer. This is to accommodate the extra 38lb weight of the fairing, bigger tank, brackets etc, and also because the rider is sitting further rearward. These shocks are still the one-way damped Cerianis we complained about when we tested the 900SS (Nov 78) and don't match the superlative performance of the double-action Marzocchi forks. These absorb bumps without wallowing, track accurately through even the longest sweeping bends and provide gallons of feedback on what the Pirelli Phantom tyres are up to — usually gripping like hell. They run at high pressures, 29lb/sq in front and 36lb/sq in rear.

With the full fairing having such good aerodynamics, the Replica ran up to the red

Continued on next page

line in fifth gear easily for the top speed tests. Ducati repeatedly advise that 7,900rpm is the absolute limit with maximum power at 7,000rpm. But it's probably from the bottom line that the Duke's power is best exploited. The desmo valve gear allows a ridiculous amount of valve open time (and there's special racing cams available which extend this even further), and power simply floods in.

The Replica comes with standard SS gearing, having a 15/36t final drive but all sorts of other sprockets are available including a 35t which would raise top speed by about 3-4mph. This would also further increase the miles per gallon which is already pretty fantastic at an overall 56mpg including several hard riding sessions. First gear is fairly tall, needing more clutch slip than the average Jap to pull away, but after that the gears are closely spaced.

Ideally, the Hailwood Replica, like the standard 900SS, is for the biker who either has alternative rat transport for mundane things such as getting to work, picking up spares and collecting the washing, or who lives within walking distance of all these routines. Obviously, you've gotta have a lotta dough as well and, at £2,899, you're not really getting much for your loot. It's a fairly basic package — no mirrors, for instance — with a confined, selected role. Now, why am I determined to get mine this year?

The DESMOGOGUE

CAFE RACER: POSEUR'S PENIS SUBSTITUTE or epitome of functional biking, depending on your point of view. With me it's the latter, but I'm open to argument if you don't mind beds with wheels. Perhaps the zenith of roadgoing, high-speed utility in current production is the Ducati 900SS. I know, I've got one. However, nothing's perfect or unique and, particularly at Glen Maye last TT week, they were common as muck. Something had to be done. This is it.

Your friendly scribe's Desmo started life as one of the worst ever made — Lafranconi silencers and 32mm carbs — but it was at a knock-down price. The dealer threw in a pair of Contis and sleight of hand produced a pair of 40mm Dell'Ortos at a very reasonable price. So the bike became at least *respectable*. The easy route then would have been to flog it straight away to buy a Hailwood Replica. Replica indeed! Did you see Mike indicating to right as he entered Parliament Square? Ergo, I had to go my own route.

The obvious bits were easy: Hailwood fibre-glass tank seat unit, second-hand, but unused — £90 (plus a written-off Honda Civic, a crumpled Vauxhall Cavalier and an embarrassed *Bike* ad-manager, but that's another story). Fitting it was a bitch — it slots straight on if you don't mind Italian gas-piping knocking shit out of a fibre-glass, but I was determined not to do a tatty job. Eventually, courtesy of BL Mini exhaust rubbers, Hoover belts, judicious cutting and welding and a bit of head scratch, positive location was assured. The whole issue can be removed in 45 seconds, handy if you want to change a fuse.

The fairing — the '79 type with the pronounced 'chin' — was similarly easily obtained at a modest discount, and installed on home-made alloy brackets for the 'lowers', complete with Dzus fasteners. The front mounting posed a bit of a problem, but eventually comprised two bits of gas tube, the one a sliding fit in the other, and a clevis pin. Various bits and bobs were added to mount instruments etc. The fairing now comes off in

Mac McDiarmid will be well remembered by Ducati freaks as an original member of Team *Bike*, that roving bunch of speed lunatics travelling to race meetings around Europe. At last he's got a decent bike, a 900SS, but he wasn't satisfied with the standard version . . .

under a minute, complete with twin Cibies.

That was the easy bit. Catch any Ducati twin owner topping up his oil and you'll find a guy with oil on his boots. The filler hole's located where a honey bee couldn't reach it, and the problems worse with a fairing. Answer: weld on a two-inch tube at rear of clutch casing, install suitable plug (ex hot water bottle in my case) and drill and tap an oil level hole at bottom of said casing. Much to my surprise, it all works.

All but the early Desmos have left-side gear change, involving intricate linkages and bags of slop. Install rose joints and you have perfect gear selection. Because of the radical seating position and my long legs, the footrests had to move back to where the silencer mounts used to be. The lugs were drilled and tapped to take early model Desmo plain steel footrests and a GT860 gear lever shortened and fitted backwards. The box thus becomes upside-down but what the hell. The idea on the other side was to make up a super-trick alloy brake lever, but I didn't get round to it,

so the original steel item was transposed to the destined location. This puts it too near the master cylinder, which therefore has to be moved, in my case on a welded-on lug above the swing arm spindle.

Desmos run out of ground clearance before even I get scared. Slightly longer shocks (ta, Dave) — the originals are crap anyway — helped, but junking the centre stand was the real solution. A clip-on side stand resides inside the fairing.

Next, the 'go' department. Lesson one is that it's futile persuading any Desmo to develop more gee-gees 'cos the clutch'll slip. 450 Desmo clutch springs, at about £1.50 a set, are the complete answer. They do make the clutch slightly stiffer, but if you ride a Ducati twin you'll have a left-hand like that green guy with the funny contact lenses anyway. A cable-oiler helps matters.

Secondly, if said Duke goes quicker, it's likely to crunch its big end quicker as well, unless you have a late model with a supposedly bullet-proof crank. *Very* frequent oil changes are a sine qua non of Duke ownership, but an oil cooler is no bad idea. Besides, standard Dukes smell 'orrible after a good thrash. An oil cooler was therefore procured from Redline Autos, the plumbing from Goodridge, and rubber-mounted on the front fairing mount. Gas flow is helped (according to, er, *MCM*) if the bellmouths are cut to half their original length. In my case, having seen the havoc wreaked on unprotected bores, this is strictly an IoM mod; K&N filters are fitted the rest of the time. A conservative amount of gas-flowing was done — generally smoothing and polishing, obtaining a steady taper from carb to valve, and getting a better conformity between manifold and inlet tract.

The exhaust system just had to be 'personalised', particularly as Contis are out of production and I wanted to save the originals and all other bits for the Vintage Race of the Year at Mallory in 2003. Steve Wynne of *Sports Motorcycles* reckons on a pipe length of 24in from exhaust valve to silencer. Presumably this places peak power at around 8,000rpm, a big giddy with suspect pistons as standard and crank-pins at £200 a throw. Consulting the learned tomes, I settled on 28in for maximum effect at about 7,000rpm or so. These were adorned with nasty but cheap short reverse cone megas from Abasport which do, however, retain the crisp boom of the originals. Thanks a bundle to Campbell Geometric, too.

With all this additional poke and penetration, Dr Freud, me gearing was all to cock. In fact, it was in the first place, as the plot would pull 400rpm into the red in top *wearing waterproofs*. So the original 38T rear sprocket was discarded and a 34T job made up by Pagehiln.

The end result is so voluptuous, so esoteric and so . . . Val d'Oise, that I'd happily give up drugs, booze, fags and even women were I not such a devout hedonist. Completely bloody impractical, of course, for anything but having fun on but, Christ, that's why I did it. What will it do? Well, the new gearing is spot on, so work it out for yourself.

DUCATI HAILWOOD REPLICA

Engine	ohc V-twin
Bore x stroke	86 x 74.4mm
Capacity	864cc
Compression ratio	9.5:1
Carburation	2 x 40mm Dell'Orto
BHP @ rpm	n/a
Max torque	n/a
Primary drive	Gear
Clutch	Wet, multiplate
Gearbox	5 speed
Electrical system	12v 200w alternator, 36ah battery, electronic coil ignition
Lighting	55/60w headlamp

DIMENSIONS

Wheelbase	60in
Seat height	33in
Overall width	29in
Ground clearance	6½in
Weight	472lb (with 1gal fuel)
Fuel capacity	5gal

EQUIPMENT

Trafficators	Yes
Electric starter	No
Trip mileometer	Yes
Steering lock	Yes
Helmet lock	No
Headlamp flasher	Yes
Others	Full fairing, split seat, cast wheels

CYCLE PARTS

Tyres

(front)	3.50 x 18in Pirellii
(rear)	4.10 x 18in Pirelli

Brakes

(front)	2 x 11in discs
(rear)	11in disc

PERFORMANCE

Top speed

(prone)	132.1mph
(sitting up)	123.04mph
Standing ¼ mile	12.55sec/107.15mph

Speedo error

at indicated 30mph	29.3mph
at indicated 60mph	56.78mph

Braking distance

from 30mph	28ft
from 60mph	125ft

Fuel consumption

overall	50mpg
ridden hard	46mpg
PRICE	£2,899 (inc VAT)

Guarantee 6 months/12 months Autoguard
Supplied by .... Coburn & Hughes, 53-61 Park St, Luton, Beds.

The Darmah 900 SD is a civilized desmo, without the frame, fairing and other racetrack gilding of the Super Sport Desmo. But don't let that fool you. The V-twin engine—and the first winding road—will tell you the Darmah is the genuine Bologna article.

● IT'S NOT MERELY OUT OF QUIRKINESS THAT several Cycle staff members have owned Ducati V-twins over the past seven years, and devotedly hung onto them. The 750 twins—GT, Sport or Super Sport Desmo—handled with uncanny precision and, despite meager offerings in body comfort, were ridden many miles in between their owners' normal road-testing duties. Back in 1973, the editors were quick to recognize a good thing, and they were concerned the good might not last.

Though agreeable in most respects, the 750s were loud—even with effective silencers they produced a significant amount of valve train noise—and the impending gloom of DOT and EPA regulations seemed uncomfortably close even as the first units landed in America. While Those Who Cared waited, collected their favorite specimens and fiddled endlessly with valve shims and electric switch contacts, Those Who Didn't watched and waited for it all to end suddenly.

They watched every model year as more Ducatis were brought from the Bologna factory. They saw the 750s equipped with chromed steel instead of aluminum rims, steel instead of fiberglass fuel tanks (imbedded with flies and table salt), and even screw-type valve adjusters instead of replaceable Winkler caps. Was this the end coming, or just a slow fade-out of the eccentric Ducati charm?

In 1975 the first Ducati 860 appeared, and by 1976 the 750s were gone, replaced by wider, heavier derivatives. Labeled in 1977 as a "900," the twin was represented here by the SS Desmo and sport-touring GTS. The year 1978 brought the GTS, Super Sport and a model called the Darmah, also a "900," but with more conservative styling and riding position. Yet, like the Super Sport, the Darmah had desmodromic valve gear, with cams that opened its valves and pulled them shut, eliminating the possibility of valve float at high revs. The Darmah carried along a host of DOT-required bits, such as large, seamed mufflers. Too, an electric starter added weight and complexity and required a larger battery, which in turn demanded that the rear cylinder's intake manifold be angled crazily out of the way.

The Darmah, purists and owners of 750s moaned, wasn't a true Ducati but merely a facsimile. Though encumbered by an electric starter and a reasonable set of mufflers, the Darmah was still a nice motorcycle—one that connoisseurs had to ac-

cept for the same reasons they accepted their 750s.

This year, three Ducati V-twins are available in the United States: a slightly reworked 864cc Darmah, a Darmah SS and the Desmo SS. What has the world of economics, emissions regulations and safety standards done to these Ducks? Are they soft-spoken, with hinges at every frame junction, or do they bark out like in the good old days and track like the proverbial freight train?

A number of changes distinguish our black-and-gold 900 SD Darmah from its 1979 counterpart. Its saddle and tail are different—for comfort and storage space—it has "seamless" Silentium mufflers for aesthetic reasons, electric starting but no kickstarter and longer, gas-charged reservoir shock absorbers. Some 1979 Darmahs, units assembled late in the production year, had reservoir shocks but not these other changes. Minor differences include allegedly lower footpeg height (for more rider comfort), and a more rounded-profile front fender. It is said that no DOT- or EPA-mandated changes have been made.

Production Ducatis aren't world-beating drag racers; their engines are designed to deliver a broad, high-torque powerband rather than a big rush at peak revs. This generous torque spread does make the Darmah easy to ride at the drag strip. Our 517-pound test bike put in a best run of 13.13 seconds at 101.35 mph. Although that's a long way behind the 11.49-second, 116.88 mph Suzuki GS1100ET, when compared to the GS850's 12.97-second, 104.77 mph showing, the Ducati doesn't appear so drowsy. Besides, as we said, the Ducati makes a different kind of power. Though a Yamaha XS Eleven will outgun the Darmah in a top-gear roll-on contest, the Darmah will handily shoot down Honda's CB750F in the same match. And the 750 is no slouch.

No internal engine changes distinguish the 1980 Darmah from its 1979 sibling or indeed from the Darmah SS or 900 Super Sport. Three-ring pistons slide 74.4 millimeters in 86.0mm bores and provide a compression ratio of 9.3:1. To promote even cylinder-head and cylinder cooling, Ducati casts each cylinder and head differently; that allows all cooling fins to be placed horizontally.

Driving the single overhead camshafts are a bevy of straight-cut gears and spiral-bevel gears. On the engine's right side, revolutions are handed to two ball-bearing-

supported shafts with spiral-bevel gears at each end. Each camshaft has four lobes: two open the intake and exhaust valves, and another pair closes them. The first set of lobes works the valves through normal rocker arms (and Winkler-type clearance caps); the closing lobes work similarly but upside down, with forked rocker arms that pull up on collars on the valve stems. Complicated? Somewhat, but this system, in addition to eliminating the possibility of valve float, obviates the need for valve springs. One light closing spring is used for each valve; these are for starting purposes only. Gas pressure and inertia ensure valve closing once the engine is running, and then the springs have no bearing on how the engine performs.

Both connecting rods share the same crank pin, and since the rods ride side-by-side, the Darmah's forward cylinder is located slightly to the left of the rear barrel. The crankshaft is a pressed-together, three-piece affair, and the rods are one-piece forged units that center on roller bearings. Ducati uses plain bushings at the small ends; extensive racing experience has told them that nothing more is needed.

Immense quantities (5.3 quarts) of engine oil are circulated by a gear-type pump and cleansed by an honest-to-God disposable filter cartridge located between the cylinders. The unusual filter residence was acquired when the big-bore twin's ignition was switched to magnetic-triggering in model-year 1975.

The "new" ignition pickups run in oil, for no particular reason other than that there was room inside the cases near the left crankshaft end and it seemed like a good place. And why not? The pickups are maintenance-free. The alternator runs in oil too, on the engine's right side. It produces a maximum of 200 watts—enough to keep the battery charged in the worst high-drain circumstances.

Both intake and exhaust noise has gradually decreased over the years, but the exhaust note has been stifled slightly more than the intake: you can hear the Darmah's intakes pulsing through its rubber intake bellows and steel air-filter housings.

Select a gear. Second is fine for starting off, unless you're in a particular hurry. The Ducati pulls from low, low on the rev range. Depending on how you ride the Darmah, fuel mileage can be either admirable or rather embarrassing. Our best tankful trickled through at 49.7 miles per gallon—this was obtained on a sedate freeway run—

PHOTOGRAPHY: DAVE HAWKINS, ROBIN RIGGS

Braking's fade-free, thanks partly to twin-piston Brembo calipers, but requires a stout tug on lever.

The 1980 Darmah has a flip-up tail-section cover that allows access to tools—and lots of extra space.

The remote-reservoir Marzocchi shocks are fine for solo riding but underdamped for two-up cruising.

and the worst was from a spirited canyon-sprint, producing 30.8 mpg. Not including drag strip testing, we averaged 43.1 mpg, enough to take us 171 miles before pushing. Fortunately, the Darmah has twin three-position fuel taps that guarantee an extra half-gallon of gas. Given our average consumption rate, we'd need reserve after only 148 miles. Even though the Ducati gets satisfactory fuel mileage when treated gently, a four-gallon tank doesn't provide the range necessary for out-back touring.

Amazingly, the Darmah engine produces over 40 lbs-ft of torque from 3000 rpm to 6500 rpm, where it makes maximum horsepower: 52.31 bhp. Maximum torque,

45.37 lbs-ft, develops at only 3000 rpm. Above this engine speed, the torque drops, then swings upward to its second-highest peak at 5500 rpm. From this point the torque begins to fall off, and at the engine's 7800 rpm redline approximately 30 lbs-ft is produced. The Darmah engine definitely runs out of breath before its redline; you'll consistently change gears on the safe side of this speed, especially if you want to accelerate quickly.

To call the Darmah's powerband wide is practically an understatement. It gives you a choice between two gears—sometimes three—for a given situation. And you can roll on the Ducati's throttle at low revs with-

out it jolting you like a rodeo bronc. Interestingly, the Darmah's powerband is as opposite the contemporary Japanese multi's characteristics as possible. Yet both are fun to ride; each has its attraction.

Unquestionably, the Ducati is geared tall. You may find yourself trolling quite happily along the highway in fourth gear, then notice there's fifth left. Second gear is good from a standing start all the way up to 66 mph. Fifth will run you up to 116 mph at redline, and even though the engine is well past its power peak earlier than that, it'll pull right up to redline in top cog without much delay. By most motorcyclists' standards, the Darmah shifts exquisitely. The

DUCATI DARMAH TEST

DUCATI DARMAH TEST

only noise that emanates from its gearbox is a mild clunk when first gear is engaged.

Our only difficulty with the Darmah's transmission came when the shift drum detent bolt backed out, allowing the drum—and selector forks—to vibrate to any position. This made shifting, and keeping the Darmah in gear, challenging. Retightening the bolt eliminated the trouble.

A firm lever pull is a small price to pay for a smoothly engaging clutch, and once the Ducati's clutch has hooked up, you'll notice little driveline slack. Every power-transmission connection is as slop-free as possible. With a properly adjusted chain you'll be hard-pressed to detect any backlash.

Dell'Orto, as in the past, supplies Ducati with carburetors; for the Darmah they're 32mm units with accelerator pumps. Though the EPA required no jet changes for 1980, a federal law requires that any carburetor (or ignition) components which are adjustable must, at their adjustment lim-

its, allow the vehicle to pass EPA emissions tests. Ducati's answer to this regulation was to *glue* the idle mixture screws in place with what looks for all the world like fingernail polish. In any event, the Dell'Ortos are set up nicely—the Ducati runs smoothly at all engine speeds, and its idle remains constant, hot or cold.

Italian motorcycles have been accused time and again of rough-riding their pilots, and of possessing suspension springs more fit for a White Freightliner than a motorcycle. Our Ducati Darmah offered a *firm* ride, but not one we could call *rough*. The rear shocks may provide a negligible amount more axle travel than last year's units, and they're something of a compromise. Since they have reservoirs, they carry more oil. This is fine, but reservoirs and oil add weight—the unsprung kind. We don't think you were likely to get last year's shocks heated to the fade-point anyway, so there's no reason for finned reservoirs. Ducati probably got a good deal on the shocks. They do increase the already ample cornering clearance and reduce rake and trail slightly, allowing safer leaning and quicker steering.

The Marzocchis seem slightly under-damped, but only when the bike is working under the combined weight of a rider and passenger. Their spring preload can be adjusted five ways with a traditional spanner wrench, and the top position allows maximum cornering clearance without promoting undue ride harshness.

Compared to a BMW or Honda Super Sport fork, the Ducati's 38mm Marzocchi unit has a relatively great amount of stiction, making it fairly unresponsive to small road irregularities. However, the front end won't nose-dive objectionably when you yank on the front brake lever, and the Ducati won't sway around when you're trying to hustle it through a corner. The Darmah definitely rides less smoothly than some sport bikes, though it has the most successful spring and damping characteristics overall for going fast on a windy road. Distance-riding depends on your tolerance for jiggling. We found the suspension adequately comfortable for extended

Valve placement is similar to 750's; wider squish band accepts larger bore.

Beginning of the cam drivetrain: right crankshaft end turns straight-cut gears.

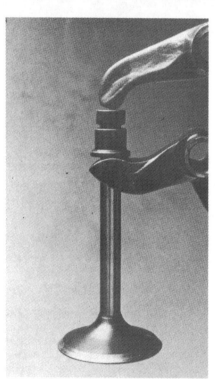

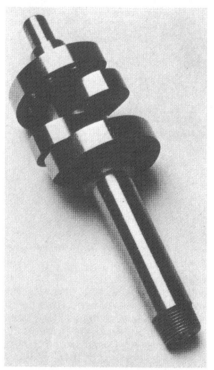

Principles of desmodromics exposed: the upper rocker arm opens this valve; lower arm closes it . . .

. . . with one camshaft. The conventional inner lobes are for opening, the larger outer lobes for closing.

Each camshaft is driven by a ball-bearing-suspended, two-piece tower shaft and bevel gears.

Both sides of the Ducati's electric starter/flywheel/primary-drive assembly: a sprag clutch inside the flywheel allows one-way engagement. This keeps the starter motor inactive during normal engine use.

Polished connecting rods are oil-fed by a common crank pin and ride on separate roller bearings.

The 900 Darmah's no-frills pistons have three rings, trimmed flanks and machined valve pockets.

A large two-piece input/output shaft is utilized. The smaller shaft couples up to allow ratio changes.

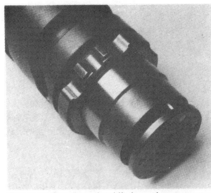

Detent scallops keep the shift drum—hence gears—in place, while steel pegs are used to rotate drum.

A Ducati V-twin piece since the beginning: inside is a labyrinth for condensing crankcase oil vapors.

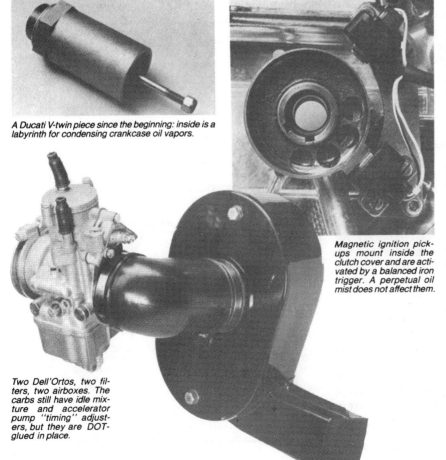

Magnetic ignition pickups mount inside the clutch cover and are activated by a balanced iron trigger. A perpetual oil mist does not affect them.

Two Dell'Ortos, two filters, two airboxes. The carbs still have idle mixture and accelerator pump "timing" adjusters, but they are DOT-glued in place.

DUCATI DARMAH TEST

trips. A long (61.0-inch) wheelbase and slow steering geometry make the Ducati extremely stable at high speeds, so it's relaxing to ride even in windy conditions or on bumpy highways.

Remember that corner you hustle through on your favorite back-road ride, the one that has a bump by the apex and a crack out by the exit? Dive into it on the Ducati and you'll swear those obstacles have disappeared. The Darmah is unperturbed by patchwork corners, fourth-gear sweepers or decreasing radius spirals. The bike requires a fair amount of handlebar force to be banked sharply into a corner, but once you're over, it seems to be on auto-pilot. Few mid-turn corrections are necessary in keeping the Darmah on-line. There are no serious flaws in the Ducati's cornering personality. The Darmah is equipped with an hydraulic steering damper, but it doesn't need one. Perhaps Ducati purchased the Marzocchis *and* the damper in a package deal.

Using the engine as an integral frame member is not a new trick for Ducati, but this does save some in weight and frame complexity. Twin front and twin rear downtubes straddle the V-twin, front and rear, and three main backbone members tie things together under the fuel tank. Although the Darmah frame has a few more bent tubes than did the original 750s, it's still nicely triangulated, with large-diameter steering head and swing-arm bearing areas. Eccentric swing-arm pivot-pin carriers allow chain adjustments to be made at that pivot instead of the rear axle: in moving the swing arm instead of the axle fore and aft, the rear wheel can't become cocked out of line with the front.

Both the center- and sidestands support the Ducati well: the centerstand is extremely easy to use; the sidestand is difficult, since it's tucked beneath the electric starter housing and the left-side exhaust header. If not careful you can knock the Darmah into gear while feeling around for the sidestand.

One of the Darmah's nicest features is its Pirelli Supersport Gordon tires, 3.50 H 18 front and 120/90 V 18 rear. They're soft and supply a wide footprint when vertical or heeled over. The front tire's considerable width helps the Darmah to slow quickly during braking; both tires contribute to the Ducati's cornering prowess. One drawback to sticky tires is rapid wear: the rear tire on our test bike required replacement after few more than 2000 miles. You may get better mileage out of yours.

Stopping the Darmah is *no problem.* A trio of Brembo calipers act on 280mm cast-iron rotors for eye-popping stops. Like the clutch lever, the front brake lever requires a hefty pull, but you get superb feel.

The rear brake pedal has one drawback: it angles back over the right-side footrest in a manner that makes it easy to hit with the side of your foot. We found ourselves ap-

DUCATI DARMAH TEST

plying the brake unintentionally, and in doing so caused unusual cornering gyrations. When we learned to expect this, staying away from the arm was easy. Even on rough roads during quick stops, the rear wheel takes some "pushing" before it will hop. Yet the rear brake is not as sensitive as the front, so it requires more care to recognize how it in turn affects its tire.

In the wet, the non-perforated front brake rotors lose their moisture film as soon as the brake pucks are applied and present no difficulties in feel or performance. The rear brake takes considerably longer to work when wet; it must be activated for a second or two before it begins to brake in earnest.

Our longest rides on the Darmah told us that whatever vibration the bigger V-twin has in excess of the 750s' levels, it's not enough to cause rider discomfort. There are no noticeable spots in the Ducati's slight buzzing—it's just there. The mild vibration won't affect your hands, feet or seat, though your passenger may notice some tingling in the passenger pegs.

Seating accommodations are a tradi-

Make and model .... Ducati 900 SD Darmah
Price, suggested retail (as of 1/28/80) $4299

PERFORMANCE
Standing start ¼-mile .... 13.13 @ 101.35
Engine rpm @ 60 mph, top gear 4026
Average fuel consumption rate .... 43.1 mpg (18.3 km/l)
Cruising range, main/reserve .... 148.0/23.0 mi.
(238.1/37.0 km)
Load capacity (GVWR less curb weight) ....160.5 kg
(354 lbs)
Maximum speed in gears @ engine redline .... (1) 46.1
(2) 66.0 (3) 85.7 (4) 103.1 (5) 116.3

ENGINE
Type ....Four-stroke, 90-degree V-twin, air-cooled with
single overhead camshafts, gear-driven
Bore and stroke .... 86.0 x 74.4mm (3.39 x 2.93 in.)
Piston displacement .... 864cc (52.7 cu. in.)
Compression ratio 9.3:1
Carburetion .... (2) Dell'Orto 32mm slide-needle
Exhaust system .... Two into two
Ignition .... Battery-powered capacitor discharge,
magnetically triggered
Air filtration .... Dry cartridge, disposable
Oil filtration .... Paper element, disposable
Oil capacity .... 5.0 liters (5.3 qts.)
Bhp @ rpm .... 52.31 @ 6500
Torque @ rpm .... 45.33 @ 3000

TRANSMISSION
Type .... Five-speed, constant-mesh, wet clutch
Primary drive .... Helical gear, 2.19:1
Final drive .... #530 chain, 2.53:1
Gear ratios, overall .... (1) 12.4 (2) 8.7 (3) 6.7
(4) 5.5 (5) 4.9:1

CHASSIS
Type .... Twin front and rear downtube frame
Suspension, front .... Coil-spring center-axle fork
rear .... Swing arm and (2) remote-reservoir
shocks
Wheelbase .... 1550mm (61.0 in.)
Brake, front .... Hydraulic, dual-disc, 280mm (11.0 in.)
rotors with dual-piston calipers
rear .... Hydraulic, single-disc, 280mm (11.0 in.)
rotor with dual-piston caliper
Wheel, front .... Cast, 2.15 x 18
rear .... Cast, 2.50 x 18
Tire, front .... 3.50 H 18 Pirelli Supersport Gordon MT18
rear ......120/90 V 18 Pirelli Supersport Gordon MT18
Seat height ....813mm (32.0 in.)
Ground clearance .... 198mm (7.8 in.)
Fuel capacity, main/reserve ..13.0/2.0 liters (3.4/0.5 gal.)

Curb weight, full tank .... 234.5 kg (517 lbs)
Test weight .... 309.3 kg (682 lbs)

ELECTRICAL
Power source .... Alternator, 200 watts
Charge control .... Solid-state voltage regulator
Headlight beams, high/low .... 60/55 watts
Tail/stop lights ....5/21 watts
Battery 12V 28AH

INSTRUMENTS
Includes ....Speedometer, odometer, resettable tripmeter,
tachometer. Indicators for sidestand position, lights,
high beam, turn signals, "generator," neutral
Speedometer error, 30 mph indicated, actual 29.14
60 mph indicated, actual 58.86

CUSTOMER SERVICE CONTACT
Berliner Motor Corporation
Railroad Street and Plant Road
P.O. Box 145
Hasbrouck Heights, NJ 07604

Engine Speed	Bhp	Torque
2500	18.50	38.87
3000	25.92	45.37
3500	29.80	44.72
4000	33.13	43.50
4500	37.02	43.21
5000	41.70	43.81
5500	47.47	45.33
6000	51.48	45.06
6500	52.31	42.27
7000	51.80	38.86
7500	50.66	35.48
8000	44.18	29.00

BHP (52.31 max.)

TORQUE (45.33 max.)

Ducati SD 900 Darmah
Test Conditions:
Barometer 30.00
Temperature
64°F Wet 74°F Dry
Correction Factor 1.038
Date of Test: 11/12/79
As Tested on the
Webco Dyno

CORRECTED REAR WHEEL HORSEPOWER

TORQUE IN FOOT POUNDS

RPMx100

Ducati Darmah

ional sore spot for many Italophiles. Ducati hasn't usually been as abusive as some other Italian companies in this department, but they aren't known for building two-wheeled couches either. And unfortunately the Darmah seat doesn't go far toward raising the Ducati name from scorn in this regard. The saddle is stylish, is padded sufficiently and has the correct width. But its shape does not get our unanimous approval. When questioned about the passenger accommodations, one riding guest replied, "Wretched. Does that describe it enough?" The seat's back slopes forward, shoving the passenger into the rider.

The pilot's portion is shaped better, although six-footers will feel something like a jockey atop the Darmah. The pilot's section definitely settles you in one spot: it slopes forward at its front *and* rear, keeping you pretty well centered.

The required riding posture is sporty, and the two-inch-rise handlebar is excellent for fast roadwork or freeway touring. We wish more bikes came with this type of handlebar: it offers advantages in steering control *and* riding comfort.

We *don't* wish bikes came with short-stalked mirrors like the Darmah's. While the mirrors themselves work fine, their stalks are simply too short to allow much more in your rear-view vision than half of your coat sleeves. Substituting long-stemmed mirrors helped us obtain a greater rear view.

Yes, it's true: Japanese-made Nippon-denso instruments flank the Ducati's moderate indicator light selection. The handlebar switches are Japanese, too, as are the electric starter, lights, turn signals, horn and engine cutoff switches. Our starter button worked intermittently—a result of some debris in the switch—requiring a couple of jabs on occasion to make contact.

The Ducati comes equipped with an outstanding Bosch quartz-glass headlight. Little else needs saying except that it ranks right behind good brakes and tires as a major safety feature. The turn signal and high beam indicators are bright enough to "leak" light through to the rest of the indicators. If you're forgetful, a sidestand-down indicator reminds you not to turn left.

True, the twin-cylinder Ducati has grown in size and power output. The Darmah weighs 48 pounds more than its 1973 predecessor, and produces slightly more horsepower and torque. Much of its weight gain can be attributed to two more disc brakes, a steel fuel tank, electric start mechanisms and a heavier engine assembly.

At 7000 rpm, the 750GT produced 49.91 bhp while the Darmah produces its maximum horsepower 500 revs per minute lower. The V-twins' power curves are similar, but at 5500 rpm, where the old 750 started to flatten out, the "864" continues producing power, and it rejoins the 750's output at 8000 rpm. From a 15 per cent displacement increase (and a much qui-

eter engine), Ducati has nudged out 4.8 per cent more peak power. The original 750GT (unladen) toted 9.40 pounds per horsepower; the Darmah has to carry 9.88 pounds—a slightly greater load. Even still, we were able to run the Darmah quicker down the same drag strip as that used in *Cycle*'s 1973 Superbike Comparison Test. The original 750 ran the quarter in 13.29 seconds at 101.12 mph; slightly slower than the Darmah.

Torque capabilities, while immense in the 750, are now even more staggering. Reflect, if you will, upon the torque capabilities of the first 750GT: it produced 38 to 43 pounds-feet from 3000 to 7000 rpm. The curve, when plotted on a graph, looked not unlike a gentle dome. Here's a rundown of the figures: at 3000 rpm, 38 lbs-ft; at 4000 rpm, 43 lbs-ft; 5000, 43 lbs-ft; 6000, 41 lbs-ft; at 7000 rpm, 38 lbs-ft.

The Darmah's torque curve, in comparison: at 3000 rpm, 45; 4000 rpm, 44; 5000, 44; 6000, 45; at 7000 rpm, 39 lbs-ft. The Darmah's torque curve is not *wider* than the 750's, but it is slightly more stout.

This explains why the original 750 would embarrass bigger, more powerful motorcycles in high-gear roll-on contests. The GT was lighter and had a wider, meaner torque spread than other bikes. The Darmah, by virtue of its relatively light weight and great torque output, is still able to hide from bikes with greater horsepower figures.

Both the Honda CB750F and Suzuki GS750 tested in this issue produce significantly more peak horsepower than the Darmah, yet their torque curves look destitute in comparison. Yet, though these Japanese fours weigh more than the Ducati (26 pounds for the Honda, 22 pounds for the Suzuki), they run through the quarter-mile quicker and faster. The reasons? Mainly, horsepower production—gearing differences may also have played a minor role in the quarter times.

Our Darmah had few poor-quality items among its components, but one that should be mentioned is the gas cap. When the tank is full, the cap allows gas to seep out. Too, if you're tucked down on the motorcycle and touch the cap release button with your helmet, the cap can fly open, drenching you with North Slope premium.

Drooling gas caps and finicky starter switches aside, the Darmah's stay at *Cycle* was a pleasant time for our test riders. The Ducati V-twin certainly has changed in seven years, but its charm has not faded nor been buried under a pile of chrome-plate rims or CV carburetors. Our Darmah test bike was for the most part thoughtfully equipped, it ran beautifully, and didn't leave us musing about where $4299 worth of quality was hidden.

Those Who Care will continue to collect specimens and fiddle endlessly with valve shims and electric switch contacts—and one of the specimens in their collections will be a Darmah. It's not only perversity that makes people hang onto Ducatis.

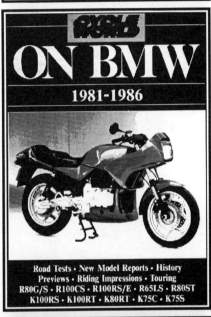
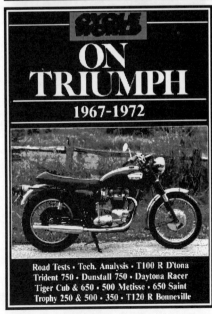

The Odds-On Duke

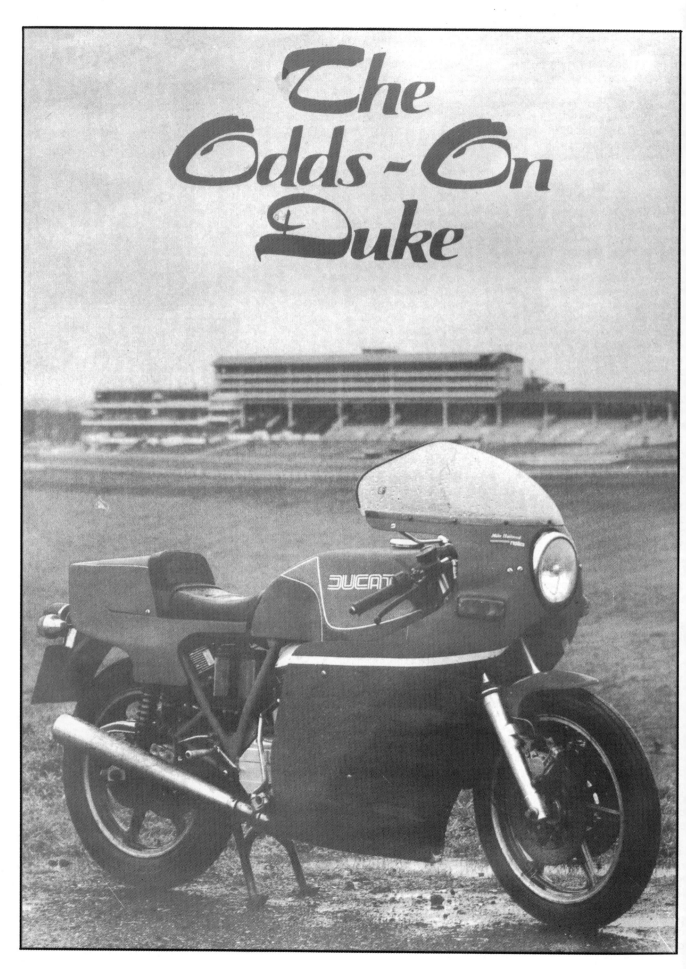

Hailwood's TT Is Over - But The Bass Line Lingers On

Like Italian Coffee, Ducati's Factory Cafe-racer is Strong, Hot and Expresso. Mike Maxwell Scorches His Superlatives

A cold breeze was blowing across the open grassland causing the taller tufts to beckon frantically at me. Leaden clouds were billowing in omnipresent majesty across the skyline. The rolling boom of thunder echoed across the pre-historic plateau as the cumulus masses clashed, with jagged forks of lightning casting a bizarre yellow pallor momentarily over the landscape. As the first few swollen tears plummeted from the pregnant heavens and shattered on the dull black surface of the road I shivered in anticipation of the impending elemental wrath.

The steady pulsing throb of the big vee-twin re-assured and comforted me as the clouds began to unleash their burden, and the words of the 23rd Psalm began to course their way through my mind. "Yea though I walk through the valley of the shadow of death. . .", and the rain fell harder and faster. The headlight beam cut a path through the sheet of water as we wound our way along the narrow road, illuminating the roadside and etching the falling drops in front of the fairing.

I began to realise slowly that I was actually enjoying being out in this, eating up the miles of undulating road in total solitude, feeling the solid and dependable Ducati motor turning effortlessly beneath the exquisitely sculpted petrol tank. The harsh suspension fed the contours of the road surface to my body, and each was processed through my mind and responded to, with minute corrections to the steering.

A tight left-hander loomed up in the headlight beam, the sinuous black strip ahead of me falling away steeply and out of sight. Automatically I dropped down through two gears and bunched myself behind the screen. Throwing out my knee I began to negotiate the bend, gingerly cranking the bike over, fearful of the well lubricated blacktop.

As the bend began to tighten, I nervously edged more of my body out of the saddle, until I was hanging my rear over the machine like some primitive human outrigger. Inexorably the road continued to contort itself. I felt I was coming dangerously close to the limit of my wet weather riding ability.

With no alternative left, save more leaning of the machine, I began to lay it down. Almost certainly I was about to part company. Yet the Pirelli Phantoms clung tenaciously to the slippery road until it straightened out abruptly, leaving me with an excess of adrenalin in my bloodstream and a renewed confidence in the sheer roadability of the machine.

It's not difficult to road test the Ducati Hailwood Replica – that in itself is unadulterated riding bliss. But to avoid rendering superlatives redundant one has to be extremely judicious in their use.

The roadholding and steering alone encourage a superfluousity of praise from even the most jaded of scribes. The freedom from flex in the rolling chassis, the precise way in which it can be steered, the taut feel of the suspension; they all add up to make the Duke *the bike* when it comes to outcornering the opposition. Naturally, there are a few minor flaws when you come down to the sordid practical realities of day-to-day commuting, (since this particular variation on the Ducati theme is uncompromisingly for hard 'n' fast riding), but leave them for now.

The most important single point to bear in mind when testing any race replica machinery is this: it is exactly what it purports to be. While the styling and design is obviously heavily influenced by the original racing machine, it can never amount to an exact copy since racing practice necessarily precludes itself from the open road. When a machine has to be fitted with lights and a self-generating electrical system, and when the engine must be in a lower state of tune for optimum reliability, certain compromises must be made which deny the visual promise of the real thing. However, all that being said, this particular

replica is a very fine example indeed. While it is not as fast as the TT winning machine, it feels as though it could be competitive as a proddy scratcher, and it certainly encourages you to pay more attention to your riding than any other road bike I can think of. This is as it should be, when you consider the replica's ancestry. No, not Hailwood's TT bike, for it is only a descendant in appearance. Rather you must look back to the original 750 SS, the common ancestor from which both bikes are derived.

The Replica itself comes via the 900SS, in fact it *is* a 900SS. The frame has a different part number, but only because it's red. There are even brackets for side panels, though they are redundant because of the seat-cowl. Hailwood's race-bike had a one-off racing frame, though it differed little in major design aspects.

Anyway, nothing wrong with being a 900SS in smart clothes, for the 900SS is reckoned by many (myself included) to be God's own motorcycle. The Replica adds a slender racing fairing to the recipe, which already includes clip-on bars, rear-sets and milled metal footpegs. The fairing itself is well mounted and free from distortion, even at the bike's top speed, and has an additional bonus in that it keeps the worst part of the elements off the rider. Normally race-fairings don't offer much weather protection, but because of the seating position and tank shape, the rider is remarkably well tucked-in on this little number. It also functions very effectively as a streamlining device, with excellent penetration.

The other difference is the seat-cowl, which judiciously displays frame tubes and electrical components normally concealed behind side covers. "Purposeful" is the visual message, but I have my doubts about the wisdom of exposing Ducati electronics to English rain. The notorious susceptibility of these items to failure manifested itself in two areas on the test bike. The first was the ignition switch, which showed a tendency to cut the supply of electricity to the system quite independently of the rider's control, which was a little irritating. The second failure was the tail light bulb, brought to my attention by the driver of a candy-striped Rover, which was a little embarrassing.

listen to it. Throttle blipping is a childish pastime I found hard to avoid.

The engine itself is the traditional and conventional (in so far as any Duke can be described as such) desmodromic overhead cam 90-degree vee-twin, displacing 864cc. With a comparatively moderate compression ratio of 9.5:1 it has an even tickover and will rev happily to the 7900rpm redline in all five gears. The motor is said to produce a mean torque figure of 57.9 lb/ft at 5200rpm, which is spread very evenly throughout the rev range. It pulls effortlessly from low engine speeds and slipping the clutch in the high first is fun, but hardly necessary.

The tall gearing gives the bike a deceptive sense of undisturbed calm as it trundles along. It doesn't feel fast, until you look at the speedo. It never loses this sense of composure even at three figure speeds. The red and green Duke can easily top a ton in third. Changing into fourth while roaming the city streets is nigh on impossible, unless you want either to lose your licence, or enjoy the spread of torque at very very low revs.

The engine vibrations are a unique combination of aural imbalance and mechanical smoothness. As the pistons bang out their power strokes the machine sounds like it should shake itself to death. Yet the rider feels a smooth, almost liquid, power plant which transmits no mechanical disharmonies through the frame. There's just a soothing sense of omnipotence, noisily proclaimed.

A smooth wide-range motor and superlative steering and handling; one is struck by the machine's sense of coordination. It simply feels right! The Marzocchi front and rear suspension is stiffly sprung, and at times feels under-damped, but it keeps the wheels on the road and the machine tracks accurately through the bends. Hitting a severe bump at speed however, tends to be a little disconcerting, since your derriere is lofted from the seat and your feet are prone to rise from the foot pegs.

Hailwood's Replica comes equipped with a dual seat and passenger footrests. Both of which are unfortunately placed distressingly close to the rider. The passenger's feet, in particular, compete for lebensraum with those of the driver, which can be a nuisance in traffic or under braking. The bike is far more fun to ride alone anyway.

The switchgear is fairly well laid out and accessible once one has got used to it, although I found the indicator switch tended to go over centre. While griping about hand controls, I would like to suggest Ducati employ dog-leg levers, since the position of your hands on the clip-on handlebars means a full stretch of the fingers is exhausting, especially in traffic, when a lot of weight is thrown on to the wrists.

Surprisingly, the bike proved to be quite comfortable on longish motorway runs, since I for one have come to associate clip-ons and rear sets with long distance discomfort over the past ten years of motorcycle riding. With a 70mph wind cushioning the body, I could happily endure three or four hours motorway cruising at a stretch. The long-limbed Duke could sustain high speed riding with ease and returned an amazing 50mpg on a particular dash down the A3.

Petrol consumption was most encouraging, even when riding around London, where it never dipped below 42mpg. This was probably due to a

There is also a clip-on glassfibre conversion that changes the dual seat into a single perch. Pity it doesn't double as a helmet: you could then draw up alongside that beautiful hitch-hiker, and give her legal headgear by the very act of making room.

As you prod the kickstart lever and the engine roars into life, the throaty throb emanating from the minimally restricted Conti exhaust pipes (one could hardly describe them as silencers!) lets all the world know this machine was born to run. There is no hint of American emission control emasculating the gutsy motor. It issues a defiant roar to all-comers, the twin 40mm Dell'Orto carbs sucking greedily at the atmosphere through the wire mesh of the unfiltered carb trumpets.

This is a free breathing machine that revels in its own sonorous growl, a paean to the gods of speed. The only trouble with a bike that sounds so rorty is that one never misses an opportunity to

combination of its comparatively light weight (450lb with a gallon of fuel) and the fact that it out-accelerated most of the traffic without going over 4500rpm in first and second gears. By sticking rigorously to speed limits and being very cautious with the throttle, the fuel consumption could be reduced to a stunning 74mpg! After a plethora of gas-guzzling Jap multis it was a real pleasure to find a performance bike that didn't eat a hole in one's wallet every time it needed petrol.

The clutch and gearbox were smooth and crisp, with the gears engaging positively every time, although neutral ocasionally presented problems at traffic lights unless it was selected while cruising to a standstill. The gear ratios are very widely spaced, which means one tends to spend a lot of time in each gear between shifts unless one is riding particularly hard. I found I never got beyond third in a 15 mile trip traversing London from south to north. The big Duke has tall gears!

The Pirelli Phantom tyres I have already lauded for their tenacity. They cannot be faulted for their road holding ability. I confess to having a predilection for this particular brand of rubber, and my experiences with the Ducati only serve to strengthen my already high opinion of them as road tyres. Naturally they wear down fairly quickly, but then again any high hysteresis compound is going to wear out fast. It's one of the penalties one pays for good roadholding; besides, tyre replacement is cheaper than falling off.

One problem was the limited steering lock. With a lot of desperate footwork, U-turns could be achieved in three or four point manoeuvres, although narrow streets meant more heaving and hauling. Like all things, one gets used to these minor irritations, and compensates for them. It is a problem that exists, and the top Duke has it in common with most race-faired machines. Another tedious aspect of the fairing is that it must be removed in order to check the sump-oil level.

Brakes were dependable and efficient, with a pair of 11 inch discs at the front and a single 11 inch disc at the rear being arrested by Brembo hydraulic calipers. The cast iron discs were less prone to delay in the damp than their stainless steel counterparts, although not entirely exempt. I'm sure the drillings in the brake face help rapid dissipation of moisture.

The general finish of the bike was to a high standard, with well-cast metal parts, neat Japanese switchgear and German lighting, and excellent detailing of the glassfibre. The sculpted tank is an exceptionally beautiful piece of metalwork. The total package is only marginally marred by the fact that the eye-catching red, green and white paintwork looks like it could have done with clear lacquer to finish it off.

All in all, the Ducati Hailwood Replica is a lovely machine to ride. It is swift, reliable and manoeuvrable. It can be thrown around with abandon and it encourages you constantly to test your riding ability. As a machine that can be ridden

hard and fast on public roads it has few equals, and yet it can be used as an ego massage any time you care to mention it. It is sad that it is going to be a limited production issue, but then again for those who can wheedle the necessary finances together – almost three grand – it represents a classy and usable bike that won't ever feel outranked on the road or outside the poseur's bars. I only wish I could afford one.

Ducati 900SS – Mike Hailwood Replica

£2899 inc VAT

PERFORMANCE
Maximum Speed – 129.3mph
Standing Quarter Mile – 12.57sec
Fuel Consumption – Hard Riding – 46mpg
        Cruising – 63mpg
Best Full-Tank Range – 310 miles

ENGINE
Type – air-cooled 90 degree V-twin, desmodromic valve gear, SOHC, roller bearing crank
Displacement – 864cc
Power – 68.5bhp at 7000rpm
Torque – 57.9lb/ft at 5200rpm
Bore & Stroke – 86mm × 74.4mm
Compression Ratio – 9.5:1
Induction – two 40mm Dell 'Ortos with accelerator pumps
Exhaust – twin Conti megaphone silencers
Oil System – wet sump, gear type oil pump
Ignition – 12 volt twin coil Bosch electronic ignition

TRANSMISSION
Clutch – wet, multiplate
Primary Drive – helical cut gears
Final Drive – chain
Gears – 5 speed gearbox

CHASSIS
Frame – spine-type, using engine as frame member
Front Suspension – telescopic forks, Marzocchi
Rear Suspension – pivoted rear fork with two Marzocchi shock absorbers, 5 position adjustable preload on springing
Wheelbase – 59in
Ground Clearance – 4½in
Seat Height – 31in
Weight (wet) – 490lb
Fuel Capacity – 4.9gall
Tyres – Front 18in Pirelli Phantom 100/90 V18
    Rear 18in Pirelli Phantom 110/90 V18
Brakes – Triple 11in drilled cast iron discs. Brembo calipers calipers

INSTRUMENTS
150mph speedometer with trip meter, rev counter with redline at 7900rpm, warning lights for indicators, oil pressure, alternator, neutral, high beam and lights

EQUIPMENT
Electrical – 12V 36amp hour battery, 200W alternator
Lighting – 60/55W headlight

OPTIONS
Single and dual seat

Test bike supplied by Coburn & Hughes, 21 Crawley Road, Luton, Bedfordshire.

The Special Special

A Very Noble Duke

We didn't know what to call this bike. The Duke was no good – we already had our own Darmah and the test Hailwood Replica in the car park. In an earlier incarnation, it had itself been a Hailwood Replica. But we had to rule that name out, because the factory bike pre-empted it, and it had changed anyway. So we called it the Replica Replica. Just to avoid confusion, see.

Didn't work.

So we dubbed it the Special.

But that didn't last, either: not after I'd spent a sodden day and a half on the road with it, in company with the factory Replica and in search of ultimate biking.

No. From then on, only one name would do. The Special Special.

This bike – this lean, spare, rorty, raunchy desmo Duke – really is that. Light, powerful and beautifully prepared, it's an honest grease-monkey's caff-racer.

That's a compliment, because I mean the good kind of grease-monkey. The guy who knows bikes backwards, and loves them. He's the kind who strips his bike of everything superfluous (note that skeletal silhouette). Who's not afraid to change or improve on factory detail design (note the under-slung back brake, and clean cockpit. One rev counter, one speedo, one switch.) He builds engines so they feel they'll stay built. He's not afraid to experiment. And he does a real neat job.

Just look at that profile. Daylight shows through, but you can see how the skimpy open-cradle Ducati frame uses the full-bellied vee-twin to provide strength and rigidity. There's not a lot else, after lights and the SS fairing. Just wheels, a bit of frame, and lots of engine. Topped with the sculpted 5-gallon Ducati racing tank, made of glassfibre and with that clear strip so you can check the level at a glance. This is the stuff of legends, a racer with lights. What is much, much more . . . it's a Ducati.

The engine is just what you'd want for the super-neat bicycle. It even has a history. Started life as a 750SS (as did the frame). Along with the passing of time (1975 to 1980), it grew. New barrels brought the capacity to 846cc, same as the 900SS. The desmo valve gear was just fine, especially with Imola road-race cams making the perfectly-controlled valve timing just a little radical. The crankshaft fly-wheels were lightened. And the heads got, just, worked. You know, ported and polished, though not skimmed. It breathes in through the 40mm throats of Dell 'Orto's finest pumpers, and shouts out through Conti's tailpipes. A free-breathing engine that lacks only high-compression pistons to make it a fire-breathing engine.

But then it is a London motorcycle, and the very gentle 7.5:1 compression ratio makes it much easier to live with around town which compensates for the loss of top-end performance. Even the gearing is for London: a two-tooth bigger sprocket makes the wide-ratio gears notably shorter. It snorts away from the lights in first, and bellows its way through second. Yet fifth is still tall enough to run at the ton for as long as you like without over-revving.

It's really a very fast motorcycle through London. Or Manchester, come to that. It's narrow, so without even slowing you can take the gaps that leave Gold Wings gasping. It really jumps when you wind on the throttle, too. It goes almost without saying that the brakes are

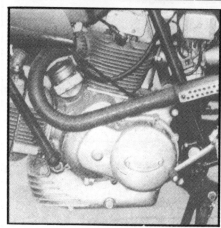

superb (they're Lockheed up front, and even more sensitive and dependable than Brembos). And boy can you make up ground round the one-way systems! It leans without scraping anything; until you fall off, I presume. It steers just exactly where you put it, and stays there. Out of some fast company, the only bike that rivalled it – or even came near – was the other Ducati.

There's a trade-off or two, though. Comfort, mainly. Those original 750SS front forks, Ducati's own early leading-axle jobs, are stiff like air-forks are soft. Since much of your weight is on the clip-ons, your shoulders take a fair pounding over big bumps.

Sadly, I had only a limited period of this discovery and enjoyment. Motivation

Motorcycles would only part with the bike for one day, and then only with a 6000rpm rev limit (bedding down after a top-end rebuild). and my fervent promises of warming it up and wiping its bits. We'd scheduled a hell-for-leather test-track bonanza *mit* photographer and a galaxy of bikes. Naturally enough, that was the day it rained non-stop. Then they closed the only interesting part of test-track anyway. It was a dejected Ducati that splashed around like a performing seal so photographer Rajah Phillips could work his magic.

But not for long. Because this bike is too good to be put down by a bit of wet. Michelins – M45 up front, wet-weather racing at the back – do a grand job of holding on to wet pavement. and the brakes didn't mind. And while conditions like that would have had me quailing had I been fiddling with 105bhp and 600lbs of feisty Honda CBX, they made a great showcase for the Duke. This, folks, is when the virtues of light, torquey, twin-cylinder motorcycles come to the fore. Real motorcycles, for real motorcyclists, who don't go home when it gets too wet.

The two Dukes put some memorable miles up round the lanes of Surrey that too-short day. By the end, Max and I were so wet and cold that to stop was agony. Just keep booming on, and you're way too busy to notice that your gloves are soaked through. Only, in the end, seriously deteriorating vision made the weather the enemy.

There were some interesting comparisons to be made. The factory bike was consistently faster, even when it was also held down to 6000rpm. It simply makes more power – the substantially higher compression pistons see to that. Only from the line the short gearing give the Special Special some edge.

It was never truly outpaced, though. And in some ways the Special Special was quicker. Engine response, certainly. The flywheels have been skimmed, and the engine dangles on the end of the throttle cables like a live thing.

It was a little rougher, too. The lighter flywheels, perhaps, changing the balance factors. Or maybe just advancing age.

Certainly, the Imola camshaft is less refined, though again lighter flywheels would contribute to its slightly ragged response at low revs. On any Duke, though, low revs *means* low revs. Even this rorty, sporty motor pulled smooth and strong from a mere 2000rpm.

There wasn't much to choose between Replica and Special Special in handling. In the dry, the factory bike's Pirelli Phantoms beat the combination of Michelins. That super-wide, soft-compound, wet-racing rear was prone to drift on the aforementioned one-way systems. In the wet, obviously, the situation was reversed. But not much. Those Phantoms are *good* rubber.

In the end, there wasn't a lot to choose between them. They reflect different styles of Duke-dom: do it yourself quick chic, or buy it ready made.

Thanks to the folks at Motivation Motorcycles in Grange Road, Bermondsey, for the loan of the bike, which they'd prepared for a customer. Thanks to him, too. And see, I didn't crash it, not even once. Next time, lend it to me for longer, and let me rev it above 6000. Then we'll see if the Special Special can beat the factory special. **MS**

Ducati's Pantah 500

An owner reports

IN 1970 Ducati made a prototype 500 cc vee-twin (or "L-twin" as they like to call it). By the time it was put into production it had grown to 750, and later 900. Hopes that a 500 vee would one day become available were dashed when the 500 parallel twin was announced. A fast bike, no doubt, but, as D.L.M. wrote a few issues back ("Some People", March — Ed.), it sounded wrong, looked wrong, vibrated; and very few were sold. Rumours of a new 500 vee-twin with toothed-belt drive to the camshafts began afresh three years ago, and were confirmed when a prototype was shown in Italy. In August 1979 a Ducati Pantah was on show at Earls Court, and it was then that I decided I had to have one.

Continued on next page

Ducati's Pantah 500

Finally on 7 May 1980 I took delivery, from Sports Motorcycles in Manchester. This particular bike was to have been raced in the island as Sports Motorcycles' entry in Formula II, but a special works-prepared 600 cc Pantah had been promised from Italy, so the machine could be sold to a customer after all . . . to me. Naturally I agreed that my bike could be raced in the TT if the works 600 did not turn up.

As the bike is extracted from its crate and PDI'd by Pat Shinn's efficient crew, I hover around, pestering. Flashing indicators are left off on request — useless appendages — but the machine is otherwise totally standard, at this stage.

Now I set off to begin the running-in procedure. The handbook recommends not exceeding 6,000–6,500 revs for the first 300 miles, and goes on to say, ". . . we suggest travelling on hilly and tortuous roads, along which engine, brakes and suspensions are well tested and run-in." Since the specified rev. limit works out at over 90 mph in top (fifth) gear, I start with a short tour of the Peak District, taking in Matlock and Buxton; the A6 should be hilly and tortuous enough for anyone! It turns out that the boring running-in period I have experienced with 500s in the past does not arise. On the contrary, the main problem is finding roads where I can take the motor up to the recommended level without breaking my neck!

First impressions are of smoothness, quietness, docility. The engine starts at the touch of the button, every time; ticks over reliably at 1,000 revs; is quieter than a BMW; does not vibrate perceptibly at any speed. Just like riding a Japanese bike, really, and the Nippon Denso speeds and tach reinforce the impression. Compared with my 750 SS, the most striking differences are that handling the 500 through corners takes less effort, but keeping the PJF engine on the boil requires more. The shorter wheelbase, lower weight and quicker-steering geometry of the Pantah make chicanes and unexpected changes of line effortless, although none of the renowned stability of the 750 has been lost. No steering damper is fitted, and none is needed on any public road. Naturally the engine seems to be lacking in grunt, but the 750 is after all half as big again and exceptionally torquey for its size. Furthermore, noticeable inflexibility later turns out to be a characteristic of a new, tight engine. Fully run-in, the motor will accept more throttle at lower revs and the minimum non-snatch engine speed in top gear falls from 4,000 revs to below 3,000.

A minor but baffling problem holds me up for five minutes at a petrol stop; if the engine kill button, which is a rocker switch, is not pressed all the way into the "RUN" position, the bike will not start. When the petrol tank is filled to the brim from just on reserve, it takes 3½ gallons, so the half-gallon reserve makes up nearly the 4.18 gallons claimed in the manufacturer's handbook and the 20 litres permitted by Formula II regulations.

Although Pirelli tyres had been expected as a standard fitment, when the crate was opened they turned out to be Michelins. Never mind —

an opportunity to explore the handling properties and roadholding limits of the bike would be found later, when the original boots wore out (which did not take many miles) and tyres with a reasonable amount of stability and grip could be fitted. Opportunities to discover whether the brakes worked came sooner, however — they do work, just as well as reputation would lead one to expect three Brembo discs to; consistently, without fade, in wet or dry conditions regardless. The calipers are of the small, single-pin type fitted to other Italian 500s. Only the rubber hydraulic hoses mar the picture by allowing a barely-detectable trace of sponge, which will be cured as soon as I fit Aeroquip braided-steel hosing. Suspension is by Marzocchi, with exotic-looking bright red remote-reservoir shocks at the rear, complete with a Schrader valve for altering the air pressure inside. Wheels are gold anodized cast-alloy, six spoke Campagnolo-type but specially made for Ducati. I am happy to report that the spokes are straight; the recent fashion for bent spokes is one for which I have yet to hear an engineering justification, and indeed bent spokes are something many of us have spent a lifetime trying to avoid! Rear rim width is an incredibly generous WM4.

Sitting on the Pantah ought to be uncomfortable, from the look of the narrow seat, tall tank, clip-on handlebars and rear-set footrests fitted as standard. But remarkably a wide variety of differently sized people unanimously find the riding position comfortable. The seat, unusually, is of a shape which roughly corresponds with that of the part of the rider's anatomy into contact with which it is intended to come, and the footrests lie vertically below the saddle where they can best support a share of the rider's weight. The comparatively short wheelbase allows the traditional stance for clip-ons (i.e., stretched out

Opposite page: P.J.F. trying not to drop his week-old bike at VOC Cadwell in May. Opposite left: Frame consists of four horizontal tubes braced by several cross-members and gathered up to a generously gusseted steering head. Right: Neat pivoting lifting handle (lower left) makes using centre stand effortless, with no need to tug at the GRP enclosures. Below: Three-quarter fairing is fitted as standard

across the tank) to be avoided, and the controls to be reached easily. Passengers have more of a problem, though. Pillion footrests are provided and the seat, at first glance solo only, can be converted to accept a second person in one minute with a screwdricer (or or 2p piece will do), but the dual-seat is cramped and two full-sized adults would find a long journey arduous.

If you're getting impatient, hold on because I'm just getting to the important bits, like the frame and the engine. Both are recognizably in the Ducati style, both are totally new, and neither is anything like any frame or engine made by any other manufacturer.

The frame consists of four horizontal tubes braced by several cross members and gathered up to a generously gusseted steering head at the front, rather like the jib of a crane. The lower pair of tubes run along the *top* of the crankcases, which are suspended beneath them. If the lower rear part of the frame appears to be lacking in strength, it is because none is needed there; the pivoted fork (or "swinging arm") pivots not from frame lugs but from a boss on the back of the crankcases, in bushes which are continuously lubricated by the oil in the engine and are, therefore, expected to last indefinitely. Frame stresses are transmitted from crankcases to frame at three widely separated points on each side, in typical Ducati fashion. A very substantial set of chain-adjuster components, incorporating the Seeley-type alloy split clamps used on 900 SSs, adds the rigidity of the wheel spindle, wasted in so many designs, to that of the pivoted fork. However, it did not take Ron ("Maxton") Williams long to suggest improvements in the frame design — for a start, he said, the cross members could be arranged so as to make triangles instead of squares, and could be attached to the horizontal rails nearer to the engine-mounting points. On the other hand, he noticed, the superb ease of access to the carburettor, exhaust pipes, rocker covers and battery, among other things, would thereby be lost. Any motorcycle is a mass of compromises, and Ducati have already achieved both an exceptionally rigid frame structure and a high degree of accessibility. It would hardly be worth sacrificing the latter for a small enhancement of the former.

The engine is, of course, a 90° vee-twin, with a single overhead cam to each cylinder and desmodromic valves. Ducati's system for allowing themselves to use more radical cam profiles than anyone else by doing away with valve springs is too well-known now to need a detailed description here, and too successful to need justification. Cylinder dimensions are 74 mm bore by 58 mm stroke, oversquare to an extent typical in modern sports engines. Capacity is 498 cc and compression ratio 9.5 to 1. The cooling fins are cast longitudinally on the horizontal cylinder, circumferentially on the vertical one, and have numerous rubber inserts for the usual purpose of cutting down noise. Big-ends are side-by-side plain shells while the helical gear primary drive is on the right for the first time on a Ducati.

Camshaft drive arrangements are unusual, to say the least, and deserve a detailed description. From the left side of the crankshaft a pair of helical-cut spur gears, with 25 and 50 teeth, drive a half-time idler shaft which crosses to the right side of the engine along the crutch of the vee. On the end of the idler shaft is a toothed-belt pulley 1½ inches wide which drives two separate belts, each ¾ inch wide, to the camshafts. The back of each belt runs over a small fixed plain pulley on its working run, and over a slightly larger pulley mounted on an adjustable bolted up plate on the return run. These pulleys, ingeniously, consist simply of sealed ball races. Yes, that's right, the outer surfaces of the ball journals themselves serve as pulleys! Grit and rainwater are kept off the belts by simple cast-alloy covers, which of course do not have to be oiltight. Attached to each cylinder head, serving as the inner half of the belt cover, is a substantial black rubber casting. I confess I cannot recall any manufacturer who has ever used a sizeable rubber casting in an engine before — but no doubt some more knowledgeable reader will write in to enlighten me.

Ignition is mainly Bosch, but the electrical equipment is remarkable for the variety of proprietary manufacturers Ducati have employed. Two hundred watt altenator and voltage control: Ducati Elettro technica; ignition pickups and amplifiers: Bosch; coils: Nippon Denso; ignition switch and idiot lights:

Aprilia; fuse box: Hella; battery: Yuasa. The mixture works well, and most of the components are of the highest available quality. It is depressing that Joe Lucas has not managed to get in there somewhere.

Gear ratios fitted as standard result in calculated speeds, at the manufacturer's recommended rev. limit of 9,050 rpm, of approximately:

First Gear: 51 mph
Second Gear: 73 mph
Third Gear: 95 mph
Fourth Gear: 117 mph
Fifth Gear: 138 mph

In standard trim, the bike will certainly pull to the red line in fourth gear, but that is the highest speed obtainable, and top has to be regarded as an overdrive for long-legged motorway cruising. After certain modifications, though, and on certain downhill parts of the Isle of Man TT circuit, it will very nearly pull top gear. Still, for normal purposes the bike is vastly overgeared with the standard 38-tooth rear sprocket so I propose to run normally with 40 teeth for better acceleration in cities, and less need for gearchanging on open roads.

Detailing, a feature on which Ducati have fallen down in the past, is in the main excellent. Rubber mountings are used everywhere, including the rear mudguard bolts, the alloy plate on which the major electrical components are mounted, and the bulb holders inside the tail-lamp assembly. The entire wiring harness is well provided with multi-pin plugs so that dismantling and reassembly become foolproof. The petrol tank, although fully rubber-mounted, can be removed without tools in one minute — but only if you know how! The electric starter pre-engages when the engine stops turning, so there is no gnashing of Bendix drive pinions when you start up the next time. Exhaust pipes are double-skinned, Honda fashion, so no trace of bluing is visible.

Just in case you're wondering if the machine has no faults, the various deficiencies and much needed modifications will be discussed next month, together with accounts of racing a Pantah twice: part 1, an amateur at Cadwell, and part 2, a professional on the Island. P.J.F.

High Performing Italian 500s

Ducati Pantah

EXHIBITING PRE-PRODUCTION PROTO-types at motorcycle shows is a chancy business. If the bike is a show stealer, as Ducati's Pantah was when it first flashed a thigh at Cologne in 1978, it arouses a frenzied discussion whenever motorcyclists meet in pub, club, or at those kerbside Saturday socials outside the local dealer. The photos in the bike mags become torn and oil-stained as they circulate round the gang like the last bottle of wine at a party. Riders of other brands trash the factory's promises on horse-power and performance; the already-converted accept these claims just as surely as they know the sun will rise tomorrow. What the new bike now has to do is deliver when it hits the streets.

It's when a fanfared machine turns out to be a limp-wristed flop that the risk element in pre-launches becomes gruesomely evident to a factory. The critics chant 'Toldyaso', while the former disciples furtively cancel plans to trade in for the new model. Total disillusion-ment sets in. I wonder how many proponents of the Wankel engine actually laid out money for Suzuki's short-lived RE-5 once the grapevine told of its excessive fuel consump-tion and chain wear, the engine's weird back-firing effect and its gross complexity?

But the Ducati Pantah makes no mistake. This middleweight V-twin from Fabio Taglioni represents the best of everything that has come to be associated with Italian motor-

cycling, only more so. Italy's motorcycling renaissance has been in full swing for a decade now, and its factories have used that experience to become competent at produc-ing rounded-out bikes. In the early seventies their efforts were typified by delightful engines and chassis marred by tacked-on and often malfunctioning detail accessories. The Pantah is a polished, fully-fitted road traveller as well as a finely honed sports 500.

Yet virility hasn't been sacrificed in the transition to maturity. As with earlier Ducatis, a red-blooded engine is the focal point of this bike. And, also in the Ducati tradition, the unit is a 90-degree in-line Vee relying on a chain for final drive. Ducati's familiar desmodromic system opens and closes the valves, but the use of rubber belts in place of shafts and bevels to turn the single overhead camshafts is a new departure. The belts are cheap to make and silent in operation.

The 74 x 58mm engine breathes through a pair of massive — by 500cc standards — 36mm carburettors, and is claimed to produce 46bhp at 9,050rpm at the back wheel. It really is a beautiful motor. It's smooth, flexible, quiet, devoid of crude humps in its power curve — yet undeniably quick.

It shouts up to the 9,000rpm redline — OK, 9,050 for the fastidious — even at a rash 10,000rpm there is no hint of valve bounce or impending mechanical implosion. Precise control of the valves at very high speeds is one of the benefits of desmodromic opera-tion, which substitutes cam-directed rockers for springs for the closing function.

In top gear at 7,000rpm the Pantah is cruis-

ing — the word is deliberately chosen — at an indicated 100mph. The crudely optimistic speedo means that the true road speed at those revs is around 90mph, but that remains an impressive steady-rolling rate for a 500. In everything it does the Pantah's engine leaves an unmistakable message: it's Unburstable (though only time will tell).

This untiring performance is assisted by unusually tall gearing in an era when quick quarter-mile times are accepted as crucial sales propaganda. Getting a Pantah away from rest requires a little more clutch slip than is normal with a 500. And on long climbs or in the face of a strong wind the bike will some-times prefer a drop to fourth when most half-litre machines would pull through in top.

But riders with a taste for long distance motorcycling — and most Ducati owners seem to fall into that category — will gladly trade the chance to go traffic light drag racing for the Pantah's remarkably long-legged feel on the open road. In top gear it bowls along as effortlessly as many a four-cylinder bike of half as much capacity again. But then, a well-designed two-cylinder engine of the right layout — and that implies an opposed or a V-twin — will always feel less frantic than a four. Unlike most of the Japanese parallel twins, the Pantah has no balancer shafts and doesn't need them; its basic concept means that it is smooth enough without them. And, despite that highish gearing, it's not exactly a slouch when pointed up the drag strip.

Perhaps as impressive as the Pantah's per-formance is the lack of noise it makes. The contribution of the camshaft-drive belts has

Civil servant Peter Fisher (29) took his Pantah over to the TT as a spectator and was 'persuaded' to lend his bike to the Sports Motorcycles racing team who'd problems with theirs. Unfortunately, though the bike handled well and went well, rider Eddie Roberts had to retire with a slipping clutch. Peter has raced his in club events with the following mods: bell mouths instead of air filters on the carbs, strategic placed holes in the exhaust though all the baffles are still there, a 41t (standard 38t) rear sprocket to help it pull top gear, Girling Gas Shocks — changed because Girling had spare springs available at the TT and Marzocchi didn't, mirrors and indicators removed and a Dunlop KR124 racing tyre up front. It was slightly faster through our speed trap at 120.8mph but was still accelerating. An rpm check showed it to be doing 125.6mph at 10,200rpm.

already been noted, while the liberal use of rubber bungs between the cylinder fins plays a part in the sound-deadening process. But the Pantah is also inoffensive at its rear end, despite the Conti brand-name carried ominously on the silencers.

Some of the bigger Ducatis are equipped with Contis, and are generally credited with giving Europe more sleepless nights than almost anything. Maybe the silencer makers are feeling some remorse at this reputation, but whatever, they've arrived at components that allow the rider to slink home at night without leaving behind a trail of rattling window panes.

Yet here again sophistication has been gained with no loss in machismo. The flanks of the Pantah's fairing bounce the battle cry of the desmo Vee up to the rider's all-too-willing ears, and if you fling the tacho needle towards the red sector you are rewarded with an aural phenomenon not unlike a supercharged V8 drag engine howling towards 200mph from beyond an adjacent hill. Making the motor pull hard in a high gear at 4,000 to 6,000rpm results in a noise like one of the great old single-cylinder engines — G50 Matchless or Manx Norton — assaulting the Mountain Mile on the Isle of Man. The Pantah is a most entertaining bike to listen to, yet the stereo effects can be shut off on demand.

Those natty rubber belts, incidentally, need replacing every 20,000 kilometres (12,500 miles) — or so the handbook insists. And at £23.60 a pair plus VAT they suddenly don't seem such a cost-effective proposition after all. Yet belts performing similar jobs in car engines enjoy much longer lives, and one can't help wondering if Ducati haven't erred on the side of caution until they discover over a prolonged period of production just how durable these items can be. Checking for tension every 5,000 miles is accomplished by removing the seven screws attaching the two handsome cover plates to the right side of the engine.

The Pantah's vibrant engine is matched by superlative qualities of handling, steering and braking. The frame is based on the layout used on the bigger Dukes, conventional bottom rails being rejected in favour of a banana-shaped trelliswork. The lowest main frame tubes curve around each side of the upright cylinder, while further back extensions support the footrest, and the swinging arm pivots on the rear of the engine casing.

Suspension is Marzocchi all round, with an excellent set of front forks matched by gas shocks with separate reservoirs at the rear. Those rear legs contribute immensely to the satisfaction of riding the Pantah. Popular myth says that Italian bikes are plank-hard at the back end, but it's a stigma that newer Latin street racers like the Pantah are shaking off. The five-position Marzocchis ride the bumps well without ever degenerating into sogginess. On the softer settings the frame still has enough rigidity to hold the bike on line, while even on the next-to-hardest position there is almost none of the whack-on-the-backside punishment meted out so liberally by the old 450 Ducati singles.

Pantah handling is so fine that it's quite difficult for the average rider to approach its limits, especially on unfamiliar roads. There is

Above: The Pantah has a similar solo/dual humped seat as the Hailwood Replica. Three screws attach the seat — the toolkit is in the hump (for which you need the screwdriver to reach).

Above: The two 36mm Dell 'Orto carbs are fitted with remote choke and no ticklers.   **Below: Shades of Jap convenience — an oil level window. Ducati making things *easy*?**

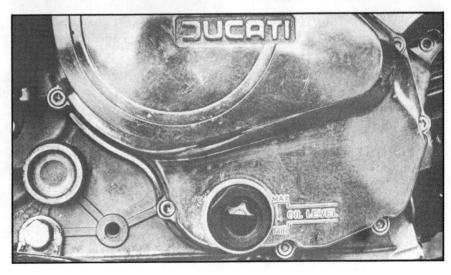

High Performing Italian 500s

no flex, wobble or weave with this bike. In fact the Pantah is so good that on initial experience it can even irritate. Lesser machines can be made to squirm quite easily, making the rider feel he's performing well by approaching the limits. When the Pantah is pushed, it simply responds. The chassis remains rigid, and the narrow engine makes for so much side clearance that you virtually have to be falling off before anything grounds.

I had a vivid illustration of Ducati handling qualities when fast-cruising the bike at 80 to 95mph along a sinuous road. Understand that I was distinctly *not* attempting to street-race, a fact that may explain my rather stupid inattention to the rear-view mirror. When I did snap a glance at it, I slowed at the sight of a white box in the far background. Too late: the 2500 Triumph hove to alongside with blue lights flashing and a black-sleeved arm inviting me to take a breather by the verge.

The driver stepped out to inform me that in that motor he was able to catch most things, but he hadn't been able to keep pace with the racy looking bike I was riding. And I stress, I hadn't been belting the Pantah that hard! Anyway, this friendly cop was certainly impressed by the Pantah's lines — so much so that he didn't even ticket me. In view of my gross violation of the two-lane 60mph limit his magnanimous act made me feel horribly ashamed of every snide comment I've ever spoken or written about the law . . .

All the Pantahs that had arrived in Britain at the time of writing had been shod with Michelins, but as an experiment the importers had fitted Pirelli Phantoms to the test machine. These covers are perfect for flipping the bike from side to side along a snaking back road, while their broad grip allows the rider to explore the Pantah's ground clearance to the full. They declined to wiggle even when poked into cat's eyes at 80mph on a streaming wet motorway.

Braking is handled by triple Brembo discs that work so well there is little to say about them. You squeeze the levers, they slow the bike; the more you squeeze, the faster they shed speed. But as well as being strong they are sensitive, so that the locking-up point can be approached without being crossed.

During the test mileage I spent two four-hour stints in the Pantah's saddle, periods that would be jail sentences on most clip-on equipped bikes. But Ducati know about riding positions; they know that you can't make clip-ons acceptable without a low seat height and properly located footrests to spread the rider's weight around all the body's contact points with the bike. At 32 inches the Pantah's seat height is not exceptionally low, yet it's still a comfortable machine. Thus 250-mile rides are no problem, while that spartan-looking seat offers quite generous support.

Top right: Fairing on the Pantah is effective and makes high speed cruising a cinch. Inside is a bit naff however.

Top left: It could only be a Ducati . . .

Right: Trellis frame and ancillaries suspended from it except air filter on top — that black rounded tube. Electrics are all packed in tight and access to the desmo valvegear is limited.

Rider stamina is assisted by the fairing, which at first seems a couple of sizes too large for a 500. But the screen tosses the wind neatly over the head, while a cruising range of about 170 miles minimises the hassle factor in long journeys.

For riders of average height the Pantah's detachable seat squab has no practical value, as no production 500 has sufficient kick-in-the-pants to make a backrest essential. But it's a good styling gimmick, and is easily removed by applying a coin to three screws. Then the three ragged-edged screw holes are visible along the edge of the main seat base — a set of grommets would be useful to plug these. Passengers have to take their chances on a skeletal pillion seat — and there's no grab rail, although, admittedly such a fitting would detract from the bike's looks.

Just a little of the old Italian abandon in the

provision of ancillary equipment still lurks about the Pantah. Efficient switchgear and big instruments are by Nippon Denso — but the rev counter is as fitted to a 900 Duke and hence incorrectly red-lined at 8,000rpm. Steering and tank locks are supplied — but the seat squab, seat and tools carried in the tailpiece are not vandal-proof. Electronic ignition and sight windows in the engine cases for checking the oil level and using a strobe light will ease maintenance chores — but the brake fluid reservoirs have basic and unprotected screw caps.

Generally, however, the Pantah is a fine motorcycle that can only add to the Italian industry's mounting prestige. It's horrendously expensive for a 500 — just £100 more will buy you a *v. des.* GSX1100 Suzuki — but a minority of bikers will always be prepared to pay for something special.

MIKE HAILWOOD would have cried. After only two days of "ownership" the Hailwood replica Ducati was falling apart around my ears.

Compression was down on the front cylinder, the clutch cover was chucking oil out over the back tyre and there was more smoke coming from the exhaust than you would expect from a TZ750 on full power.

After a day of testing at the Motor Industry Research Association track, in company with the Kawasaki Z1000H, the evil John Robinson surveyed the two machines parked side by side. "Yours is looking decidedly second-hand" was his only comment. Sure enough, the Ducati was dripping oil from one of its cam box covers.

The answer was to take the bike back and start again. Dave Martin, workshop supremo at Coburn and Hughes, had been on holiday when the Ducati *wasn't* checked out for our road test. He soon had the bike sorted out, cured the oil leaks and fitted a new front cylinder head to rectify the lack of power.

Make no mistake: this bike had had a hard life. The clock showed 8000 miles of press use — or should that read abuse? It had been both thrashed and crashed, not

SHOWMAN'S SPECIAL

to mention generally abused and we feel that this is the reason for the rather slow top speed of 126mph — although it didn't feel that slow when the fuel filler cap burst open, spraying petrol straight into the riders face!

The machine is basically a Ducati 900SS production racer which the factory have "tarted up" with Sports Motorcycles/Mike Hailwood style tank, seat and fairing.

Cafe racers normally have very cramped riding positions but the Ducati is such a big bike that you have a fair amount of room to shift about and get reasonably comfortable. There is a lot of weight on the wrists, but then you always get that with clip-on bars.

No electric starter is fitted and when using the kickstart lever you have to be a man. Kick the Ducati in half-hearted way and it will kick you back! No chokes are fitted to the 40mm carbs and to start from cold you give it two handfuls of throttle which causes the carbs to pump a couple of squirts of neat petrol into the bores.

Once it does fire up the exhaust note is lovely. It is the sort of bike that gathers crowds when it is parked, and there is always a little so-and-so who stands too close and has to touch the controls. Kick the bike into life with an extra big handful of twistgrip and the sudden crash of the exhaust will send him scuttling back as the rest of the crowd rock back on their heels. It costs you petrol but it's good fun.

Riding about in town traffic isn't quite such good fun because the clutch is very heavy — this may have been especially "doctored" for *MCM* because we had a lot of trouble with the 900SS clutch when we tested that model. With high gearing you tend to use only the first couple of ratios for moving from one set of lights to the next and the restricted lock isn't condusive to weaving in and out of queues.

On the open road the bike comes into its own, taking to motorways or country lanes like a duck to water. The ride is very hard, even with the suspension on the softest setting but I was quite prepared to put up with that in order to retain the "tight" feel, and the superb steering.

On the motorway the bike is as solid as a rock and through long sweeping bends it is dead steady. It doesn't flick from left to right like some lightweights will, but this only adds to the safe feeling.

At most roundabouts you don't have to slow at all, just shifting the weight to the inside and pointing a knee into the bend is all that is required. The Pirelli tyres are as good as any road tyre I have tried and will take a lot of power with the bike cranked over. Steering on the throttle is quite easy and never gives any "nasty" moments.

Above anything else you are left with the lasting impression of a safe, solid feel. Other bikes go just as quickly around the corners but they don't *feel* anything like as good.

Total straight line performance isn't shattering but it is quick 12.77 seconds for the standing quarter isn't a disgrace for a bike with such a high first gear. Getting off the line in a hurry is quite difficult. Not enough revs and clutch slip makes the engine bog down, while too much lofts the front wheel in the air and you lose time. Changing to second at peak revs also lifts the front wheel.

What you can't measure is the easy power delivery that makes the bike so nice to ride on the road. Although the 40mm carbs won't take full throttle below 70mph in top, you can feed in real pulling power at low revs giving the motor more and more gas as the rpm build up.

We tried a top gear roll-on against the Z1000H and the Duke with a sick motor would just about hold its own up to 100mph — pretty good against the most flexible Z1000 that Kawasaki have ever produced — and it has a 140cc capacity advantage.

All Ducatis have a special feel that is hard to define and the Hailwood replica has that bit more going for it. Once aboard you can't help showing off. Coming up behind

Below: Chain adjustment is simply a matter of loosening the spindle nut and screwing up the adjuster nuts.

Right: Brembo discs give instant stopping power from light lever pressure. Marzocchi forks are stiff and sure.

Big tank and broad fork yokes give the Hailwood Replica a wide feel. The fairing costs £500 give or take a few bob.

a family saloon car I always held back waiting for the "audience" to take notice. It was never long before at least a couple of expectant faces appeared at the back window.

Cruising along in top gear I would wait for several seconds to elapse so that the finger pointing and waving could take place and then make my move. This always follows a set pattern. First off I would have a very obvious look up the road which told my admirers that I was about to overtake.

Having put that idea in their minds I would give the motor a good "bark" to change down a gear, the "audience" catches its breath but I would hang on for a

Below: Giant 40mm Dell'Ortos feature primer pumps. No chokes are fitted. Bellmouths are plastic.

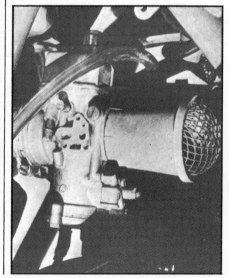

second to let their expectation build and then go down *another* gear and blast past.

As any great showman will tell you: timing is everything.

Another way of showing off was to use the superb braking power — shooting past a row of cars and other bikers going into a roundabout, slamming the brakes on at the last instant, maybe making the tyres squeal if I really wanted to put on a show.

It's just that sort of bike. It isn't sensible in any aspect. It's just a great big expensive toy that gives endless hours of riding pleasure — I loved every minute of it.

Dave Walker

Testers verdict *(points out ten)*

Performance	8
Economy	8
Handling	9
Comfort	6
Appearance	9
Equipment	7
Braking	9
Value for money	7

Solid state regulator/rectifier is made by Ducati Electronica. Ignition is electronic.

This portion of the seat unbolts to reveal pillion space.

ENGINE
SOHC, 90 deg V twin with desmodromic valve gear. Magnetic transducer/CDI ignition, two 49 mm Dell'Orto carburettors, wet sump lubrication, 12V alternator, 12 Ah battery.

displacement	863.9 ccm
bore x stroke	86 x 74.4 mm
compression ratio	9.5:1

GEARBOX
Helical gear primary drive to multiplate clutch, five speed gearbox and final drive by chain.

primary reduction	70/32
final reduction	16/36

gearbox ratios: 2.237; 1.562; 1.204; 1.00 and 0.887

CHASSIS
Front tyre	3.50/V18
Rear tyre	4.25/85V18
Wheelbase	59 inch
Castor	60.5 deg
Trail	n/a
Overall length	87.4 inch
Overall width	26.6 inch
Dry weight	415 lb
Fuel tank capacity	5.6 gal

List price inc. VAT and delivery £2,399.
Warranty: 6 months/6,000 miles plus 1 year Autoguard (engine and gearbox only).

PERFORMANCE
Maximum speed	127 mph
Standing ¼-mile	12.77 secs

Speeds in gears at 7,900 rpm (note: wide range of optional sprockets available.)

1st	55 mph
2nd	79 mph
3rd	102 mph
4th	123 mph
5th	139 mph

FUEL CONSUMPTION
best			58 mpg
worst			40 mpg
average	over	test	49 mpg

TOP SPEED
Hailwood Ducati	127 mph
Suzuki GS1000	126 mph
Honda 900 FZ	125 mph (wet track)
Kawasaki Z1000 A3	131 mph
Yamaha XS1100	126 mph

SS ¼ MILE
Hailwood Ducati	12.7s
Suzuki GS1000	12.4s
Honda 900 FZ	12.7s (wet track)
Kawasaki Z1000 A3	12.3s
Yamaha XS1100	12.3s

AVERAGE FUEL CONSUMPTION
Hailwood Ducati	49 mpg
Suzuki GS1000	44 mpg
Honda 900 FZ	37 mpg
Kawasaki Z1000 A3	43 mpg
Yamaha XS1100	39 mpg

PRICE
Hailwood Ducati	£2899
Suzuki GS1000 EN	£1995
Honda 900 FA	£2099
Kawasaki Z1000 A3	£2049
Yamaha XS1100	£2280

rpm	bhp	torque lb-ft
4000	39	52
4500	47	55
5000	52	55
5500	56	54
6000	59	51
6500	62	50
7000	66	49
7500	67	47
8000	65	43

WHEN THE DUCATI FIRST APPEARED on our streets in 1977, it was a new departure for the Bologna firm in that all the parts that had previously let the rest of the bike down by virtue of their inferior quality were replaced by imported components. Out went the notoriously ropey Aprilla electrics in favour of Bosch equipment from West Germany; the ridiculously small Veglia instruments were replaced by larger, more accurate clocks from Japan. The switchgear received similar treatment and so, the criticisms that had been justifiably aimed at Ducatis were not applicable to the Darmah.

The 1980 Darmah differs only a little from the first model, so it seems that the mix was right. The kickstart has gone for this year and the pretty tail fairing has been modified so that it now lifts up to give access to a small compartment for stashing the odd item. Cosmetically, the most important change has been to drop the ugly, seamed silencers and replace them with a much smarter pair. Over the three years of its production run, minor changes have made the Ducati a refined and quite desirable bike and all it needs now is a more durable finish to make it a hundred percenter.

The suffix SD stands for Sports Desmo which tells you that the Darmah is fitted with a soft version of the fire breathing SS motor. It still has the unique and unburstable Desmod-

DARMAH:
The Open Road Beckons

Ain't no place like home — and that for the Ducati Darmah is
thundering along a twisty lane. Test by Jim Lindsay.
Photography by Colin Curwood.

DARMAH: The Open Road Beckons

romic valve gear of the SS but the power output, which remains Ducati's secret, is lower due to the 40mm Del'Orto carburettors having to breathe through the emission conscious air filtration system as opposed to the gaping bellmouths of its compatriots, a lower compression ratio and a pair of mufflers that reduce the Darmah's voice to a polite V-twin thump rather than a raucous bellow.

A kickstart would have been useful on the few occasions during the test when the electric instep only just managed to nudge the motor into life. It only happened after short urban hops so, presumably, the battery needs a few milesworth of charging to recover from the drain the starter motor puts on it. The Darmah is not intended as a town bike so the criticism is not a severe one, but it is one hell of a weight if you end up having to bump start it.

The odd hiccough apart, starting is an easy business provided you quickly get used to contorting your hand to reach behind the left side panel to flood the rear carb. Yes, the Darmah is ticklish like the other Dukes, apart from the Pantah. It's as traditional as flooding the monoblocs on a pre-unit Trumpet though a bit fiddly for a bike purporting to be a tourer.

Flooding is only necessary when the motor is stone cold; when warm, a couple of twists on the throttle to let the accelerator pumps on the Dell'Ortos squirt in some extra gas is all that's needed before thumbing the starter button.

It's a large motor so it takes about ten miles before it's good and hot and able to deliver its full performance. Power delivery is completely different from the 900SS — it's a much easier engine to live with, whether you want to lope along two-up at sixty or charge illegally along the highway like a maniac. It hasn't much more breath left at the ton, but it'll keep that up for mile after mile. Heavy handed hammering of this type does lead to oil mist developing on some parts of the engine, mainly around the clutch cover sealing faces, the gearstick shaft boss and, wettest of all, on and around the rev counter drive gearbox on the top of the front cylinder head. You may call this unforgiveable in these oil-tight days, it seemed to me to be an acceptable hassle of owning a Duke.

Maintaining Ducati engines is not an easy task especially when it comes to setting the valves of the desmo mills. The engine has to come out of the frame before the rear head can be worked on — not a mammoth task but a bit of a bind if you have to do it once every 5000 miles.

Small stuff you can do yourself is also a bit on the wrong side of awkward; like checking the oil. The box spanner in the toolkit for removing the hexagon headed dipstick-cum-filler plug can only just be persuaded into place and once you get it firmly on the nut, you've got to rotate the spanner anticlockwise — not as simple as it sounds 'cos the tommy bar hits everything in sight. One fine Wednesday morning, I threw up my hands in despair then rode to the tool shop to buy a 20mm combination spanner.

Better tell you about adjusting the chain while we're on the subject of awkward maintenance tasks. The Darmah swingarm is mounted on eccentric cams which are sec-

ured in their housings by pinch bolts. To adjust the chain, you move the swinging arm backwards or forwards and therefore, unlike almost every other road bike, the relative positions of the wheel and the swingarm remain constant. The advantage is that it rules out the possibility of getting the back wheel out of line. The disadvantage is that it can be a bitch of a job to do. The tool in the kit supplied for rotating the cams broke the second time I used it, whereafter I had to lash up a weird system with Mole grips and a massive screwdriver; it worked and caused no damage but it was an unnecessary nuisance.

Ducati freaks are more than prepared to put up with the odd, tedious idiosyncrasy though. Fatuous as it may sound, it all adds up to the mystique of what is a Very Wonderful Motorcycle.

To people used to slant-eyed clutches the action of the Darmah clutch will be a bit heavy. Don't let that put you off though, it's not actually in the wristbreaking class. You've no doubt heard of the tendency for Ducati clutches to slip when fed full power. Don't let the stories worry you. It's only the SS models that produce too much power for their clutches. Brutality on the test strip and repeated replays of the traffic lights grand prix failed to produce the slightest hint of slip. It takes up the drive nice 'n smooth and is a pleasure to use, good solid stuff y'know.

The ratios in the gearbox are well picked but the test bike we had suffered from a notchy change that was a drag in traffic on the occasions when it just plain refused to downshift. That's worrying when you're bearing down indecently quickly on a line of traffic and needing the box to slow you up. It's even more alarming when you're careering full tilt at a corner leaving the retardation until the last possible second, you want third and you can't get it. You know the scene, accelerated heart rate, heavy braking and finally lugging the brute out of the bend in too high a gear, thoroughly choked off about the devalued quality of that piece of riding.

The overall gearing is tall but the immense torque of the engine means that this isn't a problem. When threading through town traffic around 40 per, third is the best ratio to use since it allows reasonably smooth progress while leaving enough acceleration to cope with most situations.

Unlike its Japanese counterparts in the world of touring bikes who, by and large, are happy enough on the urban circuit, the Ducati does not like towns. It gets hot and bothered, the gearbox action become sticky and the suspension which is harsh compared with the squashy setups on Jap machines, starts to get on the rider's nerves at low speeds when he can feel every irregularity on the road surface.

Above: Latest Marzocchi rear shox have a separate fluid reservoir. Apart from looking trick, they're compliant and nicely controlled.

Below: Lockable seat hump toolbox is surprisingly large — room for a chain lube aerosol.

Take the Ducati for a lengthy blast on twisty open roads however, and you'll really appreciate the firmness of the ride. It's not in the SS class but it still tracks like a train on bends no other big tourer does half as well. What you get is constant feedback through the seat of your pants and through the handlebars. Two up, luggage laden, high speed razzling is always fun on the Duke and never the alarming trip that it can turn out to be on lesser motorcycles.

Dashing up the A420 from Bristol to Didcot one Sunday en route to Uncle Bunt's with a friend on the back, I executed a quick crazy by taking a line of motors on the outside of a fast (can't tell you just how fast) uphill left hander. We hit a series of potholes, the bars

Above: Darmah is now equipped with 'tame' version of the Desmo 860cc engine and breathes through air filters and normal silencers.

twitched violently from side to side, 'Oh dear' I thought to myself, 'don't like this very much'. In due course, the twitching stopped, we'd passed the line of cars and the bike hadn't moved away from the line I'd chosen. That type of handling gives you tremendous confidence to hurl the machine about as if it weighed 350lb instead of the 500 it does tip the scales at. Man, you got to be a real idiot to fall off a Darmah.

The Darmah has a different chassis from its quicker brothers and when you crank it hard over at high speed, there's a noticeable little twitch but not so much as to be alarming. More ground clearance would be useful, the centre stand had been quite extensively modified by left hand corners. It was interesting to compare it with the Laverda's Jarama — soft 'cooking' version of the 1000cc triple — on one trip we made together. I was very conscious of having to push the Laverda through the roundabouts, leaning hard to make it go over while Barry on the Ducati was flicking in

and out of the same roundabouts effortlessly with a big grin on his face.

When you approach a hazard on the Darmah, thought and action are inseparable. Decide how you're going to get through and almost before you're aware of any action having taken place, the bike has done exactly what you intended to with no hiccoughs or hesitation.

The Pirelli Phantom tyres are capable of coping adequately with all degrees of rider insanity whether the roads are bone dry, slightly greasy or soaking wet. On the minus side, the rear boot, which was virtually new when I collected the bike, was suffering from premature baldness some 2000 miles later. That's an excessively high rate of rubber consumption but seems the necessary premium to pay for top performance. Want longer tyre life? Have to suffer less grip then.

The Marzocchi remote reservoir dampers keep the back end doing what it should, and forks from the same manufacturers take care of the business up front. They work well; on fast and bumpy lanes no evidence of fade rears its malevolent head, even under severe pressure.

Considering that the SD is a tourer, the pillion portion of the seat could do with thicker padding and contours less inclined to hurl the passenger against the rider's back under even quite gentle braking. Also with the tourer theme in mind, a modest grab rail would be a useful addition even if it might slightly spoil the pretty lines of the back of the seat.

The electrics were remarkably well behaved throughout the test. The left indicator warning light packed up, as did the propstand warning light. The Mickey Mouse switch on the latter system was to blame, giving up the ghost after its first outing in the rain. Why all bikes aren't fitted with a Bosch 65/55 Watt headlamp is beyond the power of my poor brain to grasp. It's a superb unit with enough throw and penetration to steam along A roads in the dead of night in perfect safety. The illuminations are all controlled by ND switchgear which is reliable and easy to lay your hands on. There's one criticism I have to make: the on/off switch and the dipswitch are side by side on the left handlebar cluster and operate in the same plane. It's possible to turn out the lights instead of merely dipping — pretty scarey on unlit roads.

The finish on the Darmah is appalling. Even after a thorough clean up, the bike looked about two years old rather than the 1980 machine with a mere three grand on the clock. Bad, bad news. The list is thus: poor chroming on the exhausts and mudguards, more bloom than you'll see in Springtime Spalding on the gas tank paintwork, rust on the frame tubes in several places and unsightly corrosion on the crankcase castings. Ain't good enough for a cycle that'll cost you in the region of two and a half Gs to put on the road.

The 900SD has got what it takes to tour in comfort, or most of it at least. It's not dramatically fast but it'll pull a steady 85 per all day two up without flagging. The motor is ninety degree, vee smooth. Stick on a fairing, a set of panniers and a better seat if two up riding is the game, and you're set to have some fine fun that won't come too pricey on the gas.

The Darmah Bums
Zen Beat Goes On

Zen Object Lesson Number One – Some Ducatis Break Down Some Of The Time. Ergo – never trust a Ducati. Especially if it's yours and especially if it's been running perfectly.

Take heed, be warned, that the yin yang nature of the Ducati teachings is such that it equates joyfulness with misery. Every high is positively tempered by a low. Every soulful mile down the road is mated with yet another nail in the heart at the roadside. For every Isle of Man legend there is a first lap loser.

Ducatis are both exotic and esoteric. They yield their secrets only after considerable study. They will steal your emotions as surely as they will steal your money. They seem to exist at the very meeting point between two parallel worlds. Twin domains of excellence and excruciation. Ducatis are not for born suckers, but they impart great lessons of suckerdom during ownership.

Zen Object Lesson Number Two – Don Juan never rode a Darmah.

Or if he did, he certainly never rode ours. It not being hard to forget about romantic and mystical pilgrimages to Ixtlan, when you're doing your best trying to make Islington by nightfall.

Yet, as a fully paid-up convert and subscriber to the Ducati cause, I know that the rewards of owning one far outstrip the penalties. Being of The Faith, baptised in hellfire and boiling sump oil, I am aware that the transcendent buzz one can attain on a Duke is of the purest, sweetest and most sensual nature this side of teendream carnal knowledge.

But there is screwing and there is being screwed. And in this case it's being inflicted by a laughing, fat Ducati demon of malicious and dubious pleasures.

Final Object Lesson – not all the fire-engine red things in the perfumed garden are roses.

Of course, there's a lot you can do to avoid the weeds and the thorns. Weekly maintenance of a thorough variety helps considerably. Common ownership where the bike gets treated like the oldest whore among bros does it no good at all.

Anyway, I was thinking about Zen and Ducatis while admiring the stationary view from the driving seat of the office Darmah on a sweaty Friday afternoon in rush hour London. It was not healthy. The deal was for me to take our own Darmah to Luton in order to collect the spanking new '80 Darmah for

test. The signs were bad. Maybe I was just tempting fate and the fat hobgoblin. Maybe our own Duke wasn't too impressed with the scam. Whatever. . . . This bike was might sick, yet again in a life that has been wrecked with silly, nagging complaints.

There was a curious metal, but muffled knocking noise coming from the front pe being amplified back by the fairing. Was a piston or a big end? The clutch wa on the fast escalator out anyway. The cable broke, it slipped and needed constan adjustment, you couldn't find neutral eve with the precision needed to operate the ha a gearchange that remained. We had new clutch plates and springs, but hadn't go round to putting them in.

Up top, the electrics were a mess – n warning lights, only one of the twin Cibi beams working, no ignition keyhole, just plastic switch and two loose wires. N wiring loom for the headlights, just a snak puffball of wires stuffed behind the consol and held together and down with odd bits o Sellotape. No indicators of the workin variety, and a defunct speedo.

There was very little tread on the rear tyr and the awful possibility of a slow punctur or leaky valve. The throttle cables snappe with hideous precision. This one was si weeks old and way overdue. I feared for i life. The back brake was working but the dis so badly scored and pitted that it didn matter much. The swing-arm bushes ha been shot for a long time.

The real trouble was that this bike had fou nurses and no doctor. It's easier to hate and avoid it rather than repair it. And doin the easy bits is no substitute for care an cure.

I sat in the traffic queue and contemplate the rust on the filler cap and my inhuman lot. There is a depth to futility – it is perhap the greatest Zen lesson of all.

I never made it to Luton on that Frida afternoon. About five miles short of th motorway, the main ignition wire fell out an everything died. By the time Uncle Bodge and myself had sussed the Ducati Esoteric Electric problems, and cured a few bypasse and dead ends along the way, it was too lat to go anywhere except home.

"Oh mama . . . can this really be the end To be stuck outside of Highbury with th Darmah blues again."

This road test was timely. After nearl three years of dogged and faithful service our own staff Darmah is due for retirement And I for one shall miss it.

A fabled, fated and much abused beast the office Darmah has earnt its release from the daily stresses of inner city journalisti life and is looking for a new and quiete existence. There's nothing much wrong with it that can't be fixed, and it's being primed fo action right now.

A new Darmah is something else though something to be relished and savoured That's how it is with the all-encompassing Duke experience. At its highest level you have to reach for the word-jar labelled "superlatives". Pseuds Corner is but the first hurdle on the road to true Ducati under-standing. At its lowest level you have to reach for a fistful of tools and an encyclo paedic knowledge of the marque's mechanics that can only, repeat *only*, be gained from owning one. It's not hard, it jus has to be done – and it's educational and re warding, most of the time.

Taking hold of a new Ducati after month of faceless Jap bikes is like scoring a smoke after a three week drought. It clears you head and hones your perceptions. It also does wonders for your riding. You're back in the world of real motorcycles see? This one even handles like a real motorcycle. And brother, for that one essential quality, I can forgive a lot.

The 1980 Darmah Sport Desmo offers quite a few changes from previous models. And it is almost certainly the best yet in a chequered career where year by year, the Ducati factory perversely release an updated revision, never ever taking any notice of previous worldly criticism. Nope, they never take any notice of the changes that *need* to be effected, but they just blithely bring out a new and different and usually better model all the same.

The performance hasn't changed though. It's still that strange combination of medium to good acceleration, reasonable top end and perfect handling. Smooth and exciting almost everywhere.

By today's ultrabike standards this bike is slow. More relevantly, it's slow compared to the Darmah Super Sport, the SS and especially the Hailwood Flyer. But that's because this is the soft option, the softly tuned engine. They bill it as a tourer (joke).

Does 62bhp at 7000rpm and a realistic top speed of 110mph sound slow to you? It shouldn't. Because this bike will beat the living shit out of any 1-litre Jap iron over a series of good and twisty country roads. Other bikes may be quicker, but no Oriental steed can live with it where it matters, in the bends and the turns.

Neither ultra-quick nor slouchy, the Darmah Express begins with an almost perfect power/weight ratio (62bhp/498lb wet). Most of that weight is low. There's a low centre of gravity and a low seat height (29 inches). And it's also narrow, everything being held classically and longitudi-nally within the semi-spine frame.

The Darmah's heart can be found in that tireless old performer, the 864cc 90 degree Vee-twin engine. The drive from the crank begins with reduction gears, is carried through helical bevels to a single overhead camshaft that lifts the opening and closing rockers of the desmo valves. Perfect.

The result is 864cc of slugging, gritty and high performance torque which picks up really low down from around two grand pulling to a peak of 47.8lb/ft at 5750. Once it's rolling, the high gears help it stretch right up to and just past the 8500 red-line. At 5000 it's topping 80mph, at the ton it's nudging 7500 and still feeling under-stressed. The bevel gears whirring happily, the desmo valves closing positively, and the hungry mill just eating the miles.

Changes this time round amount to the absence of the kickstart (the cover's blanked off, but you may well be able to fit a pinion, springs and pedal). Then there's some nice fat 40mm Dell' Ortos. These pumpers don't seem to have affected the perform-ance much, except perhaps in cleaning up some earlier breathing problems. The old model carried 32mm carbs and seemed a bit slow coming on to the main jet at low revs. It always felt like it was choking unless you really wound it up. The new Darmah pulls like a train everywhere, so the major benefit has been better breathing in the low to middle range.

The frame is classic Darmah which in turn is classic GTS, with the top tubes and rear subframe curved to drop the seat height. If there was ever a perfect frame, this one comes close. It must be one of the sturdiest around. The open cradle spine format has the twin downtubes bolting directly on to the crankcase at the front. Under the tank,

there's a single tube which runs from the top of the chunky headstock to meet a pair of smaller tubes which run back from the bottom and are cross braced all the way. At the very back there's a trick triangular section for the rear footrests. Strong, light, very well designed and superbly crafted, the frame will die for you rather than flex a millimetre.

Suspension this time out features trusty Marzocchi units front and rear. The front forks are the same beautifully chromed and well sprung items as before, but there's an extra spacer because of the increased height at the back. The rear 'zocchi units are all new and offer five-way preload as well as adjust-able damping, courtesy of the remote reservoir which runs at 28psi. This makes the back suspension firmer than before and is just right for the weight. With increased rear wheel travel, the whole back end now stands so high that they've had to fit a bigger centrestand just to get the wheel off the ground. On the road you get deliciously precise damping. No bounce, no pitch, nothing but perfectly regulated spring control. With the preload on three and the damping as standard, the bike was easily keeping pace with a fast Laverda around our small and snaky test track.

The Pirelli Gordon front and Phantom rear stuck tenaciously to a line, while the suspension dealt firmly and without fuss with both the large bumps and the angle of attack. Again, the sturdy Ducati swing-arm needs praise for this. And again its eccentric mounting means that chain adjustment can be effected without the wheels ever possibly going out of alignment. Perfect.

The seven-position steering damper is still there and still has precious little effect except at high speed where it helps avoid a weave above 105mph. It isn't really necessary even then because the bike has a long wheelbase (61 inches) and sits down comfortably at speed.

The steering is extremely light though. Sitting up high, superbike style, poised between the flat bars, the bike can be effort-lessly flicked from line to line and angle to angle.

Cornering is very much a matter of how fast you want to go, because at any speed it goes through smoothly and on a perfect line. The real trick is to get the power on early coming out of the turn, getting the bike up and letting it rip through the gears until that inevitable moment when the clutch starts slipping.

Ducati clutches are unique. What else has a nine-piece ball, roller, pushrod and actuating arm system, three points of cable adjustment and eight working plates that need regularly boiling in detergent to

preserve any semblance of steely grip?

Mechanically beautiful, but only mechanically wonderful sometimes, the importers, Coburn and Hughes had tried the time-honoured method of fitting bigger 450 springs to this one to eliminate the dreaded slip. This worked fine for a while, you had to engage neutral from a rolling second and develop extra muscles along your left arm, but other than the slightest hint of top gear, high speed slip, it was dandy.

Over two weeks, it got worse. It could be adjusted. Then the cable broke. We replaced it. It broke again. And again . . . Ducati allow for virtually no free play in their cables. The bigger springs made the assembly tight anyway, but the puny cables don't help. Result – a big Zen lesson in trauma and utter disbelief.

The throttle cable broke the first day we had it, but that's about par for the course.

You can always get home though. The Darmah has so much low torque that the clutch is just a convenience for traffic lights. The throttle cables are weak, but then so is the idea that it should be a one into two (via a junction box) arrangement.

Only believers bleed. But as an owner you're going to have to take care of that clutch system like no other. Set it up right and keep it adjusted and it will probably never let you down.

The bad things about the Darmah amount to poor cables, a sensitive clutch and some doubtful electrics. That's it. That's the whole list. And the rest is so wonderful, you're soon going to forgive these minor complaints. The electrics aren't that bad really. The neutral light comes on in third, but the Nippon Denso dials and switchgear all work fairly well, if not accurately. The riding position's nice too. The wide flat bars are slightly angled upwards and out, and you can get a good grip on the 3.3 gallon tank with your knees. The gearchange is fast, and the back brake has considerable travel. And the Brembo brakes are, of course, . . . wait for it . . . superb! (I knew you'd be surprised.)

Ground clearance on both sides is hampered by the pegs. This baby corners so low, and with such little fight or effort on the part of the rider, it's wise to keep your feet well tucked in and out of the way.

Other changes include a new seat/duck-tail styling, more streamlined than before with a folding and lockable stash space at the rear. Unfortunately the seat now bolts down via two fiddly Allen screws underneath. The tasty gold wheels aren't Campagnolos, they're made by FPS, are all aluminium alloy, look and feel just as good and are considerably cheaper. Exhausts are Ducati Silentiums which are OK, but tend to rust over the years. Contis are better, noisier

and inevitably, more expensive.

Finally, there are new standardised fuel taps. Up for reserve, down for on – all very sensible I suppose, but I liked the old fashioned flow system of one forward, one back. Silly innit?

Fuel consumption, despite the bigger carbs, remains good. We consistently returned plus 40mpg figures on a variety of roads and even at the track the worst figure was only 36mpg.

Any colour you like as long as it's red or black/gold (the paintwork is a treat). Yours for a shade under £2400, which is cheap for such an exemplary ride.

What more can you say? This is one of the most finely balanced motorcycles you can buy. It's got faults, but they are by far outweighed by the virtues. Even Zen teaches that excellence is many-faceted. It's a safe, smooth and exhilarating ride.

The very best road riders are smooth, fast and unobtrusive. You don't notice them until they're past you. It's a matter of control and concentration. Getting the best out of a Darmah isn't hard because it's relaxing to ride fast, and so obviously outperforms almost everything else on the road. The Darmah Super Sport is better. The SS is better still. The Hailwood Replica is the finest of them all. It's like a royal ancestral family. A dukedom. The standards start high and just get higher.

And now, sadly, ours is up for grabs, and we shall all miss its performance and its personality. Somewhere there exists a perfect Ducati. I've seen them. Some of them are still being raced in Formula One. By definition, the perfect Ducati is owned and cared for by someone who knows and loves what makes Ducati motorcycles such a rare and sweet experience. One day I'll find it. Because one day it will be mine. **JC**

Ducati Darmah 900 SD
£2399

PERFORMANCE
Maximum Speed – 110mph
Standing Quarter Mile – 12.4 secs
Fuel Consumption – Hard Riding – 40mpg
– Cruising – 45mpg
Best Full-Tank Range – 148.5 miles

ENGINE
Type – 90 degree Vee twin, air-cooled, single overhead camshaft desmodromic valve gear
Displacement – 864cc
Power – 62bhp at 7000rpm
Torque – 47.8lb/ft at 5750rpm
Bore & Stroke – 86 x 74.4mm
Compression Ratio – 9.3:1
Induction – two Dell 'Orto, 40mm
Exhaust – two into two with balance pipe
Oil System – wet sump
Ignition – Bosch (electronic)

TRANSMISSION
Clutch – wet, multiplate (see text)
Primary Drive – helical gears
Final Drive – chain

CHASSIS
Frame – open cradle, spine type
Front Suspension – telehydraulic forks (Marzocchi)
Rear Suspension – swing-arm and shox (five-way adjustable spring preload), adjustable damping in remote reservoir (Marzocchi)
Wheelbase – 61in
Seat Height – 29in
Weight (wet) – 498lb
Fuel Capacity – 3.3 gall
Tyres – Pirelli Gordons front 3.50 x H18; rear 4.25 x H18
Brakes – triple Brembo discs

INSTRUMENTS
150mph speedo, 11 000rpm tach red-lined at 8000rpm; warning lights for sidestand, lights, neutral, main beam, generator and indicators

EQUIPMENT
Electrical – 12V 36 A/H battery, 200w alternator
Lighting – Bosch H4 headlamp

Test bike supplied by Coburn and Hughes, 51-61 Park Street, Luton, Bedfordshire

OWNER SURVEY
DUCATI V-TWINS

Handling Alone is Worth the Price of Admission.

Surely there is no motorcycle more specific in design and intent than the Ducati. It's not a multi-purpose or dual purpose machine. A Ducati is used soley for sport; it's made to carry an excited rider down a snake-like road satisfying a lust for speed.

How satisfying the Ducati is can be answered by the owners. Responses to this survey came from owners of 55 Ducatis,

including 16 750 GTs, four 750 Sports, one 750 Super Sport (desmo), 13 860 GTs, five 900 GTSs, 11 900 Darmahs and five 900 Super Sports. Eighty percent of the bikes were bought new.

Fewer than half the Ducatis (42 percent) are used for daily transportation and predictably, even fewer (35 percent) are used for touring. The Duck's real forte is sports riding and this shows in the fig-

ures—91 percent of the Ducatis are ridden for pleasure. This makes Ducati the most single-purpose machine we've surveyed, edging the Honda Goldwing (90 percent used for touring). Sixteen percent of the Ducati owners race on the streets and canyons (a new record) and 8 percent participate in organized road races.

Even when they aren't racing, Ducati owners push their machines harder than any of the other machines we've surveyed, even harder than the Kawasaki 900/1000 owners. Twenty percent of the owners ride very hard, and 51 percent ride moderately hard. Of the remainder, 22 percent have an average riding style and only 7 percent ride gentler than average.

As back-road barnstormers, Ducatis don't pile up the miles as fast as most other brands. The used Ducatis average only 6200 mi. and the new bikes average only 11,300 mi. (the highest mileage was 50,700 on a 750 GT), so overall, the Ducatis have covered an average of 10,200 mi. On a yearly basis, Ducatis are ridden from 1000 to 15,000 mi., averaging 5600 mi. per year. Fuel economy figures ranged from 30 to 50 mpg with a 42.5 mpg average.

Ducati dealers are hard to find in many parts of the country, so a large number of owners do their own maintenance. Forty seven percent of the owners always work on their bikes and the same number usually do. The remaining 6 percent sometimes service their cycles and none of them always leaves the servicing for a dealer.

They do most of their own work on their Ducatis but the owners don't seem to mind. Forty one percent rate the work very easy and 52 percent call it average. Only 6 percent say the work is difficult. As for the valve adjustment, one rider commented, "Desmo valves aren't as bad as you might think; mostly different. If you are careful and have the right shims, they're no worse than a Japanese multi."

Maintenance problems are few on the Ducati and a third of the owners said they had no problems. The same number said they had problems adjusting the valves and the only other problem mentioned by more than 5 percent of the owners is the electrical system, mentioned by 6 percent.

There are eight areas of other than routine maintenance mentioned by 5 percent or more of the owners and 22 percent say their bikes need only routine servicing. The same number (22 percent) had problems with the electrical system. Most of the electrical problems were with shorts or melted fuse blocks (fixed by one rider by carving a new fuse block out of wood and using Radio Shack fuse holders.)

Twenty percent had problems with excessive valve guide wear. Nine percent frequently break the throttle cable and 7 percent do the same with the clutch cable. A fix for these problems, which also reduces clutch effort, is to use a Yamaha Power Cable Injector (about $4) to squirt lubricant through the entire cable until it comes out the other end.

Other problems, all mentioned by 6 percent of the owners include the ignition system, the brakes, the transmission and the handlebar switches (fixed by several owners by substituting switches from any of the big four Japanese brands).

A quarter of the Ducatis have been idle

while waiting for parts and the waits ranged from a week to eight months, averaging 58 days, the longest of any of the bikes we've surveyed. In rating the parts availability, 19 percent said they are always available, 46 percent said mostly available, 31 percent said sometimes hard to find and 4 percent said they are always hard to find. These are poor figures, but parts aren't totally unavailable and in fact, the percentages are only a little worse than for the Yamaha XS 750.

Under hints, one rider suggested, "Learn to think like an Italian." While you're figuring out how to do that, some practical hints include using automotive coils with a wider plug gap (.035–.040 in.) for easier starting and better idling (don't forget to use a ballast resistor or you'll burn up a set of points); on the kick start 860s, use the starter button to operate a set of airhorns; replace the intake valve seals when the carbs won't stay adjusted as the seals get hard and leak; add grease fittings to the swing arm pivot; loosen the dipstick and the drainplug with an impact driver and a sparkplug socket to avoid stripping them; use the kickstart lever from the 900SS and remove the spring from the right footpeg so it will fold to make kickstarting less painful and finally, if the wiring gets wet and the bike won't start, disconnect the green wires going to the coils. These go to a relay behind the headlight which grounds the ignition system to stop the engine.

There may not be many Ducati dealers, but they do fairly well according to the owners. Twenty six percent are very good, 45 percent are good and 22 percent are fair, so 93 percent of the Ducati dealers are doing at least a reasonable job. No dealers got a poor rating and the remain-

ing 7 percent are very poor.

Do Duck owners modify their bikes? Is the Pope Catholic? Individual owners did everything from changing the coils to installing nitrous oxide injection and only 7 percent said they left their bikes stock. Thirty one percent changed the exhaust system (most adding Conti mufflers), 22 percent changed or modified the carbs, 19 percent changed the coils (usually to Bosch or automotive coils), 15 percent installed quartz-halogen headlights and the same number replaced the handlebar switches with Japanese units, 13 percent changed the handlebars, 11 percent put on a smaller mirror or an extra one, 7 percent each changed the gearing or did internal engine modifications (cams, pistons, etc.) and 6 percent each rejetted the carbs, replaced the electrical system, changed the handlebar grips or had the cylinder heads modified or ported.

The sporting instincts of the Ducati owners show in their choice of accessories. The most popular add-ons aren't fairings or saddlebags, but air filters. Forty three percent of the owners changed air filters (usually K&N or Uni), 31 percent added fairings (usually sport, not touring models) and 26 percent switched tires. Nineteen percent mounted aftermarket shocks, 15 percent added a pack or tank bag, 9 percent added a luggage rack and 6 percent mounted saddlebags. Thirteen percent added no accessories.

Only four products were rated as especially good accessories. Conti mufflers got four raves and one rider complained they are too loud. Three riders each like S&W shocks and K&N air filters and two riders are impressed with Dunlop K-81 tires.

Reliability of their machines isn't much

Ducati Owner Survey

Bought new?	80%
Bought used	20%
Average mileage	10,200 mi.

Types of riding

Commuting and transportation	42%
Touring	35%
Pleasure	91%

Riding style

Very hard	20%
Moderately hard	51%
Average	22%
Gentler than average	7%
Miles per year	5600
Fuel economy	42.5 mpg

Serviced by owners

Always	47%
Usually	47%
Sometimes	6%
Never	0%

Ease of maintenance

Very easy	41%
Average	52%
Difficult	7%

Parts availability

Always available	19%
Mostly available	46%
Sometimes hard to find	31%
Always hard to find	4%

Dealer rating

Very good	26%
Good	45%
Fair	22%
Poor	0%
Very poor	7%
Ever broke down	11%
Had to wait for parts	25%
Average waiting time	58 days

Maintenance problems

Valve adjustment	33%
Electrical system	6%
Need factory tools	3%
Checking oil level	3%
Chain adjustment	3%

Best features

Handling	87%
Torque	35%
Smoothness	35%
Brakes	22%
Looks	19%

Worst features

Electrics	20%
Lack of comfort	15%
Quality of finish	9%
Controls	9%
Sidestand	9%
Would buy another Ducati	96%
Same model	60%

of a problem for the Ducati owners. Only 11 percent of the bikes broke down and stranded their owners, placing the Ducks well up on the list, just behind the Kawaski 900/1000 (10 percent). Melted fuseblocks, ignition problems and broken throttle cables were the most common causes for the breakdowns.

Best features? There's no argument here. Handling tops the list of the Ducati's attributes with 87 percent of the owners calling it a best feature. One rider said, "I've let some friends take her for a spin. Soon I won't be the only one in town with a Ducati!"

Other favorite aspects of the Ducati include the torque and the smoothness (35 percent each), the brakes (22 percent), the looks (". . . picking up girls, turning heads, having people in Ferraris giving you a thumbs up.") at 19 percent, the uniqueness (15 percent) and the power (13 percent).

The owners also like the sound (11 percent), the feel (9 percent), the fuel economy (7 percent) and the gearbox, the reliability, the quality of construction and the responsiveness (6 percent each.)

There is less agreement on the Ducati's worst features. Twenty percent don't like the electrics, 15 percent say it lacks comfort, 9 percent each complain about the quality of finish, the controls and the sidestand and 6 percent each don't like the noise, the footpeg position when kickstarting, the lack of dealers, the low speed handling and the cold starting characteristics. In addition, there were a few comments highly critical of the Ducati distributor, Berliner Motors.

Nothing was the most common answer to "What would you change if you could?" with 15 percent of the owners saying to leave the Ducatis just as they are. Thirteen percent each want better electrics or a more comfortable seat, 11 percent think the switches could be improved, 9 percent each want a better riding position or better brakes and 6 percent each want a larger fuel tank, improvements in the shocks or better quality control. One rider said, "If it had a driveshaft, I'd keep it forever."

After all the individual comments on plusses and minuses have been counted up, the Ducati owners almost unanimously agree on one thing. Ninety six percent said yes, they'd buy another Ducati. This places the Duck near the top of the list in owner loyalty, behind the Suzuki GS750 (98 percent) and the Yamaha XS750 (97 percent). Sixty percent said they'd buy another of the same model with the rest hoping to move up to one of the faster Desmo models.

What do the owners think of their Ducatis? "The only bike of any make that draws an instant crowd when its in a crowd of other bikes." "the only production racer I can buy as a stock bike" ". . . a thick cut above Japanese clone-bikes" and "if only every road were curved."

Pantah Looning
Belting Along On The Deep-Breathing Duke

I'd been out there for two weeks when they found me. They said I was tired, violent and desperate, they said they were going to look after me. They said I was in big trouble this time but that it would all be OK if I did what I was told. Then they lifted my wretched body out of the saddle, took away the keys and locked me in this room. There's nothing here but this typewriter. No stimulants, no diversions, nothing but a bright red Olympia portable and a mass of scribbled gibberish which I believe to be notes I made while I was out there. Nothing but unintelligible cyphers and an icy deadline staring me in the face. And now they expect me to tell you what it was like. But Sweet Jesus, how can I tell them that the answers are all Out There . . . on the road? Don't they recognise a bad case of white line fever when they see it? Why don't they just give me the bike back and let me get the hell out of here?

Well . . . yes, and here we go again. One more time over the top in an orgiastic word-lust frenzy of overkill motoring journalism. From the outer limits to the inner city ring roads and back. I'll put my metaphors on "stun" and my cliches on "devastate" just so you get the severity of my drift. But let's begin simply with a few obvious considerations. The Ducati Pantah 500 Desmo is good. This bike is the fastest and best handling street contender in the 500cc class. It has a pedigree. It has innovation. It has speed. Everybody who's ridden it thinks it's pretty godamm immaculate. And it is.

But is there really any way I can even begin to describe what it's like to live with? How it can completely dominate your life, so that all you ever want to do when the roads are dry is ride? Just ride away. No purpose, no point, no particular way to go except hard and fast. Shall I scorch superlatives supreme and adjectives aplenty about Ducatis as a breed and over high speed excitement as the drug? No . . . I did that last month, and anyway maybe it might be more fun to try and justify the £2300 bottom line by investigating the facts. Since you, I and every greasy punter in the land already knows that this bike is *the* hottest thing around at the moment, maybe the cliches aren't necessary, maybe the physical rolling truth is enough.

Mike Scott filled you in on the wonderful facts of the Pantah experience when he scooped (some would say stole) the prototype last year. This one's the production model, but there are very few changes. Still this is the one you'd get if you had £2300 and if the importers, Coburn and Hughes, had any left, which they haven't at the time of writing, since the initial batch were immediately swallowed by wise and trusting desmofreaks.

For Ducati lovers everywhere the announcement of the 500cc Pantah was sweet news indeed. Way back in 1970 there'd been a paper Pantah, a 500cc vee-twin prototype that eventually got junked in favour of developing its larger brothers, the 750 and 900. The 500 twin they *did* release was a 180 degree parallel job, a desmo for sure, which ran fast enough (112mph/ 13.5 seconds) and looked every inch a Duke, but somehow failed to appeal to the market. Everybody wondered why there was so much space in the front of the frame.

The 1980 Pantah is the real thing — a 90 degree air cooled vee-twin combining the best of the old traditional 860cc engineering with some new and impressive ideas.

The 498.9cc mill (well oversquare at 74 x 58mm and running 9.5:1 compression) retains desmo valve operation and a SOHC for each pot, but uses a toothed rubber belt for the drive. The 3/4 inch

rubber belts get momentum from a crank driven pulley. On their way to the camshafts they pass over and back two tensioning pulleys, one of which is adjustable. Timing comes courtesy of a pair of crank driven helical spurgears on the left. The belts are a lot quieter in operation than whirring bevel drive, though they aren't expected to live as long and replacement every 12400 miles could be expensive.

The desmo valve gear is more familiar. One cam, four rockers, two valves being opened and shut mechanically. Rocker adjustment as usual is easy enough for the opening pair, but involves nil millimetre adjustment for the closing duo via half rings. Frequent adjustment is unlikely though in view of the precise timing system. Whether the belt driven cams are better than the bevel/shaft arrangement remains to be seen, but in 1500 miles, the engine revealed not a hint of tuning or timing loss despite being regularly run to the blood line.

The engine revs as freely as any Jap multi and is a damn sight quicker at picking up the power. The red-line on the dial at 7500/8000 is wrong and the handbook specified limit of 9050rpm is right. The power just boils around the clock and comes in very quickly. Running a maximum back wheel figure of 46bhp at 9000rpm (it's about 52bhp at the crank) the Pantah's obviously no slouch in the acceleration/power stakes. Breathing through two enormous (for a 500) 36mm Dell' Orto pumpers, the bike cracks 90mph in third gear and is really fast in mid-range with an almighty punch of acceleration anywhere above 6000rpm.

Since it's massively overgeared, keeping it on the boil is necessary around town. The bike will red-line in every gear except fifth where it just won't take full bore throttle. By the time you've wound it on that far though, you're travelling at a meaty 110mph.

The constant mesh box might provide better results with a 40 tooth rear sprocket (38 is standard). There again, the bike seems to be generally geared for maximum speed in true Ducati style — a high first and a quasi-overdrive in fifth. During testing, the clutch was slipping a little anyway and nobody was silly enough to see if it would run faster in fourth than it would in top. Having respect for red-lines on Ducatis doesn't come from fear of valve bounce, but rather from a deep rooted fear of clutch destruction.

The answer is probably yes, the lower gear gives you more speed, but who cares? It's fast enough.

Since there's been some wildly varying top speeds quoted for this bike (everything from 108 to 125mph) we'll add our own cup of hot fat to the cauldron of confusion by stating that on a reasonable day we got a best of 113.5mph, which we'd be willing to call 115mph because of the clutch slip. A maximum of 120mph is easily possible via minor alterations to the air intake and exhaust system. Either way it's a lot faster than the Darmah, and what it lacks in 860cc torque it more than makes up for in its incessant ability to rev and rev hard. The half pint Pantah engine is beautiful to drive in the upper half of the dial and it's so hungry for revs that you just have to let them out. The low weight (432lb wet) and the whole v fine balance of the motorcycle lead to inevitable excess. It's just so exhilarating and so sweet to spin the motor that quick. In town driving/cruising using only three gears and three-quarter throttle gets you around your local street circuits faster than you'd ever thought possible. Too fast really to wind it up and continually get away with it. The nightmare drivers our capital breeds and our society allows will get you sooner

or later. There again, the riding pitch the Pantah provides sets you thinking about survival of the fittest. A near fatal illusion in these neurotic times. Better then, to aim it out towards the country and just revel in the bends. Slingshotting the Sunday drivers into the turns and roundabouts, where there's enough room for both of you, and where maximum acceleration and roadholding are the key.

Averaging 50mpg with a low of 38 at the track, the Pantah mill breathes deeply but without greed. Electronic ignition is by Bosch and Ducati have thoughtfully provided two sight levels, one for a timing strobe to check the advance and one for the oil level. Cute eh? The oil sump itself holds 3.3 litres with a disposable filter cartridge living under the right-hand side.

Ignition is reliable (there's no kick) and the mill idles quietly and happily at 1200rpm. Vibration is very much a matter of acquaintance. For some reason, I found that my right arm would seize up after half an hour or so, but it never deterred me from riding and isn't noticeable except on a long hop.

With its futuristic (for Ducati) long and lean engine cases, the powerplant hangs perfectly braced in the frame. The old and the new blend perfectly in the 1980 Pantah picture. Expensive, but solidly mechanical and toughly built with precision assembly. Make no mistake, it also needs someone to keep it that way, to maintain perfect tune from the beginning. But such a pretty little engine deserves some loving attention.

The vee-twin mill has always played a special part in Ducati frame building since the bottom loop of their cradles is always completed by the engine itself. With the Pantah though, they've excelled in experimentation by dispensing with the cradle altogether and opting for a spine frame consisting of four cross braced tubes which make two ladders, one each side of the engine, each one running back from the huge headstock down to the top of the crankcases. The mill itself gets connected at three stressed points on each side.

The really trick bit's at the back though, where the swing-arm pivots inside the half rear crankcases. The bushes get lubricated by engine oil, hence minimal bush wear.

Though the eccentric cam method of chain adjustment has been lost, the whole back end is as strong and well balanced as before. It just oozes confidence.

Suspension front and rear is Marzocchi. What at first appeared to be a steering fault under fast cornering was traced to a slight oil weep from the front fork seals. You expect that sort of thing on a demo bike cos they get ridden hard, but generally the long stroke forks are vice-free in action, no striction, good travel, controlled springing and damping.

The back end's tougher — the wide swing-arm taking care of most of the heavy action supplemented by the Zocchi spring-shox, five way adjustable for preload and with a "shocking" red remote air reservoir, for really solid damping. The ride is firm — too firm for some of the disgraceful dirt tracks our leaders call city roads, but fine for high speed rolling thunder when the rough bits have to be dealt with quickly and efficiently.

Wheels are by FPS for Ducati and are gold anodised cast alloy. Brakes and hydraulics by Brembo with triple drilled 10.2 inch cast iron discs. Surprisingly, they fall short of the traditional *SuperBike* "superb" epithet and are merely "extremely good". The front seems a touch spongy for heavy braking and I have no idea why. They reach an adequate retardation point sooner or later, but sometimes it's a bit too late. The back brake's fine though with oceans of travel.

The standard tyres are Michelins, but we had Pirelli Phantoms, a wise choice of tyre with astonishing grip. Curiously, after 1000 miles of rigorous driving, the left-hand corner tread of the rear boot began breaking up badly, the fabric tearing rather than wearing. It may have been the ease with which the Pantah slid (slightly and predictably) down at the track, most likely though it was just a duff tyre.

The three-quarter race fairing is one piece glassfibre mounted by two brackets off the downtubes and by two more off the extended headlight assembly. It's of real benefit at those illegal speeds where the Pantah likes to prowl, taking much of the wind pressure away from and

above the rider, who's tucked into a prone position behind the clip-on bars, lying on the spacious 4.2 gallon tank and perched on the rear sets.

The riding position the bars give is low but comfortable in its own *Man of Iron* way. Your back suffers a bit if you're tall but you can soon persuade your spine to adapt. Controls, levers and cables are all surprisingly good (for Ducati) and the bar mounted mirror is sharp enough for a quick glance at the old world moving backwards movie.

The seat meanwhile is a plank with a fake ducktail which turns out to be the solo/dual seat *à la* Hailwood Replica. Pillion passengers can forget it. This is best as a solo mount.

Under the right-hand sidecover lives the battery. Under the left sits the rear carb and generally, working access is pretty good because of the overhead frame.

The styling/paint exercise is a showstopper and anyone who argues otherwise is an unaesthetic blockhead. The quality of the Italian silver blue paint seems a lot thicker with a better lacquer/gloss finish than seen on previous specimens. The red and blue flashes are just street racer audacity. It's as pretty a bike as I can ever remember seeing anywhere. Girls will go wild over it. Pimply youths will cream their jeans. Old men will die happy. Policemen will pull off the road and weep.

Like I said, a real showstopper. Everywhere you go makes you the new kid in town with a difference.

Right. Listen.

The 500cc class of street bikes available today is the most exciting of them all. The best of them, the Montjuic and the Pantah share the same sort of good things like fabulous power, immaculate roadholding and rugged individualism. They're mighty, meaty bikes matey and they share a common exotic price tag. Other than that though they're wholly different. The Pantah stands alone as the modern wonderful expression of the fast vee-twin engine, integrally and intelligently built into a revolutionary frame, coupled with a short wheelbase, low weight and quick steering. The bits that go together to make up the motorcycle are enough to guarantee a fine ride. The word is balance and the answers are still all out there on the road. Ride one and believe in magic. When they finally let me out of this writer's decompression chamber I'm going to take the first train to Luton and steal it. And this time there ll be no coming back. Ever.   JC

Ducati Pantah 500 Desmo
£2299

PERFORMANCE
Maximum Speed — 115mph (see text)
Standing Quarter Mile — 14.1sec
Fuel Consumption — Hard Riding — 38mpg
                                   Cruising — 54.8mpg
Best Full-Tank Range — 230 miles

ENGINE
Type — 90 degree, air cooled vee-twin, belt drive SOHC, desmo valves
Displacement — 498.9cc
Power — 46bhp at 9000rpm
Bore & Stroke — 74mm x 58mm
Compression Ratio — 9.5:1
Induction — 2 x 36mm Dell' Orto pumper carbs
Exhaust — two into two with balance pipe (Contis)
Oil System — wet sump
Ignition — Bosch electronic

TRANSMISSION
Clutch — Multiplate wet
Primary Drive — gear
Final Drive — chain

CHASSIS
Frame — overhead cradle or ladder spine type (see text)
Front Suspension — Marzocchi telehydraulic
Rear Suspension — Swing-arm pivoted on engine, Marzocchi shox with remote reservoir
Wheelbase — 60in
Seat Height — 32in
Weight — 432lb wet
Fuel Capacity — 4.2 gall
Tyres — Pirelli Phantoms 4.10 x 18 front and rear
Brakes — triple drilled Brembo discs (10.2in)

EQUIPMENT
Electrical — 260W alternator, 12 volt battery
Lighting — 55/60W/H4

Test bike supplied by Coburn and Hughes, 51-61 Park Street, Luton.

Pride and Prejudice

DUCATI 900SS

Ridden hard,
Crashed spectacularly,
Regarded respectfully

By Andrew Gilchrist
Graham Monro pics

MY DUCATI SS900 has been raced, ridden hard, regarded respectfully and crashed spectacularly. It's had its problems, but given me an endless amount of joy. Like a good wine, it's getting better with age.

The 900 isn't the first Duke I've owned, but it is probably the one I'm proudest of. Before it came a GT860 (and before that a Yamaha DT250A, but I'd rather forget about that); unreliability haunted the 860, to the extent that anyone sane would have shed themselves of it quickly. Me? I really dug that bike, because when it went it *ran!* The first day after handing out $2000 to

Fraser's in Sydney the electrics burnt out and a tyre went flat. For the next two years it was in and out of Fraser Motorcycles, until one day a valve wandered carelessly into a piston; following a recommendation it was repaired by Gowanloch Motorcycle Engineering in Sydney, the beginning of a satisfactory relationship between Ducati and repairer.

After a reassembled bottom end —

and later the top end — modified electrics and some knowledgeable tuning, it became quite a reliable machine. A twin-headlight John Player Norton fairing was fitted, as were twin discs. All in all, $1500 was spent on repairs and modifications.

Compared to the 900, the 860's suspension was softer, the handling felt less precise and the throttle less sensitive, the engine slower and plusher — the 900 communicates that it is the tauter, sportier and more powerful bike.

Bought late in 1978 for $2600, the 900 had 22,000 km on the clock and gave every impression of being a low-flying missile. It soon developed an electrical fault that manifested itself whenever the engine was hot. The generator was replaced, but the bike's state of tune continually bordered on abysmal, so forever after it was put in more tender and careful hands.

The initial problems were basically minor and the fun of savouring the Ducati began. Weekend blasts along winding country roads highlighted the

bike's surefootedness and superb braking.

Soon I began considering modifications. I wanted to swap the 32 mm Dellorto carburettors for something larger, and for about half the price one dealer quoted, Gowanloch replaced the disc pads, fitted 40 mm carburettors, polished and matched the ports, re-seated and shimmed the valves and fitted Metzeler C88As back and front — all for $250. The increase in performance was amazing. The bike was far more responsive, vibrated less, had more torque, was stronger in mid and top-end pull and gave slightly better fuel consumption.

Unfortunately, the bliss of it all was short-lived. A month later on my way home a car took a right-hand turn where and when it shouldn't have. The driver provided the immovable. I became the stoppable.

The impact of the collision swung the car 180 degrees and pushed it back 20 metres or so. The 900 was a mess — the front end demolished, save the wheel hub, disc calipers, tacho and speedo (oh, and the headlight which shone crazily on as the machine wept oil onto the glass-strewn road).

I was okay, but abused the driver to make me feel better. The police arrived, booked the driver, who then made the mistake of abusing the police; one of them said later that he'd never seen anyone so off-hand about nearly killing someone. It takes all kinds, doesn't it?

Mysterious ways

Repairs totalled abut $1600, including straightening the frame and adding NCR-style frame braces. Most front-end parts that you can think of were replaced and the bike, from such a bad accident, was off the road for an unbelievably short time of only three weeks.

But having never been involved in an accident where a bike has sustained so much damage, I was more than sceptical about how the repaired article would handle, and how reliable it would be. Fair questions I reckoned.

If you'll take my word for it, the 900's handling was slightly improved, and the steering even smoother and more precise. Roadholding was much, much better, the bike rock steady, tracking beautifully over rough roads at rather faster speeds than usual. I take my hat off to the mechanic.

And as for reliability, well, a month after the crash I was off on a 10,000 km jaunt through NSW, Victoria and Queensland. Six weeks of living out of a pack rack and saddlebags, of trailriding, cruising and blasting along places like the Great Ocean Road.

Through all of it the 900 cruised effortlessly at 140 km/h. One remarkable happening should be noted; with the Tomaselli throttle friction holder in place on roads such as the Hume, the bike was capable of returning fuel consumption of about 25 km/h (70 mpg!) That's amazing!

Electrical problems? On the last day of

the tour a small, grey wire popped its socket in the fusebox while I was blasting along a roughish road at 160 km/h. At the time I was running with some bikes from Tamworth. The bike stopped dead, the fault was found and remedied. That's the electrical story.

Back in the city my thoughts turned to racing, and with licence in hand I fronted at Oran Park one day for practice. After two hours of riding I was ready to call it a day, but just two more laps I thought. On the first of those last laps the left-hand header pipe scraped hard, lifting the rear wheel, and off I went for a slide.

The pain to the bike, my pride, wallet, leathers and arse was immeasurable. The fairing was scratched and scraped and the ducktail crumpled.

The 900 was now looking tatty, and with 30,000 km on the clock was at the head of the queue for a big end failure. Gowanlochs pulled the motor down and fitted a modified big end capable of withstanding significantly more stress. Gearbox and bevel gears were re-shimmed, the crankshaft rebuilt and aligned. An Imola cam was installed, resulting in a smoother and peakier motor, and the fairing, frame and other sundry parts were either repainted or rechromed. The worn primary drive gear and several clutch plates were replaced soon after.

The 900 was now almost perfect, needing just Imola pipes to solve a clearance problem, compliment the cam and give a sizeable power boost.

It was now competitive on the racetrack and raced at a five-way club meet at Oran Park. Amaroo soon followed — on Michelins rather than the Metzelers.

In day-to-day riding the 900 has proven very reliable. It's used as a commuter, although a long time aboard it around town causes tired shoulders, sore backside and drumming ears but it's a small enough price to pay for such a superb machine.

The small fairing is effective in preventing buffeting by wind and does keep the upper half dry in rain. Starting is no problem, just one or two kicks and it's running, and the extra low-down torque of the 40 mm carbs makes the bike more rideable while improving fuel consumption.

The 900 is an excellent all-rounder. It handles racing, city hacking and touring with aplomb. It's my machine and I love it. Maybe one day I'll have the skill to exploit its potential to the full. *

The 900 original (above) and twice-modified (left). It's still used around town, Imola pipes, cam and all.

Hailwood's TT Replica

It may be a carbon copy, but it looks and performs almost as well as the original . . .

One look at the Ducati 900 Hailwood Replica tells you that it's going to be impractical, uncomfortable, uncivilised, unreliable and anti-social. One ride tells you different. It's fast and fun.

For sure it's noisy, but it's not anti-social. Old men appear out of cracks in the pavement with a gleam in their eyes, wistfully telling you about their AJAYs, Matchlesses, Rudge Ulsters and Indians of their past. Little old ladies stop sweeping their paths, smile and tell you what a nice bike you've got. On the road, Dads swing two wheels of their Allegros into the ditch as they wave you past while the kids lean out of the rear windows to stick enthusiastic thumbs up.

Impractical? Uncomfortable? Uncivilised? All the things you expect from a cafe-racer special? Not this one. The riding position is a racing crouch but the seat, tank and footrests blend together perfectly. Long-legged riders couldn't get their knees into the tank cutaways, which serves them right. God obviously meant me to ride a Ducati when he gave me stubby little limbs.

Until they get used to it, your wrists are going to ache around town, but at speed the balance between body weight and wind pressure is relaxing. A few minutes with a two-pence piece unscrews the dummy single-seat tail to reveal an equally pleasant-on-the-eye dual-seat with generous padding so your best friend can share the fun. The passenger only has you to hold on to so choose your partner carefully.

Getting started from cold can't be hurried because the only way to get a rich mixture is to flood both carbs with tickler buttons. Reaching the front carb is a tight squeeze behind the fairing and at night it is hard to tell when the fuel is overflowing, but once this fiddling about is over the engine starts first or second kick. Straight away it ticks over perfectly and runs sweetly at any speed. Beat that with your in-line four.

The gearing is high, so you're not likely to get much further than third in town. Running at tickover in top gear gets you over 30mph. In very heavy traffic this can mean wrestling with the very heavy clutch, but otherwise there's no problem because the motor can run so slowly. Only when it gets below 2000rpm is there any snatching. Gearchanges are rather noisy, but light and very positive.

The test bike's clutch would sometimes slip under hard acceleration, but it always seemed to sort itself out after a few high-speed miles. Not many Italian clutches survive our standing-quarter runs, so we left the Ducati's drag starts to the end of the day. Even so, we decided to begin with one gentle run to give us some sort of a figure before we had to pack up with a broken bike. From not much more than a traffic-light start we got up the quarter mile in 13.6sec.

Trying harder, it should have been easy to knock off another second. Revving to about 6000 and slipping the clutch gave us 13.07 straight away. Much better. Revving higher only got the engine more bogged down in the clutch, so the times were slower. Next we tried dumping the clutch lever suddenly, at about 5000rpm, hoping the shock would break traction at the rear

Hailwood's TT Replica

wheel and take the strain off the overworked plates. But the plates slipped anyway and we were back to square one.

Trying the same thing at higher revs got the clutch so hot that it couldn't disengage. We had to give up then and abandon the pillion runs. The clutch returned to normal after being left to cool down, although we had to take the locknut off the cable adjuster to allow it to screw in far enough to get some freeplay at the lever. Our Ducati was old by test bike standards, having covered 10,000 performance testing miles, and Coburn & Hughes claim it's using the original clutch. If that's true, it hasn't done badly.

None of this matters on the road, though. Getting away from traffic lights is quick without any need for fussy revs or too much playing with the clutch. Out on the open road the gears snick up and down without a clutch, so you can give the bar-mounted Bullworker a rest. Finding neutral was easy while rolling or with a dead engine, but the slightly-dragging clutch made it a bit of a chore at traffic lights, not helped by a neutral warning light that quite often lied. The chain needed adjusting a number of times during the test. Two spanners are needed to stop the axle turning, but the nyloc adjusters are easy to use and the whole adjustment system is very solid and neat.

Magic note

For quick riding and safe overtaking, all you have to do is make sure the revs are over 4000. At 16mph per 1000rpm top gear is almost an overdrive, so if you feel like living up to the Hailwood legend, you'll find yourself going down to third for roundabouts or equally slow-moving cars. There's magic in the changing note of a big vee-twin going up through the ratios.

For normal riding there's no need to change out of top until the speedo drops below 50mph. Riding lazily, it is easy to forget to change back up again because the engine is only turning over at 5000rpm at 70mph in fourth. It will rev freely past the 7000rpm power peak to the 7500 red line and beyond in the lower gears, but there isn't much point in changing any later than 6000, even when riding hard.

Ah, riding hard. Forget about struggling to recover from one twitching exit only to find that you've gone too fast into the next

bend but daren't touch the brakes. On the Ducati every manoeuvre is relaxed, unhurried. Even if you've changed down a gear or two, the engine is loping along with a steady beat that's far more exciting than a zillion whining revs. By the time you enter a bend, you've got it sussed and are looking ahead to the next one. Gentle pressure from your knees takes you down and a gentle pull on the offside bar with a little more power on lifts you out. Whether your style is to brake early, brake late, brake too late, or not brake at all, the bike will stay on the line you've chosen. There's no hint of understeer or oversteer. Changing line in mid-bend to avoid potholes or pathetic motorists is always fuss-free.

Flexing is something the frame doesn't know about. The tubes are beefy and every line is a straight one. Even the twin downtubes are straight because they don't have to form a cradle. They just spread wide around the front cylinder and bolt to the crankcase. There's no way that engine casting is going to flex.

Straight fat tubes

No gimmicky box-section rear end for this bike either. The swinging arm is made of more straight, fat tubes with an extra brace as far behind the pivot tube as it can be without fouling the tyre.

Hidden inside the fairing are much skinnier fork tubes than the massive sliders lead you to expect. Once or twice, in bumpy bends, I thought I felt them twist. I could be wrong because, at those times, I was twisting quite a lot myself. Which brings me to my only serious complaint. Riding hard might be fun, but not when the suspension does the same. Both ends of the Ducati felt rigid when the going got rough. It's all very well keeping the wheels in contact with the road, but it is also nice to keep the rider in contact with the bike. Hailwood must have felt pretty shaky by the end of Sulby Straight.

Apparently the 900 Replica has 20mm more rear suspension travel than the 900SS, which sends my heart out to 900SS owners. Even with the extra weight of a passenger, the softest rear pre-load setting is too hard. I'm not made of strong enough stuff to find out what happens when the other four settings are used.

There's no doubt that Pirelli Phantoms have just the right image for a race-replica road bike. They look like cut slicks, they act like racing tyres and rumour has it that they wear out almost as quick. I soon got used to taking each day's first few bends gently, waiting for the rubber to warm up. Once up to working temperature, they added to the bike's

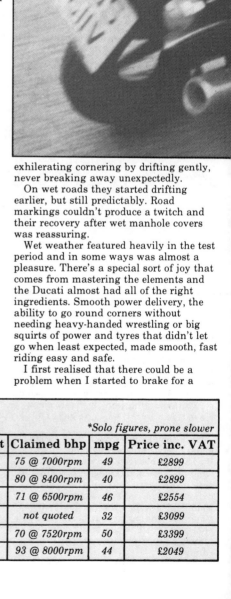

exhilerating cornering by drifting gently, never breaking away unexpectedly.

On wet roads they started drifting earlier, but still predictably. Road markings couldn't produce a twitch and their recovery after wet manhole covers was reassuring.

Wet weather featured heavily in the test period and in some ways was almost a pleasure. There's a special sort of joy that comes from mastering the elements and the Ducati almost had all of the right ingredients. Smooth power delivery, the ability to go round corners without needing heavy-handed wrestling or big squirts of power and tyres that didn't let go when least expected, made smooth, fast riding easy and safe.

I first realised that there could be a problem when I started to brake for a

COMPARISONS

Solo figures, prone slower

	Speed prone	SS ¼ mile (Prone)	Dry weight	Claimed bhp	mpg	Price inc. VAT
Ducati 900 Replica	125mph	13.07sec/105mph	452lb.	75 @ 7000rpm	49	£2899
Benelli 900 Sei	116mph	13.02sec/101mph	485lb.	80 @ 8400rpm	40	£2899
Moto Guzzi Spada	119mph	13.58sec/93mph*	460lb.	71 @ 6500rpm	46	£2554
Laverda Mirage	130mph	12.12sec/113mph	499lb.	not quoted	32	£3099
BMW R100RS	121mph	13.44sec/100mph	463lb.	70 @ 7520rpm	50	£3399
Kawasaki Z1000 MkII	126mph	12.49sec/109mph	540lb.	93 @ 8000rpm	44	£2049

TECHNICAL SPECIFICATION

Engine

Type: *Air-cooled, desmodromic SOHC, four-stroke vee twin.*
Bore x stroke: *86.0 x 74.4mm.*
Displacement: *864cc.*
Compression ratio: *9.5:1.*
Carburettors: *Two Dell'Orto PHM 40mm slide type. No air filters.*
Max. horsepower: *75bhp.*
Max. torque: *63.5ft. lbs. @ 5800 (Max. revs 8500).*
Lubrication: *Wet sump with pressure feed by gear pump and gravity return. Sump capacity 5 litres (approx. 9 pints).*

Transmission

Type: *Five-speed, constant mesh.*
Primary drive: *Helical gears. Ratio 2.19:1.*
Final reduction ratio: *2.40:1.*
Overall gear ratios: *1st 12.43, 2nd 8.66, 3rd 6.66, 4th 5.55, 5th (top) 4.94:1.*
Gearbox sprocket: *15 teeth.*
Rear wheel sprocket: *36 teeth.*
Drive chain: *Regina Grand Prix, ⅝ x ⅜in. 136 links.*
Clutch: *Wet, multi-plate.*

Frame and Forks

Frame: *Welded tubular. Twin downtubes with engine as structural member.*
Front suspension: *Telescopic fork with coil springs and hydraulic damping.*
Rear suspension: *Swinging arm controlled by twin oil-damped coil springs with five spring pre-load settings.*
Front travel: *4½in. approx.*
Rear travel: *3in. approx.*
Fork oil capacity: *230cc each leg.*

Wheels and Brakes

Front tyre size: *100/90V18.*
Rear tyre size: *110/90V18.*
Front brakes: *Twin hydraulically-operated, 280mm dia., cast-iron discs.*
Rear brake: *Single hydraulically-operated, 280mm dia., cast-iron disc.*

Electrics

Ignition: *Bosch electronic, with battery and coils.*
Battery: *12V, 12Ah.*
Alternator output: *200W.*
Headlight: *55/60W, H4.*
Tail/stop lamp: *5/21W.*
Indicators: *21W.*
Warning lights: *Generator, lights on, high beam, neutral, turn, 5W.*

Dimensions

Seat height: *800mm (31.5in.).*
Length: *2200mm (88.6in.).*
Width: *700mm (27.56in.).*
Height: *1280mm (50.39in.).*
Wheelbase: *1510m (59.45in.).*
Ground clearance: *128mm (5in. approx.).*
Dry weight: *205kg (452lb.).*
Fuel tank: *20 litres (4 gall.).*

The meaty vee-twin motor which produced a delicious throbbing exhaust note was surprisingly easy to kick-start, provided the front pot carb hadn't filled with rainwater

Hailwood's TT Replica

roundabout soon after a cloudburst. Nothing happened for a couple of seconds. Luckily, the tyres could cope with braking a bit later than planned.

The real trouble came at much slower speeds, in traffic queues. At 40-50mph it took much longer for the pads to clear the water from the cast iron discs and twice I had to go around cars that braked unexpectedly, when I would have preferred to have stayed behind. Hopefully, Dunlop or Lockheed make all-weather pads to fit Brembo brakes.

When dry, the brakes are up there with the best. Adding a passenger affects their performance less than on most bikes. At first, the rear brake felt dead, but I soon came to appreciate the feel it gave. It took our crash stops at MIRA to lock the rear wheel for the first time. By the end of the brake testing session, my right hand ached painfully from the effort of supporting my weight at the same time as squeezing the lever as hard as I could. But on the road, two-finger pressure is usually enough and a bit of extra grip with my knees took a lot of the strain off my arms. Braking hard on a bumpy road left me wondering which way was up due to the violent nature of the rock-hard forks, but neither wheel locked or hopped.

Top speed is something of an obsession with the Italians. The obsession is shared by Italian-bike owners, although I can't think why. Going ever so fast on straight-line motorways is best left to Japanese stratocruisers. Not that the Ducati isn't fast. The 125mph top speed shown in our performance figures doesn't tell you about the 131mph best-one-way figure in top gear. Riding into the wind always knocks off more speed than you gain by riding with the wind and the test day was sure as hell windy, which explains why the fourth-gear top speed is also 125mph. Given a better day, the high-geared top ratio could easily push the bike nearer to 130mph average.

But who cares? Using the Ducati on motorways is a terrible waste. It cries out for the twistiest road you can find. Even here you'll be surprised to see you're doing 100mph quite often if you care to look at the speedo.

On a rock-steady bike that only needs to rev to 6000 in top, 100mph is cool. Give it a bit more of a twist in fourth before changing up and 110-plus is yours on the shortest straights, still cool, still stable.

The only frightening part of our high-speed runs came while braking. I had my

Smart and practical seat hump came off after undoing three screws

head tucked inside the screen and when I braked the chinpiece of my helmet knocked the release catch of the crude non-locking fuel cap. Petrol emptied itself over the instruments, filling the fairing. With a full tank the cap leaked under braking, even when closed.

Even in top gear, adding 20mph to your speed takes less than ten seconds. Despite the tall gearing, overtaking in top gear on the Ducati is as quick and safe as on most 1000cc bikes. Opening the throttle too quickly at low engine speeds makes the slide-type carbs gasp but, since we're talking about revs barely more than tickover speed on a Japanese multi, the problem is academic. You wouldn't normally be in top gear at those times.

Carrying a passenger knocks off more speed than you'd normally expect, but it's not due to any lack of guts from the engine. We didn't do solo and prone runs because the rider is so tucked away at all times. But a passenger is sticking up at the back like an air-brake, which can be quite a strain.

All this clock-watching showed up another of the Ducati's plus points — the accurate speedo. Being only two-mph out at 100mph is rare. Like Laverda (not to mention Hesketh) Ducati have chosen to buy the bits the Japanese do best. Nippon Denso supply the instruments, warning lights and handlebar switchgear. The instruments and switches never failed, although I would have preferred to have the lights on/off switch on the empty right-hand bar, where I couldn't accidentally hit it with my thumb while looking for the dip switch.

The test bike's warning lights looked as though somebody had hit them with a hammer. As a result, the winker warning and pilot/dip warning were erratic. Since

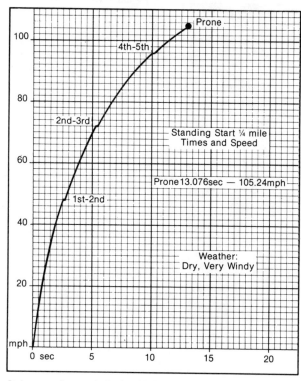

Hailwood Ducati 900

Prone

100

4th-5th

80

2nd-3rd

Standing Start ¼ mile
Times and Speed

60

Prone 13.076sec — 105.24mph

1st-2nd

40

Weather:
Dry, Very Windy

20

mph

0 sec   5   10   15   20

MAXIMUM SPEEDS and SPEED RANGES

Gear		mph max	mph min	mph 1000rpm
1	solo	57.16	8.21	6
2	solo	83.21	11.35	9
3	solo	109.75	15.74	12
4	solo	125.22	23.06	14
	pillion	113.04	,,	,,
	prone	—	—	—
5	solo	125.37	30.30	16
	pillion	109.82	,,	,,
	prone	—	—	—

Best one way speed: 131.50mph

FLEXIBILITY IN TOP GEAR (sec)

mph	30-50	40-60	50-70	60-80	70-90	80-100
solo	6.64	6.43	7.73	6.18	8.84	9.10

BRAKES (both)

mph	solo ft	pillion ft
30	30	37
40	57	70
50	88	106
60	125	149
70	188	211

SPEEDO

ind	true
30	27
40	37
50	47
60	57
70	67
80	78
90	88

Milometer
Accurate

Oil used
Negligible

MPG

mph	solo	pillion
30	Figures	
40	not available	
50		
60		
70		
Overall	49	

Performance figures obtained at: M.I.R.A. Test Track, Nr. Atherstone, Warks. Test Riders: Bob Goddard, Neil Millen.

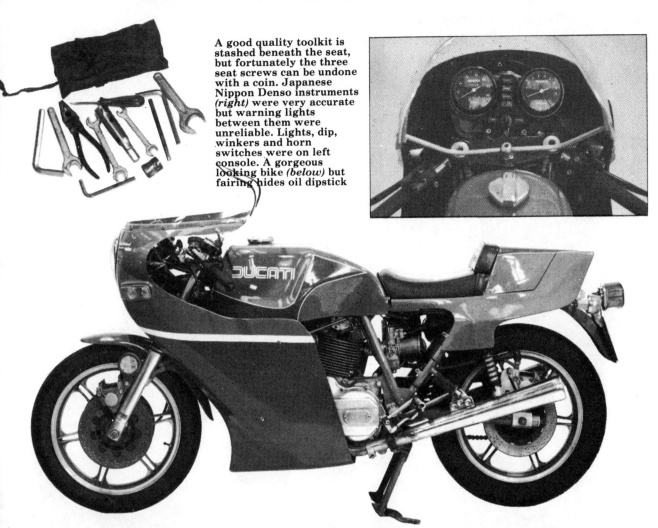

A good quality toolkit is stashed beneath the seat, but fortunately the three seat screws can be undone with a coin. Japanese Nippon Denso instruments *(right)* were very accurate but warning lights between them were unreliable. Lights, dip, winkers and horn switches were on left console. A gorgeous looking bike *(below)* but fairing hides oil dipstick

the backs of the winkers were visible inside the fairing and most bikes don't have a pilot/dip warning light anyway, these are no great problem. A side-stand warning light is fitted but no side-stand so, not surprisingly, it didn't do much.

For me, one of the biggest surprises of the Ducati was that there isn't a vibration problem. The big vee thumps powerfully but never harshly. It's a strong enough sensation to be an essential part of the bike's character without having any unwanted side effects.

The first shock was that the bar-mounted mirror works. It gives a good field of view — an excellent field of view if your passenger is wearing a skirt — without any blurring. The next shock was that all of the lights worked all of the time.

I ran the test bike with the lights on in daytime and never had to replace a bulb. The 55/60W CEV Halogen headlamp was good enough for 70mph in dark country lanes but Coburn & Hughes deserve a slap on the wrist for not replacing it with a left-hand dipping unit. Instead, it had been angled far too low in order to avoid dazzling oncoming cars.

Nicely-sorted details continue with a conventional-pattern gearchange on the left-hand side. The linkage was a bit sloppy and towards the end of the test, the positive-stop return spring needed a little help to get the lever back to the centre position.

The various glass-fibre bits were racing-thin, but of high quality and nicely

finished, apart from the crude cutting-out around the fairing. Constantly removing and replacing the three screws that held on the dummy single seat and dual-seat wasn't doing much for the condition of the various bits involved.

Some sort of quick-release design would have been neater and would also have speeded up the process of getting at the toolkit. However, this is a minor problem compared with checking the oil level. To get at the dipstick-cum-filler plug, the fairing has to come off unless you've got very thin, four-foot long arms. A removable panel would be so much more sensible. Perhaps that's why the sump has a nine-pint capacity.

And talking of capacity, the Ducati has a large capacity for going a long way. For a large-capacity, high-performance bike the Duke is very economical at 49mpg overall. With its 4½-gall tank this gives a range of 220 miles. Unfortunately, our Petrometa went on the blink, so we can't bring you steady-speed consumption figures this time.

Summary

If you're into riding for its own sake here's your bike. Light, low, powerful, near perfect handling. Add stunning looks and you've got a lot of motorcycle. You can get most of these things elsewhere, but not often such a sorted-out package.

The Ducati 900 Replica is comfortable and practical as well. It is rideable in traffic as well as ideal for long distances

one or two-up, as long as you can stand the hard suspension. You can even strap a small tank bag behind the filler of the huge tank, neatly avoiding the fuel spillage problem. All the electrics work, it keeps going in the rain and nothing fell off. Not many cafe-racers do those things. You get 37lb more bike than the 900SS, but it costs you £240 more at £2899. Even so, it compares favourably with other superbike prices and you get much more character. I'm glad Hailwood didn't do it on a Honda.

— Neil Millen

Now that motorcycle designers have charted the outer limits in terms of cylinders, power, weight and complexity, some people seem to have returned to earth orbit in their thinking. The virtues of low weight, usable power and good handling are once more being exploited in Japan as well as Europe. But nowhere has the synthesis of style and logic been displayed more effectively than in Italy, where a whole new breed of middleweight half-litres has emerged. Are they what motorcycling is really all about? We set out to evaluate two superficially similar designs — Ducati and Moto Morini's 500 sports V-twins — to discover if this is where it's at in the 1980s

Ducati Pantah

We're all familiar with the reputation that Ducatis have built up for themselves in this country: fast, temperamental engines in frames that handle like a racer's, but with the whole package let down by poor attention to finish and detail. Instruments were farcically inaccuarate, electrics tended to give up the ghost for no apparent reason, chrome fell away in record time and paint faded if you so much as mentioned an English winter.

Yes, you had to be a dedicated Ducatiphile to get the best from one. Certainly they were immensely satisfying when functioning properly, but you had to be an enthusiast with a really comprehensive range of tools.

Now we have a new approach from Ducati. For in the Pantah the factory have produced a machine in which almost all the components from lights to engine meet one very high standard. No longer can you describe

for two...

a Ducati as 'absolute perfection dressed in tatters' as someone once did as he sought to characterise the early 750 V-twins. This 500cc, 90 degree V-twin has a character made up of Italian temper without the tantrums, reliability without a trace of blandness. It's all Ducati, but the Ducati which critics thought they could never produce.

The new approach is evident at first glance. Where you'd expect to see two tubular covers for the shafts that drive the camshafts there are two wide, flat, highly-polished castings concealing pulleys and toothed rubber belts. And the electrics, once solely Italian, are a world-ranging mixture of Italian, German and Japanese components. The headlamp is a Japanese Stanley H4 unit, yet the indicators, rear light and instrument warning lights are Italian CEV components. And while the electronic ignition unit and fuse-box comes from Bosch, the battery is a Yuasa. Nippon Denso instruments are complemented by a switch cluster from that company on the left, but on the right the switchgear/twistgrip unit is made in Italy by Verilicchi. That's buying on a world market, all right. And, more importantly, this weird mixture — the fuel taps are from Italian suspension makers Paoli! — answers just about all the criticisms made by customers and press about Ducati components of days past.

Careful examination of the engine reveals quite clearly that this is not, repeat not, a scaled-down 900SS motor. It has so many carefully-considered

Gearchange linkage features only one Rose joint, but note removable panel to reach rear carburettor and crankcase window for easy timing

The superb chassis revealed, along with the cams' toothed belt drive: belt life is a pessimistic 12,000 miles. Note air filter under tank which let in water

One reason why the Pantah seems to handle so well — air-assisted Marzocchi dampers. Conti silencers are fairly muted for a Ducati

Vee for two...

details quite apart from the use of toothed belts to drive the desmodromic valve gear. And that, in itself, is nothing new when you consider Morini and Honda (Gold Wing) practice. Look at the little window in the crankcase to check the oil level: very Japanese. But look at the larger window on the other side through which you can strobe the timing: very advanced for anyone. No kickstart is fitted; the starter proved totally reliable.

It's a lovely engine to work on, desmodromic valve gear or no. There's a car-type, screw-in oil filter and small panels can be detached from the large glass fibre moulding at the rear so that you can get at the fuses on one side or the rear cylinder's carburettor on the other.

Out on the road the engine is beautifully smooth and revs to a 9050rpm redline with a will in all but fifth gear. As the valves are both opened and closed mechanically using the desmodromic valve gear developed by Ducati in the 1950s, piston speed obviously becomes the critical factor in engine performance.

So the Pantah's 499cc motor has massively over-square dimensions with a bore of 74mm against a 58mm stroke. Our test machine came with an incorrectly marked revcounter and we were assured that — for the purpose of discovering the machine's absolute top whack — that we could regard 10,000rpm as the limit. At that frenetic pace in fourth gear the Pantah put in a series of 114mph runs on the mile straight at the Motor Industry Research Association testing ground and then a best of 115.39mph on the longer banked circuit. An impressive performance, especially from a test bike with 7250 very hard miles under its belt.

Yet absolute top speed and more than adequate acceleration

— an average 14.5 seconds for the standing quarter-mile is certainly that — don't even begin to describe what the Pantah feels like on the road.

For a 500 twin the Pantah is remarkably light at 440lb (198kg), especially when you consider that it carries a man-sized four-gallon tank. But weight-saving isn't always a recipe for good handling. If you don't get the frame and suspension to harmonise with this lack of bulk it can lead to all sorts of unpleasantness. Naturally Ducati, famed for their expertise in this area, have got it right; and how.

The chassis and suspension are wonderfully sensitive to each slight correction in course you make. Once you've been in the saddle for a while it seems that all you have to do is think of the optimum line through the next bend and the Pantah receives the impulse by some kind of extra-sensory perception. It doesn't take miles to appreciate that here is a rolling chassis designed in a logical, coherent fashion. Unlike the situation — as I imagine it — in some Japanes factories, the men who build the engines at Ducati talk to the men who build the frames and select spring rates.

Engine and chassis complement each other perfectly. The handling and roadholding enable you to make (almost) full use of the fairly modest 46bhp available. It seems so right on the move. Everything is where it should be and operates with the minimum of quirkiness. You really would have to do something incredibly stupid to fall off this one — although it does tempt you to explore the outer limits of your skill and nerve. The Brembo brakes will rescue you from almost any disaster, come rain or shine.

I can't see how you could get a footrest on the deck on a Pantah without being right on the rag-

ed edge of the Pirelli Phan-oms' adhesion, which is con-derable. Incidentally, Ducati fit Michelins to Pantahs as original quipment, but the con-essionaires had fitted the Pirel-s on our test bike. They be-aved impeccably. The only time ey so much as stepped out was n a fast downhill left-hander quipped with a large white LOW sign across the whole ne. The fact that it was raining ard didn't help, either. Or the ct that Watson was breathing own my neck on the Morini.

Only occasionally was I trap-ed by the tall gearing and rced to slip into a lower gear as e hurtled across the Midlands search of yet more high-speed rills at the Long Marston drag rip. The gearing is curious: first quires a certain amount of utch slipping (worrying in view f the reputation of Ducati utches), while second, third nd fourth are closely grouped r fast getaways from tight urns. Which leaves fifth, a real verdrive ratio in which the en-ine will almost always refuse to ev past 8000rpm against wind nd gradient. That's well over the gal limit in miles per hour, but d like to see a rear sprocket fit-ed with a couple of teeth fewer an the one currently installed.

But what actually makes the ing handle so well? The frame self consists of a well-riangulated space frame into vhich the motor bolts as a tressed member. In fact the winging arm is—à la Guzzi V50 — actually mounted on to the ear of the crankcase. The pindle bushes are shrunk into ach crankcase half and the pindle is constantly lubricated y engine oil.

Up front, the Marzocchi fork is known quantity of proven vorth. The rear suspension is lso by Marzocchi, but with air-ssisted damping from remote eservoirs. Very flash they look oo — red body with black prings — but I can assure you hat it's not all show, for they eally do work. There's plenty f travel available and, more im-ortantly, it's under superb con-rol. I spent a short time follow-ng Watson when he took the Pantah for a gallop and watching he rear suspension movement vas quite fascinating. The springing soaks up the bumps very nicely and the damping is o controlled that the rest of the ike doesn't appear to react at ll. And that's just how it feels vhen you're on board.

Of course the riding position oes help considerably. The clip-ons and rear-set pegs are deally positioned. Since we pan a fairly remarkable range f heights in *The Biker* office it

was interesting to note that the Pantah's lovely angular, waisted tank and removable bum-stop suited everyone, without excep-tion.

Perhaps surprisingly, in view of its angular 'little 900SS' looks, perhaps not in view of its overall civility, the Pantah isn't an especially noisy machine for a Ducati. If you've ever heard of 900 on those Conti 'silencers' at maximum revs, you'll appreciate what the Yanks mean when they call four-strokes 'boomers'. The major component of the Pan-tah's row is induction roar. It's mechanically quiet thanks to silent belt-drive for the cams, with just a snickering from the valve gear and the Contis on this one make a real attempt at silence.

In fact, induction noise wasn't the only thing to come out of the barrel-shaped air filter under the tank. Some water got in there, ran down the rear carb's intake hose and gave us problems for a couple of days. Watson now claims to hold the world record for dropping the float bowl off a 36mm Dellorto. If you have pro-blems with one, we suggest you drill the filter housing and pipe off the excess fluid.

Detail points that jarred the senses slightly amongst this near-perfection were few. The three-screw fixing for the seat hump — remove it to convert the saddle into an intimate dualseat — looks a little tacky. The inside of the fairing could be better fin-ished and we'd like *two* Rose joints on the rear-set gearchange linkage, please. This set-up is a great improvement, but it's still too sloppy.

Apart from those points, the machine looks simply superb and will keep its looks too. We were very agreeably surprised at the standard of paint, chrome, glass fibre and ABS (used on the front and rear guards in a funereal black).

So where do Ducati go from here? This is without doubt the engine they'll be developing, in the same way that the men at Moto Guzzi are working on the V50's power unit in preference to older designs.

It is known that a 720cc ver-sion exists (I want one!) and that the British importers concluded their assessment of the Pantah by requesting a 750 in the same chassis.

In the Pantah, Ducati have combined their undoubted skills as engine and frame builders with an almost Japanese reliability without sacrificing the character of a truly European motorcycle. It's difficult to see how they could improve on such an effort, but if they do we'll be delighted to ride it.

One thing saddens me, how-ever. It's the price you have to pay for this sort of engineering. £2299 is one hell of a lot for a 500, even one as good as the Pantah. Try not to ride one if you can't afford the payments. Otherwise you'll just break your heart every time one whistles by you with some lucky cuss in the saddle.

Julian Ryder

Moto-Morini Maestro

Market research, as a woman for whom I was tasting marmalade in Croydon remarked, exists to give the customer what he wants. Or at least what he says he wants, I thought as I idly picked a piece of ersatz orange peel from bet-ween my teeth. For market research usually comes up with this simple formula from the biker in the street when he's asked what improvements he'd like to see made to his machine: more of the same, only make it bigger and faster. And look where that got us.

This then is the Morini dilemma. For a company famed for its tiny but magnificently rapid four-stroke singles — any-thing from ohc 123cc road bikes to 246cc dohc racers developing 35bhp at 11,000rpm — small and light is obviously where it's at. Provini's 250 single was timed at 137mph; Rome is knee-deep in ageing ohv Morini road singles.

But when you build a phenomenally-quick ohv 350 V-twin like the 3½ Sport, which comes equipped with a chassis that feels like it could handle a 750 motor, you have a problem. People will constantly ask for more of the same — more cubic centimetres, more power and a lot more speed.

It's impossible to resist this kind of marketing pressure,

however much you might like to. And anyway, the 3½ was designed as a 500 but cut down to 344cc to cope with one of those weird capacity/tax classes with which Europe — and es-pecially Italy — seems to abound. Yet if you launch a 479cc version of something that is incredibly quick for a 'mere' 350 four-stroke twin at not far short of the ton, it had better deliver something extra in terms of performance, right? Wrong.

If the Morini V-twins were built in Japan — improbable, as they're as Italian as a stiletto in the back — then the two 3½ models would have been drop-ped on the British market when a 500 appeared. There's no tax or insurance advantage over here for a 350 and only a paltry £210 currently separates the 3½ Sport and 500 Maestro. Slightly strange from a marketing point of view, for potential customers will obviously want to know what the 500 has to offer over and above the 350, other than 134.6cc.

In a nutshell that is the question that testers have been asking themselves when they've tried to come to terms with the Maestro while their heads were still full of 3½ Sport. They've seen the 500 and 350 V-twins as competitors when in fact they're alternatives. It's that simple, and the slight price dif-ferential emphasises that this must be the correct approach to the Maestro. You have to try and forget the 3½ Sport and con-centrate on the Pantah/Maestro split.

And what a difference there is here. All that unites the two machines are the facts that both are four-stroke V-twins made in Italy by folk who know how to build motorcycle frames.

But that wasn't what I was thinking about in the bath at 7am on a recent summer's morning. What I was thinking was that after the two inches of rain that had fallen overnight it could be that the Motor Industry Research Association's proving ground was under a few feet of water. Just as my daughter threw a plastic duck past my ear from the taps end the lady on Radio 4 who brings gloom and despondency into my life every day of the week reported that there was a three-mile tail-back of cars on the M1. I made a noise like a sick sea-lion and reached for a towel.

Out on the street with the Maestro and encased in leathers and rainsuit I cursed the day as the electric starter failed to fire the 72-degree V-twin. As furious kicks on the left-mounted kick-starter failed to elicit more than a faint cough the language got worse. Snicking the five-speed box into second I pushed off down the road. Then I pushed it up the road. Then I thought about throwing up into my Bell, but resisted the upward flow of recently-ingested breakfast. Eventually it fired into raucous

life and I eased off the handlebar-mounted choke control as a large puddle of sweat gathered round the waistband of my Y-fronts.

I cannot remember having a test machine in such a strange state of tune. Once mobile it was fine: it would kick over hot at the first prod and pulled fairly well up to the 7500rpm redline. But it still felt a trifle slow at the top end. I felt angry and hurt. Angry just because that's the way you get with bikes that won't start; hurt because I've ridden enough Morinis and know enough people who own them to want one for myself. It was all so untypical, so annoying.

On a sodden A5 heading north for MIRA, with Mr Winfield on the Pantah, we soon got going. Very shortly we were motoring at speeds that would have had other machines sliding brakeless under oncoming trucks. The road was alternately flooded and coated in wash-outs of mud, gravel and hedgerow. Both bikes

just laughed it off, braking impecably, taking curves like cats running across roof tiles, feeling very, very safe in appalling conditions. At the track both were down on performance: the Pantah refusing to make more than 105mph, the Maestro 95mph. Hasty phone calls to both importers arranged re-runs with the results you can see.

Of course it's partly the Maestro's fault that it had received such a hammering in the hands of the press hacks. The bike's handling and brakes are so good and so much 'faster' than the engine that it gets wound out to the point where you think that connecting rods must start appearing from under the fuel tank, mile after mile, after mile.

The Morini differed from the Ducati quite markedly in terms of riding position, suspension and power delivery. The Maestro's footrests are far too far forward, just as they are on both the 3½ Sport and Strada. it's not too uncomfortable, and you do get

used to it, but now that th original 'touring' spec 500 is n longer offered you can opt for Maestro with a top fork yoke th will accept a nice flat handleba as an alternative to the blac clip-ons. It's certainly the way I want to go, despite the rad looks of the clip-ons with th neat Morini fairing, a £62.5 extra.

The Maestro's Marzocchi for is a superb piece of equipmen as are its three Grimeca dis brakes. In fact they're almost tc fierce, and require gentle app cation. However, the simple o damped Marzocchi re dampers with their rock-lil springs are outclassed by th Ducati's more expensive unit The Morini's rear-end comp ance over rough roads is limite so that although the wonderful stiff chassis keeps everything line, you get a bumpy ride.

Something else that wou help at speed is rubber mountir for the clip-ons. Although the i evitable vibration that resu from the out-of-balance forc inherent in a 72 degree V-tw design — as opposed to Ducati 90 degree alternative — doesn numb you bum or shake yo boots off the footrests, it do come through to your hanc quite strongly at high revs.

Talking of revs it's interestir to note that the Maestro pr duces its 46bhp at 7500rpn This is where it differs noticeab from the 3½ Sport, redlined 8500rpm. The 500 Morini much torquier than the 35 with a smooth flood of pow uninterrupted by a 3½ Spo type power step. So there's r need for a six-speed gearbox quite as much footwork wi your right boot.

One problem associated wi the Morini's parallel valves, fl head and bowl-in-piston co figuration is the restriction places on valve size. The 3 Sport runs 25mm Dellortos, th Maestro 26mm. So whether yc attribute the Ducati's superi performance to valve size or i ability to rev so freely witho fear of valve bounce, the Mori is obviously losing out som where. By way of recompense delivers excellent mileage p gallon.

Out on the road the differen in performance is not nearly marked, as we discovered. T Ducati may be smoother, mo comfortable and mechanica quieter, but it cannot shake th Morini off, especially in fif gear.

The Maestro's worst featur are its toolkit, which contains th cheapest of cheap stamped-o spanners; its headlight (than goodness for Cibié) and thinly-coated black exhaus

	Ducati SL500 Pantah	**Moto-Morini 500 Maestro**
PERFORMANCE		
Maximum speed	115.39mph	104.30mph
Standing ¼ mile	14.5sec / 95.15mph	15.30sec / 83.45mph
FUEL CONSUMPTION		
Overall	48mpg	56mpg
Best	50mpg	61mpg
Worst	45mpg	51mpg
Average full tank range	201 miles	196 miles
SPEEDOMETER ACCURACY		
At indicated 30mph	25.87mph	29.03mph
At indicated 60mph	54.74mph	58.06mph
BRAKING DISTANCE		
From 30pmh	34ft (10.4m)	36ft 6in (11.1m)
From 60mph	139ft (42.4m)	139ft (42.4m)
ENGINE		
Type	Desmodromic ohc 90deg V-twin	Ohv 72 degree in-line V-twin
Bore x stroke	74 x 58mm	69 x 64mm
Capacity	499cc	478.6cc
Compression ratio	9.5:1	11.2:1
Carburation	Two 36mm Dellorto	Two 26mm Dellorto
Claimed bhp at rpm	46 at 8500	46 at 7500
Claimed torque at rpm	N/a	32ft-lb (4.42kgm) at 5500
Transmission	Gear primary drive, wet multiplate clutch, 5-speed gearbox, chain final drive	Gear primary drive, dry multiplate clutch, 5-speed gearbox, chain final drive
ELECTRICAL SYSTEM	200W alternator, 12V, 14Ah battery, electronic ignition, 55/60W H4 headlight	140W alternator, 12V 15Ah battery, electronic ignition, 40/45W headlight
CYCLE PARTS		
Frame	Tubular space frame using engine as stressed member	Duplex cradle
Suspension	Telescopic front fork, pivoted rear fork with 5-way adjustable air-assisted dampers	Telescopic front fork, pivoted rear fork with 5-way adjustable dampers
Wheels	6-spoke cast aluminium alloy	7-spoke cast aluminium alloy
Tyres	4.10 x 18in Pirelli Phantom front 4.10 x 19in Pirelli Phantom rear	3.50 x 18in Pirelli Phantom front 3.50 x 18in Pirelli Gordon rear
Brakes	Twin 10.25 (260mm) discs front 10.25in (260mm) disc rear	Twin 10in (254mm) discs front 10in (254mm) disc rear
DIMENSIONS		
Wheelbase	57in (1448mm)	57.5in (1460mm)
Seat height	31in (787mm)	31in (787mm)
Overall width	26in (660mm)	28in (711mm)
Ground clearance	7.5in (190mm)	7in (178mm)
Weight (with 1 gal fuel)	440lb (199.6kg)	420lb (190.5kg)
Fuel capacity	4.2gal	3.5gal
PRICE	£2299 inc VAT	£1735 inc VAT (fairing £62.50)
Warranty	12 months/unlimited mileage	6 months parts
Supplied by	Ducati Concessionaires UK Ltd, 51-61 Park Street, Luton, Beds	Harglo Ltd, 462 Station Road, Dorridge, Solihull, Warks.

Morini tacho is electronic | Pushrod motor is easy to work on | Rear dampers make for a 'sporting' ride

secondhand Morinis and Ducatis are often no advertisement for new models in terms of finish. And selling such a machine without a Ducati-like handlebar-end mirror will soon lose you customers as they forfeit their licences.

However, these are pretty small considerations when you're in heaven, dragging the sole of your boot on the road through a tight curve. It's so selfish, so sophisticated and yet still a little raw. When you're ready, Maestro . . .

Peter Watson

In conclusion . . .

If one motorcycle can impress — not to say delight — a whole office full of journalists, then it must possess wide-ranging appeal. We all loved the Ducati Pantah, which says a great deal for the many ways in which it differs from earlier Dukes. Yet it still manages to retain a very distinctive character and a very attractive one at that. Its only significant drawback is price. At

£2299 you might be tempted to go for something of twice its capacity from Japan. But beware — you could get blown into the weeds through the curves while attempting to get that super-techno, whizzo-whirro 1000cc four on line.

The Maestro remains something of an enigma. Although it is what it appears to be in one sense — more of the delightful 3½ Sport — it feels

to have been left at the lights by the Ducati in terms of top speed, suspension and reliability. It is less well equipped — and its £1735 price tag reflects this. We felt that while the 500 Morini is an immensely enjoyable machine it still needs many of its rough edges smoothing down. It remains a true uncompromising 'enthusiasts' mount.

However, if you do choose either of these machines you can be assured of owning a motorcycle of distinctive character. And one that represents, to us at least, a superlative blend of power and handling. You can use all the performance, nearly all of the time. So after you've found the money, keeping your licence could be the major problem.

500 DESMO

DUCATI PANTAH 500SL

It's a Ducati, a desmo and a mobile Italian flashgun; so what's so new? Everything! Engine, bike and all.

● THE DUCATI PANTAH IS THE MOST important motorcycle to come out of Europe in the last five years: important because this motorcycle demonstrates the direction in which Europeans are likely to aim their machinery, because the Pantah indicates what Europeans can and cannot do in the realm of motorcycles in the 1980s, because this 500 V-twin is the first genuinely *new* European bike in a long time. Furthermore, the Pantah bears the engineering stamp of Ing. Fabio Taglioni, who has been Ducati's one-man engineering *tour de force;* the 500 stands at the end of a long, cast-aluminum line that extends deep into the 1950s, and almost all of those products bear his mark.

The front half of the gas tank usually hides the ganged electrics; the cylindrical airbox resides under the rear portion. A detachable side cover gives easy access to the battery for routine maintenance chores.

Two overhead ladder frame sections form a box under which the engine fits. The engine "hangs" from six tabs, and the tubular-section swing arm pivots on a pin that passes through bushings in the rear of the crankcase.

The huge 36mm Dell'Orto carburetors draw air through a paper filter. Air headed for the rear carb must flow through two 90-degree bends in the air boot; air for the front carb has to deal with only one sharp turn.

DUCATI PANTAH 500SL

One could argue, and persuasively so, that the Taglioni-designed Ducati GT750s and 750 Super Sport Desmos, first seen in the United States in 1972 and 1973, re-legitimatized the V-twin concept, and ended once and for all the hoary assertion that V-types belonged to the days of Indian and Vincent. Those first 750 Ducati V-twins demonstrated to enthusiasts and the enthusiast press that V-twins were an effective way to power a modern sporting motorcycle.

Being first is only that and nothing more, first. This has not been lost on Italians. Fiat pioneered the front-wheel-drive econobox with the 128 sedan (Anglophiles will kindly spare us cries of Austin Minis); the Germans perfected the arrangement with the Golf-Rabbit; the Japanese made them better and cheaper; and Fiat, a bit worse for wear and dusty, wondered where everyone went. Thus Taglioni and Ducati, having been first, knew that having been first would be no guarantee in the end against having been had. The 500 Pantah, then, isn't an updated or revamped or redone 750-series engine. The Pantah is a new engine in a new motorcycle.

At first glance the 499cc Pantah engine appears to be a shrunk-down 750, a tighter, squatter engine with characteristically Ducati heads and cylinders. Resemblance, yes; but that's it. Wave goodbye to the old gear-and-tower camshaft drives. Inside the Pantah, rubber toothed belts drive the desmo valve gear. Toothed belts have the advantage of being light, quiet and easy to install and maintain, and they can be quite durable. With the Pantah, however, Ducati recommends replacing the belts every 12,500 miles or two years, whichever comes first. These frequent changes are probably designed as a safeguard to preclude belt-failure problems.

Past Ducatis used spiral-bevel gears to drive the single overhead cams through towershafts, a system that was an adaptation from the single-cylinder bikes dating back to the late 'fifties. When Taglioni designed his first overhead cam motorcycle engines, a toothed belt solution wasn't viable, and the drive options were chains or gears. Bevelled gears and towers made Ducati engines very labor-intensive to build; the 750 twin, for example, had shims everywhere. Furthermore, noise control increasingly became a concern in the 1970s, and a dozen gear faces meshing didn't help.

The new belt technology not only solved the noise problem, it made the Pantah engine less labor-intensive and therefore less expensive to build. That's the whole point of being able to take advantage of new technology to redo an idea: you get a better product than before, and it costs less.

While the toothed-belt drive is the prime example of updated technology in the Pantah, the new engine fairly bristles with changes. The powerplant has been engineered to be built efficiently, to put the greatest number of parts in the least amount of space, and to save weight wherever reasonably possible. (With a curb weight of 433 pounds fully gassed, the Ducati is lighter than all Japanese 500/550cc bikes, excluding the single-cylinder Yamaha 500.) The result is a motorcycle that's surprisingly compact, light and simplified—and has room for further development.

The toothed belts and valve gear are driven off a jackshaft that takes power off the engine's left side via gears. The jackshaft runs between the cylinders—and turns belt pulleys on the right side. The jackshaft helps to keep the engine extremely narrow (14.8 inches wide) since the camshaft drive no longer forces the alternator far out on the end of the crank. The crank can be shorter and stiffer than would otherwise be the case. Two aluminum belt pulleys mount on the right side of the jackshaft; in the timing belt cavity the pulleys and rubber belts are sealed off from dust (outside) and oil (inside the crankcase).

Beneath the timing belt cavity on the right side is a very Ducati-looking multi-plate wet clutch, which is driven by helical-cut primary gears. On the left end of the crankshaft there are two drive gears. One spins the jackshaft gear, the second connects to a sprague clutch, through an idler gear and thence to the electric starter mounted at the lower front of the crankcase. Outboard of these gears is the crank-mounted capacitor-discharge ignition rotor and the small permanent magnet rotor for the alternator.

The Pantah has a one-piece crank, unlike the pressed-together cranks used in other Ducati engines. One-piece cranks can't tweak out of alignment, and it takes fewer production steps to build them. The crank is stronger, and in production it's easier to control the distances between the interior faces of the main bearing journals; we suspect that the Pantah crank is much easier than 900-series Ducatis' to shim to proper clearance in its vertically split crankcase.

The switch to one-piece cranks dictates the use of two-piece connecting rods with plain-bearing big ends and a high-pressure oil system compatible with plain-bearing engines. Plain-bearing big ends (Pantah mains are ball bearings) may cause Ducati traditionalists to wrinkle their noses, but there's nothing wrong with plain-bearing big ends as long as they get high-pressure lubrication and the oil film between bearings and journal doesn't break down. And as long as you have hell-for-strong two-piece rods, which the Pantah does: short, squat tough-looking pieces.

Like the pumps used on the 750/900 engines, the Pantah pump is a gear type; but its 78-92 psi flow rate is much higher than the 15 psi of those other pumps. To

New technology comes to Bologna: innovation in the form of jackshaft-powered rubber belts to drive the camshafts, and conveniences such as an automotive-type spin-on oil filter and a small view window for monitoring the crankcase oil level.

The ignition rotor and a permanent-magnet rotor for the alternator mount on the left side of the crankshaft. The swing-arm pivot pin that mounts in the cases is visible to the right of the countershaft sprocket.

Helical-cut gears that transfer power from the crank to the jackshaft lie behind the rotors. The electric starter mounts in front of the engine and spins the crankshaft through an idler gear and a sprague clutch.

The Pantah uses an all-indirect-drive gearbox. Gears on the input shaft that carry the heaviest loads ride outboard near the bearings for better support.

The two-piece connecting rods ride on plain bearings and require high-pressure lubrication. The one-piece crank must be shimmed in the vertically split cases.

New Ducati engine uses cylinder heads with a 60-degree included valve angle. Present 74mm bore diameter allows the Pantah room to grow in displacement.

The pulley-driven camshaft actuates two valves through four rocker arms: two "normal" arms push the valves open; two forked arms pull the valves closed.

The right side case houses the clutch, primary drive gears and the 78-92 psi gear-type oil pump. Twin belt pulleys mount on the right side of the jackshaft.

Inside view shows stout construction: cast-in webbing adds case strength, crank spins in angular thrust bearings as per standard Ducati 750/900 practice.

DUCATI PANTAH 500SL

understand how radical this switch is, you must consider that the Italians have only recently switched from wire-mesh oil strainers to the vastly superior disposable paper element filters. Like the newer Ducatis, the Pantah features a spin-on automotive-type paper filter; it's located under the right side case and is very accessible.

As expected, the Pantah's 74.0 x 58.0mm bore and stroke (very similar to the classic 250's 74.0mm x 57.8mm figures) make the 500 far more oversquare than the 86.0 x 74.4mm 900. The Pantah runs happily near 10,000 rpm, a figure beyond the road-going big twin, though the Ducati isn't in the same oversquare world of the three-valve 10,000-rpm Honda CB400 (70.5 x 50.6). It's irresistible to speculate about how oversquare this engine *could* get: 80mm x 58mm would produce 583cc, and still that would only yield a safe 3800 piston feet per minute.

Boring the Pantah engine out wouldn't be easy. The aluminum cylinders lack the iron liners used in Ducatis from time immemorial. Instead, the 500's cylinder walls are Gilnisil, a plating that contains tiny silicon and carbon particles. This super-hard plating wears like diamonds, saves weight and greatly improves heat transfer (see BMW road test, March 1981). The stuff is actually Nikasil, which is becoming much more widely used as cylinder wall material; Gilnisil is, we presume, one trade name for the plating. Should a cylinder become damaged or excessively worn (unlikely), replacement is the only cure; plated cylinders cannot be honed or rebored. However, the Gilnisil cylinder's increased durability should offset the cost differential of replacement in the long run.

Except for the method of power drive, the Ducati desmodromic valve gear design remains unchanged. Each head uses a single four-lobed camshaft and four rocker arms to actuate the single exhaust and intake valve. Fairly conventional-looking rocker arms open the valves, while forked rocker arms close the valves by lifting up against special valve-closing collars that clip on the valve stems. This positive, mechanical method of valve actuation eliminates the need for conventional valve springs as well as eliminating the possibility of valve float at high-rpm levels. Light auxiliary springs are necessary to close the valves and ensure sufficient compression for combustion during starting. Once the engine is running, these springs are too weak to affect engine performance.

The most significant factor in the cylinder heads is the 60-degree included angle between the valves. For a long time, one limiting factor in the race development of Ducati big twins was the 80-degree included valve angle; that angle

made it almost impossible to get a lot of compression and a good piston design—one that would not demand a high dome that split the combustion chamber in two and ruined flame propagation. Moreover, less valve angle and a shallower combustion cavity in the head allows better inlet and exhaust tract shapes for better flow. The valves, 37.5mm intake and 33.5mm exhaust, need deepish pockets in the pistons, and the perimeters of the pockets (at the edge of the piston) and the valve placement in the chamber suggest that this engine has room to grow in bore size without resorting to an unfashionably wide squishband.

Huge 36mm Dell' Orto carburetors feed the Pantah engine; they mixed less cleanly than we would have liked. Our Pantah ran very rich. Cold starting was always difficult because full choke was too rich on even the chilliest mornings. The cam-type on/off enriching lever, located forward in the fairing, doesn't lend itself to partial settings. We usually ended up playing with various throttle openings to get the bike started, especially since the choke lever is so awkward to reach. Furthermore, the Pantah would run faster on the top end with the throttle partially closed rather than wide open, and increased elevations magnified the annoyance. Finally, the 500's jetting richness hurt the bike at the drag strip. Since full throttle doesn't necessarily produce maximum power, we had to experiment with different throttle settings, a tactic that just as easily hinders times as helps.

The drag strip isn't the Pantah's bailiwick. Besides the rich-running engine, there's the matter of gearing. An incredibly tall first gear (52 mph @ 10,000 rpm) works against rocket launches and dictates the use of high engine speed and much clutch slipping in order to get off the line decently. Even with heartless disregard for the clutch, we bogged the Pantah every time coming out of the hole. Luckily, the 500 is blessed with a stout clutch; it endured over two dozen launches without a whimper.

Shifting at the 8000-rpm redline produced a sluglike 14.51-second quarter. Since the engine felt willing and Italian publications had used 10,500 rpm in their performance testing, we worked by feel. We never entered the land of five-digit engine speeds, but 9800 rpm was close. Our best time of 13.66 seconds (trap speed 98.14 mph) is quite respectable for a 500cc twin, though it pales when compared with the new-wave 550 four-cylinder bikes from Japan. To give a frame of reference for performance, the Ducati is midway between a Suzuki GS450 (14.13 seconds @ 93.16 mph) and the Yamaha XJ550 Seca (13.16 seconds @ 99.44 mph). The Kawasaki GPz550 (12.86 seconds @ 102.62 mph) is the quickest and fastest of the lot at the drag strip. All you get here are bald comparisons because the Ducati's jetting,

gearing and streamlining skew any direct comparison. Jetted perfectly, the Ducati engine would have responded crisply and the bike would have been quicker and faster at the drag strip; but make no mistake: the Ducati at optimum isn't a 12-second quarter-miler.

The Pantah's drag strip performance surprised us—the bike felt slow on the road. The engine's incredible smoothness, its presumably flat torque curve, and the fairing's still-air pocket make a seat-of-pants gauge read "slow." But feel and actual performance can be two different things.

Even though the engine never leaps upward in a cammy rush, the engine revs willingly. It starts working at 2500 rpm, picks up at 7000 rpm, then pulls as far into redline as you dare to take it, except in top gear; in fifth it will only pull to the 8000 rpm redline and only after a long run down a billiard-table-flat road. Although we tended to stretch the throttle cables, we averaged a miserly 48.1 mpg (despite the jetting), good for 240 miles with the huge five-gallon tank.

The Ducati gearbox will be a revelation to those raised on a strict diet of Trans-Pacific machinery: the shift action is wonderful, the best thing we've tried since the 788 MV Agusta. The Pantah shifts with low effort; it's smooth and crisp with a positive detent for each gear, and no false neutrals lurk in hidden corners. There is virtually no driveline snatch to complicate shifting or low-speed maneuvers. The ratios are spread a useful distance from one another and never form too wide a gap for road riding, especially if you're willing to violate the low redline. That high first gear would be a problem in town were it not for the Pantah's broad spread of power.

What you will notice in town and everywhere else is the draw pressure at the clutch lever. It's as high as anything in recent memory. The effort level is acceptable for 1971, not 1981. The limited amount of clearance between the centercase and the right side case makes the clutch actuating lever arm shorter than it might have been, which reduces the amount of mechanical advantage available. This may explain why the clutch takes a lot of pressure at the hand lever. Regardless of reason, Ducati needs a mechanical redesign here.

The Pantah violates the American sense of good ergonomics in other ways. The clip-on handlebars, firm (and thin) saddle and high footpegs result in a stretched-out, semi-road-racing riding position. If you are the right size, the riding position is effective for a short backroad thrash; outside that environment, specifically on freeways and in town, the Pantah has its rider suffering from aching wrists, nagging back and numbing butt before much time or mileage has rolled by. The Pantah's sporting position gives us pain just as surely as the begging-dog

139

DUCATI PANTAH 500SL

position characteristic of cruiser-type motorcycles. We think bikes should be comfortable in more than one mode. Agony knows not cause, just agony.

Given our druthers, we'd have the Pantah done in the "Darmah" trim rather than the "Super Sport" configuration. That would produce a riding position that would be comfortable for a full afternoon's travel.

No matter how fast you take the Pantah down a winding road, the bike is stable. The 57-inch wheelbase is long for a mid-sized bike and the 30.5-degree steering-head angle is greater than most other motorcycles' regardless of size. These two figures combine to make the bike track with rock-solid assurance, although at a cost in increased steering effort. You can't casually flick the Pantah into corners; when riding quickly, proper technique requires handlebar pressure (counter steering) to get the Pantah into the corner. Lighter-steering Japanese bikes, such as the Kawasaki or Yamaha 550s, follow the rider's weight and need a less-conscious effort at the bars. And once the railroad-car-like Ducati is on its cornering course, the rider must exert a fair amount of pressure to get the Pantah to change lines, assuming that's necessary. To those accustomed to Japanese motorcycles, riding the Ducati will seem like switching from a car with power steering to one with manual steering: it's not necessarily more difficult, but the feel

Cycle
Test Specifications
DUCATI PANTAH 500SL

Make and model .... Ducati Pantah 500 SL
Price, suggested retail (as of 3/4/81) $4549

PERFORMANCE

Standing start ¼ mile .... 13.66 @ 98.14
Engine rpm @ 60 mph, top gear 4156
Average fuel consumption rate ...... 48.1 mpg (20.4 km/l)
Cruising range, main/reserve .... 240/24 mi.
Load capacity (GVWR less curb weight).......... 140.6 kg
(310 lbs.)
Maximum speed in gears @ engine redline .... (1) 41.6
(2) 60.6 (3) 78.0
(4) 96.8 (5) 115.5

ENGINE

Type .... Four-stroke 90-degree V-twin,
air-cooled with single overhead
camshafts, belt-driven
Bore and stroke .... 74.0 x 58.0mm (2.91 x 2.28 in.)
Piston displacement .... 499cc (30.40 cu. in.)
Compression ratio 9.5:1
Carburetion............................. (2) Dell'Orto 36mm
Exhaust system .... Two into two
Ignition .... Battery-powered, inductive,
magnetically triggered
Air filtration .... Paper element, disposable
Oil filtration .... Paper element, disposable
Oil capacity .... 3.0 liters (3.2 qts.)
Bhp @ rpm .... NA
Torque @ rpm .... NA

TRANSMISSION

Type :............. Five-speed, constant-mesh, wet clutch
Primary drive .... Helical gear, 2.23:1
Final drive .... #530 chain, 2.53:1
Gear ratios, overall :.......... (1) 14.09 (2) 9.66 (3) 7.51
(4) 6.05 (5) 5.07

CHASSIS

Type .... Overhead, tubular-ladder frame
Suspension, front .... Center-axle, coil-spring fork
with 126mm of travel
rear ..Swing arm with (2) dampers adjustable
for preload, yielding 90mm of travel
Wheelbase .... 1448mm (57.0 in.)
Rake .... 30.5°
Brake, front .... Hydraulic, dual-disc 260mm
rotors (10.32 in.), with single-piston caliper
rear .... Hydraulic, single-disc 260mm rotor
(10.32 in.), with single-piston caliper
Wheel, front .... Cast, 18 x 2.15
rear .... Cast, 18 x 2.15
Tire, front .... 3.25 H 18 Michelin S41
rear .... 3.50 V 18 Michelin M45
Seat height .... 792mm (31.2 in.)
Ground clearance .... 155mm (6.1 in.)
Fuel capacity, main/reserve ....19.0/2.0 liters
(5.0/0.5 gal.)
Curb weight, full tank ....196.4 kg (433.0 lbs.)
Test weight ....269.0 kg (593.0 lbs.)

ELECTRICAL

Power source .... Alternator, 200 watts
Charge control .... Solid-state voltage regulator
Headlight beams, high/low .... 60/55 watts
Tail/stop lights .... 5/21 watts
Battery... 12V 14AH

INSTRUMENTS

Includes...............Speedometer, odometer, tripmeter,
tachometer with 8000-rpm redline. Indicators
for lights, high beam, turn signals, neutral, "generator."
Speedometer error,
30 mph indicated, actual 29.23
60 mph indicated, actual 56.35

CUSTOMER SERVICE CONTACT
Berliner Motor Corporation
Railroad Street and Plant Road
P.O. Box 145
Hasbrouck Heights, NJ 07604

Cycle's *Schenk dynamometer, long residing at Webco, Inc., in Venice, California, is in the process of being moved and re-installed at a new location. Consequently, this motorcycle could not be dyno-tested at this time. Figures for this motorcycle will appear in Cycle in an upcoming issue.*

Ducati Pantah

is distinctly heavy. This trade-off, heavy steering for rock-solid stability, makes it easy—or at least reassuring—for most riders to go quickly. But it's worth noting that at least two staffers would have much preferred a Ducati that required less steering input effort.

In keeping with Ducati tradition the Pantah uses Italian Marzocchi suspension components at both ends. They complement the stable steering characteristics by supplying a firm, sport-oriented ride that comfort-oriented types would consider too stiff. The shocks feature nitrogen-pressurized reservoirs that hold extra oil to prevent heat fade. While we can question the necessity of reservoir shocks on a 500cc street bike, they certainly do have sales appeal. The Marzocchis offer five settings for spring preload; the springs were a little stiff, but they didn't overwhelm the adequate damping action.

The 35mm fork tubes, smaller than those used on the 900cc Ducatis, are sufficient for the Pantah's weight. Like the shocks, the fork is stiffly sprung but offers good damping action. The fork had too much stiction and its responsiveness to small road irregularities such as freeway expansion seams suffers. The Ducati lacks the suspension adjustability of contemporary Japanese sports bikes. In view of this, Ducati has set up the suspension on the stiff side. The Pantah is such a one-dimensional sports motorcycle that its lack of adjustability may be understandable, if not forgivable. The Pantah remains calm and controlled when traversing patches of less-than-perfect pavement at speed. Bumps, cracks and dips leave the 500 unruffled, taking some of the fuss out of high-speed backroad riding.

Generally speaking, ground clearance will not limit your riding the 500 hard. By deleting the sidestand, Ducati has eliminated this traditional cornering bugaboo, but convenience in parking does suffer. We would have preferred that Ducati retain the sidestand and mount it out of harm's way. The centerstand tang on the left grounds with some regularity. If you bang the centerstand out of the way, next come the pipes on each side. If you're dragging these as a matter of course, find a racetrack: a sponsor must be looking for you.

The three disc brakes do an admirable but not perfect job of stopping the 500. Brake actuation is linear and feedback, good; but the twin front disc brakes take an unusually firm squeeze to maximize stopping. The square edges on the front brake lever also annoyed some testers.

Although past Ducatis used the engine as a stressed member, the Pantah frame uses the engine as an actual load-bearing member by merit of the swing-arm pivot that passes through the rear of the crankcase. This feature and the unique ladder-configuration frame demonstrate the extremes to which Ducati went to keep the Pantah as compact as possible. The longish engine and wandering exhaust plumbing left no room for downtubes. The engine "hangs" from the ladder, bolting to the frame by six tabs: two forward tabs in the crotch of the cylinders and four (two high, two low) aft of the gearbox.

By appearances the chassis shouldn't work; the Pantah doesn't follow the time-honored tradition of rigidly tying the swing-arm pivot area to the steering head. Think about it: The swing arm feeds loads into the crankcase which, in turn, may deflect (relative to the steering head) slightly in the frame. What should work or shouldn't in theory is one thing; what does is another. In stock configuration the Pantah frame works well. It may be that the Pantah doesn't have enough power and/or weight to load the chassis enough to distort the steering head in relation to the swing-arm pivot. If this chassis is going to show a handling problem it will take more power than the Ducati has now to reveal any shortcoming.

The body pieces that attach to the chassis are also somewhat unusual. The seat fastens to the seat platform with three screws that also secure the detachable mono-posto subsection. Set up for solo riding, the saddle does hold you in place—if you happen to be exactly the right size. None of our testers happened to be that particular size. We rode with the full-length option.

A small storage compartment, suitable for a pair of gloves, is integrated into the tail end of the seat platform. The platform's fiberglass work extends forward over the frame rails to the rear of the tank and down to the detachable fiberglass side panels. The seat platform bolts to the frame, but you'll rarely need to worry about removal because almost all maintenance items are located behind the side covers or under the steel gas tank. Removing the left side cover gives access to the rear carburetor, while the battery rests behind the right. Even though only two rubber straps hold the tank in place, removing the tank is awkward. Tight clearances and friction between the tank and the rubber frame cushions inhibit movement. Removing the tank exposes the electrics and the cylindrical plastic airbox that houses the paper air filter.

The Pantah shows that Europeans won't build motorcycles in the classic UJM form. Trying to go head-to-head with the Japanese would kill the Europeans. The Pantah message is clear. Using the most current technology available to them, Europeans can build motorcycles that are innovative and original. These machines will stress lightness, a virtue that's far more obtainable for Europeans than the complexity of six cylinders and signal-seeking radios. Furthermore, the Europeans must be clever engineers, in order to get the maximum number of displacement models out of the same basic engine and cycle parts. Engineering finesse must carry the Europeans rather than reliance on corporation size.

In one way or another, these factors commit the Europeans to low production numbers by Japanese standards and to narrow-spectrum machines with well-defined clienteles. It becomes a case of matching volume and buyers. If you're going to build very few of something, it had better be built for The Few because it will be expensive. The Pantah is certainly that: $4549.

It is apparent that European motorcycles like the Ducati Pantah are not going to be better than Japanese machines in objective measurements. Any of the new Japanese middleweights will run with, if not away from, the Pantah, and anyone looking for ultimate performance at the Pantah's price level could buy a Suzuki GS1100 and have $550 in change for gas money.

If not better than the Japanese standard, European motorcycles will be different. Different, expensive, low-volume and narrow spectrum are qualities that add up to one word: Elite. The Ducati is perfect for the individualist who believes that the Japanese are much too sensible to build anything like the Pantah. ◉

141

Duke of Earl

Ducatis, it is commonly asserted, suffer more than most from the effects of inclement weather. To be specific, they rust. Less now than previously, so we're told; but the problem still exists. If you had seen our staff Darmah when it was finally laid to rest you could have been excused for thinking it had spent 50 years moored off a North Sea oil rig instead of three and a bit years motoring (sometimes) around our sun-kiss'd isle.

When taken to task on this matter, Ducati executives merely shrug their shoulders and say that their motorcycles shouldn't be ridden in the rain anyway. All very well if you have alternative transport, I suppose.

Luckily, the owner of this pretty little 750GT does indeed possess wet-weather transportation. Which means that this particular Ducati has never felt the bite of council salt or the merciless lash of low-pressure precipitation. It is clean in both the aesthetic and the physical sense, so clean in fact that you could eat your dinner off it (if you could get close enough with your saucepan).

Bob Greenacre bought this bike way back at the tail end of 1975, when the asking price was a far-from-piffling £1166. This put you in line for one of the last conventional valve spring 750 Ducatis;

although later 860s continued the tradition, the old 750Vs, GTs and Sports were all eventually superseded by the 750SS Desmo which had scored first and second places at Daytona in 1972.

Desmodromoid or no, the 750GT had the legs of the later 860 by virtue of its more mountainous cam profile. An all-up weight of around 400lb gave the GT rider a speed potential on the right side of 120mph and easy 75mph cruising with just four grand showing on the Veglia tacho. Plus of course the symphonic thunder of twin Contis burtling down yer lugs; was this the ultimate biking experience?

Purists might cast a disdainful eye over Bob's GT and answer in the negative, for by no stretch of the imagination can it be described as original. But the changes that have been made are, by and large, well in keeping with the spirit of the original pre-Tartarini design. Only the Campbray wheels are mildly offensive to the eye, in the same way that Mona Lisa wouldn't look quite right wearing a flat cap. For the rest of it, criticism seems churlish. Tomaselli clip-ons and grips are wholly appropriate, while the substitution of the old single cable throttle by a dual-lead arrangement is simply a sensible move, if only from the point of view of carburettor adjustment (32mm PHF

Dell'Ortos on the GT, now fitted with alloy bellmouths).

Two nasty bits of bent wire on the original machine — the mudguard stays and the rear shock absorbers — have been ditched in favour of rather more rigid spars and Konis (respectively). The ubiquitous Suzuki switchgear sits behind an RD400 clutch lever, the latter chosen for the convenience of its integral 'ole into which the lawnmower-style choke control neatly pops. A Lockheed disc replaces the old Scarab unit, and the centrestand has had a dip in the chrome-plater's tank.

The sole engine mod, and one which Bob reckons was worth every penny, was the introduction of Lucas Rita electronic ignition. Must say our Darmah never sounded anything like this one, even when the crank was still working, ha ha ha (sob). Just lean on the kickstart and off she goes; boff-boff-boff-boff. Lovely.

Bob's been offered two-and-a-half Big Ones for his 750GT, but as you've no doubt gathered he turned it down. With less than 8000 miles up from new, and in this condition, I reckon I'd feel hard pressed to accept twice that amount myself. Or even thrice. Money-based valuations seem gross when applied to this machine, don't they?

TM

ZENYATTA DUCATI

MIKE SCOTT RIDES THE LAST OF THE REAL MOTORBIKES

You can take a few things for granted about Ducati's SS. That it is fast. That it handles. That it is beautiful. That to ride it is to love it. That any road test will be strung with superlatives. That this is the last of the real motorcycles.

All this, and more, is true.

I shall try to keep these statements of superlatives to a minimum. It won't be easy.

Perhaps the best way to cut the Duke down to size would be to pick a few worthy Japanese rivals, and compare them point for point.

Fast? The Duke will pace its long legs out to a workable top speed around 130mph, with more to follow given a long, long road. Kawasaki's GPZ1100 and Suzuki's GSX1100, to name but two big multis, can add five easy miles an hour to that, and then more. And even though the SS can lift its front wheel, you don't even want to talk about acceleration.

Power? The Ducati's venerable twin chuffs out 58lbs/ft of torque at 5200rpm, and 69bhp at 7000rpm. Both the Suzi and the Kawa handsomely exceed those figures, with 99 and a massive 108bhp respectively.

Equipment? In 1981, Ducati's Super Sport has indicators, and old-fashioned Suzuki-style Japanese switches. Even so, it remains spartan. No electric starter. No sidestand, no helmet-hooks, a crappy tool kit under a tacky seat-lock. The Jap multis are generations ahead, with efficient self-cancelling indicators, and even (on the GSX) an electronic multi-function-check.

Service? The Jap bikes are complex, but usually require a minimum of attention beyond regular maintenance. The Ducati is more mettlesome, and likes to be fettled frequently. And the traditional simplicity of a twin is as of naught when it is fitted with desmodromic valve gear.

Money? The Ducati will cost you £2899. The Kawasaki GPZ1100 costs £2476, and you get fuel injection. Suzi's GSX costs about £200 less.

So. On paper, Ducati's Super Sport is better in pictures than it is in words (for there's no question that it looks a great deal prettier than either Jap monster).

All of which goes to prove just one thing: that words are words, and motorcycles are motorcycles. And if you want to compare motorcycles, you should do it on the road rather than on paper.

Here, the Ducati will feel a great deal more at ease, even when faced with just such formidable opposition. On the road, the Ducati can shine as it never can on a spec sheet. On the road, the Ducati can prove that it is not what it does that is important (not that 130mph is *slow*) it is the way that it does it.

I don't think there's a single SS owner in the country (I class myself among this esoteric company for the week or two of road test) who would be afraid to take up the challenge of the latest, hottest Japanese superbike. Given anything other than a flat out motorway blast, the Duke would find many opportunities to assert its dynamic superiority.

Under braking, cornering, even in instant command of engine power, a well-ridden Duke SS is virtually unbeatable. I again include myself among those who ride well, immodestly perhaps, but there is something about the Super Sport that brings out the best in your riding ability. By reacting so directly and correctly to your riding input, it sharpens up your whole approach. It also makes you plan ahead (not least because of its sluggish steering), for it covers the ground very fast indeed. Your anticipation must be redoubled, and all the while your journey progresses effortlessly, at a relaxed but high average speed that has your Jap merchant working hard, and living dangerously.

And even on the aforementioned M-way blast, the Ducatiste stands a fair old chance, despite giving away both acceleration and ultimate top speed. For the Duke is designed to travel easily at top speed; rider balanced deftly against the 125mph headwind, tracking straight and true. It has a warp-speed confidence a compromised Jap bike cannot offer, and an ability to stop from those speeds a heavy Jap bike cannot rival. There are often times when such confidence is worth at least another 5mph.

With good aerodynamics, very tall gearing, and lots and lots of low-end torque, all this is achieved with an economy of effort that is reflected in the fuel consumption. I was amazed to better 50mpg on one tankful that included some fast work in the country, up to and including top speed. All this on pumper carbs, too.

Balance all this, if you like, against the perils of Ducati ownership. There is the knowledge that if it is almost unbearably pretty now, it will not look so in one or two year's time, unless you invest long hours in care for its cleanliness. The lacquer on our test bike's tank was so soft it was damaged by my waterproof buckle while I was prone on the tank (honestly, officer, I was only lying flat to improve fuel economy). There is the need for careful and costly servicing – though if you are an able and confident mechanic, they say it only takes three or four practice runs before you can set the valve gear up right.

While on our catalogue of woes, our test bike was beautifully prepared, the big pumper carburettors synchronised to perfection, the engine clean and sweet from its low thumping idle to its mellow bellow 8000rpm red line. Even so, it lost oil here and there, in small but messy quantities; one centre-stand mounting bolt came out on a long journey, joining the seat lock somewhere in Suffolk. A footrest came loose, as did the speedo. All these little niggles would only happen once if you owned the bike, for you'd soon find a way to solve them. But they do indicate that Ducati's SS is not the sort of bike you park and ignore.

Which leads neatly to the final assertion of my first paragraph: that the Ducati 900SS is the last of the real motorbikes.

Only one thing challenges this claim: the imminent arrival of the Hesketh, which is shaping up to be a worthy high-cost rival, and has promised to emerge in super-sport guise.

Until then, the SS stands supreme; not just the last but probably the best of the real motorbikes.

Whatever it might be that makes such a machine, the SS has plenty of it. It shows in the way it looks – spartan and spidery, with lots of blue sky visible in its profile. It's certainly there in the sound – that crisp, off-beat bass bark, a world away from a wailing four. Ducati noise provokes fond nostalgia in people who never had the experience in the first place.

The kickstart is another badge of a real motorbike. Do it right, and the Duke fires first kick every time. Do it wrong, and you're likely to get a kickstart pedal buried in your calf muscle.

But mostly the reality is in the way it behaves; lithe, fast, safe and responsive, an extension of your mind and body, rather than a conveyance for them. Light weight, a low centre of gravity, a stiff frame, manageable engine power, precise controls and good tyres all take a hand in this. I believe there is something more; the evident art of the man or men who designed it. And this quality, identifiable in this Duke, the Triumph, a few good British-framed specials, and to a lesser extent in nearly all European bikes, can never be found in a committee-designed and computer-developed, mass-produced Japanese motorcycle.

In real motorcycles, art is all. And Ducati's SS has plenty of art.

Not to dwell too long on old ground, the art is that of Dr Fabio Taglione, Ducati's chief engineer and purist supreme. It is another Italian whizz-kid who has influenced other Dukes, notably the stylish Darmah and heavily-dressed Pantah, Dr Tartorini (or Tart-Up Toni, if you prefer). His hand is evident in the Super Sport's latest dual seat, a crude (though pretty) piece of glassfibre. Happily, Dr Taglione's favourite child has escaped too much of the tart-up treatment. It's pretty pure.

The straightback frame tubes are still there, for instance, even though they force an unusually high seat. The other changes from Dr Taglione's sparse original are small, and mainly for the good. Like the indicators, which come along with a Bosch electrical system and H4 headlight like that on the Darmah. Like the new Nippon-Denso switches, of the simplest type but with proven reliability.

These things aside, the SS remains as it always was, an exuberant celebration of desmodromic

elaboration, an expression of artistic engineering for its own sake, and with impeccable results.

Enough has been written about desmodromic valves, but they cannot be ignored. I will repeat my assertion that the desmo gear (valves positively closed by cams instead of passively by springs) is only there because it is so interesting. The SS revs only to 8000rpm, and it is the weight of the 86mm pistons combined with the distance they must travel (74.4mm stroke) which prevents it spinning faster. Certainly, valve spring technology is well up to those revs, and it is only on the 500cc, 10 000rpm Pantah that the desmodromia starts to make sense.

It does allow big valves, but it's a toss-up whether Dr Taglione might not have found more horsepower by fitting two more smaller valves to make a four-valve head.

But then he wouldn't have had the exclusivity of the world's only production desmodromic engine: which has given Ducati a lead in technology that may now be coming back into favour. I quote no less an authority than Keith Duckworth, designer of the formidable Cosworth DFV 3-litre V8 formula one car engine, who spoke of desmodromics as a way of getting more revs and horsepower from that doughty 15-year-old design to combat the new generation of turbocharged cars. That was on BBC2's *Horizon*, and the engine they used to demonstrate desmodromic valves was (you've guessed) a Ducati 900SS.

There's one big change to the 1981 SS that I've neglected to mention so far – very remiss. It's the pipes. Gone are those defiantly loud Conti straight-through silencers. In their place, a pair of Silentiums, with external seams and a heavily restricted chuffing sound. I have forgotten to mention them because they have a readily removable baffle at their tail end. We removed it readily, and the results were good. Not as noisy as Contis, they still released plenty of boom and plenty of power. With them fitted, the factory say that some bottom-end torque is lost, but that peak torque and horsepower are not changed.

This test has been thin, so far, in the dry detailed assessment you might have expected. I make no apologies. The Ducati is as much a personality (or metallic expression of personality) as a machine, and has characteristics that cannot be assessed except by conversational exploration. Here, anyway, are some brief but essential facts.

Ducati's SS demonstrates the best of the motorcycling conventions of a time before heavy weight and many cylinders. It tips the scales at 454lb full of four gallons of fuel and nine pints of oil. Because of the almost horizontal front cylinder, much of the engine's weight is below the axle line, a classic formula for precise handling.

Simplicity extends to the spine-type frame, which dispenses with a full cradle by using the engine as a stressed member. There's nothing trick about the swing-arm, either, a simple tubular construction, with plain phosphor-bronze bearings. Which reminds me: an unkind Japophile once said "Ducatis handle well because they aren't very powerful," which is true in a way but rather misses the point. It's not how much horsepower you have, chum, but how you can put it on the road.

Certainly, the suspension is as simple as you like. While heavyweight Japs search for better control via air springing and even rising-rate lever monoshock systems, the SS gets by on a pair of handsome but straightforward unprogressive springs on Marzocchi gas shocks. The point is made again: light weight doesn't need complex suspension to achieve good roadholding. By the same token, the ride is unsophisticated. Or should that just read "hard". There's little room for a monoshock, with the back cylinder in the way. Still, a more sophisticated suspension would only make the Ducati still better, for it could add comfort to the pin-sharp roadholding.

Up front, it's 'Zocchis again; not the new adjustable-damping type and devoid of air caps, or any other trickery of the '80s. They perform just fine, riding firmly and resisting flex.

The test bike wore Michelin M45 tyres on its gold Campagnola wheels, instead of the Pirelli Phantom's expected. Aside from a strange uncertainty straight-ahead at low speeds (a bit like an over-tight steering damper), they performed impressively and predictably wet and dry.

The clutch clutched throughout, our best Ducati clutch so far, though the lever was quite heavy. You soon learn to find neutral *before* you coast to a stop; the gears are otherwise crisp and quick.

And (a *SuperBike* record) almost the end, without a single mention of "superb Brembo brakes".

Ducati's SS is as close as you can get to a traditional racing four-stroke on the road. It is Very uncompromising, yet remains easy enough to live with. Or maybe you just put up with a lot, in exchange for the pleasure of each ride.

And that is the final impression. Enjoyment SS style comes not from having a bigger power output, but by using a smaller one to maximum effect; and the end result is one of the fastest tar-road point to point machines in the world.

Enjoyment Ducati-style also includes safety. Sure, it takes you hard and fast. But it seldom takes you out of your depth; and even then there's a good chance it will rescue you.

And you can't ask for more than that.

Ducati 900 Desmo Super Sport
£2899

PERFORMANCE
Maximum Speed — 128mph
Fuel Consumption - Hard Riding — 44mpg
Cruising — 51mpg

ENGINE
Type — 90 deg air-cooled Vee twin, shaft-and-bevel-driven 550hc, desmodromic valve gear
Displacement — 863.9cc
Power — 68.5bhp at 7000rpm
Torque — 58lb/ft at 5200rpm
Bore & Stroke — 86 × 74.4mm
Compression Ratio — 9.5:1
Induction — two 40mm Dell'Orto carbs with accelerator pumps
Exhaust — two into two with balance pipe
Oil System — wet sump, 8.8pt
Ignition — Bosch electronic

TRANSMISSION
Clutch — multiplate wet
Primary Drive — helical gear
Final Drive — chain
Gears — five-speed constant mesh

CHASSIS
Frame — open cradle spine, with engine as stressed member
Front Suspension — Marzocchi tele-hydraulic forks
Rear Suspension — swing-arm, five way spring preload, Marzocchi dampers
Wheelbase — 59.5in
Ground Clearance — 6.5in
Castor — 29.5 deg
Seat Height — 31in
Weight (wet) — 454.7lb
Fuel Capacity — 3.95 gall
Tyres — Michelin M45, 3.50 × 18 front; 4.25/85V × 18 rear
Brakes — triple cast-iron discs, Brembo calipers

INSTRUMENTS
10 000rpm rev counter, red line from 8000 to 8500rpm; 150mph speedo with odometer, no trip meter; warning lights for generator, indicators, high beam, neutral, lights

EQUIPMENT
Electrical — 12v 12Ah battery, 200w alternator
Lighting — Cibie or Bosch 55/60w headlamp

Test bike supplied by Coburn and Hughes, Park Street, Luton, Bedfordshire

MONZA V PANTAH

DUCATI 500SL PANTAH

Fragile but fun

The sleek, silver blue 500SL Ducati bears more than just a family resemblance to the mighty 900SS. The 117mph V-twin extracts more performance than its power output would suggest and, like the big sportster, it focuses all its attention on going places quickly.

Its single-minded nature is emphasised by Tony Rutter's F2 win in the Isle of Man, a circuit to which the 500 would be well suited.

One of the modifications to the race bike was stronger clutch springs because, again like the 900, the clutch is the bike's weakest point.

With an already heavy lever action (the 500, apparently, has an hydraulic clutch lifter) more spring force would make the machine unbearable for any sort of city riding. But it would seem to be the only way to drive the back wheel with any predictability.

When we tested the 900SS the clutch failed and a new unit started slipping as soon as we began using full power. Earlier this year we collected the 500 and the clutch failed almost immediately. The bike went back to the concessionaire, Coburn & Hughes, where it was decided to put another machine on the test fleet as the original had already covered a fairly high and not too gentle test mileage.

It took some time to get the replacement, but when it arrived, resplendent in new Pirelli Phantoms, it seemed worth waiting for.

On the first journey, two miles out of town the clutch failed! Not in a big way — at the first large handful of throttle the clutch spun

as soon as the revs got up near peak power.

It proved easy enough to control, feeding in more throttle gently and shifting up before 8000 and, as the clutch got hotter, it seemed to improve. It made the Ducati difficult to ride, particularly in traffic, leaving a very short rev range which made it essential to be in the right gear with the right amount of throttle before the twin would accelerate properly.

The clutch would grip well at low engine speeds but the motor wouldn't take a lot of throttle below 4500, it just spluttered and

died if the throttle was opened too quickly.

It was a nuisance but not unrideable and as it could still be eased up to more than 80mph we decided to use the bike anyway. There didn't seem a lot of point — based on past experiences — in having anything done about the clutch.

Despite the artificial limitations, the Pantah proved to be agile and very swift, eating up country lanes at a rate which was guaranteed to wear a hole in anyone's driving licence.

The suspension was too hard (on such a bike, what else could it be?) and the riding position only emphasised the low-speed impracticality of the bike. But a short way on the far side of the speed limit, a transformation took place. Metamorphosis isn't just for tadpoles and butterflies. As it got into its speed range, the Pantah changed just as dramatically, becoming very easy to handle and very nice to ride.

Perhaps the suspension didn't help; in fact it didn't really seem to do anything at all, but the handling was just about all you could want. The tyres are nearly as good as race tyres; they hang on tightly in the dry, they give steady, precise steering in the wet and, in 1000 fairly rapid miles, they didn't seem to have worn too badly.

In Snetterton's fast and bumpy curves, the Pantah was as quick as anything we've ridden. But its absolute performance was put into perspective by an RD250 — it was a real

Left: Ducati's tidy fairing mount carries the instrument cluster and choke control.
Below left: Toothed belt drive to the overhead cam and desmodromic valve operation distinguish the 500.
Below: Slim lines and low weight give the desmo Ducati its biggest advantages.

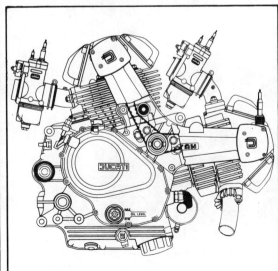

MONZA V PANTAH

struggle to catch up and pass the smaller bike. The 500 was apparently peaking and the tacho was reaching the red line before the clutch let go, so there didn't seem to be any more performance to come. I was hooking it up through the gears a few hundred rpm below the red and using the brakes, handling and tyres to make up in the turns what the Pantah was losing along the straights.

The brakes are superb. Forceful yet with a lot of feel, they held the bike hard and could even be used quite safely in the wet.

The slim engine gives a lot of ground clearance and all the hardware along the sides of the bike is well tucked in. It can be heeled over long way before anything touches down but when it does, the exhaust smacks against the floor good and hard.

The bike feels light, in reality it is 45lb lighter than a Z550GP, 14lb lighter than the XJ550 but 60lb heavier than the V50 Guzzi. And it responds quickly like a short wheelbase machine, yet Ducati quote 57 inches. The steering is heavy, not with the heaviness that comes from a lot of weight, but the sort caused by a lot of steering castor or trail.

It makes the Pantah very stable at speed and gives a steady, reliable feel in long curves. The only difficulty was in fast S-bends when the Ducati needed a lot of force on the handlebars, so much that when the bike was pushed even harder the front wheel would twitch rapidly from side to side.

It had seemed that as the bike was used harder, the clutch improved — when cold it would slip quite easily. The first top speed

run at MIRA showed that the 500 was going to pull into the red in top, and would reach an engine speed where the clutch would slip. Before the throttle could be backed off it let go and the engine spun on to an indicated 9500, where surprisingly, it gripped again.

We assumed that it had gone over peak power, and the power had then dropped to a point where it was no longer too much for the clutch. Running the engine above clutch-slip speed, we took it up to 117mph, with the help of a slight tail wind.

Something in this treatment seemed to agree with the clutch, which gripped like it never had before. We even ran standing quarters — at 14.1 seconds the high-geared Ducati isn't doing badly. The biggest surprise was the top gear roll-on. Although it would not take full throttle and the power had to be fed in gradually until the bike was under way, its times were quicker than the supposedly flexible Moto Guzzi.

Now that the Pantah could use power, its performance changed quite radically. It was much crisper to drive and the handling tightened up as it could be powered through corners more easily.

The dyno test — which we'd deliberately left until last — showed what had happened. Two factors had combined to deceive us about the 500's true performance. The power curve has a peculiar shape, it flattens off at 7000 and then jumps up with a really violent surge to its true, 42bhp peak at a true 8400 rpm. If this sudden flood of power were allowed to hit the clutch all at once, the clutch just gave up.

The second part of the deception was that the tacho read very optimistically. At 7100 true rpm, the tacho showed 8000. So it was easy enough to believe that the engine had peaked out, at 31 horsepower, and had run into the red band. No wonder it was a struggle to get past the 250 Yamaha!

In fact the Pantah had another 2000rpm and another ten horsepower to go. As long as this was presented gently enough not to upset the clutch, it completely transformed

The Brembo brakes were powerful but the linked set-up played up during the test.

the Ducati's performance.

At the other end of the speed scale, the 500 is not set up to cope; below 50mph the riding position puts too much weight on the wrists, the suspension is much too hard, the engine is well below its power band and the bike doesn't do very well at all.

I attempted a longish trip at low speeds just to see how economical the V-twin could be; it was too uncomfortable to be a realistic test. At 45 to 50mph, plus frequent bursts up to 60 or more to relieve the pain, it gave 63.3mpg compared to a norm of about 50mpg. The slim tank, taking 3½ gallons plus reserve, gave a range which was only compatible with the bike's level of comfort if it were ridden fairly quickly.

The final and perhaps most important aspect is the Pantah's styling which makes it one of the most attractive bikes around. There are lots of neat or useful touches around the bike, such as the detachable hump on the seat or the folding handle for lifting the bike on to its stand.

The Monza was spoilt by awkward controls and the high pressure suspension.

Anyone longer than 5 foot 10 inches will probable find that the fairing makes the bike a bit cramped. And most riders will find that the screen deflects a lot of weather straight into their faces. So although the 500 is visually excellent, there is still room for improvement.

Dipped beam had failed early in the test and, by the end of our mileage a slight oil leak was beginning to seep through to the outside world.

The practicality of the Ducati aside, it is still a very satisfying machine to ride although the clutch has to be seen as a major failing. Other than that, there are only detail irritations trying to spoil the Pantah's promise of performance.

MOTO GUZZI V50 MONZA
adequately rapid . . .

Moto Guzzi's sporting 500, the V50 Monza, feels extremely light after the heavy-steering Ducati. In comparison it seems like a 250 and it isn't just the steering that's lighter — the bike weighs a lot less. Looking around at competitors in the same capacity class, the Guzzi is anything from 40 to 100lb lighter.

That is a big advantage which shows up mainly in the Monza's taut handling and fast steering. It also allows very good road performance from what is a modest engine output. With a shade under 35bhp, the Monza isn't going to win any prizes in the power stakes. But when you put the whole thing together on the road, it is adequately rapid.

At MIRA it reached a speed of 107.7 mph although it is handicapped by over-gearing, being scheduled to pull 113mph at peak power and 117mph at the 800rpm yellow line. In fact by the time the revs get up to the yellow and red zones the power is all over.

On the road the usable performance is better. The bike as a whole, likes to travel at 70mph and top gear punch is good in this range, as the motor is just getting on to peak torque.

It may not have a headline-making top speed but its power is developed to give good response at typical road speeds and, combined with the handling and light weight, gives the Guzzi performance which is enjoyable and effective.

The bike is spoiled, in this respect, by the poor layout of the switches, which make them hard to find and use quickly, and by the gearshift. This has a heavy and vague action which demands slow gear changes and even then it doesn't always go through or

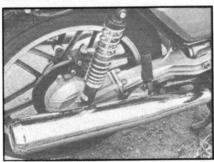

Swing arm pivots on gearbox. Wheel can be removed leaving disc on bevel box.

engages with a sudden jerk and a clunk.

There is a lot of flywheel effect, which doesn't help to match the revs before changing gear. It can also make the bike lurch and twitch if the rider makes a mismatched gear change in a corner.

Normally the Monza's stability was very good and the precise steering was one of the bike's best features. When we first got it the steering would go very light at high speeds and it would develop a slight weave.

This was cured by lowering the rear suspension, which also made the steering a bit heavier. The Monza has air-assisted units front and rear, but the suspension is much too hard for road use and the only noticeable difference made by adjusting the air pressure within the recommended range, was to the feel of the steering.

The suspension works at unusually high pressures — between 40 and 70 lb/in^2 — which makes it more than usually difficult to adjust. There is such a small volume of air in the forks that the slightest touch on the valve releases nearly all of it.

In the end I gave up and ran all four units at zero pressure. It was the only way I could be sure they were all equal and, from a ride comfort point of view, it gave the best setting anyway.

The riding position is fairly good, making a reasonable compromise between low-speed and high-speed comfort, although it would have been better generally if the footrests had been further back. I would also have preferred the pedals to be closer to the footrests but the worst problem was a partial failure of the linked front and rear hydraulic system.

Initially this gave remarkably good stopping power and I am always mildly surprised by the controllable progression of

Guzzi's linked brakes, which allows you to use them on poor surfaces and in corners without locking the wheels up.

But after a series of hard stops from top speed at MIRA, the brake lost power and the pedal could be pressed down until it fouled the exhaust pipe, without giving much braking effort. After it had cooled down more brake appeared but it was never quite the same again.

The wheel has to be removed for the dyno tests and, to fit a drive-line adaptor, we also had to remove the disc which normally stays attached to the bevel box. Replacing the wheel afterwards, we found that the brake pressure had disappeared once more and the pedal didn't seem to have enough travel to "pump up".

It seemed likely that air or vapour had got into the linked circuit, but the prospect of bleeding it does not look easy. The individual front disc operated from the handlebar lever still worked perfectly well.

Of the remaining controls, the throttle was too stiff, making its operation fairly heavy and refusing to snap closed when released, even though the friction screw was backed right off.

The Monza always fired up easily, which is more than I can say for the operation of the starter button. This is cunningly positioned so that you can't easily hold the throttle and reach the button at the same time.

It took a long time to warm up and usually had to be ridden about half a mile before the choke lever could be released. As the test progressed it began to show more signs of running weak, banging in the exhaust, spitting back through the carbs and not running too well at low speed.

When the symptoms took a sudden turn for the worse, we examined the motor more closely and found a split in one of the carb mountings. The worm-drive clips which hold the rubber mounting to the intake stub were of too good quality! They allow too much purchase and over-enthusiastic tightening makes the clip bite into the rubber and tear it.

It may have had a beneficial effect — that particular tankful of fuel gave us 52.9mpg, whereas the Guzzi would usually run in the mid-40s. Admittedly, that was with a strong tendency to run at fairly high speeds, egged on by the Monza's fine handling. More subdued use gave a good response in economy — better than 70mpg on one steady, cross-country trip.

On varied journeys we got a range of

MONZA V PANTAH

anything between 150 and 180 miles before needing the tank's reserve. This and the firm but comfortable seat made the 500 quite an attractive long-distance runner.

There are many changes which distinguish the Monza from the earlier V50 II — such as the reversion from electronic ignition to contact breakers. Oxford Motorcycle Engineers, who run a useful service school for Guzzi owners, explain this both as an economic step and for reasons of changing the advance curve to avoid a low-speed flat spot. I don't know why cb bobweights couldn't be used with the Bosch electronic pick-up; and the Monza still has a flat spot just below 3000, so maybe the reason was an economic one after all.

At the end of the test period there were various oil stains seeping out around the engine and the crankcase breather seemed to be over-active. The biggest surprise was that the Michelin rear tyre was down to 1mm of tread, despite the fact that the bike had done only 2600 miles.

As a light sports tourer, the Monza has a lot of promise; it goes well, it steers very well and it can be quite economic. But, like so many other Italian machines it is spoiled by the lack of attention to detail.

John Robinson

Ducati 500 Pantah

Moto Guzzi Monza

Specification
Moto Guzzi Monza
PERFORMANCE

Maximum speed	107.7 mph
SS ¼-mile	14.1s/89.4 mph
30mph top gear roll-on, ¼-mi	17.0s/76.6 mph

speeds in gears at 8000 rpm

first	39 mph
second	62 mph
third	89 mph
fourth	109 mph
fifth	125 mph

fuel consumption:

best	72.7 mpg
worst	44.8 mpg
average	50.8 mpg
CLAIMED OUTPUT	48 bhp at 7600 rpm.

ENGINE AND ELECTRICAL SYSTEM

Type: OHV, 90-degree V twin.	
Displacement	490.3 cc
Bore x stroke	74 x 57 mm
Compression ratio	10.4:1
Fuelling	two PHBH28 Dell'Orto
Ignition	twin cb and coil
Lubrication	wet sump
Generator	12V, 280 VA alternator
Battery	12V, 20Ah
Headlamp	12V, 45/40W

TRANSMISSION
Gear primary drive, single plate clutch with diaphragm spring, five speed gearbox, final drive by shaft and bevel gears.

primary reduction	1.466
final reduction	3.875
gearbox ratios: 2.727; 1.733; 1.277; 1.045 and 0.909	

CHASSIS
Air assisted suspension, front and rear.

Front tyre	3,25S 18
Rear tyre	3.50S 18
Wheelbase	55.9 inch
Castor/trail	NA
Overall length	82.3 inch
Overall width	27.6 inch
dry weight	352 lb
fuel capacity	3.52 gal
oil capacity	2.5 litre

Horsepower at rear wheel and effective torque at crankshaft, measured on the Heenan Froude DPX3 chassis dynamometer at LEDAR, 10 School Lane, Baston Lincs.

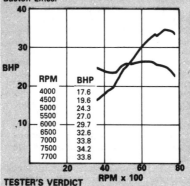

RPM	BHP
4000	17.6
4500	19.6
5000	24.3
5500	27.0
6000	29.7
6500	32.6
7000	33.8
7500	34.2
7700	33.8

TESTER'S VERDICT
Good points: handling, lightness and road performance.
Bad points: awkward or heavy controls.

Performance	acceptable, good mid-range.
Economy	can be very good.
Handling	light, firm, positive.
Comfort	good but suspension hard.
Braking	good, initially, deteriorated.
Equipment	fly screen, linked brakes.
Value	costs more than Jap 500

PRICE inc car tax and VAT £1669
WARRANTY: 12 months unlimited mileage
IMPORTER: Coburn & Hughes, Park St., Luton, Beds.

Specification
Ducati 500 Pantah
PERFORMANCE

Maximum speed	117.3 mph
SS ¼-mile	14.1s/95.6 mph
30mph top gear roll-on, ¼-mi	16.1s/79.4 mph

speeds in gears at 8500 rpm:

first	45 mph
second	66 mph
third	85 mph
fourth	105 mph
fifth	126 mph

fuel consumption:

best	63.3 mpg
worst	38.8 mpg
average	49.6 mpg

ENGINE AND ELECTRICAL SYSTEM

Type: belt-driven SOHC desmodromic; 90-degree V twin.	
Displacement	498.9 cc
Bore x stroke	74 x 58 mm
Compression ratio	9.5:1
Fuelling	two PHF 36 Dell Orto
Ignition	Bosch electronic
Lubrication	wet sump
Generator	12V 200W alternator
Battery	12V, 14ah
Headlamp	12V, 60/55W

TRANSMISSION
Helical gear primary drive to multiplate clutch, five-speed all-indirect gearbox. Final drive by 530 chain (Regina GP 136)

primary reduction	2.2258
final reduction	2.533(38/15)
gearbox ratios: 2.50; 1.714; 1.333; 1.074 and 0.900.	

CHASSIS
Marzocchi front and rear suspension

Front tyre	100/90H 18
Rear tyre	110/90H 18
Wheelbase	57.1 inch
Castor/trail	NA
Overall length	84.6 inch
Overall width	26.4 inch
Dry weight	396 lb
Fuel capacity	4.2 gal
Oil capacity	3.33 litre

Horsepower at rear wheel and effective torque at crankshaft, measured on the Heenan Froude DPX3 chassis dynamometer at LEDAR, 10 School Lane, Baston, Lincs.

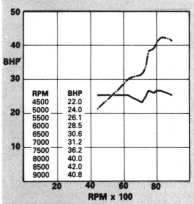

RPM	BHP
4500	22.0
5000	24.0
5500	26.1
6000	28.5
6500	30.6
7000	31.2
7500	36.2
8000	40.0
8500	42.0
9000	40.8

TESTER'S VERDICT
Good points: handling, braking, styling.
Bad points: clutch, suspension/low-speed comfort.

Performance	good but hard to find
Economy	average
Handling	bike's best feature
Comfort	good at high speed
Braking	lot of power, lot of feel
Equipment	neat fairing, convertible seat
Value	price is competing with bigger bikes.

PRICE inc car tax and VAT £2589
WARRANTY: 12 months unlimited mileage
IMPORTER: Coburn & Hughes, Park St., Luton, Beds.

The most desirable 500 lotsa money can buy

When you spend £2700 on a Ducati Pantah you're not simply paying an over-inflated price for a sports motorcycle, you're buying a piece of living art. You could maybe justify packing it away in mothballs as an investment, a hedge against inflation, or you could mount it on a dias in the living room as a monument to mechanical engineering at its most sensual. But either way you'd be missing the Pantah at its best.

Y'see, while a lot of pretty machines are a let down when you come to ride them, out there on the open road is where the Ducati really excells. If the 500cc Pantah is beautiful stationary, in motion it is pure poetry. All the time I was riding the

By the time I arrived at work I was in love. The Ducati had purred through traffic, swooped through roundabouts and bends and roared on the open road. Over the too-few days of the test that followed, I rode the Pantah at every opportunity and schemed in vain of ways to buy one.

The heart of the Ducati is an all-new 499cc short stroke, V-twin engine. Toothed rubber belts drive overhead cams which operate the valves desmodromically, that is one rocker arm opens each valve and another closes it. With a 9.5:1 compression ratio, this motor produces a claimed 52bhp at 9500rpm, giving it 750cc performance. Ducati dealers will tell you this is a 120mph motorbike and, on the right day, on the right road with the right conditions, so it is. We clocked a 116mph best-one-way speed wearing one-piece leathers at MIRA and the

bike was still accelerating with 500rpm to go when it tripped the timing lights.

A tall first gear which demanded lots of slipping from the painfully heavy clutch hindered rapid starts for our acceleration tests, but the Duke still averaged 13.82sec/93.4mph prone, which equals the Yamaha XJ550. The five close ratio gears are well chosen to make best use of the motor's power and contribute to the racer feel. Neutral was easy to find and the cogs swapped quick and slick, except third to fourth which often needed two attempts. This and a jerky first gear were probably due to a previous ham-footed tester's abuse.

Clip-on handlebars provide a very direct and sensitive control to the steering which was faultless. The Pantah heeled into bends and straightened out of them again with no

no cinquecento

delightful little Duke, I wished I was standing by the roadside as well, so that I, too, could gape, open-jawed at the silver blue spectacle flashing by and hear the exhaust bark fade into the distance.

If all this sounds a little exaggerated, let me put it in perspective. After you've road tested a few hundred motorcycles over a few hundred thousand miles, your appetite for new bikes becomes a little jaded and you are not easily impressed. That's why when we collected the Pantah from Coburn and Hughes' Luton emporium on Friday, I didn't get round to riding it until Monday. All weekend it stood gleaming in the drive, while I did necessary odd jobs around the garden.

Monday morning came and, half expecting a disappointment, I walked over to the patient Pantah. Having turned on both fuel taps and located the choke under the headlamp shell, I searched for the kickstarter. But, unlike the 900cc Hailwood Replica which requires booting into life, the Pantah has no alternative to its push button starting. With a single prod of this civilised device, the Duke hummed into life. Yes, hummed. No rattle of tappets or clatter of cam chain, no gasps from the huge 36mm Dell'Orto carbs, and no window-shaking crackle and roar from the exhausts. Just a gentle, muted woofle filtered through the silencers when the throttle was blipped.

First gear clicked into place and the Pantah slipped into the morning traffic without fuss. Even cold the beautiful polished aluminium motor would pull from 2000rpm and was so tractable, smooth and silent it was hard to believe. When the throttle was opened the bike leapt forward and surged ahead on a stream of power, the gentle throb of the exhaust building up to a crisp bark as the revs raced for the red line.

Colour page: Paint and glass-fibre finish is near perfect. Engine cases are beautifully polished. Single-seat cover unscrews to reveal tricky pillion butt bruiser. Note fold-away grab handle in front of Marzocchi shocks with air-loaded damping

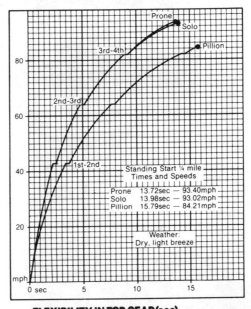

PERFORMANCE CHART

(Graph: acceleration curves — Prone, Solo, Pillion — with gear change points marked 1st-2nd, 2nd-3rd, 3rd-4th; vertical axis mph 20–80, horizontal axis 0–15 sec)

Standing Start ¼ mile Times and Speeds
Prone 13.72sec — 93.40mph
Solo 13.98sec — 93.02mph
Pillion 15.79sec — 84.21mph

Weather: Dry, light breeze

MAXIMUM SPEEDS and SPEED RANGES

Gear		mph max	mph min	mph 1000rpm
1	solo	43.71	8.67	5
2	solo	64.96	12.03	7
3	solo	82.21	17.45	9
4	solo	104.04	21.36	12
	pillion	98.59		
	prone	104.04	''	''
5	solo	105.52	25.04	13
	pillion	92.41		
	prone	112.47	''	''

Best one way speed: 115.89mph

SPEEDO

ind	true
30	28
40	38
50	48
60	57
70	66
80	76
90	86

Milometer — Accurate

BRAKES (both)

	solo	pillion
mph	ft	ft
30	30	35
40	63	71
50	98	104
60	133	139
70	158	170

MPG

Best	56
Worst	38
Overall	47

FLEXIBILITY IN TOP GEAR (sec)

mph	30-50	40-60	50-70	60-80	70-90	80-100
solo	9.01	8.50	9.40	13.70	15.95	—

Oil used — Negligible

Performance figures obtained at: M.I.R.A. Test Track, Nr. Atherstone, Warks. Test Riders: Bob Goddard, Neil Millen.

COMPARISONS *High winds gave low performance test results.*

Make	Speed prone	SS ¼ mile prone	Dry weight	Claimed bhp	mpg	Price inc. Tax
Ducati Pantah	112mph	13.72sec/93mph	397lb.	52 @ 9500rpm	47	£2700
Moto Guzzi Monza	105mph	14.53sec/90mph	370lb.	48 @ 7600rpm	58	£1669
Laverda Montjuic	110mph	13.86sec/95mph	370lb.	50 @ 8500rpm	51	£2579
Kawasaki GP550	118mph	12.50sec/104mph	440lb.	58 @ 9000rpm	50	£1614
Yamaha XJ550	107mph*	13.72sec/95mph*	410lb.	56 @ 9500rpm	48	£1639
Honda CX500	105mph	13.89sec/93mph	441lb.	50 @ 9000rpm	54	£1429

conscious effort on the bars. The Ducati handled the way only an Italian bike can: impeccably. Either upright or fully cranked, under full power or with the brakes crammed on, the Pantah performed as if it didn't know what instability was. We only once persuaded the back end to weave and then discovered that one of the air/oil damped, piggy-back Marzocchi rear shock absorbers had no pressure. With both units pumped up to their recommended 28psi and the spring preloads in the middle of their five positions, there was no further misbehaviour. Top notch settings were favourite for two-up riding to avoid bottoming and although both front and rear suspension was generally firm, the effect wasn't uncomfortable. The bike's toolkit did not contain a C-spanner for adjusting rear spring preloads and the damper reservoirs made the job far from easy.

Michelin M38 tyres were fitted to the Ducati's cast alloy wheels and combined good grip with high speed stability. They felt perfectly safe with the Ducati's exhaust pipe's scraping the tarmac, which seemed like ninety degrees from vertical. We encountered no rain during testing, but from previous experience with M38s we know them to be safe on wet roads.

The bike's riding position is one of its most appealing features. Well rear-set, folding footrests and clip-on handlebars produce a comfortable racing crouch which is not too stretched for poodling around town and lets you see well over the screen. Knees fit snugly against tank contours and bum butts up against the removable solo seat hump. Bending your elbows tucks you right inside the fairing and the screen offers a good, undistorted view. The overall feeling of blending with the motorcycle adds enormously to the thrill of a hard thrash down country lanes.

The seat which converts for solo or dual use, or removes completely for access to the toolkit in the tail, is too thinly padded for travelling any distance. The edges of the plastic seatpan dig into tender parts noticeably after an hour's ride and pillion passengers become numb-bummed after thirty minutes. High pillion footrests and no grabrail mean passengers have to hang on to the rider.

Carb behind panel. Note timing window

Tidy chain adjusters and spindle clamps

Powerful twin Brembos stop gold cast front wheel

This and the enforced intimacy of too small a dual seat with a hump at the back, means most owners will spend much time kerb-cruising for likely wenches to ride pillion.

A hefty grab of front brake is a certain way of getting to know your passenger. The Pantah's twin 10.2in. drilled disc Brembo front and single disc rear brakes were powerful enough to lock either wheel, but had sufficient feel to permit safe and rapid stopping. We managed to haul the bike to a halt in 158 feet from 70mph (74 indicated) which is as good as you'll get on any bike. The front brake would be even nicer to use if it had a dog-leg lever to reduce hand stretch and strain and the same goes for the Bullworker clutch lever.

Japanese switches were as easy to use as the Nippon Denso instruments were to read. Speedo error varied from three to six percent and surprisingly was most accurate at top speed. Warning lights for indicators, lights, main beam, neutral, oil, generator and sidestand (optional) hint at overkill at night due to internal light spread.

Talking of light spread, the Pantah's halogen 60/55 watt headlamp was a dismal disappointment. Unlit roads limited speed to 60mph and I could have believed the bulb was nearer 35 watts. The indicators and rear lamp were well up to standard. A 200 watt alternator feeds a 14 amp hour battery via an electronic regulator and it has Bosch electronic ignition.

Despite the motor's rorty performance and tunnel-like carburettors, the Pantah averaged 47mpg over the test, giving a 180 mile range from the 3.96 gallon tank. As delightful as the Duke is to ride, it will be a well-padded rider who uses a tankful of juice without a stop.

The Pantah's beauty is not merely skin deep. A very high standard of finish was evident, from welding neatness and paintwork to the sparkling shine of the motor's alloy castings.

Perhaps the most lasting impression the Pantah made was its degree of sophistication and total lack of the crudeness that has marred road-going racers before it. I've learned to live with the fact that I can't afford to buy one. I just hope one day I'll get to ride one again.

Bob Goddard

TECHNICAL SPECIFICATIONS

Engine

Type: Air-cooled, 90 degree, in-line V-twin, SOHC desmodromic four-stroke.
Bore x stroke: 74 x 58mm.
Displacement: 498.9cc.
Compression ratio: 9.5:1.
Carburettors: Two 36mm Dell 'Orto slide type.
Max. bhp: 52bhp @ 9500rpm.
Max. torque: 29.48ft.lb. @ 7500rpm.

Transmission

Overall gear ratios: 1st 14.09, 2nd 9.66, 3rd 7.52, 4th 6.06, 5th 5.07:1.
Clutch: Wet, multi-plate.

Frame and Forks

Frame: Tubular cradle suspending engine below it.
Front suspension: Double-damped telescopic fork. 5.1in. travel.
Rear suspension: Swinging fork, twin units with five pre-load and air/oil damping. 3.5in. travel.
Castor angle: 59 degrees, 30 minutes. **Trail:** 5.1in.

Wheels and Brakes

Front tyre size: 3.25 x 18.
Rear tyre size: 3.50 x 18.
Front brake: Twin hydraulic 10.2in. dia. discs.
Rear brake: Single hydraulic 10.2in. disc.

Electrics

Ignition: Bosch electronic with battery and coils.
Battery: 12V/14Ah.
Alternator: 200W.
Headlight: Halogen 60/55W.
Tail/stop lamp: 5/21W.
Indicators: 21W.
Warning lights: Turn, lights, main beam, neutral, oil, generator and sidestand (optional).

Dimensions

Seat height: 30in. **Length:** 89in.
Width: 30.7in. **Height:** 42.9in.
Wheelbase: 61in.
Ground clearance: 6.5in.
Dry weight: 397lb.
Fuel tank: 4.62 gallons.

DUCATI 900SS and YAMAHA TR1

yesterday's hero and the young pretender

The V-twin has long been recognised as a classic motorcycle powerplant. Ducati's 900SS and the Yamaha TR1 approach the concept from totally different angles. But how long can the Duke remain in its present guise now that the factory are concentrating on a new range based on the Pantah? And is the TR1 really a viable alternative to the Japanese multi? Mat Oxley finds out

YAMAHA TR1

When rumours of Yamaha's TR1 V-twin first started to circulate in the British press, learned bike hacks thought that the Japs had finally got their priorities right. At last here was a machine that would fulfil the true ideals of a motorcycle — good power-to-weight ratio, nimble handling and low running costs.

Yamaha were so keen to impress upon us the significance of the TR1's arrival that an exclusive press launch was arranged. Amidst much uncorking of vino Mike Winfield and others were flown out to Sicily to ride the new V-twin. Mike came back suitably impressed. But he admitted that it would take a full test on British roads to assess the machine's true abilities.

The TR1's motor is obviously what attracted so much interest when the world was first informed of the bike's existence. The inline V-twin represents a major change in policy for Yamaha. While the remaining Big Three continue to churn out across-the-frame fours with monotonous regularity Yamaha have had the guts to step out of the power struggle and look objectively at the needs of the real motorcyclist.

Yamaha were first attracted to the V-twin configuration because they wanted a large capacity mill which would produce great lumps of torque without the attendant vibes of a

parallel twin. The factory was not over-worried that such a machine wouldn't cut it in the power stakes. The real concern was that it should provide ample power without the unnecessary complexity of umpteen valves per cylinder, double overhead cams and rows of finnicky carbs.

Yamaha have certainly achieved their goal. The 75 degree motor employs single overhead cams driven by chain and operating two valves in each head. Costs have also been kept down by using identical castings for each barrel and Yamaha have effectively solved rear cylinder overheating by moulding an air scoop into the right hand side panel.

The result of such a technically conservative design is a motor that produces a piffling 70bhp. But where the bike really scores is torque — a massive 60ft-lb (8.3Kg-m) at 5500rpm. And if all that stomp seems a little high up the range to be of any use don't worry. The TR1's torque curve is about as flat as Mia Farrow's chest with useable power available from below 2000revs right up to the 7000rpm red line. There's nothing to stop you whizzing up and down through the five well spaced gear ratios but there's little to be gained by such frenzied activity. The bike is so soothingly easy to ride that you'll find that cogswapping becomes a forgotten art — it just

ain't necessary.

If such characteristics will endear the TR1 to touring riders' hearts the lack of shaft drive won't. For some strange reason Yamaha have stubbornly ignored current trends and fitted a fully enclosed chain. Okay, so the chain runs in a litre of lithium grease and should last for anything up to 30000 miles. But there's no doubt that a shaft would make a much better long term solution. Yamaha have said that the power loss and torque reaction associated with shaft drive determined their decision but since the TR1's little brother — the XV750 — uses a shaft to good effect it's difficult to see the

logic in Yamaha's reasoning.

If Yamaha have treated th question of the engine unit in refreshingly different manne they've come up with the weird est of frame designs. Looking the bike for the first time yo won't notice anything unusua about the framework. But be neath the sombre Stateside in fluenced styling is a frame tha consists of no less than fou separate sections. The moto acts as a stressed member and bolted to a pressed steel back bone via the front cylinder hea and the rear of the gearbox. Th rear segment of the frame taken care of by a pair of heavil engineered footrest plates an

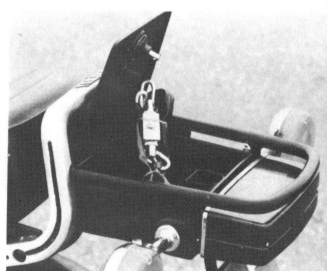

Rear 'boot' contains neat padlock and chain

tubular loop supporting the seat and mudguard.

The suspension itself is nothing out of the ordinary by Yamaha's standards. A hefty air-sprung, oil-damped de Carbon type monoshock unit controls the rear end while the usual air-assisted telescopic forks do all the work up front. Yamaha have gone to great lengths to make sure that adjusting the monoshock is a simple operation. Both the spring rate and damping can be altered by remote controls sited on the right of the seat. This means that it should be no problem to have the suspension set up just right, whatever the conditions.

Unfortunately the proximity of the monoshock to the rear cylinder causes overheating problems with the damping fluid. Yamaha claim that the specially designed magnesium damper rod expands to compensate for any loss in the fluid's viscosity. But there's no doubt that on long and hard runs the suspension loses its efficiency.

Even before the bike began to show signs of over reacting to road surfaces it became obvious that the TR1 suffers from an acute lack of ground clearance. Getting the centre stand on the deck requires no heroics and two up it's virtually impossible to negotiate a bend without removing large amounts of metal from the stand's feet. This might be faintly amusing at times but over enthusiastic owners could well find themselves in trouble now and again.

With such limitations on ground clearance it was difficult to tell just how the TR1 would handle when pushed hard. But despite the bike's sensitivity to suspension settings and damper fluid temperature it seemed to hold its line through all but the worst corners.

Braking is taken care of by a pair of ten inch discs up front. And though the Nips finally seems to have conquered the problem of disc lag in the wet they are still a long way behind on tyre development. The Mag Mopus' fitted on the TR1 just don't inspire the sort of confidence necessary for safe and enjoyable wet weather riding.

On the equipment side the TR1 is well up to Yamaha's usual standards — the massive 7½in headlight is without doubt the best I've ever used.

Other detail touches like the handlebar mounted choke and steering lock cum ignition switch all make the TR1 an easy machine to live with. And that seems to be the TR1's forté. It's like so many other Japanese machines in that it neither attracts adoration nor hatred. Yamaha were hoping that the TR1 would give them a machine that would attract the same kind of cult following that Ducati and Harley Davidson do. I'm afraid that they haven't succeeded on that score even though in some respects they have produced a better motorcycle.

But with a few minor modifications the TR1 will certainly appeal to today's motorcyclist who wants healthy performance without crippling service bills. The bike is going to be of particular interest to the touring rider who will find the comfy riding position, undemanding motor and good fuel economy perfect for long distance jaunts. In fact I'm sure that the TR1 will succeed for the same reasons as Honda's much maligned (but very popular) CX500. It offers different but practical everyday transport. And at just under two grand it's going to leave a lot of people wondering whether their latest 130mph hyperbike is really worth all that extra loot.

DUCATI 900SS

Few motorcycles produced today are aimed at such a limited market as Ducati's 900 Super Sport. The 90 degree V-twin represents a total contrast to the mild mannered and supposedly mass-marketed TR1. And though few people will ever own one of these Italian masterpieces you can be assured that the Duke is universally admired as one of the few motorcycles that can perform alongside Japan's best and still retain a character and feel that is just not there in most modern machines.

The Duke's real home is on the track — a fact that is made all too obvious while riding the bike around town. But surprisingly pootling through traffic was not quite the torture I had expected it

to be. Sure there's barely any steering lock, a neutral light that continually lies, a riding position that is uncomfortable below 60mph and a motor that is lumpy and cumbersome at low speeds. But anyone who's going to lay down his three grand for such a bike is not going to let such minor drawbacks get in the way of what just has to be the ultimate in racers on the road.

For all the Duke's associations with racing (the machine's ancestry lies with the successful F750 mounts that Paul Smart and Bruno Spaggiari campaigned in the early seventies) there is precious little evidence that the 900 can still cut it with the best on the track. Go along to the next Streetbike

Not an inch of space wasted on the TR1. But note the weird rear end styling thanks to the swing arm mounted mudguard

Redesigned seat, Silentium silencers and new paint job are the only external changes for 1981

round and I guarantee that there won't be a Ducati in sight. Indeed at the Mallory Park Post TT the whole damn grid consisted solely of across-the-frame fours. The few riders who had optimistically started the series with a Ducati were rapidly convinced that the Dukes could no longer hold their own and reluctantly adopted a policy of 'If you can't beat them — join them' that sent the disillusioned Ducati freaks scuttling down to their local Big Four dealership in search of the latest piece of oriental techno-wizardry.

That doesn't mean to say that the Duke has had it as a roadster. It's not often that you have to contend with Ron Haslam and CB1100R on the A303, but it just indicates that the Japs have now made up enough lost ground on frame development to press home their long held power advantage. On open twisting roads the 900SS is unsurpassed for its ability to allow the rider to ride in total safety at speeds that would be dangerous on other lesser machines. Such attributes as light weight, superlative brakes and easy going engine characteristics make all that possible.

There's no doubt that the desmo motor that powers the Duke is not ideal for town work. But once the mad hordes are out of the way the mill is easy and rewarding to use. Power flows in from 2000rpm and from then on the 900 will out torque any of its multi-cylinder rivals. Desmodromic valve-gear also makes a nonsense of the redline since bending a valve is almost impossible with the desmo system. Admittedly I didn't try — it's just reassuring to know that missing a gear on full bore won't result in instant disaster.

At 72bhp, power output is nothing earth shattering but what the Duke loses in outright horses it more than makes up for in low weight and minimal aerodynamic drag. The Duke recorded 129mph through the timing lights — a figure very similar to Honda's 900FZ which has an extra 20 horses on tap. Standing quarters were also comparable though we took things easy in case the dreaded Ducati clutch slip arose. It didn't which must be thanks to the redesigned unit.

Of course in true Italian tradition the Ducati is *loud*. The evocative rumble that comes from the Silentium silencers and gaping 40mm Dellortos is one that will warm the heart of any real motorcyclist. Actually the Silentiums are a good deal quieter than the outrageously loud Contis that were once fitted as standard equipment and I can

see many purist owners bolting on a set of Contis before you can say Fabio Taglioni.

If all that noise and those massive carbs conjure up visions of car like fuel consumption, you'll be surprised. Try as hard as we might we couldn't rush a gallon of four star through the

Dellortos in less than 45 miles. With a restrained rider on board something in the region of 55mpg must be a reality but we only managed 49mpg since the Duke was never designed with the energy crisis in mind.

That's especially true on winding A roads where it is impossible to ride the Ducati in any other way than was originally intended. There can't be many motorcycles around that encourage you to take the longest and most demanding route between A and B. But on the Ducati I found myself going miles out of my way just to take in some particularly entertaining stretch of road. The long wheelbase and riding position make slow corners a bit of a problem, though it is possible to take fast sweepers at such superior speeds that you soon forget about any difficulties encountered on the previous bend. Trick air suspension and monoshocks are conspicuous by their absence and indeed the only limit to the brilliant handling and sticky Pirellis seemed to be the centre stand on left handers and the silencer clamp on right hand corners. These only made contact with the deck during some enthusiastic bend swinging — the sort of antics that would soon have you in trouble on many a Japanese projectile.

The Brembo brakes also do their bit in making the Ducati one of the fastest and yet safest machines on the road today. During braking tests at the MIRA proving grounds it was quite possible to lock the front wheel and hold it there without the slightest hint of drama. Again the sort of thing that would be,

Desmo motor produces just over 70bhp but the Duke will still run with Japan's best

er, interesting on an oriental mammoth.

Predictably finish is not all that it should be but the Italians are still learning. The chrome and paintwork resisted all temptation to flake off and only some ham-fisted hack from another mag had managed to spoil the finish on the tank. Electrics are still a sore point at the Bologna factory and though we did suffer one minor problem we can't really see the average 900SS rider worrying about the Mickey Mouse instruments and idiot lights.

You see, owning a Ducati is much more than just possessing a motorcycle. It's a way of life. The 900SS will take up considerable amounts of your time in keeping it in fettle. If you're used to riding a machine from A to B and then forgetting it, steer well clear of the Ducati. Not only will it entice you out onto the open road when you should be behaving like an honest citizen but it will also change your whole character. Never again will you set out without a plastic bag to protect the open carbs from the British weather. You will develop abnormal calf muscles to start the thing and people will realise that you've finally lost your marbles as you set out at sunrise with no particular destination in mind. But my God you'll enjoy yourself.

READOUT

	DUCATI 900SS	YAMAHA TR1
PERFORMANCE		
Maximum speed	129.69mph	120.94mph
Standing ¼ mile	12.73secs/106,44mph	13.25secs/100.64mph
FUEL CONSUMPTION		
Overall	47mpg	45mpg
Best	49mpg	48mpg
Worst	45mpg	41mpg
Average fuel tank range	183 miles	188 miles
SPEEDOMETER ACCURACY		
At indicated 30mph	26.59mph	29.21mph
At indicated 60mph	52.96mph	57.46mph
ENGINE		
Type	90 degree ohc V-twin	75 degree ohc V-twin
Bore x stroke	86 x 64.4mm	95 x 69.2mm
Capacity	864cc	981cc
Compression ratio	9.5:1	8.3:1
Carburation	2 x 40mm Dellorto	2 x 36mm Hitachi
Claimed torque at rpm	58ft/lb (8kg/m) at 6500rpm	60ft/lb (8.2kg/m) at 5500
Transmission	Gear primary drive, wet multiplate clutch, 5 speed gearbox, chain final drive	Gear primary drive, wet multiplate clutch, 5 speed gearbox, chain final drive
ELECTRICAL SYSTEM	200 watt alternator, 12Ah battery, CDI ignition, Cibie 60/55W headlight	AC generator, 20Ah battery, Mitsubishi TCI ignition, 60/55W headlight.
CYCLE PARTS		
Frame	Twin down tubes using engine as stressed member	Pressed steel spine
Suspension	Marzocchi front fork, pivoted rear fork with Marzocchi dampers	Air assisted telescopic front fork, air-sprung, oil damped rear monoshock
Wheels	Twelve spoke cast alloy 100/90 V18 Pirelli Pantom front 120/90 V18 Pirelli Phantom rear	Ten spoke Yamahà Italic 325/19 Bridgestone L303 Mag Mopus front 120/90 18 Bridgestone S714 Mag Mopus rear
Brakes	Twin 11in (279mm) Brembo discs front Single 11in (279mm) Brembo disc rear	Twin 10in (254mm) discs front Single 9in (228mm) drum rear
DIMENSIONS		
Wheelbase	59in (1499mm)	60.6in (1540mm)
Seat height	32.5in (825mm)	30in (762mm)
Overall Width	30.5in (775mm)	29in (740mm)
Ground clearance	6.5in (165mm)	4.5in (114mm)
Weight (with 1 gal fuel)	452lb (205kg)	472lb (214kg)
Fuel capacity	3.9 gal (17.7 litres)	4.18 gal (19 litres)
PRICE	£3129	£1999
Warranty	12 months/unlimited mileage	12 months/unlimited mileage
Supplied by	Coburn and Hughes, 53-61 Park Street, Luton, Beds	Mitsui machinery sales, Chessington, Surrey

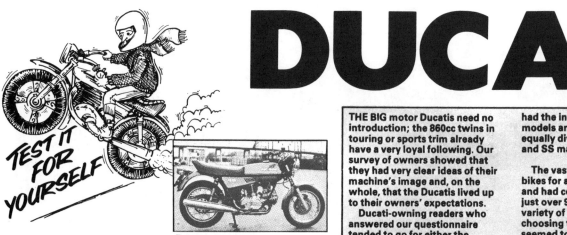

DUCATI

Forerunner of the present models, the 860 has a conventional ohc cylinder head.

THE BIG motor Ducatis need no introduction; the 860cc twins in touring or sports trim already have a very loyal following. Our survey of owners showed that they had very clear ideas of their machine's image and, on the whole, that the Ducatis lived up to their owners' expectations.

Ducati-owning readers who answered our questionnaire tended to go for either the touring GTS models or the sporty 900SS. Only 20 per cent had the in-between Darmah models and the rest were fairly equally divided between GTS and SS machines.

The vast majority had had their bikes for a year or slightly longer and had covered an average of just over 9,000 miles. A wide variety of reasons was given for choosing the Ducati; overall it seemed to boil down to a taste for "traditional' motorcycles, in particular something different to

Performance

OFTEN given as the reason — or part of the reason — for buying the bike, performace was assessed very realistically by the owners. Top speed was barely mentioned although much was made of the "usable power", the ever-present torque and the general swiftness in getting from A to B.

The harder riders were consistent in getting 45 to 50mpg although many mentioned that 60mpg was possible and quite a few ran their machines in the high 50s as a matter of course. Oil consumption seemed to vary with engine age; up to 5,000 miles it was usually zero, increasing to a pint of oil for 1,500 to 2,000 miles. Only one machine used a lot of oil, at 600 miles to the pint.

Handling/braking

THIS section produced the shortest, most succinct answers of all. "Superb", "best I have ridden" were fairly typical replies. Don Upshaw summed up the general feeling about the Brembo brakes with his comment, "Superb, wet or dry, plenty of feel."

The Darmah SS is basically similar to the 900SS but has more graceful styling and an electric starter.

The late Mike Hailwood proved just how well a big Ducati can go on the occasion of his TT comeback in 1978.

Reliability

A surprising number of cables (clutch and throttle), switches, bulbs and fuses had to be replaced. Other items mentioned less frequently were ignition stators, various engine oil seals, broken rear mudguard, and Marzocchi units which blew their seals. A few readers mentioned bad paint on the tank, sidepanels and mudguards. The life of tyres and chains seemed to be about average for a big bike.

Despite a lot of minor faults or failures, most owners saw their machines as basically pretty reliable. Ease of maintenance was considered good with the exceptions of access around the rear cylinder, awkward oil filler and desmo valve clearances!

Poor dealer back-up and long delays in obtaining parts were mentioned by a couple of owners. Spares prices were regarded as cheaper or no worse than Japanese parts but some readers maintained that this only applied to routine items and, as John Starr said, the price of "bodywork is a bit naughty". David Trott added that frame parts were "extortionate" while Mathew Stenhouse complained of parts being "expensive and slow to arrive".

The most exclusive of the Ducati range is the Mike Hailwood Replica. This amount of style will set you back by over £3,000. Engine and cycle parts are the same as the 900SS.

Suspension/comfort

THIS was the other side of the coin for many riders, who pointed out that they were prepared to suffer too-hard suspension in return for such tenacious roadholding. Almost all said the suspension was at least firm — most adding that the front forks were good but the rear units were much too hard. Many had changed their Mazocchi struts for Girling or S & W air shocks.

Most liked the riding position — at least for solo use, apparently it gets a bit cramped with a pillion and passengers had complained about having no grab rail. The most common complaint was that the seat was too hard and narrow, for rider and passenger alike.

V-TWINS

the Japanese multis, plus good performance and handling. Four-fifths of the bikes were bought new.

About a third of the machines were used purely for pleasure — weekend trips, rallies or visits to race meetings, usually involving fairly long journeys. The remaining two-thirds were used for everything — going to work, weekend runs, touring holidays — even though most of the owners either had another motorcycle or a car.

Asked about the bike's suitability, the general concensus was that it was good for long runs but the heavy steering and high first gear was not so well matched to city traffic, making it "lumpy around town", as Bryan Kerswill put it.

The questions gradually revealed two factions among the owners — the very serious, "all-purposes" riders who obviously put their machines to pretty hard use, and the pleasure-riders who were more aware of the bikes 'posability'. The latter tended to gravitate towards the SS models.

Asked about their next machines many owners of sports models wanted a tourer, while touring owners plumped for the sports bike, although always a Ducati!

But all of the riders were obviously very impressed by the looks and styling of the bikes which Brian Clarkson described as "aesthetically perfect".

The average age of the owners was 25 and almost all had been riding since the age of 16 — or earlier in a few cases. About 90 per cent of them did their own servicing and repair work, although a few confessed to leaving major jobs and anything to do with desmo heads, to their dealer.

Equipment/details

STARTING — could be tricky unless the right ritual was observed. Awkward kickstart.

Lighting — some early models had right-dip headlamps — 900SS considered to be a vast improvement on GTS. Some owners had fitted Cibié Z-beams.

Gear shift — the lever was thought to be too long or to have too much travel and gave clunky gear changes at low rpm. Neutral was difficult to find while at a standstill.

Vibration — only at low speeds and then very slight.

Instruments — generally considered to be poor, erratic and inaccurate. The warning lights were criticised for being too dim to be noticeable.

General finish — quite a variety of replies here. On the whole the frame and alloy was praised, while the paint and chrome on the cycle parts was criticised.

Cranks on some earlier models were a bit suspect. Later units had beefed up crankpins.

450 Desmo springs give the clutch more bite.

Conclusions

OUR sample of owners obviously had a clear idea of what they wanted and of what the Ducatis offered. In this respect most were satisfied with their machines and, in reply to our question asking which bike they would buy next, they almost always said Ducati. However most of them pointed out that they exppected to keep their present machine for quite a while yet.

They were a bit more cagey when asked if they'd recommend it to a friend, usually saying yes, but only if he was able to maintain it, or only if he wanted a sports bike.

It seemed that they thought the Ducatis were about right in standard trim and didn't need many modifications. Where bikes had been altered, the most popular items were: clutch springs from the 450; Cibié Z beam light; Girling gas shocks.

Asked what modifications they would like to see made at the factory, the most-mentioned improvements were to chain life, access to rear cylinder, softer seat, adjutable handlebars like the Jota, better finish, better instruments and a sidestand on models not fitted with one.

Useful tips gleaned from hard experience included regular use of WD40 on electrics and to cover the open right-hand bellmouth if the bike is parked in the rain. Several owners mentioned that it was a good idea to join the Ducati Owners Club as this was a source of much useful information as well as having a spares scheme.

For most of them, though, Ducati riding had obviously become a way of life. Michael Bryant said: "There is the same distance between riding Japanese and riding a Duke as there is between motorcycling and not."

And we'll let Stephen May sum it up with this parting comment: "Ducatis seem to instil a strange loyalty even if it is born of a dogged determination to conquer the oddities of Italian biking."

LET US KNOW WHAT YOU THINK
How do you rate your bike? What problems have you had? What are its best points?
In the next few issues we'll be producing readers' tests on:
● Suzuki GP125/100
● Honda CB900
So if you own one of these models, send us a large SAE and we'll return it with our questionnaire. Write to: MCM Reader Test, Bushfield House, Orton Centre, Peterborough.

Far and away the most popular of the big Dukes, the 900SS has a pure racing image that appeals to riders who want something different from the crowd.

Ducati Pantah 600
SPAGHETTI FUNCTION
On the road with the big-bore Duke

Way back in December 1979, *SuperBike* shocked the establishment with Mike Scott's scoop test of the first 500 Ducati Pantah in Britain. A quote from that article seems appropriate.

"Best way to describe the test bike's power is that there was plenty there, but it would have been nice if there'd been even more".

Thus began the dreaded Curse of Scott. In the October 1980 issue there came another portentous pronouncement, this time about the BMW R65.

"Another five bhp would be the minimum required to fulfil the potential of what is almost a very exciting and rapid bike".

What happened next is history. Noting that the Curse was on, Ducati and BMW set to with a will and a wrench to rescue their machines from the awful consequences of prolonged Scottish disapprobation. From Munich came the new R65, complete with the requisite extra 5bhp. From Bologna now comes the 600cc Pantah, a motorcycle which is more than simply an intermediate step between the progenitor 500 and the projected 750. It is instead a 500 with more heart, a Pantah with poise *and* poke, wrapped in a mid-size package which might just make the bigger and smaller brothers look a touch redundant (perish the thought).

We make no secret of the fact that, generalising a little, we're pretty keen on Italian machinery here at *SuperBike*. Write-ups we've done in the past usually have a kind of rosy

glow about them; we even tend to dismiss Italian bikes' shortcomings as nothing more than charming quirks or amusing diversions. Purveyors of Italiania have therefore been known to respond magnificently to our requests for bootleg bikes in the past. On this occasion Steve Lilley of Jack Lilley's Italo-bike shop in Shepperton High St dusted off his brand new, zero-mile showroom 600, topped up the vital fluids and nailed on a numberplate. To him, we are extremely grateful: and why not? Would *you* let a motorcycle journalist loose on *your* new Pantah?

Of course, the trouble with new bikes of any sort is, they need some running in. This is especially true of thoroughbred V-twins, so we were not unduly surprised at Steve's wish that we should take things easy. This pill was made easier to swallow by the news that we were to have the use of Coburn & Hughes' fully-run-in 600 during TT fortnight, heh, heh.

January in Croydon is not really the same as June on the Island (I hope). Still the Pantah looked every bit as appetising in the frozen wastes of 1982 as it did when it was first displayed to a salivating public at the Cologne Show in '78. The main external difference of course is the new fairing, which is now an ABS moulding instead of hand-laid fibreglass as on the old 500s. The big bonus of ABS is a much smoother finish on the *inside* (the fibreglass fairings were terribly rough), as well as the equally obvious advantages of easier

production techniques. There is a marginal weight penalty, but most Pantah owners would tolerate this so long as they're getting the quality which by rights should have been there in the first place.

The lower half of the fairing is different too, with the trailing edge now ending above the line of the bottom trellis tube. The front part of the fairing lower slopes forward now, providing for a pronounced air-scoop aperture and improved ventilation for the rear cylinder. A protruding lip creases the side sections, cleaning up the airflow and reducing any tendency for the front end to lift at speed. Another minor change has been occasioned by the use of a new 154mm Bosch headlamp, as used on BMW's R45/65 series. The overall visual effect is slightly more conservative than the old 500's racerish image, rendering the 600 into more of a gentleman's carriage. Admirers of the original Pantah appearance will be dismayed to learn that the new fairing will also feature on the 500 from now on, a logical move really, although it's still not cheap by any means (over £500 plus VAT).

Physically, the rest of the bodywork is unchanged, except for the new 1982 colour of silver metallic with red and black highlights. Very becoming it is too. The mudguard is new, and colour-matched to the rest of the paintwork (earlier Pantahs had black mudguards). It's in the engine and transmission that most of the effort has gone. Bore has gone up from 74mm to 80mm, increasing the advertised power

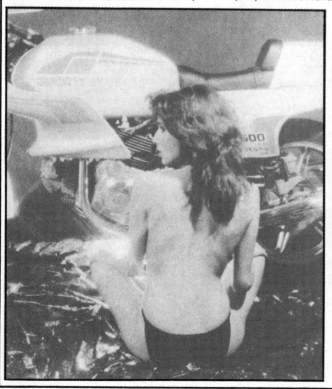

output from 52bhp at 9000rpm to 58bhp at 8500. Pistons on the 900 Dukes are 86mm across, but the rumoured 750 Pantah will have a longer stroke as well as a bigger bore; 750cc is regarded as the largest practicable engine capacity using the present Pantah crankcases.

Torque is naturally up as well on the 600, although no figures are available to confirm by how much. On the road the difference is hinted at by a noticeable push beginning lower down the rev range than on the cammy 500, which would only produce real power over 6000rpm. In this respect the 600 promises a combination of the 500's lightness and feel with something of the engine characteristics of the 900 at the bottom end.

This is not to say that the Pantah's willingness to rev will be compromised, however. Maximum power is still developed high up at 8500rpm. Much more meaningful are the transmission changes which enable the 600 to make the most of its performance. The first 500s had 15:38 sprockets and a 1:0.9 top gear ratio which endowed them with a *theoretical* top speed of around 138mph; in practice the maximum was more like 115mph, and that was in fourth because the 500 couldn't pull anything like max revs in top. Later 500s, and now the 600, have modified fifth gear ratios of 1:0.931. On the 600, this makes the theoretical top speed around 122mph using the new 36-tooth rear sprocket, and an informed guesstimate of 120mph *actual* top end. Obviously, a much more satisfactory state of affairs. Club racers will now be able to discard all those 41-tooth sprockets they've been stockpiling.

Early Pantahs were plagued by gearbox trouble, brought about by slipping backlash dogs which were given to destroying first gear under certain circumstances. This catastrophe was especially likely to happen if the man shimming up the vertically split crankcases at the factory was having an off day and failed to keep to the engine's very exacting tolerances. By dispensing entirely with the backlash dogs and adopting racing-type gears on the Pantah, Ducati hope to have laid this particular ghost once and for all.

Cush drives in the transmission have not been modified, which means that the slight jerkiness on moving off from rest, so typical of Pantahs, is still present on the 600. We noticed a fair bit of chain wear on our test machine, the great majority of which was almost certainly due to this snatchiness, despite slipping the clutch to get under way in the high first gear. The new hydraulic clutch is rather heavy, and might promote wrist ache during prolonged spells of town riding; personally, I was more grateful for the knowledge that I wasn't about to be stranded somewhere holding one end of a snapped clutch cable, the bane of our old Darmah (which, if anybody's interested, can now be seen sporting a new white paint job and, would you believe, a Windjammer fairing, somewhere in the South London area). Gearlever action is a delight, and on the open road the transmission is hard to fault.

As is the whole machine, really. Engine sound is definitely more subdued on the 600, no doubt due to the more substantial construction of the fairing. At a steady 80mph (around 5000rpm) the Pantah is very quiet indeed; just a whisper of rushing air over the screen and a muted hum from the Conti exhausts and the odd sharp intake of breath from the 36mm Dell'Ortos on acceleration to remind you that this is definitely a Duke you're riding.

May I quote from a "rival" test of the 500 for a

moment? "Even at a rash 10 000rpm there is no hint of valve bounce". Hmmm. Such is the wonder of desmodromic valve operation. . . .

Should you require your 600 to go faster than the average 600, you may opt for a special race kit which should be available here by the time you read this. New pistons, cams, carbs, jets, sprockets and exhaust pipes will transform your bike. Price? Oh, £1405 plus VAT. Bargain.

Another bit of engine expenditure you won't be able to avoid is the replacement of your cam drive belts every 12500 miles, which your dealer will replace for around forty notes. Some chaps prefer to perform such duties themselves, including the periodic adjustment of the pulley tensioner. There have been instances of belt failure in the past, caused by well-meaning owners checking the belts when cold and being alarmed at their apparent slackness. If you have the Special Tool, you can do the adjustment; if you haven't, all the aluminium engine parts tend to expand when the bike is warmed up, leading to drastically high tension on the poor belts. So beware.

In most other respects, the engine presents few problems for the DIY-er, with electronic ignition and a very accessible spin-on type oil filter sitting under the front cylinder. All the body parts remove easily for access to the electrics, which I am pleased to relate functioned perfectly on our test bike. Nothing fused or broke off.

Alert types might have noticed something different about the front end of the Pantah 600. Got it yet? Well, for a start the brake calipers are now mounted *behind* the fork legs, and what's more they're the bigger calipers from the 900 instead of the Guzzi V50-size Brembos previously used. The forks themselves are Paiolis, not Marzocchis. Marzocchis have not been abandoned by Ducati; just that the demise of Ceriani has placed a considerable extra burden on the Marzocchi factory which sometimes leads to shortages. So, although we didn't have them on our bike, Pantah owners might also find Paioli shock absorbers at the back (they have an aluminium finish and squarish remote reservoirs). Rest assured: our Paiolis performed flawlessly, and personally I feel safer riding a bike with brake calipers mounted behind the fork legs anyway.

Similarly, Michelins or Pirellis may be supplied depending on availability (the shortages here usually affecting Pirelli). During the worst weather of the year I never felt less than safe aboard the Pantah, which I suppose is some kind of tribute to the bike's tremendous rideability. The tyres are always in tactile contact with the road surface, and provide total communication for the grinning pilot. Although the seat is not particularly close to the ground, shorter riders will have no bother getting their feet down because the Pantah is so slim. It's one of those bikes that allow you to sit upright at traffic lights with your arms folded and your boots up by the front wheel somewhere.

I enjoyed the 600 Pantah. There *is* a 750 on the cards for the future which promises much; after all, the Formula Two 600s are already putting out over 70bhp, a healthy amount in a motorcycle weighing less than 400 pounds dry. But the 750 is going to have to be good to upstage the 600. That's the problem when you're trying to produce an "improved" version of something that's already a standard by which others must be judged. Let's hope that the 600 gets a fair chance to make its mark in history before the usurper arrives. Somehow, the idea of discounting 600s seems strangely heretic. **TM**

DUCATI PANTAH 600
£2799

PERFORMANCE

Maximum Speed – 120mph (est)
Standing Quarter Mile – 13.4 (est)
Fuel Consumption – Cruising – 55mpg
Best Full-Tank Range – 230 miles

ENGINE

Type – 90-degree air-cooled vee-twin, belt-driven SOHC, desmodromic valve operation
Displacement – 583cc
Power – 58bhp at 8500rpm
Bore & Stroke – 80 × 58mm
Compression Ratio – 9.5:1
Induction – two 36mm Dell'Orto pumpers
Exhaust – two into two with balance pipe
Oil System – wet sump
Ignition – Bosch CDI

TRANSMISSION

Clutch – hydraulically-activated wet multiplate
Primary Drive – gear
Final Drive – chain
Gears – five-speed constant mesh

CHASSIS

Frame – twin overhead ladder type
Front Suspension – Paioli/Marzocchi tele forks (according to availability)
Rear Suspension – Paioli/Marzocchi remote reservoir shocks and swing-arm
Wheelbase – 57.1in.
Ground Clearance – 6.5in.
Seat Height – 32in
Weight – 407lbs (½ tank petrol)
Fuel Capacity – 4.2galls
Tyres – 100/90 × 18 front, 110/90 × 18 rear (Pirellis or Michelins)
Brakes – triple 10in Brembo discs

EQUIPMENT

Electrical – 200watt alternator, 12V battery
Lighting – 55/60W Bosch

Test bike supplied by: Jack Lilley Motorcycles, High St, Shepperton, Middx (Tel. 98-24574).

Pantah 600 — a big

Pantah fairing has been re-designed for the 600 to inc

Contrary to popular belief, particularly within the Morini Owners' Club, I like Italian bikes. They can be brash, they can be different and they often embody more of the magic that makes motorcycles attractive to interesting people such as motorcyclists.

The Ducati Pantah 500 we tested last August was all these things, with a degree of refinement previously only available from Europe by accepting the less stunning performance of BMWs and Guzzis. The Pantah 600 increases this performance edge without any sacrifices.

That their chassis' handle with assurance and steer with rewarding precision is a foregone conclusion. That their V-twin engines are long-legged and strong and respond in a satisfying way to the delight of an enthusiastic rider is perhaps only to be expected. These things are Ducati's strengths. The difference with the Pantahs is that these things are unspoilt by crude peripherals.

Starting is push-button, instant and reliable. The switches are simple and weatherproof, other electrics including the headlamp, are powerful. The engines are smooth apart from the characteristic V-twin throb and even that lovable sensation fades at higher revs. The riding position is as comfortable as a clip-on crouch can be. To describe the standard of the finish is to

Marzocchi shocks have air adjustment

drool, from the neat wiring, through the quality glassfibre to the sparkling paint, chrome and polished alloy casings.

The Pantah 600 has been created to sell alongside the 500 by making small but effective changes. Bore has been increased from 74 to 80mm, taking the capacity from 499 to 583cc, and compression is substantially more keen at 10.4:1 instead of 9.5. The effects are that power peaks 8bhp

stronger, 400rpm lower, and torque gets a big hike — 29.5 to 37.4lb.ft. at the same 7500rpm engine speed.

In case any rider might have the balls to push the already-excellent brakes closer to their limit, the front discs are 20mm bigger in diameter, but otherwise the chassis and secondary mechanicals such as the internal gear ratios are unaltered.

The 600 has stronger clutch springs to cope with the extra power, compensated for by the expensive complication of hydraulic operation. The action is smooth but still heavy.

Riding the 600 was as effortless as it was exhilarating. The electric starter would easily crank a cold engine into an even and subdued burble, only needing a few seconds of the cold-start lever buried inside the nosecone. Straight away the engine ran clean and pulled reliably.

Engaging first and subsequent gears was never silent, but always smooth and almost always positive. Perhaps once a day I found a false neutral when changing down from third. Clutchless changes were too messy to be acceptable, but the heavy clutch action was only noticeable when it had to be fully disengaged and that was necessary only in traffic.

To suit the relaxed, throbbing nature of

GLIA
ING

off the 500 block

V-twin power, the gear ratios are tall, including first. But getaways were still rapid with none of the jerkiness Bob noticed when riding the 500 Pantah. It was possible to take fifth (top) gear down to about 35mph without snatching but in practice 3-4000rpm was the minimum for a reasonable ride with useable throttle response in the higher gears.

If riding at no less than 30mph in third gear, 40mph in fourth and 50mph in top sounds like the recipe for an inflexible handful, forget it. The Pantah hummed happily to its 9000rpm red line (still 100rpm short of the power peak) and beyond, without feeling strained. Torque peak is at 7500rpm but throttle response was instant and felt just as strong down around 6000. And the beauty of it was that the motor sounded and felt as though it was running at half that speed.

Having no temperamental power band to fall out of, the Pantah stormed out of bends even if I messed up the entry. Better still, within very few miles the chassis had impressed me enough to make my riding style uncharacteristically confident. When you believe in a bike mistakes are less noticeable.

In the Pantah's case, some normally hazardous actions ceased to be mistakes.

PERFORMANCE CHART

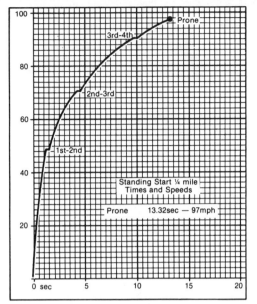

Standing Start ¼ mile Times and Speeds

Prone — 13.32sec — 97mph

MAXIMUM SPEEDS and SPEED RANGES

Gear		mph max	mph min	mph 1000rpm
1	solo	50.4	7.05	6
2	solo	73.8	11.83	8
3	solo	95.4	17.33	11
4	solo	118.8	25.58	13
5	solo	123.04	32.78	16
	pillion	—	—	—
	prone	—	—	—

Best one way speed: 126.08mph

SPEEDO

ind	true
30	29
40	38
50	47
60	57
70	67
80	77
90	87

BRAKES(both)

	solo	pillion
mph	ft	ft
30	30	35
40	63	71
50	98	104
60	133	139
70	158	170

Figures for Pantah 500

Milometer

Accurate

MPG

Best	51
Worst	48
Overall	50

FLEXIBILITY IN TOP GEAR (sec)

mph	30-50	40-60	50-70	60-80	70-90	80-100
solo	—	8.55	9.80	9.85	12.58	—

Oil used

Negligible

Performance figures obtained at: M.I.R.A. Test Track, Nr. Atherstone, Warks. Test Riders: Bob Goddard, Neil Millen.

COMPARISONS

Performance figures for R65

Make	Speed prone	SS ¼ mile prone	Dry weight	Claimed bhp	mpg	Price inc. Tax
Ducati Pantah 600	123mph	13.32sec/97mph	414lb.	60 @ 9100rpm	50	£2799
Ducati Pantah 500	112mph	13.72sec/93mph	397lb.	52 @ 9500rpm	47	£2469
Laverda Montjuic	110mph	13.86sec/95mph	370lb.	50 @ 8500rpm	51	£2399
Kawasaki GPZ550	118mph	12.50sec/104mph	440lb.	58 @ 9000rpm	50	£1699
GS650G Katana	117mph	12.70sec/102mph	481lb.	73 @ 9500rpm	45	£1728
BMW R65LS*	108mph	14.07sec/93mph	412lb.	50 @ 7250rpm	48	£2434

ow-level spoiler. H4 headlight is superb

Instruments are clear but speedo reads in kph

On most bikes I consider it reasonable to expect a nasty reaction if something unexpected forces me to shut off the power in the middle of a bend. The Pantah's frame stayed firm and steered unerringly on line, so why not shut off? Or even brake hard? The bike didn't seem to care, so why should I? Having so much of my attention free to read the road made every journey smoother and safer. This was particularly

true at night when potential hazards appear with less warning, or on wet roads when the best line is often marred by manhole covers or dubious-looking patches of tarmac.

Near perfection, there's just enough room for improvement in the Pantah's chassis to make a MkII model worthwhile in future years. Bob had found the 500 Pantah's rear end inclined to wave gently at times, but had managed to tune out the effect by paying careful attention to the air-pressure balance in the rear suspension reservoirs. A similar waving motion in long, fast bends proved more stubborn on the 600.

Unique to the 600, the front end felt light coming out of bends under power. And with the bigger engine's stunning mid-range response it was possible to come out of bends under a *lot* of power. On dry roads the effect was usually nothing more than a slight widening of line. On wet roads the front wheel could slide noticeably, particularly when powering out of uphill bends. But the Michelin tyres recovered and pulled the bike straight at the instant the power was rolled off.

The Pantah's secondary safety systems were equally impressive. Rain at the MIRA track ruled out our measured brake tests. But on the road, the slightly bigger front discs delivered exactly the right amount of stopping power at the command of two fingers. No surprise, no disappointment and

FAMIGLIA FEELING

no delay when wet. Some riders thought the rear brake lacked bite, but I preferred to be able to concentrate on the front end without having to worry about the possibility of locking the rear wheel. The rate at which hundred-plus speeds could be cancelled without fuss was impressive.

Backing up the predictable and adaptable handling, the headlamp had the power to see well ahead with a beam spread that tucked light into the corners. Not pointing into turns can be a serious drawback with lights in frame-mounted fairings, but not for the Pantah 600.

Well controlled fork dive ensured that the illuminations weren't turned into a spotlight for the front wheel when braking for bends. Similar suspension control kept the rear

end firm but, unlike most Italian bikes, it wasn't at the expense of suspension movement. The Pantah could hardly be said to have floated over rough roads, but it didn't shake out my fillings.

Not having to make apologies for the suspension of an Italian sportster is a refreshing change. Being able to back up some of the performance claims of Italian bike owners is an almighty relief. The Pantah 600 has far and away the highest top speed in its class, still with a healthy rpm safety margin thanks to a slightly taller top gear ratio than the 500, giving an extra 0.5mph/1000rpm.

Quick one

It is the acceleration that is most impressive on the road. Tall gearing tames the standing-quarter-mile times, leaving the 600 with a result that is respectable but behind the Japanese. A closer look at the graphs, however, shows the Pantah to be much quicker up to a useful 50mph. It can run up to 50 in bottom gear while the Japs are screaming for second gear at about 30mph

and the result is much cleaner getaways out of bends and in traffic. Top gear is too tall to make our flexibility figures worth discussing; anyway, for quick riding through country lanes third and fourth are the most commonly used ratios.

Fuel consumption was good at around 50mpg. On our test the 600 was more economical than the 500 but that could have been due to a lot of wet weather. Anyway, being able to go fast without screaming the engine meant that the thirst didn't vary much. Getting about 180 miles out of a tank before going on to reserve encouraged long, quick trips without any feeling of being rushed.

Back-seat writher

As I implied at the opening of the test, impractical and/or badly executed details are few. Perhaps the bike's biggest practical drawback is that the pillion seat is thinly padded and therefore chronically uncomfortable, in contrast with the rider's perch. Luggage isn't as much of a problem as it may at first appear because, although throwover panniers would scuff the paint off the bodywork, there's room for a small tank bag and I know that Krauser UK have successfully fitted pannier racks to Pantahs.

All Pantahs are imported with kph speedos. The inner mph scale is too small

SPECIFICATIONS

ENGINE

Type: *Air-cooled, in-line 90 degree V-twin, SOHC, desmodromic four-stroke.* **Bore x stroke:** *80 x 58mm.* **Displacement:** *583cc.* **Compression ratio:** *10.4:1.* **Carburettors:** *Two 36mm Dell'Orto slide type.* **Max. bhp:** *60 @ 9100rpm.* **Max. torque:** *37.4ft.lb. @ 7500rpm*

TRANSMISSION

Overall gear ratios: *1st 14.09, 2nd 9.66, 3rd 7.52, 4th 6.06, 5th 4.91.* **Clutch:** *Wet multi-plate.*

FRAME and FORKS

Type: *Tubular space frame with engine suspended below.* **Front suspension:** *Telescopic fork with coil springs and hydraulic damping.* **Rear suspension:** *Swinging fork controlled by twin coil springs with air/oil damping. Five spring pre-load settings.* **Front travel:** *5.1in.* **Rear travel:** *3.5in.* **Trail length:** *5.1in.* **Castor angle:** *59 degrees, 30 minutes.*

WHEELS and BRAKES

Front tyre size: *3.25 x 18.* **Rear tyre size:** *3.50 x 18.* **Front brake:** *Twin discs, 11.0in. diameter.* **Rear brake:** *Single disc, 10.2in. diameter.*

ELECTRICS

Ignition: *Bosch electronic.* **Battery:** *12V, 14Ah.* **Alternator:** *200W max.* **Headlight:** *60/55W H4.* **Tail/stop lamp:** *5/21W.* **Indicators:** *21W.* **Warning lights:** *Turn, lights on, main beam, neutral, oil pressure, generator and sidestand (optional).*

DIMENSIONS

Seat height: *30in.* **Length:** *89in.* **Width:** *30.7in.* **Height:** *42.9in.* **Wheelbase:** *61in.* **Ground clearance:** *6.5in.* **Dry weight:** *414lb.* **Fuel tank:** *4.6 gallons.*

This year's Pantahs have revised fairings. Three bolt-together parts give smoother lines and a built-in spoiler.

to read at a glance in daylight and near-invisible at night. The odometer and tripmeter are also in kilometres, of course.

No mirrors are supplied, despite the fact that the lever clamps have threaded holes built in. Someone had bent a Jap mirror to the necessary shape for the test bike and it worked without blurring or fouling the fairing, so mirrors ought to be fitted as standard. On Pantahs a side stand is an optional extra, which I didn't miss because the bike is light and easy to pull on to the centre stand.

The clip-on bars are surprisingly comfortable on the move, but U-turns can be an embarrasingly long process due to the restricted turning circle. Clearance between the hydraulic clutch reservoir union and the ignition key is tight; with a bundle of extra keys to fit the steering lock and fuel cap, trying to turn 180 degrees right can kill the engine. Last moan, honest, is that the dipswitch moves illogically forward for dipped beam, back for main.

At £2799 including VAT the Pantah 600 is expensive — that's a Kawasaki GPZ550 with £1100 in loose change. It's even expensive by BMW standards. Whether or not it is worth over £300 more than the 500 Pantah depends on the value the rider puts on having a performance edge but, once paid for, you'd have to be very fussy or very boring to be disappointed.

Neil Millen

Right: As a single seat the Pantah is comfortable but, with the tail section removed, passengers suffer too much for long trips. The tail is held by three coin-sized screws which have to be removed to get the toolit also.

Below: 600 Pantah has bigger front discs with amazing stopping power but the action is still light, giving controllable braking under any circumstances and without any wet delay.

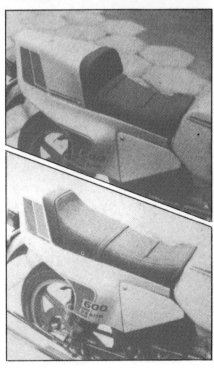

There's no noise. No engine clatter; no penetrating staccato exhaust blast. The slinky-smooth silver beast is a new breed.

Enter The Panther...

Still very much the specialist sportster, Ducati's smallest V-twin is rewardingly different, but has sacrificed nothing of its heritage. To ride it is to immediately assume a sense of great purpose. To buy one is to understand the extra cost of the essence and mystique of Italian character.

ITALIAN motorcycles are considered by many to represent the pinnacle of achievement in style, handling and character (no-one said anything about practicality or comfort). Although the oriental superbikes have eclipsed the Ducatis, Guzzis, Benellis and Laverdas in terms of sheer performance and have been improved to the stage of matching (if not surpassing) their handling qualities, the Italians still command considerable respect for their ability to produce bikes with eye-catching looks, bikes that retain loads of character. Over the years Italian motorcycles have improved, but unlike a lot of their oriental counterparts they haven't been refined to the point of blandness.

The Pantah follows in that vein: Undeniably a very pretty motorcycle with all the mystique and personality of its predecessors. While the 500 hasn't the brutish sound or the butch looks of the 900 SuperSports it still packs a punch visually. In fact during our time with the Pantah we were constantly but pleasantly pestered by people wanting to know more about the bike. We had to agree with their commonly-voiced statement — "what a beautiful motorcycle".

Most *Ducatiphiles* will recall the sad day when the company decided to discontinue production of the 250, 350 and 450 cm^3 singles. To fill the gap it released two 500 cm^3 parallel twins, a sports model with desmodromic valve actuation and a standard model with conventional rocker arm/valve spring set-up. To dedicated enthusiasts it was a sell-out to Japanese design: A Ducati with more than one cylinder could only have two and these must be inclined at 90 degrees!

The 500s failed. They weren't convincing, and also gained a reputation for poor reliability.

It came as no surprise when Ducati decided to return to the successful formula and rumours circulated as early as 1975 that the company was seriously considering designing and producing a 500 V-twin sportster. The prototype finally surfaced at the Cologne motor show in 1978 and production models made it to Australia in 1980. Undoubtedly consumer response to the new Pantah has been favourable — for good reason. Arguably this bike is the handsomest and best-handling Ducati, and, considering that all the alternatives are big-bore, it's probably the model with broadest appeal.

As well as having legendary Ducati impact, the Pantah carries the flag in more important areas. It's light, agile and behaves exactly as one has come to expect from the Italian factory — brilliantly. Overall, the bike's road manners are a touch better than the Dukes of old; and it's when the going gets rough that the Pantah shows considerable superiority. We have yet to lay our grubby mitts on a Hailwood Replica or the new SuperSports so we can't comment on the 500's behaviour in that illustrious company, but it's better than a stab in the dark bet that the little Duke would be up there with them and perhaps might even show a clean pair of heels through the tight stuff.

There's often pitfalls associated with adhering to tradition. The Pantah has some typical Ducati features which are not to be admired. Shoddy finish is one of them. The fibreglass was not well finished, the fairing was rough around the edges and sported some ill-fitting components. The indicators looked like they'd been thrown in from a great distance. Paintwork was passable.

The bike lost a number of useful appendages during the test period. A screw (the metallic kind) fell out of the rear seat cowling and the mystery of rapidly diminishing cornering clearance was

traced to the centrestand coming adrift with a missing bolt. Still, the Pantah had had a rough childhood; quite a few hasty laps around Oran Park to be precise.

Once in the rider's seat though, all can be forgiven. The riding position promotes a feeling of oneness with the machine, the rider blends in with the bike to produce a single functional unit. People look good riding Pantahs, unless of course they're approaching the 180 cm (6ft) mark. Tall specimens will find the riding posture quite cramped. No doubt about it, a real boy racer special.

Mechanically speaking

Well, time to fire up. Pull on the choke hidden away in the fairing, find the starter button (awkwardly located on the underside of the right hand switchblock) and press. The Pantah immediately bursts into life — albeit very quietly. There's no *suck-bang* so reminiscent of the '76 model SS with its 40 mm bellmouth Dell'ortos and free-breathing Contis; just

a muted whisper through the Continentals and a very quiet murmur from the motor. The beat though, is unmistakably Ducati.

If the motor is surprisingly quiet, it's also amazingly revvy. The tacho needle can be sent well past the red, to 10,000 rpm and beyond without a hint of protest from the internals and the engine puts out good power at high engine speeds. Maximum power, a claimed 37.3 kW (50 hp), comes in at 9050 rpm, 50 rpm past the stated red line. The larger-capacity Ducatis produce maximum power at much lower engine speeds.

A motor with the engineering to rev to those extremes certainly benefits from a desmo valve drive (separate rockers open and close the valves, banishing valve float caused by springs which, at high revs, lack the capability to completely close the valve before the next intake or exhaust stroke). These days though, valve spring technology has advanced to such an extent that motors with more conventional heads can rev to 10,000 rpm and beyond without any problem (the Yamaha XJ550 has a 10,000 rpm redline), and considering the comparative difficulty involved in setting valve clearances with the desmo system it's probable that the Pantah could have worked just as well with the simpler valve spring/rocker head.

But then a Ducati just wouldn't be a Ducati without the desmo, would it? At least it makes more sense with the very revvy little 500: The motor, you see, is not merely a scaled-down version of a Darmah or a Super-Sports mill. It's been redesigned from the ground up. The most obvious new feature is the camshaft drive. Each toothed rubber belt runs on an "inverted" sprocket sited on the right hand end of the crankshaft to another on the camshaft and these belts obviously contribute a great deal to the engine's quietness.

Ducati suggests the belts be replaced every 20,000 km (whether they look worn or not). Thankfully, this is quite a simple procedure. After removing the timing covers all one has to do is release the roller-type tensioner, carefully ease off the belt, replace with a new one, and retension.

Another area benefiting from the rethink is the engine cases, which now have a sight glass for checking oil level and a window to allow easy ignition timing checking. Inside there's a new one-piece forged crankshaft with plain big end bearings, and the head uses a smaller valve angle (which allows the use of bigger valves and more radical camshaft profile).

The Pantah sucks fuel/air mixture into its 498.9 cm³ of cylinder space through two large 36 mm Dell'ortos graced with accelerator pumps — no wonder the little beast performs so well! The bike isn't an XJ550 beater by any means, but it is a

very capable sportster. A strong midrange and a hefty top end make the Duke an exhilarating go-fast machine and give it reasonable tractability through suburban traffic. Of course the low-down grunt of its bigger brothers is missing, but the 500 piles the power on in a different fashion — when the throttle is twisted right to the stop.

We were, however, a little disappointed by the top speed. An indicated 168 km/h, with the tacho needle hovering near redline was the best we could do. A slightly lower fifth gear would undoubtedly help the motor to pull maximum power engine speed in top. It's also performance at a price with this little beast. The Pantah is not a real guzzler but it's not economical either. On a gentle country cruise our best figure was 17.9 km/l (51 mpg) while a sound thrashing increased consumption to 14.2 km/l (40.5 mpg). Around town it offers about 15.7 km/l (44.7 mpg).

Frame and handling

The motor is a major rethink, and the frame has received even more attention. In a complete break-away from tradition Ducati has thrown away the how-to-build-a-conventional-frame book and tried something completely different. Its trellis frame is not unique, several specialist frame manufacturers (MotoMartin for example) market similar designs, but the Pantah is the only production motorcycle with such a construction. The MKM Krauser also has a trellis structure, but unlike the Pantah, the BM powerplant is supported by two frame tubes running under the engine cases. The Duke's motor is suspended by the frame rather than supported by it. Another feature is the unusual swingarm attachment — it pivots on bushes in the engine cases. Unconventional this structure may be, but we couldn't find any handling deficiencies caused by lack of strength or rigidity.

The Pantah's suspension system certainly guarantees precise roadholding. Marzocchi forks up front and Marzocchi rear units with air adjustable damping ensure the bike copes well with every road condition. Certainly one of the best matched suspension systems around. The only criticism is the limited travel at both ends, and the lack of comfort-inducing spring suppleness.

Steering is neutral; slow at low speed but direct and reasonably responsive at higher speeds. In essence, the Pantah feels quite different to the majority of Oriental sportsters. The bike prefers a decisive riding style and predetermined lines, but once one adjusts to the bike's requirements it feels terrific in the windies, going fast around sweepers and

Instruments are large and very easy to read. Unfortunately the idiot lights are not.

Convertible seat is a sensible feature. Remove and bingo! A pillion seat (for small pillions only).

Oh, those pretty Ducati motors — somewhat hidden on the Pantah though. It's an all-new mill, not scaled down from any of its bigger, rortier brothers.

A DUCATI FOR THE LADIES?

A Norton 850 and two Suzi waterbottles into motorcycling, LYNELLE BUXTON has found a sleekly-styled and economic tourer that takes the cake!

IN four months I've covered 18,500 km including a tour around Tasmania, a trip to North Queensland for the Cane Toad Rally and a short hop up the coast from Newcastle to Brisbane for the Rain Forest Rally.

In the process six tickets for speeding have been added to my collection; thank heavens it's not an offence to lay a bike over in a corner and belt around as well! That's what the Pantah excels at. Yes, number one on the list is handling. Drop it back a gear, tuck up into the fairing and lay it over into a curve and just let the centrifugal force push you down into the seat.

Fuel consumption is equally outstanding. Even when caned almost all

everything in between. Top speed stability is excellent as is the brilliant cornering clearance.

Brakes and transmission

Both stoppers are beyond reproach, offering progressive and strong braking power with loads of feedback through the levers. Moderately strong pressure is required to operate the brakes and the front lever is a bit of a stretch for a small-handed person, but the minor aggravations are far outweighed by the brakes' outstanding reluctance to lock up — a very desirable safety feature especially for wet weather riding.

The clutch, however, did not escape criticism. A heavy action and a narrow take-up zone combined with the tallish first gear to promote some difficulty in moving the bike off the line smartly and smoothly. On the positive side, the gearbox was a snack to use, offering a light and positive change action and extreme ease of slotting into neutral. Gear ratios could have been more suitable though. All gears were a little tall so perhaps a larger rear sprocket would help, especially around town.

All the rest

The Pantah's ancillaries were not top class. The headlight was grim, the switches were below par, and idiot lights were dull and difficult to see in daylight. Instruments were okay though; large and easily readable, but we couldn't vouch for their accuracy. The bike didn't have a sidestand (but did have a sidestand-down warning light) but no great muscling was needed to heave the 500 up onto the centrestand. Ducati has thoughtfully provided a fold out handle to assist in this

procedure, but unfortunately a rider of average height will find he has to bend over too much to comfortably make use of that attachment. We found it easier to heave on the underside of the glasswork.

A very neat feature is the convertible seat. On removing the rear cowling there is just enough space for a pillion, although the Pantah could never be regarded as a good pillion bike. The seat is too narrow and a little too short — good for short, light, cuddly ladies but that's about all. Anyone who buys a Pantah is probably not going to be particularly bothered by the maintenance requirements. Throttle cables will need synchronisation, belts will need adjustment and replacement and valve clearances will need setting, and all this means the 500 will spend more time in the garage than a comparable Japanese middleweight. Fortunately the electronic ignition will make life a little easier.

Conclusion

Make no mistake about it, the Pantah is a specialist sportster. Around town wrists suffer from excess weight, a relatively heavy throttle and a bull-worker clutch, while out on the highway the narrow seat and racer's crouch can cause quite a variety of aches and pains. On the other hand the Duke has superb suspension and brakes and a good turn of speed. Definitely one of the best boy-racer machines around, so if you're prepared to pay a few hundred dollars extra for the Ducati mystique and you're a reasonable rider, rest assured many frustrated motorcyclists will see your tail light disappearing into the distance.

A mighty fine sportster and a real rider's bike — but you pay for the pleasure. ✳

the time it returns 20-25 km/l (63 mpg) on a fast run. This could have something to do with the light weight, fairing-improved aerodynamics; or good motor design. You choose, I just ride it.

Another plus point is that my feet touch the ground. I too suffer from the Julia Cullen Syndrome of short legs and tall bikes. Travelling solo I have found two good riding positions; first, feet on the front pegs, lean low over the tank, and bum hard up against the seat tail. Result: sore bum. Second, is to get up into top gear, flip down the rear pegs, and stretch forward race style on the tank, but with my head kinked up to see. Result: sore neck. The answer is to use both alternately.

When the working day is done the bike and I like to go for a ride, nowhere in particular, just cruising up and down the coast roads, cutting the corners. The Ducati-inspired freedom that I feel is hard to define, but precious. Moving along

through a warm Hunter Valley night, the headlight cutting the soft darkness, Hexham Greys (mosquitos) committing suicide on the fairing. Or perhaps giving the guys a bit of a drag down Hunter Street.

Faults?

Well, it's not perfect. The standard gearing was too high. I went from a 38-tooth rear sprocket to a 42-tooth, lowering the gearing about 10 percent. Acceleration improved, but top speed is only 195 km/h at redline. The carburetion has been a constant hassle, the Dell 'Ortos refusing to stay in tune, having alternate rich and lean spots. The Bings it now wears at their worst are as good as the Dell'Ortos at their best. A set of Mikunis may be tried in the near future.

Though it's a long way off, I have given some thought to a next bike. A Ducati? You better believe it! But this time a 600 Pantah for that little bit extra power over 160 km/h! ✳

DUCATI PANTAH 500

ENGINE

Air cooled 90-degree V-twin four-stroke. Belt-driven single overhead camshafts with desmodromic valve operation. Conrods side by side on common crankpin, one-piece forged crankshaft with roller bearing mains and plain big end bearings. Wet sump lubrication.

Claimed crankshaft power	37.3 kW at 9050 rpm
Bore x stroke	74 x 58 mm
Displacement	498.9 cm³
Compression ratio	9.5:1
Maximum engine speed	9000 rpm
Carburation	2 x 36mm slide/needle Dell 'ortos with accelerator pumps
Air filtration	Pleated paper element
Starter system	Electric only
Ignition	Electronic
Mean piston speed at redline revs	17.4 m/sec

Fuel consumption

Touring	17.9 km/l (51 mpg)
City	15.7 km/l (44.7 mpg)
Hard riding	14.2 km/l (40.5 mpg)
Average on test	16.8 km/l (47.8 mpg)

TRANSMISSION

Helical gear primary drive through wet multiplate clutch to five-speed constant mesh gearbox with one down, four up pattern. Final drive by roller chain.

FRAME & BRAKES

Welded, tubular steel trellis frame incorporating engine as stressed member. Oil-damped coilspring front forks and oil/air-damped rear units with five spring preload positions. Hydraulically-operated drilled twin cast iron discs with double piston calipers up front, and hydraulically operated drilled single cast iron disc rear brake.

Front suspension travel	105 mm
Rear suspension travel	70 mm
Front brake diameter	260 mm
Rear brake diameter	260 mm
Front tyre	Continental 3.60V18
Rear tyre	Pirelli Phantom 4.00V18

DIMENSIONS

Dry weight	183 kg
Seat height	770 mm
Wheelbase	1450 mm
Fuel capacity (inc. reserve)	19 litres
Fuel reserve	2 litres

TEST MACHINE

Manufacturer	Ducati Meccanica, Bologna, Italy
Test Machine	Norm Frazer Motorcycles, Newcastle
Price	$3999

Best points: Excellent brakes, brilliant cornering clearance and handling combine with the responsive and revvy motor to give the bike superb sports behaviour. And it really looks the part!
Worst points: A cramped riding posture, heavy clutch and tall first gear don't promote easy and comfortable operation around town. Lights switches and finish still need improvement.

SUMMARY

RATINGS	Poor	Below Average	Average	Above Average	Outstanding
ENGINE					
Responsiveness				●	
Smoothness		●			
Bottom end power		●			
Mid range power				●	
Top end power				●	
Fuel economy				●	
Starting				●	
Ease of maintenance			●		
Quietness			●		
Engine braking					●
TRANSMISSION					
Clutch operation		●			
Gearbox operation				●	
Ratio suitability			●		
Drivetrain freeplay				●	
HANDLING					
Steering				●	
Cornering clearance					●
Ability to forgive rider error			●		
High speed cornering				●	
Medium speed cornering				●	
Bumpy bends				●	
Tossing side to side				●	
Changing line in corners			●		
Braking in corners			●		
Manoeuvring			●		
Top speed stability				●	
SUSPENSION					
Front				●	
Rear				●	
Front/rear match					●
BRAKES					
Resistance to fading				●	
Stopping power				●	
Braking stability				●	
Feel at controls				●	
CONTROLS					
Location of major controls			●		
Switches		●			
Instruments				●	
TWO-UP SUITABILITY					
Passenger comfort		●			
Stability with pillion			●		
Cornering clearance two-up				●	
GENERAL					
Quality of finish			●		
Engine appearance				●	
Overall styling					●
Seat comfort			●		
Riding position			●		
Touring range			●		
Headlight		●			
Instrument lighting			●		
Other lights			●		
Rearview mirrors			●		
Horn				●	
Toolkit			●		
VALUE FOR MONEY			●		